# THE GREAT ALTERNATIVES OF
# SOCIAL THOUGHT

# THE GREAT ALTERNATIVES
# OF SOCIAL THOUGHT

*Aristocrat, Saint, Capitalist, Socialist*

Terrence E. Cook

Rowman & Littlefield Publishers, Inc.

ROWMAN & LITTLEFIELD PUBLISHERS, INC.

Published in the United States of America
by Rowman & Littlefield Publishers, Inc.
8705 Bollman Place, Savage, Maryland 20763

British Cataloging in Publication Information Available

**Library of Congress Cataloging-in-Publication Data**
Cook, Terrence E., 1942-
The great alternatives of social thought : aristocrat, saint,
capitalist, socialist / Terrence E. Cook.
p.   cm.
Includes bibliographical references and index.
1. Social conflict.   2. Social problems.
3. Democracy.   4. Political sociology.   I. Title.
HN17.5.C66   1991    303.6—dc20    91–24242 CIP

ISBN 0–8476–7683–8 (alk. paper)
ISBN 0–8476–7684–6 (pbk. : alk. paper)

Printed in the United States of America

<sup></sup>TM The paper used in this publication meets the minimum requirements of
American National Standard for Information Sciences—Permanence of
Paper for Printed Library Materials, ANSI Z39.48–1984.

From Right to Left, everyone, with the exception of a few swindlers, believes that his truth is the one to make men happy. And yet the combination of all these good intentions has produced the present infernal world, where men are killed, threatened and deported, where war is prepared, where one cannot speak freely without being insulted or betrayed.

Albert Camus,
*Neither Victims nor Executioners*

# Contents

# Acknowledgments

Any thanks for enabling me to write this book must begin with my parents who not only brought me into existence but nurtured me toward distinctive parts of wisdom: My father, Calvin E. Cook, encouraged critical thinking and some wariness of human nature, while my mother, M. Delores Cook, taught a sensitivity to the situation and needs of others and an appropriate measure of trust in human possibilities. My wife, Annabel Kirschner Cook, and my children, Andrew and Erin, have been models of patience as I worked to complete this book.

Among others in the Princeton University program in political philosophy, Michael Walzer first awakened my interest in this subject that I have since taught for more than two decades, learning much from my students. Specific contents of this book were often tested in presentations at annual meetings of the Pacific Northwest Political Science Association, where I have enjoyed stimulating critiques by panelists such as Curtis Johnson and Doug Morgan of Lewis and Clark and Peter Steinberger of Reed.

Lisa Milligan helped me edit this work as part of a project completion grant accorded through the Department of Political Science, Washington State University, Pullman, Washington. I welcome at that address any correspondence from readers that could improve any future edition of this book. Driving a long commute from the wilderness of Idaho, Lynda Billings arranged my final drafts. From the Savage, Maryland, haunts of Rowman & Littlefield, editor Jonathan Sisk, production editor Lynn Gemmell, and copy editor Patricia Merrill have shaped the final birthing of a book that Kent Moors of Duquesne University had urged them to do.

I thank the following publishers for permission to cite from their publications: Princeton University Press, which has reprinted the original Pantheon edition of the Bollingen Series edited by Edith Hamilton and Huntington Cairns, *The Collected Dialogues of Plato* (1984); Basic Books, publisher of the Allan Bloom translation of *The Republic of Plato* (1968); the University of Chicago Press, publisher of the Carnes Lord translation of Aristotle's *Politics* (1984); International Publishers, for citations from their three-volume Marx, *Capital*, and also from Marx and Engels, *The German Ideology* (New World, 1966); and New Society Publishers (Philadelphia, Pa., Santa Cruz, Calif., and Gabriola Island, B.C., Canada; 800-333-9093), for citation of Albert Camus, *Neither Victims nor Executioners*, translated by Dwight McBride (1986).

# Preface

Santayana's famous dictum that one compares
only when one is unable to get to the heart of
the matter seems to me . . . the precise reverse
of the truth: it is through comparison, and of
incomparables, that whatever heart we can actually get to is to be reached.

Clifford Geertz,
*Local Knowledge*

Searching for "the heart of the matter" among many books of human
civilization, this study compares and contrasts four very distinctive
approaches to social theory. These great alternatives of the Aristocrat,
the Saint, the Capitalist, and the Socialist are not merely ideal types,
for I shall show that many named thinkers closely adhere to the core
assumptions that define any one of them.

Advocates of any alternative readily perceive similarities among
thinkers of each rival or even among all three rivals, following the
prejudicial judgment that "they are all alike." But for their personally
favored philosophy, they like to have it both ways. When praising
their tradition, they will also celebrate similarities of its theorists. Yet
when deflecting criticism of their tradition, one shield is emphasis on
subtle differences among thinkers of their group.

For my part, I do not claim that theorists of any great alternative
are similar in *all* respects but only that they are at least similar in the
*core assumptions* that define the type.

While many prominent social theorists may be identified with one
of the four great alternatives, I cheerfully concede that some thinkers
do not neatly fit into one alternative, perhaps oscillating roughly
midway between two of them. One should not force such cases to fit,
as if demanding choice among four Procrustean beds. Yet just as the

four cardinal points of the compass are reference points for defining intermediate directions, the four primary types of social theory help describe those theorists who look for some middle way between two of them.

As Pascal said, "The last thing one settles in writing a book is what one should put in first" (Pensée 19). I will sketch the main directions of this work: As Chapter 1 shows, whether as forms of thought or approximations in practice, the seemingly incomparable primary alternatives can be compared in terms of shared problems addressed by them. While often including other goals (such as religious salvation or secular perfection of human potentials), each great alternative shared the elementary problem of doing something about human aggression—violent crime, civil wars, international wars.

Also, each saw such conflict as in large part linked to scarcity, defined as that situation when combined human wants exceed the social capacity to satisfy them. Each alternative has offered a grand strategy to confront the problem of scarcity, with a proclaimed solution that puts specific burdens and benefits on distinctive social groups.

Focusing on each strategy's preferred economic and political arrangements, I will put the same questions to each great alternative. Each alternative must be fairly defined and defended with the best arguments of its advocates. After all, it is at least possible that one of the alternatives is largely right, the others largely wrong. But no one has a right to that conclusion without first working through reasonable doubts.

If all real thinking begins with doubt, each alternative must be criticized as if it could also be wrong. Those caught up in a tradition tend to become so fond of their answers that they become blinded to any failings. Worse, they often forget the original aim and make an end out of what had been but a means. Such oblivion of purpose arises when those within a theoretical tradition have routinized their way of thinking about the primary problem of social theory. If the original, shared problem was to minimize human conflict linked to scarcity, then the more elaborate the restatement of that problem, the more it closes off possible alternative solutions. If such steps toward mental closure defeat progress against the *original* problem, then we must critically examine how the questions were phrased, for they stop rather than stimulate critical thought.

When the sleep of reason has produced monsters, its awakening may not be found in the renewed affirmations urged by advocates of the four paradigms. The Aristocrats would have us return to Confucius, Plato, Aristotle, or Aquinas; the Saints, to Buddha, Lao Tzu, Christ, or Gandhi. Ardent Capitalists may invoke Locke, Smith, Bentham, or Mill, while Socialists may urge us go back to the texts of Marx, Engels, Lenin, or Trotsky.

The spectacular popular repudiation of the Marxist-Leninist brand of socialism in Europe suggests that against any such reaffirmation—a fervent "Yes!"—one could at least consider negation: a resounding "No!" For in seeking a solution for human violence, each great alternative may sometimes make that problem worse, while also putting democratic freedoms much at risk. If so, one way out of a closed system of thought lies through a historical retracing of how its advocates got into it, perhaps through their will to power (cf. Foucault, 1980). Historical understanding and clear contrasts can expose the core premises of each alternative, which should be critiqued without partiality.

I regard myself as an outside critic of each of the four alternatives. I ask any readers who are already inside one of the paradigms to suspend preconceptions. Any who cannot may be made uncomfortable by this book. They would concur with critiques of the other three alternatives but take offense at critical review of their own. They would criticize this book in predictable ways from the predisposing premises of their tradition.

Readers comfortable with critiques of all four alternatives may yet be disturbed by my refusal to define any fifth way that could replace the others. I will recommend that we simply recognize both the achievements and the limitations of each of the four great alternatives. I further will insist on unqualified protection of the democratic freedoms, which assure that each can be publicly advocated but also publicly challenged. As a saying goes, we have all the answers, now we just need to decide which one is right. No, perhaps all of the received answers are wrong, at least when each pretends to be a self-sufficient solution to our troubles. Perhaps, by the test of historical practice, none of the paradigms viewed as a whole constitutes the truth, if truth is defined in the spirit of Charles Sanders Peirce as the confluence of independent streams of good evidence (cf. Deutsch, 1969).

While I yet believe that each alternative does contain some partial truths, I will close my last chapter by expressing doubt that the alternatives could be easily united as if fitting pieces to a puzzle. For another truth may be that the core assumptions of each alternative set it into conflict with those of the other alternatives. When the alternatives refuse to moderate their programs, they cannot all be right, since they require highly incompatible social choices. Looking for such incompatibilities among the four great alternatives will take you to the heart of the matter of both this book and the history of social thought.

# 1

# The Problem of Social Theory and Its Recasting as Four Problematics

> Increase to a sufficient degree the benevolence
> of men, or the bounty of nature, and you ren-
> der justice useless, by supplying its place with
> much nobler virtues, and more valuable bless-
> ings. The selfishness of men is animated by the
> few possessions we have in proportion to our
> wants. . . . '[T]is only from the selfishness and
> confin'd generosity of men, along with scanty
> provision nature has made for his wants, that
> justice derives its origin.
>
> David Hume,
> *A Treatise of Human Nature*

Within this chapter I want to distinguish three things: (1) shared *problems* of social theorists in handling the violent conflict of crime, civil war, or international war and in coping with the scarcities that are linked to such violence; (2) their definitions of distinctive *problematics*, by which I mean special ways of restating the problem in terms of core assumptions, constraining thought to only one kind of solution; and (3) their finished *paradigms*, by which I mean completed models or formulas of thought once the problematics are applied to questions of economic and political arrangements and rounded off with answers. Cutting in at the second level, Hume's understanding of the origin of justice reflects one of the great divides that distinguish the problematics of social theory, suggesting two alternative solutions to the scarcity that gives rise to major human conflict. Obviously, neither moderated selfishness nor increased supply is the common problem of political theory, since theorists already diverge by emphasizing one or the other as part of their solution to scarcity and associated conflicts.

Some would locate scarcity only in the past, or in certain societies only, since in many societies the means for meeting at least the basic economic needs of all are now in hand (e.g., Bookchin, 1971). But as Hume correctly understood, scarcity is not an absolute but a relative term, such that even highly egalitarian distribution may not stem the strains between aggregate, active human wants and the available supply.

Save for a few preliterate bands living amid unusual natural abundance, in most human experience the summed economic wants exceed social capacity to gratify. Further, there are also noneconomic scarcities that may keep the problem before us. Consider access to the most desirable mates. If only because of such practices as steady dating or monogamous mating, the quest for sexual gratification and steady companionship tends to engender zero-sum conflict: The win of one is but a loss to a rival. Or if hope of praise need not be zero sum, the pursuit of fame almost surely is so, at least in the sense that we cannot all be famous during the same 15 minutes.

Yet it is not so much scarcity as conflicts of interest arising from it that define the more immediate problem. Seeking to gratify their wants, different sets of persons want to produce or prevent changes in the status quo that simply conflict. At least many of these conflicts of *interest* lead on to conflicts in *action*, often violent. Most of the greatest specimens of social thought were produced against a scene of actual or anticipated mayhem. Murderous misuse of human beings has been a shared concern of virtually all significant social theorists, even those such as Machiavelli who teach a more efficient use of violence.

### Interhuman Predation as the Shared Primary Problem of Political Theory

Civilization is restraint. But restraint is what our species learns only with great difficulty. If Freud was right, even when precariously attained, restraint endures only with some tendency toward neurosis. Restraint is incomplete even within the conditions of life called "civilized," at least as a figure of speech. This is not to deny our essentially social nature but only to say that even within social life some people act as if they regarded others on the model of predator to prey. Under conditions of extreme scarcity such as literal starvation, even our sociality may be undermined, as when children tear food from the mouths of their grandparents (cf. Turnbull, 1972).

From emergence of the Acheulian axe through the atomic bombing of Japan, our species has killed its own kind. There have been moments of progress, as when gatherer-hunter bands or even peoples of field agriculture ceased to regard other humans as appropriate food (cf. Harris, 1977). Some observers such as Kropotkin would remind us that our histories or our newspapers distort the record in publicizing the mayhem, forgetting the more normal, peaceable cooperation among human beings. Yet much of our most disciplined cooperation has been to improve predation against others. Verdun, Gulag, Auschwitz, Hiroshima, and Kampuchea remind us that ever larger projects of mayhem remain possible, such as nuclear Armageddon.

In the spirit of Kant (who followed Rousseau), we can define the predatory attitude as that in which certain categories of others are regarded *merely* as means to ends, with the other's body or bodily well-being accorded no independent value. Predation as a practice emerges in any severe or often murderous misuse of human beings, especially when expressed in the various forms of aggression such as wars between peoples, civil war, or ordinary crime.

1. *The predation of wars.* Even if our earliest ancestors were living in internally cooperative bands, wars among peoples were probably rather commonplace in prehistoric human experience. While the evidence either way is thin, perhaps such violence of hunting-gathering bands was not normal but exceptional—when crowding occurred, and when food supplies were in unusually short supply. If so, it would parallel the occurrence of collective violence among bands of chimpanzees—as observed by Jane Goodall—although one must not assume that any other primate species constitutes a model of our own "nature." In any event, the violence of civilized, political communities has in its scale and savagery vastly exceeded the dying in wars between bands of known preliterate peoples, where informal rules have often limited the killing. City-states, empires, and now the nation-states have escalated the scale of warring, as recently illustrated by the loss of a least 1 million lives in the Iran-Iraq war. "Normal men," conservatively estimated R. D. Laing, "have killed perhaps 100,000,000 of their fellow normal men in the last fifty years" (Laing, 1969, 28). Coordinated slaughters of our own kind on such an extended scale surely constitute one aspect of the problem of any social philosophy.

2. *The predation of domestic intergroup aggression.* Another kind of predation consists in violent conflicts dividing what is usually regarded as a single society, including not only large-scale civil war but intergroup violence short of civil war. While often these have set class against class, we cannot neglect communal riots such as the resur-

gence of murderous ethnic conflicts of our time, now including the fringes of the Soviet Union. Predation arises whenever there is organized assault or murder of one group by the other, extending to assassinations, death squads, or even a genocide that spares no children. The extreme case of ethnic murder in cold blood is the Holocaust.

Not unlike counterrevolutionary theorists who say that they advocate only as much violence as is needed to restore order, revolutionaries may argue that the term "predation" is misapplied if the aim is to pass through discord to renewed concord (as argued by many seventeenth-century English or Scot Puritans, eighteenth-century rebels seeking natural rights, and twentieth-century Marxist-Leninists). Whatever merit there might be in arguments claiming justified violence, surely we may call it predation when those of one group murder the captured, helpless members of another group, including letting them starve when there is the wherewithal to secure food for them.

It can be argued that, even short of bloodshed, any severe exploitation of a group that causes injury or death is also predatory. In *The Condition of the Working Class in England*, Engels accused the British ruling class of mass murder, and Barrington Moore asks us why we always ignore misery and dying under old regimes but carefully count each corpse resulting from revolutionary overthrows (Moore, 1969, 505). But if severe exploitation or even inhuman neglect can be called predation, to include as such just any degree of unequal exchange relationship would go beyond our usage.

3. *The predation of crime.* A third form of predation is ordinary crime: largely individual acts of aggression when not performed by the mentally aberrant but rather by "normal" people pursuing some gratification in abnormal ways. While ordinary street crime may most readily come to mind, this could extend to some forms of what are now called "white-collar crime" as well, as when known but uncorrected hazards of a factory operation harm workers or nearby residents.

With possible exceptions such as Genghis Khan, Hitler, or the Marquis de Sade, few have defended wars between peoples, of part of a people against another, or individual crime as if good in themselves. Many theorists have defended use of force—especially in international or civil wars—as a necessary means to the end, but even these join in the paramount agreement of social theorists that ultimately minimizing human mayhem must be a primary aim of social theory. I am speaking here of apparent intentions, not results, since I fully agree with those who warn that theorists through their followers may have only raised the scale of human murder (cf. Berger, 1976; Fishkin, 1979). But bracketing aside any such sins of the progeny that some would visit on the theoretical fathers, most great theorists have put a high priority on pacification of human existence. Their intentions were far superior to the outcomes of their work.

Ending murder is just the beginning. Aristotle would remind us that politics should aim not just at life but rather at the *good* life—in its classical sense of virtue rather than its modern corruption. But ending murder is not to be construed as only a Hobbesian preoccupation with preservation of life against premature extinction at the hands of others. Surely Hobbes went too far in thinking that all who die for a cause are necessarily mad. Actually not even Hobbes believed that politics must have a single goal—only that it ought to have as a primary aim that of preserving life, and then shift at least toward "commodious living" as a larger object.

Maximization is madness. Literal or unbounded maximization of any single, concrete aim in life may be taken as an appropriate definition of mental aberrancy. Boundless pursuit of any specific kind of object can run into excess, frustrating even minimal attainment of many other kinds of goods. Great literary models of obsessive pursuits make this point well enough, as in Marlowe's Tamerlane, Goethe's Faust, Melville's Ahab, and the like.[1]

Any reasonable social theory would make way for a plurality of human ends, but I do not think one can always rank them in a static hierarchy as the Aristocrat would tend to do. One may want to shift emphases among them, such that after attaining certain thresholds of an object of primary need one would go on to the next priority as the dominant motivator. This sounds, of course, like Abraham Maslow's allegedly empirical theory of the hierarchy of needs. He argued from the idea of a rather general human nature, which shifts its paramount motivation once a given motive is securely reached at a sufficient threshold, as if ascending the steps of a ladder: physiological, safety, social, esteem, self-actualization, and then beta or higher needs (Maslow, 1954; 1971).

It is beside the point whether Maslow's model is empirically correct or even testable in regard to the vaguer, highest-level needs. I only mean to concur with the tendency of most theorists to defend some comparable model as an ultimate value judgment, or how we *ought* to approach possible objects of human want. That is, we ought to begin with some priority on human "physical" needs but only in order to lay the basis for a shift of emphasis to increasingly more "spiritual" needs of social belonging, self-esteem, or self-actualizing creativity. I am recommending (not pretending to discover) an ultimate value judgment: My conception of the good is to raise as many people as possible as high as possible up a Maslow-like hierarchy of needs.

Most past theorists shared at least this commitment to raising our kind beyond merely animalistic needs. They, too, acknowledged that the animal needs must be at least minimally satisfied before moving on to what is distinctively human. Aristotle, Christ, Adam Smith, and Karl Marx would agree at least on that much. To say that physical needs should have some initial priority does not imply that such precedence would always dominate practical choices, though. As Aristotle put it (in a teleological idiom I do not share), human institutions such as family or polis arose for mere life but by nature exist to fulfill the good life.

## Extending the Definition of the Problem: Predation as Caused by Scarcity

Most social theorists put some priority on physical security, here understood less as threats from natural disasters than as threats from other human beings. But some theorists—who could be called the "ruthless realists"—will be bracketed aside as not even intending to get at the causes of predation, choosing instead to secure order by what could be viewed as merely improved predation. The primarily technical advice given to princes by a Chinese Legalist, a Kautilya in India, or a Machiavelli or a Richelieu in Europe would be cases in point.

Ruthless realists aside, then, social theorists attempting to solve the problem of human predation have gone on to view such predation as at least partially caused by scarcity. Even thinkers who would also indict flawed human nature as part of the problem have usually conceded some role of scarcity behind crime, civil strife, or wars between peoples. Not all situations of scarcity have engendered predation, since often people have sacrificed for their families, their societies, and so forth; but nearly all large-scale predations have presupposed some scarcity.

By *scarcity* we mean that situation in a defined social sphere where aggregated human wants (especially when articulated as demands) exceed the present and immediately projected socially available supply. With economic goods and services as the central referent, such scarcity has been common to most contexts, although in varying degree and varying recourse to the predatory means by which some have sought to resolve the tension for themselves and their own.

If not an absolute term, scarcity must then be analyzed relative to levels of demand and powers to supply.

Looking first at the magnitude of demand, we find that there are two key components: (1) the number of persons, and (2) the scale of their demands. By demand we mean active claims on the social product, excluding from view the many wishes that do not become aspirations, expectations, or live claims.

The other side of scarcity consists in the present and immediately potential supply of what is wanted. In economic terms, supply manifests itself in two forms: (1) the existing stocks of usable consumer goods and services relevant to demand; and (2) the social productive powers, which include raw materials, infrastructure (such as roads or buildings), tools and machines, relevant technological knowledge and skills, and mental and physical labor power.

The bodies and minds of persons can thus fall on both sides of the equation, constituting the foundations of certain demands while also being productive forces. As Marx somewhere noted, the worker's body is a state of need as well as a productive force. Similarly, Mexican peasants speak of a new child not only as one more mouth but also as two more hands.

Perception of scarcity in the dual form of levels of demand and also of powers to meet those demands perhaps awaited the rise of scientific agriculture in the late seventeenth century, permitting John Locke's vision of 1,000:1 increases in productivity on tilled land over what nature would yield on virgin land. Thus, if earlier theorists understood *demand* as something highly variable and controllable, it was now understood that great variation and control was also possible on the side of *supply*.

In the eighteenth century—during the period of conscious transition from "ancients" to "moderns"—theorists came to see that both sides were important in explaining predatory behavior. Pietro Verri and the Milan school of political economy held that both demand and supply should be adjusted to secure a balance for the society. Rousseau also gave great attention to both wants and powers to satisfy them in his theory of how one could fully explain the occurrence of evil human behavior without assuming original sin or innate depravity. He believed that those who want only what it is within their powers to satisfy can have no motive to aggress against others, so all wickedness must arise from an avoidable imbalance of wants and powers. When persecuted by French and even Genevan authorities, Rousseau went into English exile with David Hume, whose recognition of duality is clear in the epigraph of this chapter. Either curtailing demand on the one side or boosting supply on the other could make "justice" no longer a problem. But very few theorists have given equal attention to both sides of the equation, which leads to the first cut in distinguishing the primary paradigms of human thought.

## Converting the Problem to Problematics: Correcting Scarcity by Either Moderating Wants or Boosting Production

With few exceptions, most theorists emphasized only one side of the demand/supply problem as posed above, even when they recognized the relevance of the other side. Thus Rousseau endorsed moderation of wants much more than any enlargement of powers. He advanced in his *Social Contract* a theory of politics that would deny any man the right to command the powers of another at his own discretion. This was meant as much to prevent growth of demand in the person exercising such despotic control as to protect private use of powers for the dominated individual's own purposes. Rousseau—whose egalitarianism stopped before gender—did not apply the same theory to women, whom he thought could be subjected to male authority without either kind of harm. In any event, Rousseau identified the causes of corruption with whatever creates an imbalance between wants and the powers to meet them. This led him to condemn most features of modernity that link to the project of enlarged productive powers, since such features risk an even greater swelling of demands. Rousseau denounced urban concentrations of population, excessive social scale, industrialization, elaborate division of labor, increased commerce and communications among peoples, and the like (cf. Cook, 1975). Although not a pure type, Rousseau was closest to the Saint formula in key turns of thought.

### Curtailing Wants as Solution: The Spirit of Buddha

The origins of the want-limitation theorists are found in the agrarian vision, and they especially emerged in those societies that did not live by plundering other peoples. Given this exclusion of conquest and colonization as a means of enhancing powers to satisfy wants, and given the usual agrarian doubts about the saving possibilities of any science and technology, the traditional mind understands that there is only just so much arable land, which can yield only just so much food and fiber. Once at least cleared and supplied with irrigation works, the land is able to support only just so many persons of strictly limited summed claims. A growing demand on the part of some persons necessarily threatens the existing consumption level of the others. This poses a situation less well described as zero-sum conflict (any winnings of some exactly match the losings of others) than as "negative sum" (any winnings of some are exceeded by the losings of others). For as we have recently observed in parts of Africa, severe social conflict devastates agricultural production.

To the extent that nearly all lose from any social conflict that causes such a failure in production, the avoidance of severe social conflict constitutes a limited common good—but not necessarily an *equal* good—in moderating wants for more. Adding to this the likely defeat of rebellion in any case, it is clear why the wisdom literatures of agrarian societies in both East and West have stressed moderation of desire as the key to personal happiness as well as social harmony.

Many observers have suggested that Eastern thought stresses the ideal of harmony more than justice. But even Western premodern thought taught a sense of justice that was in some theorists (Plato, Bodin) expressly likened to a harmony as well as to social health. A twentieth-century student of Greek antiquity puts it well:

> Ancient literature teems with exhortations to limit one's desires—exhortations to the rich to avoid provoking envy, to the poor to avoid discontent and rebellion. Here . . . antiquity was to a degree conditioned by its economic situation. Living as they did, always in an economy of scarcity, the *distribution* of economic goods was their most vital and insoluble problem. Abundance or luxury for one man meant quite literally starvation for another. (Winspear, 1940, 215)

The social project of moderating aggregate desire could only be attained if individual persons curtailed their wants. Hence there was a need to generate appropriate arguments and images to encourage individual restraint, usually identifying moderation of desire as the means to individual happiness in this life as well as any hoped-for next one. To be dominated by desire, teaches the *Bhagavad Gita*, is to be as a boat adrift in the winds. To seek happiness through indulging those desires that make us worse persons, taught Plato, is to attempt filling up a vessel with a leaky pitcher, or to be as a plover on a beach, whose life is all influx and efflux.

While I have said that such thought along with its rhetoric is most typical of agrarian societies, it retains a very lively presence in our own world. It remains quite vital, for instance, among those who still adhere to the less corrupted forms of moral and religious teachings received from our preindustrial past, especially among those for whom pacification of human existence is a central this-world objective. Thus a modern Islamic Sufi urges that the true holy war (*jihad*) must be against the evil desires of our own souls (Muhaiyaddeen, 1987).

It also arises among many postindustrial skeptics regarding the capacity of science and technology to fix more problems than they cause. Here we have the ecological sensibility that is now quite widespread, since the environmental awakening of the 1970s (cf. Ophuls, 1977; Elgin, 1981). As one observer puts it, we are being squeezed between the twin jaws of a vise, the one consisting of the drawdowns of nonrenewable resources (the "mining" of not only mineral deposits but also our soil fertility, water tables, etc.) and the other consisting of what we push back into the environment—pollution and other degradations of the life system (Catton, 1980, 10).

Aside from the sensibilities of the religious peacemakers and the ecologists (often combined in the same persons), even those trying to defend stagnating industrialized economies (whether capitalist or socialist) often return willy-nilly to the rhetoric of want limitation. Such rhetoric had little presence at the birth of the two grand models of modern thought except as temporary, tactical expedients to bolster more long-run enjoyments.

For the moderns doubted that we could ultimately limit human wants to the rule of reason. Rather, reason becomes the instrument of wants. Thomas Hobbes wrote in the seventeenth century that "the thoughts are to the desires as scouts or spies, to range abroad, and find the way to the things desired" (*Leviathan*, I, viii). In the eighteenth century, David Hume was even more emphatic: "Reason is, and ought only to be the slave of the passions, and can never pretend to any other office than to serve and obey them" (*A Treatise on Human Nature*, II, iii, 3).

### Enlarging Powers as Solution: The Baconian Alternative

Those who are not impressed with want limitation as a solution to scarcity turn to the alternative of power expansion.

Premodern forms of power expansion were usually predatory rather than productive—armed raids in quest of plunder or new territory to colonize. Often in history these have been accompanied by religious justifications, as when mercantile interests were behind the expansion of Islam as well as the reaction of the Christian crusaders. In the expansion of Europe into colonies in what is now the Third World, rationalizations about a civilizing mission were present. As Machiavelli recommended in *The Prince*, or as Lenin complained in his *Imperialism*, predatory plundering abroad could sometimes minimize predation at home. Machiavelli's horizons remained largely within a zero-sum world where wealth could not be created but only conquered, then distributed among the victorious people to unite them behind the "generous" prince (cf. Orwin, 1978). Hitler, both in his demand for *lebensraum* abroad and in his genocidal projects within Germany or Nazi-controlled territory, regressed to that pattern. And ironically, the same science and technology created with a view to conquest of *nature* has oftentimes been turned toward conquest of other people.

The philosophic contrast to the Buddha and want limitation, then, is the response of Francis Bacon, as in this passage from *New Atlantis*: "The end of our foundation is the knowledge of the causes and secret motions of things, and the enlarging of the bounds of human empire, to the effecting of all things possible." What was needed was a new method or pathway (*methodos* is Greek for pathway) to knowledge of nature. With minds freed from traditionalist "Idols" and energies turned to experimentation—described as having nature "vexed" or "tortured" to make her yield her secrets—humanity could accelerate the heretofore slow process of technological innovation (Bacon, 1955).

Through new instruments and techniques, Bacon was confident, we could thus conquer nature, turning its potential to our own purposes of economic abundance and even a longer life.[2] Through enlarged human powers and consequent supply, we could defeat scarcity and hence the conflicts of interest that in the past caused predation. But this dream for the pacification of human existence would require not only some diversion of resources from projects of war to productive research but also a major shift in human thinking: Instead of asking how we might adapt to largely beneficent nature and its cycles, we were henceforward to secure indefinite progress, rather, by adapting indifferent or almost hostile nature to our own purposes. According to Aubrey's *Brief Lives*, Bacon would often tell his servant that "the world is made for man, . . . and not man for the world."[3]

As Max Weber and others have observed, the new project of scientific conquest of nature marked the disenchantment of the world. It presupposed that human knowledge can discern regularities, discounting not only magic but even any miraculous interventions of the divine. As Kenneth Burke put it, once finished with His ordering of nature, God is converted from a capricious variable to an invariant term (Burke, 1945, 98–99). The upshot of this kind of thinking is an enlarged sphere of *human* power to manipulate the world, which Eric Voegelin likens to the Gnostic heresy holding that we can become as God (Voegelin, 1956–87). Others suggest a Faustian image of the modern project, since the legend of the pact with the Devil arose in the late sixteenth century and became widely known (Leiss, 1972, 40–41; Redner, 1982). In Bacon, Nature ceases to be mother but rather a mistress or harlot to be rudely mastered, reminiscent of Machiavelli's mastery of *fortuna* ("lady luck") in the political sphere. As if by a seduction or rape, nature must be wholly dominated (cf. Leiss, 1972, 25–26; Merchant, 1980).

The moderns abandon the traditionalist view of human limits within nature's cycles, as if we could beat all bends into linear progress. Early modernists yet understood the need for some restraint, especially as linked to population limitation (cf. Malthus, "Essay on Population," or James Mill, "An Essay on the Impolicy of a Bounty on the Exportation of Grain," ch. 2). But in the nineteenth and early twentieth centuries, some moderns even doubted the need to curb population to moderate the scope of economic demand. As late as 1949, Mao was saying this: "Even if China's population multiplied many times she is fully capable of finding a solution; the solution is production" (in Fan, 1972, 70).

Perhaps nature abhors linearity, especially in humanly created projects. Our scientific-technological knowledge may not save us from ecological and social limits to growth, or possible self-destruction through scientifically improved weapons of war. Nuclear humanicide, writes Jonathan Schell, would represent "not the defeat of some purpose but an abyss in which all human purposes would be drowned for all time" (Schell, 1982, 95).

The core of modernity in either its Capitalist or Socialist primary types consists in two assumptions: (1) that labor rather than nature creates most value; and (2) that this value creation is potentially without limit if only labor were made ever more productive, more efficiently and effectively performed. But if both main schools of the modern world—both Capitalist and Socialist—converge in these teachings, they diverge sharply on the appropriate techniques of economic organization for maximizing the potential of science and technology to give us cornucopia.

## The Second Cut in Defining the Formulas: Moderating Whose Wants or Enlarging Whose Powers?

It is one thing to choose a strategy against the scarcity that causes conflict, but another to assign the primary burdens and benefits of its implementation. This brings us to a second cut in the definition of our four problematics or formulas of thought, here focused on the question of class prejudice. Any society will have a variety of nonclass stratification dimensions, such as age, gender, ethnicity, and the like. But while these can be independently very important in shaping the details of political thought and practice in a given setting, stratifications by wealth and income have a more uniform prominence in at least civilized societies. These tend to align other stratification dimensions in political coalitions. As for wealth and income, one could differentiate strata indefinitely, and doing so would no doubt give more prominence to "middle class" identifications.

As the income "pyramid" has become more like a "diamond," the middle income groups become more important, but that middle sector was almost absent in most contexts of history. Since my point is to sketch the primary paradigms of social thought, I will not address the matter of these middling positions but more crudely ask whether theorists lean more toward up-scale class loyalties or rather more toward down-scale ones. In distinctive ways the Aristocrat and the Capitalist would put the burden of their strategy more on the humbler classes, while the Saint and the Socialist offer distinctive solutions that would shift the burden more to the upper classes. The first two, if you like, are variants of the political "right," while the latter are variants of the "left" (although these concepts date only from the late eighteenth century, when King Louis XVI sat on the right side of the dais with his followers before him in the parliamentary assembly, while revolutionary critics sat toward the left).

Among other rough rules of thumb, those with upper-class identities will tend to say that *egalitarian* attitudes or practices cause social conflict, injustice, economic ruin, or loss of political freedom, while those with lower-class identities will see *inegalitarian* attitudes or practices as causing such unwanted consequences. Or again, the former will put the burden of proof for any claimed benefit on those who would demand more equal distribution of income, while the latter put the onus of argument rather on those who would enlarge or even merely preserve the standing economic inequalities.

Clearly differentiating the polar positions gives us a workable perspective on those who may oscillate in the middling zone. Perhaps these bring an added complication as so well phrased by John Adams, who thought human nature loves "equality" when it looks up the social ranks, "inequality" when it looks down (Dorfman, 1967, 126). Any associate professor will understand that.

### The Aristocrat and the Saint

There were really two kinds of "ancients," just as there are two kinds of "moderns." Regarding the former, the main contents of want-limitation theories are best understood by distinguishing the Aristocrat, whose class loyalties are upscale (great landowners), and the Saint, whose loyalties are downscale (e.g., peasants or artisans). By definition, both models emphasize moderation of wants as the key to social peace. But while the Aristocrat emphasizes at least enough moderation of upper-class wants to permit practice of charity and to avoid stimulating envy, the paramount aim is clearly the moderation of lower-class wants to prevent class war. The Saint, on the other hand, stresses moderation of upper-class wants as the primary objective, even if it means that those born to wealth must turn to voluntary poverty to avoid hypocrisy. While this may often seem to be little more than a shift of emphasis, I shall show that it makes a massive difference in the typical thought contents of the Aristocrat and the Saint.

### The Capitalist and the Socialist

By definition, both the Capitalist and the Socialist (for the most, liberal traditions versus variants of Marxism) emphasize that the problems of scarcity can be solved by a Baconian expansion of powers over nature. But whose powers? While mutually embracing modernization of the means of production through science and technology, the two models obviously diverge over what Marxists call the "relations of production"—with the one favoring private ownership and market mechanisms, the other social ownership and central planning.

In practice, though, "private" ownership of publicly prominent corporations tends to be ownership by very few, at least by the measure of major shares of stock, proprietary voice, and so forth; while the Marxist "social" ownership may mean in practice less ownership by all—including the proletariat—than control by apparatchiks. But the Capitalist arose praising less the upper class in general—which included idle aristocrats—than the "industrious and rational" (Locke) scientific farmer, the "middling classes" (the language of James Mill), and the "captains of industry" (social Darwinists). The Marxist, like the socialist forerunners and anarchists, claimed allegiance rather to the proletariat, perhaps often less out of love of the workers than out of hatred of the rich.

I have already conceded that some individual theorists fall into the interstices. But even they will be better understood if analyzed in relation to the four primary paradigms defined by the two cuts given above and in the previous section. I sketch the four types roughly in Table 1.1 but much more richly in later chapters.

While one could readily cite advocates of each paradigm among our contemporaries, the paradigms have also been visible in most historical contexts. Indeed, sometimes they may roughly describe all of the "parties" within a context. Let us examine one such case. Among the Hebrews at the time of Christ, there were four recognized religious sects: Sadducees, Pharisees, Essenes, and Zealots. (The scribes were legal clerks attached to the first two, not a distinctive sect.)

The Sadducees, chiefly great landowners who dominated the high priesthoods in the Temple of Jerusalem, were in many known details close to what I call the Aristocrat paradigm, as in their insistence on maximal free will and retributive ("an eye for an eye . . . ") punishment to maintain firm law and order. Flavius Josephus, the ancient Jewish historian, tells us that "the Sadducees are able to persuade none but the rich, and have not the populace obsequious to them, but the Pharisees have the multitude on their side" (*Antiquities of the Jews*, XIII, x).

The Pharisees were often merchants or professionals oriented more toward the local synagogues and traditions extending beyond the written law. As Spinoza later said, they were much like the seventeenth-century Calvinists, for they let sanctimonious adherence to small duties crowd out attention to the large ones, such as extensive charitable giving. In some ways the Pharisees anticipate the modern

Capitalist model. Seeing a mix of fate and freedom in human choices, they wanted less capital punishment, emphasizing stripes or fines as sufficient deterrence. They favored abandonment of the Jubilee custom of cancelling debts, instead just carrying them forward. This may in part explain why they were denounced as "covetous" for thinking they could serve both God and Mammon (Luke 16:13–14; cf. Finkelstein, 1962; Neusner, 1973; and Bowker, 1973).

The Essenes were a mystical sect whose members were mostly celibate and lived in ascetic, largely vegetarian rural communes, where they performed manual labor and did kindnesses to wayfarers. They emphasized fate in many human choices, and hence were inclined to look for repentance and offer forgiveness, even for those excommunicated from their group. This compassionate, pacifistic group closely fit the great alternative of the Saint (cf. Josephus, *Jewish War*, II, 125, ch. 7; Ginsburg, 1956).

Finally, those eventually called the Zealots belatedly originated in the region of Galilee and were to have their last stand at Masada in 73 A.D. While the Pharisees would not dine with tax collectors (the publicans), the Zealots of the Sicarii group went further in opposing a regressive Roman tax that hurt the poor: Concealing short knives (*sicarii*) under their cloaks, they would roam the festival crowds, murdering Roman authorities and even Jewish collaborators—including Jonathan, the high priest of the Temple. Often they were caught and crucified. Zealot militancy was in part a religious or national fanaticism, as in their cry of "Sacrilege!" when money changers brought into the Temple coins bearing the image of the Roman emperor. But in their plundering raids on the property of the well-to-do, their decision to burn the Jerusalem Record Office to make recovery of debts impossible and thus make allies of debtors, their executions of many more priests and nobles when briefly in control of Jerusalem, and their contempt for most temporal government, one may see some kinship with the modern militant Socialist (Josephus, *Jewish War*, II, 264, ch. 7, and II, 425, ch. 9). Leaders of the Sadducees and the Pharisees sought the crucifixion of Christ, who shared Galilean origins and much of the rhetoric of the Zealots (cf. Brandon, 1967). But he was in many commitments closer to the Essenes, the only Jewish sect not sharply criticized in the New Testament. A violent rising of the Zealots brings death, says Acts 5, and "it will come to nought" (Acts 5:37–38).

One could easily show roughly parallel religiopolitical forms in other contexts, especially mid-seventeenth-century England. Many who study comparative human experience distrust generalization, emphasizing discontinuities across changing contexts of space and time. While appreciating what is different in human cultures, I must point out that the opposite trap is to exaggerate uniqueness. Human

**Table 1.1    Balancing Wants and Powers to Satisfy: Four Paradigm
Solutions to Problems of Scarcity and Conflict**

|  |  |
|---|---|
|  | *Buddhistic Want Limitation.* Whether in preindustrial agrarian or postindustrial ecological limitations, it assumes a steady-state economy. Given finite capacities to gratify desires, avoidance of zero-sum conflict requires moderation of wants and respect for natural cycles. Moral training must be central. |
| *Identities Lean toward Upper Strata.* If loyalties favor mid-to-upper class groups, theorists defend socioeconomic inequalities (property, division of labor, incomes) and the degree of political inequality needed to protect such inequalities. | 1. *The Aristocrat's Formula: Curtail Wants of the Lower Classes.* The burden of this solution to scarcity and conflict is primarily put on the poor, who must limit their numbers and the magnitudes of their wants. In this system of stratified expectations, none must want to live better than their parents. These theorists often themselves live in some luxury, but they usually urge at least minimal restraint on the rich, who must avoid conspicuous consumption and practice charity to minimize class envy.<br><br>Favoring minimal if any democratic concessions, these theorists would include most Confucian or Hindu classics as well as Plato, Aristotle, Xenophon, Polybius, Cicero, Aquinas, Hooker, Filmer, Burke, deMaistre, Voegelin, and Strauss. |
| *Identities Lean toward Lower Strata.* If loyalties favor mid-to-lower class groups, theorists sharply criticize inequalities of property, division of labor and incomes, while tending to demand much more political equality, if not the extreme of anarchism. | 2. *The Saint's Formula: Curtail Wants of the Upper Classes.* The burden of this solution is shifted to the rich, who are even invited to practice voluntary poverty to be closer to the sufferings of the poor. The luxury of the rich requires not only harsh exploitation of the poor but much state violence to preserve such privilege. While recognizing that the poor have little margin for any further want limitation, Saints at least expect them to abstain from counterviolence.<br><br>Usually accepting small private property, these often vegetarian pacifists tend to favor decentralized and democratic politics. They are the gentle sages of history: Buddha, Lao Tzu, Chuang Tzu, Mahavira, Christ, St. Francis, Fox, Mounier, Maurin, Day, Thoreau, Tolstoy, Ruskin, Gandhi, Schumacher, and Berry. |

**Table 1.1   Balancing Wants and Powers to Satisfy: Four Paradigm Solutions to Problems of Scarcity and Conflict (continued)**

| | |
|---|---|
| | *Baconian Power Expansion.* Instead of taking the supply as if a constant, conquer scarcity not by a vain quest for self-control but by scientific control over nature. Human productive powers may be made almost boundless through science-driven technological innovation and new techniques of economic organization. |
| *Identities Lean toward Upper Strata.* If loyalties favor mid-to-upper class groups, theorists defend socioeconomic inequalities (property, division of labor, incomes) and the degree of political inequality needed to protect such inequalities. | 3. *The Capitalist's Formula: Expand Productive Powers in Private Ownership.* Give free rein to those Locke called "the industrious and rational to recombine resources toward maximal productivity of labor. Self-interested economic aspirations are harnessed through alienable private property, the division of labor, unequal incomes, and extended free-market areas. The boosts in innovation, effort, and so forth are expected to raise economic supply, surpassing any growth in demand caused by mobility, example, advertising, and so on. When confident that the high growth can thus neutralize social conflict, theorists accept liberal competitions of ideas, of candidates, and of institutional units.<br><br>Examples include Locke, Sydney, Hume, Smith, Ricardo, Bentham, the Mills, Spencer, Sumner, Hayek, Berger and Friedman. |
| *Identities Lean toward Lower Strata.* If loyalties favor mid-to-lower class groups, theorists sharply criticize inequalities of property, division of labor and incomes, while tending to demand much more political equality, if not the extreme of anarchism. | 4. *The Socialist's Formula: Expand Productive Powers in Social Ownership.* Although sharing the Capitalist's faith that modernized productive powers can surpass any growth in economic demand, the Socialist says that the higher potential of both productive forces and human development requires an end of relations of production that have become obsolete "fetters." A more collective, cooperative economy of central planning would feature social ownership of the means of production, an end to full-time division of labor, and ultimate distribution according to need alone. A transitional radical democracy would give way to no state at all with an end to property, classes, and class conflict.<br><br>Examples include a variety of Socialist forerunners, the Socialist anarchists, Marx and Engels, and all variants of Marxism since. |

similarities are at least as interesting as their differences, and there is no good reason to slight either. Both find expression through the primary models of social thought, which offer guideposts for understanding what has been thought or done in the course of building human civilization.

There are several reasons why one finds recurring approximations of the four primary alternatives in widely varying human contexts. For one thing, the four alternatives logically exhaust the possible simple solutions to the problem of scarcity and the conflict arising from it. Also, as will become apparent, the four alternatives speak to the interests of different economic layers of societies. But finally, the four alternatives seem to resonate with distinctive aspects of our common human nature. As already conceded, some individuals may bridge at least two of the four primary alternatives of social thought, but most social theorists incline toward one. Beyond their life circumstances, possibly something in their *unique* personal natures may in part explain this attraction. Yet, if only because some individuals shift from one alternative to another during the course of a lifetime, perhaps each paradigm reflects a corner of our *common* human nature, resonating with some inclination shared by each of us even when unacknowledged. Thus, convergent causes make the paradigms keep returning across the centuries: They reflect aspects of human nature as well as recurring situations of scarcity, conflict, and inequalities.

## The Political Modes of the Paradigms

Most regimes now claim to be "democratic" in some sense. Is this good news for democracy, or is it often but the triumph of hypocrisy—another homage vice pays to virtue? (See Dunn, 1979, 11.) Before our own time, it should be noted, many theorists felt free to express hostility to democracy.

And what is democracy? One must check any impulse to claim some privileged definition, as if democracy were some existential Platonic form. It is an intellectually dubious enterprise to advance a whole political philosophy under the guise of "correctly" defining some contestable term such as *justice, freedom,* or *democracy.* Not even original meanings can lay claim to being the always privileged ones. But for what it is worth, the word "democracy" has Greek roots, combining *demos* (the people) and *kratein* (the verb, to rule)—thus suggesting rule of the people.

Perhaps the people, like constitutional monarchs, usually reign more than rule. But at least democracy is weighted toward broadened popular participation in governance, going beyond mere equality before ordinary laws to insist on at least a legal equality in basic civic rights linked to formation of the laws. There are many practiced or possible forms of democracy thus understood, but this book will ask how each paradigm relates to what we call *liberal representative democracy* as later defined (cf. Held, 1987; Held and Pollitt, 1986).

Each of the four great paradigms expresses itself in various political modes—often through different individuals embracing the formula, but sometimes even at different times in the life of a single adherent. Thus, we might find our alternative paradigms operating in any of these modes: (1) the dream of anarchy; (2) the empowerment of the enlightened expert(s); (3) support for democracy to implement or sustain the formula; and (4) acceptance of any nondemocratic form, should democracy threaten the formula.

### Anarchism instead of Democracy

In the dream of anarchy, adherents to a paradigm fondly imagine its implementation with such success that all conflict ceases, and hence the rationale for maintaining any state structure. In this vision—or perhaps illusion—any democracy is at most but a transition stage to such a condition.

The Aristocrats alone usually resist this dream, checked perhaps by a typical belief in innate human aggressiveness and the need to maintain "order" against it. But even they could imagine the select few living without need of governance. Thus, Samuel Parker—the Restoration apologist for Anglicanism and royal absolutism against the "giddy multitude"—said that if we were all "as wise and honest as Socrates" we would live wholly in our own liberty (Ashcraft, 1986, 49, 52). Sometimes leaning toward the Aristocratic vision, Ralph Waldo Emerson in his "On Politics" wrote, "To educate the wise man the state exists, and with the appearance of the wise man, the state expires."

The dream that not just the wise but everyone could—through the special formula of the paradigm—live in anarchy has stronger exemplars among the other three models, including the Saint (e.g., Lao Tzu, Thoreau, Tolstoy, Gandhi), the Socialist (e.g., Bakunin, Kropotkin, Marx and Engels), and even the Capitalist (Spencer, Sumner, and at least near-anarchy in Rothbard and Nozick).

### Expertise against Democracy

The empowerment of expertise is a very different mode, although sometimes viewed as a way station toward the stateless society. As Michael Walzer noted, "All arguments for exclusive rule, all antidemocratic arguments, if they are serious, are arguments from special knowledge" (Walzer, 1983, 284). In the present case, the "special knowledge" or wisdom is largely defined by adherence to the special formula in question.

For the Aristocrat one thinks of ideal ruler traditions, such as the story of Solomon. It may be Plato's ruler-guardians eclipsing all politics, or similar visions of rule by "the best" in Aristotle, Xenophon, Cicero, and so forth.

As for the Saint, there is Lao Tzu's vision of a ruler who lives simply and leaves the people in peace, ruling his kingdom without ruinous meddling, as one fries a small fish. Buddhist and Christian mirrors for princes suggest similar dreams of rulers both wise and gently good. John Ruskin quite surprisingly called himself a "Tory"—a lover of kings—although saying that he meant not actual kings of his own time but rather ideal kings who worked harder and took less, such as the kings found in Homer or Walter Scott (Ruskin, 1978, 5–6).[4]

If the Aristocrat and the Saint sometimes tended toward nearly theocratic versions of empowerment of the wise, the moderns are more inclined to a secular technocracy. The Capitalist variant began with the Enlightenment flirtations with the idea of the enlightened autocrat or patriot-king. Technocratic leanings have emerged among many reform currents as well: the positivism of Auguste Comte; the utilitarianism of Bentham, James Mill, John Stuart Mill; the progressivism of Lester Ward and Thorstein Veblen; or the behaviorism of B. F. Skinner.

In the Socialist paradigm, the Fabians were mildly technocratic, and the Saint-Simonians and Edward Bellamy were strongly so. Like leanings have pervaded later Marxisms as well, especially within the official Marxisms of the Soviet Union and Eastern Europe. Every Leninist is a kind of technocrat in that leading elements of the Communist party of select professional revolutionaries—"the vanguard of the proletariat"—are claimed to have the most "scientific consciousness" to put socialism in place.

### Confined or Conditional Democracy

Another political mode is that of contingent support for democracy. Each of the four formulas may accord a certain limited scope for democracy when it helps either to implement or to sustain the formula in question.

Even the Aristocrat could in the "mixed regime" theory (discussed in Chapter 3) concede some gesture of democracy as the price of popular support against the graver dangers of a brutal tyranny, of slave or helot risings, or of military threat from abroad.

The Saint, more temperamentally inclined toward democracy, will especially support democracy when it helps curtail the greeds and violence of the upper classes toward the lower.

The Capitalist of the seventeenth or eighteenth centuries embraced some degree of "popular government" to undermine feudal regimes. Even now the Capitalist in either the classical or reform variant is especially fond of democratization when it challenges communist regimes, as typified by the Solidarity movement in Poland or the strivings toward national self-determination within the Soviet Union or China.

The Socialist may espouse democratization as a means not only to overthrow a reactionary regime (Engels fought in the 1848 German liberal revolt in Baden), but also to overthrow capitalism within a bourgeois democratic regime, as typified in Trotsky's theory that "democratic demands" are the complement to transitional economic demands in undermining capitalism. But if this recalls the experience of Leninism in the Soviet Union, we are then reminded that such conditional commitments to democracy as mere means to implement or sustain a formula are perforce unstable.

### Any Regime but Democracy

The last mode of each formula is to attack democracy sharply, perhaps accepting anything but democracy. Each paradigm here generates its distinctive set of reasons for such hostility. Thus, just as there are really four theories of democratic advocacy, so there are at least four variants of antidemocracy.

Anticipating discussions in later chapters, one can forecast with confidence where each becomes antidemocratic: the Aristocrat, when it seems to inflame popular demands and threaten order; the Saint, when it seems to support with violence the greeds of an affluent minority, as when Thoreau and Garrison scorned democracy for supporting slavery; the Capitalist, when democracy threatens to choose socialism; the Socialist, when it leans toward capitalism.

All such cases will be explored as I examine each of the primary paradigms of political thought. Each tends to imagine only ideal conditions for its implementation in the world, never conceding that the formula itself could be at fault. The avatar of a formula, unwilling to concede its practical failure, instead demands its more zealous pursuit. Yes, even if freedom must be pushed out of the way.

Hannah Arendt uttered a complaint against Marx that she also applied to the radicals of the French Revolution:

> The role of revolution was no longer to liberate men from the oppression of their fellow men, let alone to found freedom, but to liberate the life process of society from the fetters of scarcity so that it could swell

into a stream of abundance. Not freedom but abundance became now
the aim of revolution. (Arendt, 1963, 58)

Perhaps underestimating Marx's concern for freedom, Arendt nevertheless correctly saw that many modern revolutionaries have so
emphasized the quest for an economic solution that they have subordinated the forms of freedom. But while Arendt apparently saw this
risk only among radical variants of the moderns, I have generalized
her insight to all four paradigms of political theory.

If all four paradigms thus push freedom aside, they may also come
to hold that those who criticize the "correct" formula, defend an
"incorrect" one, or even merely demand freedom must be exiled,
jailed, or executed.

But recall that every formula originally sought to bring an end to
human killings of other humans. As George Santayana phrased it,
"Fanaticism consists in redoubling your effort when you have forgotten your aim" (*Life of Reason*, vol. 1, 13).

In 1931 mathematician Kurt Gödel proved that, under certain
conditions of formal systems—including that of mathematics taken
whole—one cannot complete the system by proving all of its theorems
to be free of all contradiction from within the system. Rather, some
propositions are demonstrably undecidable; they are neither provable
nor disprovable by the accepted, rigorous standards of mathematics
(Gödel, 1970, 83–108).

The more informal systems of social theory paradigms present a
different problem: If one remains wholly within a system as defined
by its core premises, *everything* seems both decidable and provable.
Most of us have met dogmatists who grin to themselves before they
even hear out an objection, since they have already called up their
prefabricated reply. It is said that the strongest critiques are imma-
nent—that is, working from within the premises of a theory to trace
them to contradictions. But such critiques that do not directly challenge the theory's very ground of argument may assault the periphery
but leave the core untouched. One must more bluntly address the
core assumptions.

This is because each of the great formulas could *in principle* succeed
in solving the general problem of scarcity that results in human
aggression. While *in practice* each of the four great formulas has been,
I think, largely a failure, its core premises are sheltered and spared
theoretically by the simple tactic of invoking ideal conditions for
application. With predictable inconsistency, defenders of a paradigm
will then judge rival systems not by ideal conditions, but by either
refractory real conditions or the worst scenarios imaginable.

But when core assumptions of every paradigm are set against
relevant real conditions (let alone worst-case scenarios), experience

seems sufficient to say that what works in principle is practically impossible. If so, no paradigm can pretend to offer the best way—and certainly not the only way—to the solution of our social problems.

My own approach to social theory claims a vantage *outside*—not *over*—the paradigms. I do not myself pretend to have a superior solution to the conflicts that stimulated the emergence of the four thought models. I also doubt that one could easily combine what is best of each paradigm, as if solving a puzzle by crisply snapping all of the pieces together.

Doubt of any neat solution leads me to hold all the more tenaciously to democratic moral commitments and political procedures. As I shall show, each of the paradigms offers its own distinctive uses and abuses of democratic freedoms. Often a paradigm produces adherents who have regarded democratic freedoms as mere means to implementation or protection of their special formula. Therefore, a critique of all four kinds of critics may do much in defense of democratic freedoms, for these alone assure that each paradigm can be publicly advocated and that each can be publicly criticized.

Making a fifth paradigm of democracy itself, moreover, would promise more than democracy can be expected to deliver. Since I am not theorizing here from behind a shield of ideal conditions, I must admit that, while democracy may tend to bring civility to our conflicts, I do not think it will ever end them or solve the problem of scarcity that often sets us against each other.

In any case, it is clearly time to rethink democratic theory. Doing so, we must recognize that there have been at least four distinctive theories of democracy growing out of the paradigms discussed in this book. Just as defenses of democracy in its varying degrees have come in four forms, so have the attacks on it. Once this is apparent, we may be able to develop a defense of democracy that is not dependent on any one paradigm, but rather on the failings of all formulas that would sacrifice our freedoms.

Without offering here any new definition of how liberal democracy should be arranged, I frontally challenge those who claim to have something that is to be set above our familiar freedoms. Perhaps truth itself would merit that status. But, considered not as pristine ideals but as political models battered by the relentless tests of practice, none of the four formulas constitutes the truth. As we examine each paradigm, I will state the reasons for my doubts, but readers must decide the matter for themselves.

## Notes

1. One might counter that "justice" can never be sought in excess; but once that abstract term is given more specific definition, even it may be pressed too

far. In a different vein, Kant said that the only earthly thing that is good "without qualification" is the good will, but then went on to identify goodwill as an austerely universal attitude (Kant, 1949). But a rigid incapacity to make exceptions to general rules is in itself a kind of madness, since it precludes the special bonds of love or friendship.

2. Like Bacon, Descartes also emphasized how the progress of medical science could bring us longer lives, predicting in about 1648 that we could live an average of 175 years. By 1794, Condorcet was even asserting that our lives could be prolonged beyond any "assignable value" (Schouls, 1989, 130).

In our century, better medicine has joined improved nutrition and sanitation to bring growing populations. These have increased the scale of demand in most underdeveloped nations. And in developed nations, one impact of medical advances has been to create a burgeoning population of retirees who constitute a continuing source of demand yet no longer produce marketable goods or services. While prosperity may ultimately bring lowered fertility to match lowered mortality, the modern project has many contradictions.

3. Jurgen Habermas has written, "If the theoretically based point of departure of the Ancients was how human beings could comply practically with the natural order, then the practically assigned point of departure of the moderns is how human beings could technically master the threatening evils of nature" (Habermas, 1973b, 51). Focused on enlarged human productivity, the modern orientation requires that minds be turned from disinterested speculations of *theoria* to a science of practical applications (cf. Arendt, 1958; 1961, 17–40).

4. Thus, Ruskin was hardly Tory in any normal sense, though his leaning toward expertise did provoke a common misunderstanding about him (contrast Earland, 1971, 163, 318). George Bernard Shaw correctly saw Ruskin as telling the upper classes, "You are a parcel of thieves," but he wrongly called him a "communist." Shaw also distorted things in saying that Ruskin was like Lenin in seeing a need for strong leadership to launch reforms without the excuse for inaction involved in waiting for majority support (Shaw, 1921, 11, 22, 25, 29, 31). Ruskin was no Lenin, even if a bit overbearing within his own circle of followers.

# 2

## The Aristocrat's Problematic

### or Social Conflict as a Problem of Moderating Mass Wants

The nature of desire is without limit, and it is
with a view to satisfying this that the many live.
To rule such persons, then, requires not so
much leveling property as providing that those
who are respectable by nature will be the sort
who have no wish to aggrandize themselves,
while the mean will not be able to, which will be
the case if they are kept inferior but are done
no injustice.

Aristotle,
*Politics*

Shortly before these words in *The Politics*, Aristotle says that "one ought to level desires sooner than property; but this is impossible for those not adequately educated by the laws." Attempting to avert conflict, premodern social thought confronted the root problem of scarcity not by an apparently impossible expansion of the social supply, but by moderation of wants. However, any attentive analysis reveals that the Aristocrat asks no heroic sacrifices of the rich, putting the burden to restrain economic desires primarily on the mass population.

Any moderation of upper-class desires is the minimal necessary to prevent class war. It is less characteristic of the Aristocrat than the Saint to urge reduced exploitation in the very *accumulation* of the wealth, as in landlord exactions from peasants of labor service, payments in kind or money rents, and taxes. The Aristocrat, rather, shifts attention to *what is done* with the wealth; the usual counsel is to avoid conspicuous consumption that could cause envy, and practice conspicuous giving to private persons in need (Aristotle's "liberality") or to public projects ("magnificence") to show concern for the common good.

Unlike the Saint, who typically turns to voluntary poverty if born affluent or having become so, the Aristocrat may often live in luxury. Yet the Aristocrat is unlike the Capitalist in often expressing disdain for the vulgar ostentation of the *nouveaux riches*—not only because they emulate consumption standards of those of older wealth, but because they encourage like ambitions in the lower classes. The classic Aristocratic vision never advocates the more open classes of the Capitalist ideal, but rather birth-dependent castes, estates, orders, or ranks.

Rigidly stratified standards of living are basic to the traditional Aristocratic vision, often extending to sumptuary codes that dictate what may be worn by various ranks. All are to compare their consumption only with those of the same social rank. The lower orders, more than any others, should not aspire to anything beyond that enjoyed by their immediate ancestors. All must know their "station" or "place."

Earlier I noted that the advocates of a great alternative will all discern what they have in common and thus how they contrast with any other paradigm, yet they will also recognize many variants among themselves. Defining a basic paradigm of social theory requires some slighting of differences while underscoring the similarities in a diverse range of instances of a given type.

Caveats aside, the Aristocratic consciousness is that of such figures as Confucius, Socrates, Plato, Aristotle, Thucydides, Xenophon, Polybius, Cicero, less Augustine than Aquinas, much of Bodin, Richard Hooker, Filmer, Montesquieu, Burke (these latter two with some liberal influence), de Maistre and de Bonald, Carlyle, Disraeli, much but not all of Hegel, Calhoun, and others like them. With rare exceptions such as the Saint-like Emperor Marcus Aurelius, most premodern autocrats and their top advisers at least outwardly shared most of the paradigm.

While no longer reflected in political parties separate from the Capitalist advocates (such as the Conservative party rivalry with Liberals or Radicals in many nineteenth-century contexts), the Aristocratic outlook is still alive in our time. Varied forms include conservative Thomism, Alexander Solzhenitsyn's neo–Russian Orthodoxy, the traditionalism of Michael Oakeshott or Russell Kirk, or the more epic and elusive teaching left us by Eric Voegelin (d. 1985). As in Voegelin, all such theorists tend to display historical pessimism, viewing flawed practice as being a consequence of our having fallen away from some nobler premodern understanding of political things. This dramatistic abuse of the concept of tradition has been sufficiently criticized (Gunnell, 1979).

As successor to earlier figures such as George Santayana, Irving Babbitt, Ralph Adams Cram, and Paul Elmer More, in American academic life the most influential proponent of the Aristocrat's world view has been Leo Strauss (d. 1973). A refugee from Hitler's Germany who taught political philosophy, Strauss's influence radiated from the New School for Social Research, the University of Chicago, and Claremont University, with secondary reflections at such schools as Cornell, Kenyon College, the University of Dallas, St. John's-Annapolis, and others. Some leading followers have included Walter Berns, Allan Bloom, Joseph Cropsey, the late Martin Diamond, Harry Jaffa, Harvey Mansfield, Thomas Pangle, and Nathan Tarcov. Moreover, the Straussian movement has exercised some political influence in the United States, primarily within the Republican party. During the Reagan and Bush administrations, the Aristocratic viewpoint has been represented in bureaucratic units of primarily cultural concern, such as the Department of Education and the National Endowment for the Humanities.

The Straussians make a series of contestable claims:

1. Straussians say our world is in *crisis*, primarily understood as a threat to order that readily culminates in tyranny and murder, such as under Hitler or Stalin. While conceding that the Nazi Holocaust or Stalin's Gulag do certainly eclipse in evil many less technologically coordinated human abuses, a critic may here question whether immoral tyrannies (indeed, even immoral acts by ordinary people) are any more common now than they were in the past, before the moderns undermined classical natural-right teachings.

2. They define the alleged crisis as being basically a *moral* one. A volume by self-labeled Straussians on modern democracy quite characteristically begins thus: "The crisis of liberal democracy is best understood as a crisis of moral foundations" (Deutsch and Soffer, 1987, 1). They differ from others who see any conceded moral breakdown as but the surface manifestation of the political or economic roots of crisis.

3. They view the supposed moral crisis as caused by a *failure of modern philosophy*, which first lowered and then lost its standards, leading to mistakes in political practice and a consequent suffusion of immorality throughout the mass population. Allan Bloom's best-seller *The Closing of the American Mind* laments the lapse of standards in American education, viewing the American culture as being so committed to "openness" that it has lost all sense of higher purpose. As

in almost any work by the Aristocratic type, the book is pervaded by the imperative to rank all things as higher and lower, better or worse (Bloom, 1987). Like all Aristocrats, Bloom attacks egalitarianism, dwelling on mass immoderation in educational and cultural matters. Classic Aristocratic theorists more explicitly denounced egalitarianism in economic and political demands.

4. Finally, Straussians believe that only restoration of what Strauss referred to as the *Great Tradition* of natural right, primarily defined by Plato and Aristotle, can guide moral training and save us from the crisis as they see it.

By self-perception, the Straussians offer the only *philosophic* case for the importance of *publicly* supervised moral training against the false philosophies of modernity. In both respects, they differ from the only sometimes allied opinion of the American "social conservatives"—the religious fundamentalists focused on issues of family and sexual mores. The Straussians exaggerate their unique concern about morality by adopting a very distinctive concept of what moral training must be. If one defines the virtues in Aristotelian fashion as "praiseworthy characteristics," the Straussians adopt a distinctively Aristocratic list of them. Thus, even a defender concedes that Aristotle had no place for the later Christian virtues of repentance for sin, charitable forgiveness of the sinning of others, or other Christian virtues such as faith, love, and humility (MacIntyre, 1981, 162, 170, 172). While every variant of the Aristocrat has emphasized the importance of moral training for the good society, it is important to scrutinize what *kind* of moral training is emphasized, since, among other things, it is not the same as that of Protestant Christian fundamentalists, the Catholic Workers, and others calling for a revival of morality.

The Aristocrat, Saint, Capitalist, and Socialist types have distinctive lists of virtues and vices (cf. Table 2.1).

Even if all four formulas may at least concur that wisdom, justice, and courage are worth having, one could show that they define these concepts in highly distinctive ways, closely tied to what is central in their respective paradigms. The moral code of the Aristocrat is centered on what is necessary to prevent class warfare when, first, neither imperialist plunder nor domestic economic growth are deemed feasible alternatives to satisfy new demands that may force themselves on the scene and, second, a standing system of economic inequalities is to be left largely undisturbed, palliated by charity and contained by firm law and order.

As noted, the classic formula aims to pacify society primarily by moderation of mass wants. This especially entails the courage to resist the people, the demos, and its leaders, the demagogues, who would

**Table 2.1   Characteristic Virtues and Vices as Emphasized by the Four Problematics of Social Theory**

| | Virtues (praiseworthy characteristics) | Vices (blameworthy characteristics) |
|---|---|---|
| 1. Aristocrat (e.g., Plato, Aristotle Xenophon, Cicero) | courage, valor, pride, honor nobility, magnanimity charity, magnificence, liberality propriety, responsibility, decorum loyalty (personal sense) | cowardice, sheepishness, unmanliness shamefulness, baseness, boorishness, pettiness acquisitiveness, gluttony, swinishness, demagogy (pandering to the many) indiscretion, irresponsibility, unseemliness |
| 2. Saint (e.g., Christ, St. Francis, George Fox, Gandhi) | compassion, gentleness, humanity, kindness humility, modesty simplicity, abstemiousness piety patience candor, truthfulness, consistency | violence, aggressiveness pride, hubris gluttony, luxuriousness sycophancy (pandering to the rich or powerful) hypocrisy, inconsistency |
| 3. Capitalist (e.g., John Locke, Adam Smith, James Mill, Jeremy Bentham) | industriousness, ambition, competitiveness, independence resourcefulness, inventiveness frugality, thriftiness punctuality rationality tolerance honesty loyalty (institutional sense) | idleness complacency, timidity wastefulness, prodigality inefficiency sentimentality |
| 4. Socialist (e.g., Karl Marx, Friedrich Engels, Lenin, Trotsky) | cooperativeness class solidarity, fraternity internationalism combativeness skepticism, critical consciousness | servility, submissiveness sycophancy sentimentality patriotism gullibility, credulity, stupidity |

"pander" to such wants (especially economic ones). This dominates how the Aristocrat thinks about not only the social problem but also the place of democracy, as Chapter 3 will show. To be sure, just as Marx and Engels said they did not want to offer "recipes for future cooks," Leo Strauss cautioned, "We cannot reasonably expect that a fresh understanding of classical political philosophy will supply us with recipes for today's use." Further: "Only we living today can possibly find a solution to the problems of today. But an adequate understanding of the principles as elaborated by the classics may be the indispensable starting point for an adequate analysis" (Strauss, 1964, 11).

## Commitment to the Aristocratic Formula:
## Why Moderation of Mass Wants?

It is sometimes difficult to say why specific individuals commit themselves to a given problematic. But most historical advocates of the Aristocratic program seemed to be either of or at least closely identified with the propertied upper classes in their contexts, even if critical of the newly rich. In their quite plausible view, the first generation coming into wealth more often than not tends to love money too much. Those who have just acquired wealth, sometimes by sordid means, are readily corrupted to acquire more. They may practice a socially dangerous flaunting of wealth, and they may be quite ungenerous to the poor. After worrying about the presence of insolence, ostentation, luxury, and lack of culture among the rich, Aristotle hastens to add that this is most typical of those who have not yet learned how to be rich: "As between the newly rich and those who have long had wealth, the newly rich have all the characteristic vices in an accentuated and baser form" (*Rhetoric*, 1391a; cf. also *Politics*, I, ix–x, and IV, viii).

Nor does the Aristocrat trust the newly rich in political leadership roles, since they are likely to have flawed ethical sensibilities from their scramble up "the greasy pole" (a phrase used by Richard Nixon). The Aristocratic theorist seeks leaders among old-wealth elites, a more genteel kind of character of moderation and a larger sense of social responsibility. Such "gentlemen" or the subset of "statesmen" (revealingly, most Straussians ignore gender neutrality in language) would establish the needed social tone. Thus, Straussians uphold the ideal of Winston Churchill, although the relatively egalitarian wing led by Harry Jaffa has also admired Abraham Lincoln.

Whole societies that have been dominated by the Aristocratic paradigm quite typically encourage veneration of ancestors—or, rather, pride in patrilineal descent. In traditional China, Japan, Rome, and medieval Europe, such publicity of pedigree among the great families (often involving fraudulent genealogies) tended to diffuse downward to the middle or even lower classes. But pride in lineage has little place in the other three paradigms of social thought.

In emphasizing the need for a ruling element of superior moral tone, most contemporary advocates of the Aristocratic viewpoint do not understand themselves as especially enamored of the rich, nor even the subset of distinguished families of old wealth. But if they may not especially love old wealth, they do not conceal their marked distrust of the lower orders. If the newly rich misuse reason in greedy commercial acquisitiveness, the lower orders lack all rationality in pursuit of their inordinate wants.

Shifting from social identifications to a more cultural account, we find that many contemporary Aristocratic advocates have a background of strong religious and moral training. It seems that many Straussians were raised in either Jewish or Roman Catholic orthodoxy, but now they trust Biblical faith less than philosophic teachings of natural right. Surely, they would explain themselves as being led by urgent moral concerns rather than by any social group alignments.

Perhaps the motives for adopting this paradigm often include an unacknowledged sense of personal superiority. Any teacher of Plato's *Republic* recognizes this appeal of the book, for students usually imagine themselves among the guardians rather than in the appetitive mass. Lewis Coser suggests that Strauss was a kind of new Maimonides, advancing a modern guide for the perplexed and utilizing his charismatic hold over his student followers: "They formed a little band of people in the know, a company of the elect, who saw themselves as having access to esoteric knowledge denied to the *vulgus*." Coser sees this cult as dissatisfied with modern thought and looking for anchorage in dogmatic certainties: "Committed to the few (who do know) against the many (who do not), devoted to intellectual aristocracy and to an elite that must keep in check the vulgar thought of the demos and of those who abet its base desires, the Straussian knows that the road to regeneration of the fallen world of modernity is marked by signposts to be found in the work of Leo Strauss" (Coser, 1984, 202–7, citations from 202, 206). This has the ring of truth. However, neither the quest for certainty nor such vanity is unique to adherents of this formula, being commonplace among avatars of the other paradigms.

In addition to their trust in what Strauss openly called "gentlemen," most contemporary Aristocrats wish for a stable, moderately inegalitarian political order, not wanting violent disorder at home or abroad. But detailed positions regarding political change or nonchange normally depend on more substantive policy concerns. This is especially so regarding the economic inequalities that the Aristocrat defends, more openly in the past than today. Positions regarding redistribution of the economic pie relate in turn to views regarding whether it can or cannot grow. Either a view to limited productive technology or a modern ecological vision may favor a more or less steady-state economy and further encourage commitment to the Aristocratic paradigm.

## The Economy of the Aristocrat: Valuing the Finer Things in Life

To highlight contrasts among the rival paradigms, I will apply the same analytic categories to each. This chapter focuses on the Aristocrat's economic orientations, and the following one on the political. I discuss the development and distribution of productive property, the division of labor, the distribution of the product, and the framework within which the distribution occurs.

### *Forces of Production: The Steady-state Economic Vision*

As noted, the Aristocrat rules out significantly increased supply as the solution to scarcity and related conflicts. Among other things, this means a refusal to turn to predatory plunder abroad as the primary approach to relief of any domestic tensions. One thus brackets aside the predatory prescriptions of Kautilya or Machiavelli as not implementable, workable, or morally acceptable. Notwithstanding his own strongly stated hostility to communism, Leo Strauss often maintained that key figures in the Great Tradition emphasized the primacy of domestic policy over foreign policy. If only because Athens proved that empire can enlarge wants faster than it satisfies them, the first line of defense for both foreign and domestic security must be moral training.

#### *Static Agrarian Society*
Having rejected brigandage abroad, the Aristocratic social theorist also rules out the possibility of enlarged domestic production—or increased supply—to meet any excess domestic demand. There is here none of the great confidence of modernity that one finds in Adam Smith's capitalism or Karl Marx's socialism.

The economic circumstances of philosophic thought may involve various production arrangements, such as pastoralism, irrigation agriculture, feudalism, or even our current capitalist or socialist systems. But whatever their differences, all premodern or agrarian systems with unequal holdings of property tended to make the Aristocratic consciousness the dominant form, checked almost solely by the critical voice of the Saint.

Once field agriculture emerged some 10,000 years ago, further great strides in agricultural productivity awaited the advent of capitalized agriculture. One must not ignore the intervening projects of irrigation, which at least for a time enlarged agricultural production in China, India, the Middle East, and even Peru; but even such societies recognized outer limits on production. There was only just so much arable land, which would yield only just so much food or fiber. And this could support only so many people. When the social product was viewed as if necessarily a constant, it was imperative to limit population itself or at least its aggregate demands to avoid sharp class conflicts over distribution.

When not especially concerned that there be a sufficient supply of warriors, the Aristocrat often has emphasized population limitation, as when excess population is hived off for foreign colonization. Or this emphasis could involve curtailment of fertility, including such modes as infanticide (e.g., of birth defectives among the Spartans, or unwanted female infants in traditional China or India) or sexual abstinence (even today the only approved Roman Catholic means of birth control).

But total demand is a multiple of how many persons there are and how much they *want*. This level of want must especially be checked in conditions that suppose no conquest of nature through science and technology, no linear progress, but rather a cyclical perspective on all natural processes. The members of each generation must then live much as did their parents before them.

When such possibilities as clearing more forests or developing more irrigation works are exhausted, the sheer impossibility of increasing the supply of food and fiber is central to one's thinking. While the Aristocrat may value good management for any large agrarian estate, its improvement is not worth too great an attentiveness because very little increase in return would seem possible. Even apart from political leadership or cultivation of the finer things as being a better use of time, the improbability of productivity gains made it quite sensible for Aristotle to counsel against excess attention to accumulation for its own sake.

### Distrust of Innovation
While Cicero is a partial exception, the Aristocrat has doubts about progress in human technology, which must be subject to the cyclical rises and falls that agrarian thought applies to most other dimensions of life. Quite unlike Bacon in his vision of *New Atlantis*, Plato prefaces his tale about legendary Atlantis by imagining productive technology

recurrently lost and reinvented after fires, floods, and other disasters that prevented accumulation in scientific knowledge (*Timaeus*, 22c). Plato and Aristotle knew that some innovation does occur, but they would not encourage it. Both believed that innovation in another sphere of life could lead to dangerous innovation in politics. Distrust of technology is one way in which the mind of the Aristocrat is sharply unlike that of the Capitalist (cf. Strauss, 1959, 298).

In his *Republic*, Plato faults democracy for encouraging novelties; and in *Laws*, he warns against innovation even in children's games as likely to contaminate other spheres of his practical or second-best regime. Aristotle similarly counsels against a proposal by Hippodamus to confer honor on persons suggesting innovations that improve the state, conceding some past gains in arts such as medicine or gymnastics but denying that change in the sphere of law is normally beneficial. While some laws may be cautiously changed, Aristotle warns,

> When the improvement is small, and since it is a bad thing to habituate people to the reckless dissolution of laws, it is evident that some errors both of the legislators and of the rulers should be let go; for the city will not be benefited as much from changing them as it will be harmed through being habituated to disobey the rulers. (*Politics*, II, viii)

More consistently than the Capitalist, the Aristocrat tends to doubt the equation of change and progress, the latest with the best, holding that it is often better to endure imperfections than to risk unsettling everything. Innovation in the forces of production, even when deemed possible, is often considered undesirable, since novelty can be politically contagious. Beyond distrust of merchants, such fear of novelty often caused Aristocratic societies to regulate closely or even actively discourage foreign commerce. The Ming empire in China and the Tokugawa empire in Japan almost wholly repressed trade with foreigners.

### The Ecological Vision

Our contemporary ecological consciousness has brought a renewed warning against undue faith in the technological revolution. The ecological sensibility returns to a cyclical view of the nature of things; it questions progress. Most technological fixes only engender new problems such as environmental degradations that endanger not only human health but even the capacity to sustain high production at any level, let alone rising production. William Ophuls, who oscillates between the Aristocrat and the Saint in policy orientations, has plausibly argued that we can never do only one thing; our purposive choices usually bring unintended, unforeseen, and most often unwanted consequences (Ophuls, 1977). Thus the Green Revolution's hybrid grains accelerate the mining of the soil's fertility, requiring supplement of chemical fertilizers. Such grains also require irrigation, which tends in time to cause salinization and other problems such as hardpan. In other words, we can boost productivity in the short run only to create the conditions for steep declines in yield in the longer run. Nor can more innovation (e.g., salt-tolerant crops) be relied on to save us at the cusp. Like most other human endeavors, our projects to force more from nature face at some inflection point not only a "law of diminishing returns," but a point of net negative returns.

The Aristocratic version of the ecological point of view emphasizes by definition the solution of moderating not so much the wants of the affluent as those of the relatively poor, whether in a domestic or international frame of reference. If there is any attention paid to arresting the population explosion, it would *not* be through economic redistributions or diffused benefits of growth, which in many nations have trimmed fertility toward near replacement levels. Such redistributive stability is accelerated once most women work away from home, couples choosing to limit their family size when confident that more of their infants will survive to adulthood and that they themselves need not rely on children for present field labor or to sustain them in old age. Asking that people restrain their fertility without compensation, or even that Third World nations give up their dream of industrialization, is very much more in line with the Aristocratic paradigm, however. Such thinking looks for a solution in moderation of wants, but it places the burden of the solution primarily on the have-nots.

Whether expressly or implicitly, the Aristocrat defends highly unequal holdings of property—an arrangement that precludes certain kinds of solutions for social problems, whether economic, ecological, or moral.

### The Division of Labor as Nature's Own: The Case of Plato's Justice

Even where the social division of labor may be quite rudimentary, the traditional Aristocrat defends specializations of function and related inequalities of reward. In part this long involved the patriarchal family model, but it extends as well to sharp lines of status among adult males, keeping especially subordinate and abject any needed slaves or serfs.

Economic inequalities may be defended by many kinds of justification languages; but apart from tradition and religion, the most characteristic emphasis of most past Aristocrats, excepting the Confucians, centered on differences of class natures.[1] In the West, this grew out of neo-Platonism into the medieval image of a Great Chain of Being, descending from the most perfect nature of God through ever more imperfect forms of being (cf. Lovejoy, 1936).

The Aristocrats must delicately manipulate their rhetorics of similarities and differences. To avoid social conflict, they stress vertical bonding of the classes, an interclass unity based on "common good" purposes: the security of all from domestic or foreign aggressors, the realization of justice in the sense of securing what is due to each person, and the maintenance of worship of shared gods. Having proclaimed social unity by what is similar, the Aristocrats may shift to class differences to find further unity by the interdependency of the division of labor, whereby each makes good what is lacking to the other.

But then the theme of unity is disrupted when these and other differences are invoked to justify highly unequal distributions of social burdens (who does the hard work) and benefits (who consumes the product). At least traditionally the Aristocrat defended distinctive rights and duties for different castes, estates, or classes. The ancients' teaching of natural right focused on the reasoned duty to uphold the inegalitarian order sustaining a common good, unlike the moderns' teaching of egalitarian natural rights, which concern shared, strong passions often set against government (cf. Strauss, 1953).

### Platonic Justice

Some stratifications have been long lived, such as the yet resilient caste system of India, although other castelike stratifications have vanished with the political systems that maintained them. Plato is known to have at least admired the unchanging children's games of Egypt, but Marx in all seriousness wrote, "Plato's Republic, in so far as the division of labour is treated in it . . . is merely the Athenian idealization of the Egyptian system of castes" (*Capital*, I, xiv, 5).

Be that as it may, let us examine Plato's definition of justice in the city: "Each one must practice one of the functions in the city, that one for which his nature made him naturally most fit" (*Republic*, 433a). He directly contrasts the ideal city of rule by the guardians with that of democracy, for the latter regime creates a "many-colored" life where "each man would organize his life in it privately just as it pleases him." He "lives along day by day, gratifying the desire that occurs to him, at one time drinking and listening to the flute, idling and neglecting everything; and sometimes spending his time as though he were occupied with philosophy" (*Republic*, 557b, 561c–d).[2] As the Thucydidean version of Pericles' funeral oration makes clear, though, the Athenian democratic vision praised "versatility" or assumed competence of each male adult citizen for multiple roles.

Plato defines justice in the city as specificity of function according to natural aptitudes, regarded not merely as different but as unequal. In advancing his principle to cover what a later language will designate as the social or economic sphere, Plato was preparing to turn it against democracy in the political sphere. He knew that the pride of practitioners of crafts could easily bring Athenians to accept the view of an innate knack as well as acquired skill, and he cleverly transfers such assumptions to the role of political decision-maker (Winspear, 1940, 199; Wood and Wood, 1978, 133).

Plato's antidemocratic *Republic* mesmerizes even modern readers because it lacks effective democratic interlocutors. Competent democratic opponents would have shown how Plato's justice may be unpacked as an extended series of vulnerable choices. Since so much of later Aristocratic thought emphasizes the teaching of natural inequalities, it is important to critique the first great statement of the doctrine.

Plato's argument culminates with a class system of three or probably four tiers. Working from the top down, he categorizes all individuals into the rational (loving wisdom, the ruler-guardians alone make policy), the spirited (loving competition, victory, and honor, these are the auxiliary guardians functioning as armed forces and administrators), and the appetitive (loving economic gain and sensual pleasures, these are the depoliticized practitioners of trades). His metaphor of shepherds, sheep dogs and sheep crudely suggests that these are as if distinct species. The class designations as gold, silver, and iron or bronze in his myth of the metals similarly assert sharp differentiations of kind. Apparently Plato envisions a fourth stratum of slaves with no metal at all, consisting of non-Greeks captured in war and even Greeks with mental deficiency. As Plato writes, the wise ruler "makes those who prove incapable of rising above ignorance and groveling subservience slaves to the rest of the community" (Vlastos, 1973, 140–46; *Statesman*, 309a).

In my critique of Plato's justice, I forgo addressing his views that justice objectively exists to be discovered, that human reason is capable of such discovery, and that one knows when a definition does not admit of contrary predication. Idealists often prefer such a coherence test of truth.[3] Closer to our Capitalist paradigm, the Sophists and those trained by them would question all such premises, which seem bound up with a theistic world view. Against the democratic Protagoras, Plato held that not man but God was the "measure of all things" (*Laws*, 716c). For the sake of argument, let us stay on Plato's ground by assuming that justice exists, is knowable, and is known as known when a definition is invulnerable to contradiction.

### Following Nature?
Plato chooses to define justice as a following of nature, understood to be inconsistent with the egalitarian laws and customs of Athens.

These were reflected in such principles as *isonomia* (equality before the law), *isegoria* (equal right of free speech), and *isotomia* (equality of respect). Aside from Glaucon's brief devil's advocacy of justice as an egalitarian convention of reciprocity, Plato turns away from egalitarian consent to an inegalitarian construal of nature as the measure of right.

In passing, any exhortation to follow nature implicitly concedes the possibility of either ignoring or fighting it. Thus even if one were to concede that our natures are unequal in some respect, one could argue on other grounds that we should resist or rise above nature, as J. S. Mill later recommends ("Nature," "The Subjection of Women"). But to urge that we fight rather than follow nature supposes some other standard of valuation put above it, which would leave Plato's ground of argument.

Supposing nature is the measure of right, does Plato really follow nature? That supposes that it can be recognized and that it leads in a clear direction. Plato claims to recognize "natures," and his espousal of eugenics rules out the possibility that these are only metaphysical (i.e., Platonic forms) rather than physical. He shares our modern understanding of the natural as what is inborn or genetically endowed.

Unable to observe directly what aptitudes or inclinations are innate, Plato was forced to attempt inference from what *can* be observed. Most of such argument in any theorist is referenced loosely to observations of three kinds of subjects: (1) nonhuman forms of being, chiefly the other animals; (2) "primitive" human beings, such as preliterate peoples or children; and (3) civilized adults.

Then one may choose to define the "natural" by either continuity (similarity) or discontinuity (dissimilarity); and since that nature so defined may be followed, ignored, or fought, there are many different routes (18 pseudo-inferential pathways) by which one could selectively argue almost anything. Human-nature argument becomes especially arbitrary in tendentious selection of the more specific reference set or the relevant conduct: If arguing from other animals but not all of them, then which animals; and then if not the whole repertory of their conduct, which of their behaviors? (See Cook, 1983b.)

Plato offers no clear, complete, and consistent approach to definition of what is natural. He shifts among various possible models as it suits his purpose of the moment. This explodes any pretense of following nature, since he only draws out of "nature" what he puts into it. For example, sometimes the other animals are positively invoked, as in the argument that they show homosexual intercourse to be unnatural (*Laws* 636b–c). At other times the animals are invoked negatively, as if our nature could only be found in discontinuity with their example, as in Glaucon's complaint about the city of swine or in the rejection of Callicles' law of the jungle.

If Plato sometimes defines what is natural by what is common to us and at other times by what is different or unique, some criterion other than nature must tell him which way to turn when following nature as norm. Plato's view of nature obviously slights what is common to all of us (our *human* nature) and emphasizes what is specific to groups (e.g., the sexes, the classes) or to individuals. But why take what is distinctive rather than what is shared as the guiding norm for allocating roles and their associated burdens and benefits?

Furthermore, given Plato's choice to define the natural primarily by reference to apparent differences among humans, we may ask whether at least here he intelligibly follows nature. But once again we can see him making a set of choices that could not emerge directly from observed nature.

Although differences among persons are certainly observable, including those of apparent aptitudes, Plato assumes there are sharp differences of kind when often only degree is measurable. I.Q., for instance, is distributed on a bell-shaped curve—not three clear classes. At some indefensible threshold, Plato wholly excludes most people from any political role, although the apparent mental capacity of some of his brighter tradesmen could closely approach that of his least bright auxiliary guardians.

Assuming accurate observation of differences, do these reflect what is really innate? This is vital to sort out the rational, spirited, and appetitive characters. Whole peoples are defined as predominantly rational, spirited, or appetitive (cf. *Crito*, 53d; *Republic*, 463a; *Statesman*, 262d; and *Laws*, 637d–e). Within his city, he further categorizes individuals into their appropriate classes. While both sexes may be guardians, he adds at least minimal gender differentiation of functions among them. Within the trades stratum, he has extensive differentiations of function, as also in his second-best regime: "Each artisan in the society must have his single craft, must earn his living by that trade and no other" (*Laws*, 846d–847b).

But how can we know that any manifest differences are really innate? Plato acknowledges the great force of nurture relative to nature, as in his invalid assertion that the way we use our legs shows we are really ambidextrous and should be trained that way (*Laws*, 794e–795d). But precisely how does he claim to disentangle natures from nurturance for his educational tracking system? He believes that by scrutinizing playlike earliest education we can correctly discern natures (*Republic*, 537a; *Statesman*, 308d). He thinks that appetitive natures can be discerned almost from birth—which excludes them from his more exacting educational program—but that distinguishing between spirited and rational natures requires more extended observation (*Republic*, 455b, 412e).

Plato betrays his class prejudice in saying that unworthy suitors of philosophy tend to come from among the practitioners of trades (*Republic*, 495d–e). He simply assumes that most of the lower and middle classes are iron and bronze, while silver and gold natures are primarily of his own class, the landed nobility. This is not to deny that some of these were merely spirited (like Plato's brother, Glaucon) or even appetitive (possibly his other brother, Adeimantus, who asked that justice be pleasant).

The duller offspring of guardians would be sent down to the trades stratum, and the brightest children from the trades stratum raised to guardian ranks. When this is combined with Plato's eugenics scheme for the guardians, presumably each class would eventually breed more true, reducing the need for interclass mobility. Apparently believing in inheritance of acquired characteristics, Plato also says that nurture and nature can be interactive, as when those correctly nurtured would have progeny of ever better natures (*Republic*, 424a–b).

We are increasingly aware that such things as prenatal maternal alcoholism or malnutrition as well as postnatal protein deficiency may depress intelligence (or I.Q., at least). Further, early differences of environmental stimuli are known to register in mental development, as Plato himself seems to concede in saying that mathematical study "rouses the naturally drowsy and dull, and makes him quick, retentive, and shrewd, a miraculous improvement of culturation upon his native parts" (*Laws*, 747b). Why then omit most children from the *Republic*'s math education?

Whether they are so by nature or defective nurture, Plato would say that dullards belong in the trades stratum. But he would not want to miss potential auxiliaries or the rare ruler natures. Surely, the life experience of trades children, who learn crafts by imitating their fathers, would tend to suppress any late blooming of guardian potential. Dull jobs can make dull persons, and even Adam Smith noted the danger of confusing effects of the division of labor with innate aptitudes (*Wealth of Nations*, I, ii, and V, i, 3).

The Aristocratic paradigm is unlike the other three in its disparagement of manual labor. Although the belief that manual laborers are by nature inferior assuages the consciences of those who do no such labor, Plato is on weak ground in his classifications of persons. Even if we were to concede that the mentioned dominant motives do sort us into three groups, recognizing a type becomes complicated because Plato introduces multiple indexes to identify the guardians and then further distinguish the few of these fit for rule.

Unlike appetitive natures, philosophic natures would be like the spirited in caring little for the swinish pleasures of food, drink, or bodily ease, while manifesting ardent temperament, physical health, toughness, and even comeliness.

But ruling natures would be unlike the merely spirited in caring less about the pleasures of sex and of public applause. This last removes a prominent incentive to seek political power. The philosophic or ruling natures would not want power but prefer all kinds of learning. They are said to have superior memory, shrewd and quick minds, and a facility in learning even difficult things. Later screening would test for all of the parts of virtue, and a deep-dyed commitment to the common good. So this nature would be "by nature a rememberer, a good learner, magnificent, charming, and a friend and kinsman of truth, justice, courage, and moderation" (*Republic*, 487a).

Writers should avoid intelligibility, quipped Oscar Wilde, since one may be found out. Plato's criteria raise obvious challenges regarding their clarity and consistency. If they were never inconsistent, however, they would not all need to be listed. Plato himself acknowledges that philosophic natures may become readily corrupted when badly educated. If such traits are perhaps present in varying magnitudes, the selection problem deepens: Since nature loves degree more than crisply demarcated kinds, is Plato following nature, after all—even in pretending to find the latter? As known from our modern criteria of merit, ambiguities leave much room for arbitrariness on the part of whoever is designating "the best."

Plato, in any case, picks and chooses from what nature offers to us. When inclination and aptitude are inconsistent, he has us follow aptitude over any contrary inclination: The philosopher has the aptitude to rule but not the inclination, being "least eager to rule" (*Republic*, 520d). Plato says that excessive laughter would be unseemly for guardians. This should be no problem, since making them do what they do not want to do should suppress any gaiety. Fourier and Marx, on the other hand, prefer to respect inclination: Letting people do what they want should foster happiness as well as some derivative improvement in role performance. Plato would retort that low aptitude but high inclination means inept work. But so does high talent but low inclination. Even granting the Platonic denial that pleasure is the good, why let talent *wholly* eclipse taste? Plato says that, while we cannot always train an aptitude to fit a taste (e.g., the fool who wants to be ruler), we can often train taste to match an aptitude. In the case of the trades, at least, children's games are used to direct "children's tastes and inclinations toward the station they are themselves to fill when adult" (*Laws*, 643c–d).[4]

Plato thinks that each person has but *one best inborn talent*. Fourier or Marx would respond that each has *many* innate talents and tastes that need expression, which is possible through a rotation of roles (flitting like a butterfly, said Fourier) rather than full-time, lifelong specialization in one role. They would argue that "one person, one job" is not following nature but fighting it. Does any job in any case tap only one inclination, or only one aptitude? Why not assume the possibility of two or more roughly comparable aptitudes? Plato's reply is that, even if ties might occur, only one of the aptitudes could be *fully* developed (cf. *Statesman,* 300e). Plato himself belies this, however, having mastered both philosophy and rhetoric at least, as Cicero attested (*De Oratore,* I,i, and I, xii). Most of us know highly competent people in dual careers, or those who have changed careers several times over the course of their lives. Sometimes being involved in multiple roles is the only way for us to find, eventually, both our inclinations and our aptitudes. Finally, even if the modern role of citizen is less demanding than it was in ancient Athens, our own lives falsify Plato's denial that one can practice both citizenship and a trade.

Plato makes other arbitrary choices in determining the relevance of capacities for certain roles, even though he would not use gender to block women from guardian roles. Outside of his *Republic,* Plato is more conventional regarding sex roles.[5] He is most questionable in making a high threshold of intellect displace interest as the rationale for political rights, as if policy choices were more a matter of intelligence than interest.

The principle of following nature becomes especially confusing when Plato matches up natures and roles. He does not let the mere presence of natures-as-aptitudes determine the social roles, at least not beyond the main classes. He lacks clear criteria for the determination of what more specific roles should exist, which anticipates his old-age pastime of attempting to distinguish authentic and bogus arts through symmetrical bifurcations (in his *Sophist* and *Statesman*). In the *Republic,* he works from both ends, here constituting roles to suit available natures, there adjusting available natures to suit constituted roles. He sometimes innovates roles not found in Athens, such as the auxiliary-guardian (suited for a Glaucon, or possibly Thrasymachus) or ruler-guardian (a safer role for Socrates or his star pupil).

For Plato to assume that he would have enough natures to fill all permitted roles is strange, especially for the trades of the city. Why assume a perfectly sufficient supply of cobbler or blacksmith natures, rather than excess or deficit? Could contingencies of city location or technological change affect the matter?

Far from following nature, Plato would even shape nature to his needs through eugenics, if only in maintaining the guardian natures. As noted, the mobility of mislocated natures across class lines would diminish if eugenic breeding succeeded in creating a castelike system (cf. *Republic,* 415; *Timaeus,* 19a). Sufficient supply of the spirited auxiliaries would be less of a problem than supply of the rarer philosophic natures. His city may have as few as 1,000 citizens, and ruling natures may be as few as one per 1,000 persons, which is roughly how many now define the frequency of genius I.Q. (cf. *Republic*, 429a; *Statesman*, 293). With so little margin for error, Plato's ship could soon be without a pilot.[6]

In the eugenics of his *Republic*, Plato refines the "metals," whereas in his *Statesman* he seems, rather, to mix them as better alloys: Fighting a natural inclination of persons to marry like to like, he marries opposites in order to moderate the citizenry toward a more uniform type. The strong and bold would marry the weak and gentle, as the warp goes with woof in weaving. But we may well ask why, if eugenics will shape natures as he pleases, Plato even pretends to be following nature.

Spontaneous birthings seem to create certain natures in likely redundancy. While often at war with the inclinations of others, Plato seems guided by no more than his own inclinations in trimming back some roles: players of certain instruments such as the flute, lute, and harp; many meat-producers (he was probably vegetarian); most doctors. As to the doctors, few would be needed in the ideal city, given its policies of infanticide for defective infants, preventive medicine of improved nutrition and physical exercise, and voluntary euthanasia among those citizens who were no longer functional. While the auxiliary-guardians include soldiers, there would be fewer of them because the city would not seek empire, could exploit class conflicts in enemy cities, and would secure allies by offering them any gold plundered from an enemy.

If he needs fewer of some natures, he wants to eliminate certain others, having them debarred, banished, or even killed. Cancelled roles include storytellers or poets who would follow their own muse, the Sophists or teachers for pay, paid rhetoricians or legal counselors who would make any worse cause seem the better, and many imitative arts that would minister to luxury tastes in a decadent city.

Perhaps the extreme of his fighting rather than really following nature is when Plato would physically eliminate flawed natures. He would have infanticide not only for birth defectives but probably also for any offspring from eugenically unplanned liaisons among the guardians. Further, there are the "bad natures" of incurable criminals, who will be compelled to kill themselves (*Republic*, 410a; also, *Statesman*, 308c–309a). Plato would say that one only "harms" people by making them worse persons, and execution merely makes them not persons at all. But why believe that there are bad natures beyond any possible remedy? Does Plato follow nature when he would screen and even destroy some natures? How far should this go? Another vague Platonic phrase for justice—"To each his due"—was inscribed on the gates of the Buchenwald concentration camp.

Summing up, I have tried to show many incoherences and vulnerabilities in Plato's invocation of nature to assign roles. He everywhere makes undefended or ill-defended *choices* that pretend to be *discoveries*, so he draws from nature only what he wants to put into it.

### Consequences of Justice

Plato is even more vulnerable to logical contradiction in his claims regarding the *consequences* of implementing his justice. I will launch a syllogistic argument from the major premise that justice belongs to the class of goods that does not admit of excess. It violates at least ordinary discourse to speak of a society as "too just."[7] My minor premise is that Plato's "justice," or specificity of function according to best natural aptitude, *does* admit of excess. I conclude, therefore, that the Platonic division of labor is not justice.

In defending my minor premise, I can best counter Plato by measuring "excess" against his own claims of good consequences. To begin with, he claims that, with specialization, "each thing becomes more plentiful, finer and easier, when one man, exempt from other tasks, does one thing according to nature and at the crucial moment" (*Republic*, 370c). It would be unfair to Plato to test what are essentially empirical claims against our modern hyperspecialization of function, since rather than proliferating roles he seems to eliminate more than he adds. But even to freeze a narrow division of labor in the teeth of technological and other uncontrolled changes could frustrate all three aims of furthering production quantity, quality, and facility. Beyond some threshold, specialization becomes counterproductive, if only because it fails to use more human potentials. Many have argued that overspecialization causes not only a cognitive cretinization but also moral stunting.[8]

The second claimed benefit is that it will unify the city: "Each man, practicing his own, which is one, will not become many but one; and thus . . . the whole city will naturally grow to be one and not many" (*Republic*, 423d). Here again one may argue that Platonic justice may run to excess, being not really good for the city.

In passing, one kind of excess would be too much success, too much unity: Plato thinks that any conflict in the city is unhealthy, unlike a modern view that at least some social and political frictions foster freedom. He presses his Aristocratic stratification into our very souls, not wanting civil war there any more than in the city. But could a bit of friction within our psyches also be liberating and healthy?

In another kind of excess, his division of labor would divide more than unify, contrary to intent. As Crossman puts it, "Sacrifices are demanded from each class, but only to ensure satisfaction of its dominant interest" (Crossman, 1959, 123). Philosophers may not like to rule, but their doing so protects philosophy from the demos, obviates their being ruled by worse people, and assures their security and sustenance. The spirited auxiliaries cannot compete for public office, such as had been Glaucon's ambition; but they are freed from economic care and can express their competitive and combative natures against enemies of the city. The appetitive trades stratum alone can enjoy both private property and family life, even if they must economically sustain the guardians who rule them wisely and protect them well.[9]

Such images of cross-class or vertical solidarities are invariably strained. They underplay self-interested horizontal solidarities among members of the upper classes when considered separately and then again among members of the lower classes among themselves. Rhetoric of vertical solidarity seems suspect whenever a theorist betrays anxiety about either any disarray among the upper class (Plato holds that revolutions begin with division among the ruling class), or any organizational effort to unite the lower class (he blocks the trades stratum from all politics).

The primary paradigms of the left, in both the Saint and the Socialist modes, hold that a full-time division of labor tends to divide rather than unite. It creates conflicts of interests between rulers and ruled, as well as between nonworking owners and nonowning workers. It always accompanies an unequal and exploitative exchange between the dominant and the dominated. In short, Platonic justice and similar versions of coercively enforced divisions of labor do not really make a city one.

A democratic dialectician would have been a heretic in the *Republic*'s choir, even more than was the semi-Sophist Thrasymachus. Not impressed with Platonic rhetoric, a democratic interlocutor would have defended democracy by denying the clarity and coherence of Plato's definition of justice as well as challenging claimed good consequences in implementing it. In the hunt for justice, the quarry thus eludes Plato. Perhaps, in any case, the game prized depends on whose interests matter.

### Distribution of the Social Product: Social Gradations of Appropriate Consumption

Beyond inequalities in property and in role assignments, the Aristocrat further defends highly unequal distribution of the social product. This was subdued in Plato's utopian mode, which imagines an austerity among the guardians not historically observed in ruling classes, as attested by the notorious hypocrisy of the Spartans in his own time (black broth at home, bank accounts and luxuries when abroad). Recall that the Aristocrat is usually unlike the Saint in being personally unable or unwilling to practice sharp moderation of desires, although perhaps able to practice the token redistribution of wealth called "charity." Some—such as Socrates, Plato, and the older Augustine—apparently did moderate their personal consumption, at least in any ostentatious forms. But many adherents of the Aristocrat paradigm—such as Aristotle, Cicero, or Burke—lived a contradiction in recommending to the lower classes an austerity that they themselves failed to practice.

The hypocrisy could be glaring. One biographer notes that before the public, "Cicero affected to despise comfort, luxury and the softer side of life." But his actual life of ease was apparently financed by venality in his public offices: "If his *Letters* bear witness to any steadfastness, it is his steadfast refusal to desist from the hypocritical practice of plundering the provinces by proxy" (Carcopino, 1951, vol. 1, 76, 140).[10]

Insensitivity to the apparent contradiction shows the centrality of belief in inborn inequalities, or natural gradations of the superior and the inferior. In classical versions of the Aristocrat, this led to acceptance of formal inequalities in law (as illustrated by the varying duties and penalties for citizen, metic, or slave in Plato's *Laws*) or even distinctive expectations regarding the virtues, as made plain by Aristotle (cf. *Politics*, I, xiii). The "gentlemen"—and those of less wealth than philosophic wisdom who identify with them—are born to different standards than those appropriate for the vulgar many.

Especially when people use inconsistent arguments to defend a set of economic inequalities, it suggests that group loyalties and attitudes toward inequalities precede and structure discourse, rather than justificatory principles dominating such policy preferences or group alignments. The trick for the Aristocrats is to denounce any economic envies or greeds of the lower classes, while defending their own high consumption as if it reflected needs rather than greeds.

### The Rhetoric of Difference

From Aristotle through Hegel, one argument of the Aristocratic paradigm was an emphasis on the importance of preserving "differences" and not homogenizing society, as if to make people more similar in one respect (levels of consumption) were necessarily to make them alike in all respects (including a leveling of cultural standards). Some aristocratic societies turned to sumptuary laws to designate what luxury goods such as clothing could be displayed by different standings in the society. Some externals were limited to the royal family, as in the Western reservation of royal purple for rulers and pontiffs. Even John Adams, who primarily embraced the Capitalist paradigm, held that the rich indulge luxuries out of a passion for distinction, so moderation of consumption levels among the lower classes would result in more self-restraint among the upper classes.

The Aristocrats often differentiated themselves by their patronage of the arts. In this view, the mass public lacks both will (i.e., good taste) and capacity (i.e., wealth) to sustain great art. Even today, academic adherents to the Aristocratic formula disparage mass culture and stress the gentlemanly values found in cultivation of the finer things. As someone quipped of Wagner's music, could that be better than it sounds?

### Charity

The Aristocrat, by denouncing the nouveaux riches for flaunting their wealth, almost concedes that the manifest inequalities of society may in themselves cause immoderation in lower-class desires. Beyond their indiscretion, it is said, the newly rich are too much in love with their new money and purchases to practice the liberality that further contributes to the blunting of class animosities. In Aristotle another argument in defense of inequalities is to permit the virtues of liberality or magnificence, but such charitable giving would stop short of the Saint's mad impulse to give it all away (as in Ruskin or Tolstoy). The Saint is also unlike the Aristocrat in practicing charity as an affirmation of similarity with the poor rather than difference, and in giving personal labor rather than merely opening a purse. For many of the Saints and most of the Socialists, token charity is only a seeming altruism, for what is given was once extracted from the labor of the lower classes and helps preserve the exploitative system as a whole. The Aristocrat's charity really preserves social distance, fosters deference for the giver as an individual, and becomes a power that can be turned to political or other advantages in traditional patron-client relationships.

### Service

The Aristocrat defends economic inequality by stressing other service functions of the upper classes, such as providing management of estates, maintaining granaries for redistribution in times of harvest failure, and coordinating armed protection. But as the history of late medieval and early modern Europe suggests, even when preserving their protective roles nobles could be viewed as predatory or parasitical once their productive roles had become less important.[11]

As evident from our review of Plato, the Aristocrat rejects any simply egalitarian concept of justice, at least if that involves a merely *arithmetic* equality. For Plato, Aristotle, and later theorists in the West, justice rather lay in *proportional* equality, requiring not equal rewards to equals and unequals alike but rather equal rewards only to those of equal contribution to society. It is claimed that the upper classes contribute much more than those who labor with their hands—a view that the Saint and Socialist would challenge. Proportionality aside, the Aristocrat's justice is inequality of results, not even requiring the "equality of opportunity" of the Capitalist. Even if the Confucians favored an open examination system for bureaucratic posts, they were less attentive to opening access to the education needed for success.

Beyond military protection, supplying political leadership was long the upper classes' primary claim to service. The paradigm requires that leaders be moral—for corruption, especially as venality, would only encourage mass greed. The training of "character" was the primary objective of the Confucian Chinese scholar-bureaucrats, the Hindu Brahmans, as well as many educated elites of the Hebrew, Greek, and Roman worlds. More than these groups would ever acknowledge, the moderation of lower-class desires—especially economic desires—was the goal behind their emphasis on moral training. Originally a primarily instrumental goal, it was sometimes later understood as if entirely intrinsic.

## Does Anyone Really Love Austerity?
## The Need for the Religion of Priests

In the Confucian tradition, at most a semireligious aura surrounded veneration of ancestors, ritual, and so forth; and among the aristocratic Sadducees of the Hebrews, there was no belief in resurrection. But in most embodiments of the Aristocrat's practice, religiosity in the mass public is an important auxiliary to the moderation of desires in this life. If speaking of another class, Marx put this brutally: "The mortgage that the peasant has on heavenly possessions guarantees the mortgage that the bourgeois has on peasant possessions" ("Class Struggles in France," ii, in Marx and Engels, 1962, vol. 1, 187; cf. also Parkin, 1971, 70). But this almost forgets the Marx-Engels viewpoint that most ideology is self-deception rather than deliberate deception of others, while also slighting the dread of death—which all upper classes share with the lower.

Some consolation of an afterlife has pervaded most of history's great religions. It might be a cycle of rebirths followed by a higher state of being, as in Hinduism or Buddhism. Or it could be the earthier posthumous rewards of Christianity and Islam. As to these last two, the former envisages the resurrection of the body as well as the soul, while the latter even hints that the hereafter may not be without sex. But while belief in a hereafter could indeed have the consequence of encouraging acquiescence in this life's economic inequalities, the very human fear of mortality—both for ourselves and our loved ones—would alone be enough to account for a like belief. This explains its living presence among members of upper classes as well as lower.

As Jon Elster has argued, the very suffering of the lower classes during the course of their lives could also lead them to generate—on their own—beliefs that could help them endure. This may very well be the psychic ground of mass religion, rather than its being a "false consciousness" inculcated by the ruling classes (Elster, 1983, 164). Furthermore, while lower-class religiosity often has a central vision of an afterlife, this vision—far from justifying inequalities in this life—may often challenge them (e.g., the Zealots, the Reformation Anabaptists, or Gerrard Winstanley's Diggers). On the other hand, though religiosity could arise independently of any effort of the upper class to encourage it in the lower, it is certain that theological justifications of this-worldly inequalities may be quite self-consciously encouraged by elites, as illustrated by Plato's myth of Er.

Inegalitarian contents in the Aristocrat's religious doctrine have historically accompanied highly inegalitarian religious institutions: the hierarchies of priests. Although perhaps offering some scope for non-noble upward mobility, the highest priestly offices were usually occupied by those of high social origins, such as the younger sons who did not inherit estates in medieval Europe. While often the religion may have originated with the more ascetic model of the Saint—demanding hard sacrifices from the rich—it may be transformed over the centuries toward the Aristocratic paradigm. The highest priests would encourage magnificent buildings and elaborate ritual to astonish the many, while often living in considerable personal luxury, perhaps from involuntary temple gifts, tithes and so on.

In many historical contexts, the Aristocrat thus tended to support any coercively defended religious hierarchy and associated doctrines, even if sometimes entertaining private religious doubts. Those close to the Aristocratic paradigm still emphasize respect for religion as part of moderation of mass desires, for this is the primary objective of any political order. Irving Babbitt used to say that every child has the right to be born into a moral cosmos, that none should be pitchforked into a moral chaos. Surely, Leo Strauss also made much of the importance of piety, although close reading of his comments on Plato's piety raises some question as to whether Strauss himself inwardly adhered to the piety he publicly maintained (cf. Strauss, 1975; also, Drury, 1988, 181, 188–92). It could be part of maintaining salutary beliefs appropriate to a mass population incapable of knowledge.

But is this—the Aristocratic paradigm—a "blind alley," as one adherent to the Capitalist paradigm avows? The nostalgic return to a time when ordinary people trusted some elite rather than their own judgments may be gone forever: "Myths cannot hope to serve a social purpose if people know they are myths and seek to preserve them in a utilitarian spirit. If God does not exist, he cannot be invented" (Brittan, 1975, 157).

Reason must master passion, Strauss and his kind hold—which is to say that the reason of the gentlemen must by any means help contain the passions of the simple men. Where character formation fails, one must think about constitutional design as the second line of defense, before turning reluctantly to the third line of the ruthless realist's raw force.

## Notes

1.  The Confucians conceded a common human nature across classes, although even they assumed great inborn differences of individual aptitudes to be developed and selected through training and examinations. Yet in Confucian China the meritocratic ideal was often in practice corrupted by class privilege (cf. Brown, 1988, 47–72).

2.  Here and elsewhere I cite Allan Bloom's translation of *The Republic of Plato* (1968). Other citations from Plato use the variously translated *Collected Dialogues of Plato* (1984) edited by Edith Hamilton and Huntington Cairns. If the key to Plato's ideal society is a rigid division of labor, that of Marx's vision in *The German Ideology* is the exact opposite: "Nobody has one exclusive sphere of activity, but each can become accomplished in any branch he wishes," permitting "one to do one thing today and another tomorrow, to hunt in the morning, fish in the afternoon, rear cattle in the evening, criticize after dinner, just as I have a mind, without ever becoming hunter, fisherman, shepherd or critic." With Fourier, Marx thinks *that* is following nature.

3.  Plato would say that I could not refute him unless I show that his own words "contradict one another about the same things, in relation to the same things, and in the same respect" (*Sophist*, 230b). But my critique of Plato's chain of reasoning regarding justice looks less for simple contradiction than for unclear rules of inference and vulnerabilities at the links. Often these premises are neither strictly true nor false, nor can we address probabilities of known magnitudes. We ourselves must determine plausibility weights for Plato's claims. Even when premises are linked by valid deductions, the whole of an argument is no stronger than—and no weaker than—its weakest link (cf. Rescher, 1976).

4.  Leo Strauss and his intellectual heirs have always sought to exaggerate the unity of premodern political philosophers in order to heighten their contrast with the moderns. If in part requiring the dismissal as unphilosophic of the Sophists and other schools of thought not of the Great Tradition, part of this involves the assimilation of Plato and Aristotle—done in part by claiming comic absurdity in any of Plato's more radical proposals such as rule of the philosophers (as well as equality of the sexes and abolition of family

and property). (See Allan Bloom's interpretive essay appended to his translation of the *Republic*, esp. 407 ff.; but see also Strauss, 1963, 124.)

But there are at least two ways in which Plato could seriously imagine philosophers coming into rule: one by the accident of inheriting a throne, and the other by bringing the second-best regime with its Nocturnal Council around toward the model of the first-best regime of the *Republic* (cf. Aristotle, *Politics*, 1265a). The philosophic nature can enjoy dialectics at age 30–35; then after 15 reluctant years in subordinate roles followed perhaps by rule from age 50, the philosopher can return to philosophy upon retiring. Would a philosopher begrudge some sacrifice when the same is required of the auxiliaries (who cannot compete for the honors of high office) or the appetitive stratum (who must give over some of their product to support the guardians)?

5. At least Plato was better than Aristotle, who tended to define the natures of the two sexes as if internally uniform categories, holding that "the relation of male to female is by nature a relation of superior to inferior and ruler to ruled," although excepting cases when the male is "constituted in some respect contrary to nature" (*Politics*, I, v, 7; I, xii, 1).

6. Even having two or more pilots could raise problems. In the kingdom of the blind, the one-eyed person is king. But if two or more claim visions of the vague Platonic Good, quarrels seem likely. This Platonic unity behind the forms of the intelligible world is so evanescent that it is not defined, merely compared with the illumination of the sun in the sensible world. But the secret knowledge of Dostoevsky's Grand Inquisitor was that there was no secret knowledge.

7. Mortimer Adler, for one, agrees: "Only justice is an unlimited good. . . . One can want too much liberty and too much equality—more than is good for us to have in relation to our fellowmen, and more than we have any right to. Not so with justice. No society can be too just; no individual can act more justly than is good for him or for his fellowmen" (Adler, 1981, 137).

8. These become common themes among modern theorists of the Saint tradition (Wollstonecraft, Thoreau, Tolstoy, Ruskin, Gandhi) as well as the Socialists (e.g., Fourier, Kropotkin, the Marxists).

9. This idea of social unity not through similarity but through the complementary differences of specialization of function would be elaborated later as Durkheim's "organic solidarity" (Durkheim, 1964).

10. In defense of Cicero, it was normal for proconsuls to use their office to restore the erosion of personal finances during the payless consulship or earlier magistracies of the career of offices (*cursus honorum*). Cicero "extracted much less profit from his subjects than was considered normal among more avaricious proconsuls" (Wood, 1988, 53). Although distrusting commerce in favor of agriculture, Cicero was a man of means with extensive investments in real estate as well as collected art. He held that accumulating property was a duty, even if one should avoid avaricious excess (ibid., 105–19).

11. "The lord has abdicated from his position as head of a large agrarian and semi-industrial undertaking. . . . Politically speaking, the lord was still a leader to his men, he remained their military commander, their judge, their born protector. But his economic leadership had gone—and all the rest could easily follow. He had become a 'stockholder on the soil' " (Marc Bloch, 1973, 100–101, cited in Bowles and Gintis, 1986, 212).

# 3

# The Aristocrat and Democracy

> Society cannot exist, unless a controlling power
> upon will and appetite be placed somewhere;
> and the less of it there is within, the more there
> must be without.
>
> Edmund Burke,
> Letter to a Member of the National Assembly

Even a Whig who was harboring some Tory leanings understood, it seems, that what Eric Voegelin would later call "the problem of order" requires at least two trenchworks. The first line of defense must be moderation of mass wants; and the second, an arrangement of government such that it would not itself be responsive to mass wants but rather contain them, preferably with minimal use of force.

The alternatives of moral constraint and coercive restraint were clear in traditional China's contrast of the Confucians and the Legalists, although it left out the intermediate possibility of an effective constitutional order such as the "mixed regime" (as described later in the chapter). Hindu political thought also worked both themes: the *dharmasastra* emphasis on training in the exacting *dharma* (socially integrating duties) of caste, family, or other status; and the *arthasastra* techniques of *danda* (discipline through force and fear). The former was the relative specialty of the Brahman or priestly caste, while the latter was that of the allied Ksatriya or ruler caste (Parekh, 1986).

While the problematic of the Aristocrat emerged in very distinctive socioeconomic settings, conservatives in any steady-state economic setting interpret the problem of political order as the quest for some arrangement that assures social betters will be able to contain their inferiors. As earlier noted, the proclivity to rank all things is a distinctive signature of this grand strategy against scarcity and its conflicts, and it invariably includes the ranking of persons.

53

With the self-understanding of being the champion of moral character and the leadership that embodies it, the Aristocratic conservative in practice defends wealth, especially older wealth. Recall that moderation of wants is necessary in a steady-state economy where burgeoning economic demands could only mean zero-sum conflicts. More for one class must mean less for the others. Paradoxically, the more zero-sum the situation, the more urgent the teaching of a common good, requiring both inward and outward discipline.

> Most "ancient" and "medieval" political orders developed out of a long background of violence and misery; were maintained with violence, although internal misery may have been alleviated for considerable periods; and disintegrated with violence and misery. In preindustrial societies, most persons perforce saw the world as one of limited resources, unavoidable scarcity, inevitable hardship. For many people through most of recorded history, even minimal safety of life and limb depended upon authoritative protection by the strong, and even minimal subsistence depended upon an enforced order. Out of countless experiences with scarcity, violence and acute social dependence, there evolved such hierarchic world views as the medieval Christian doctrines or the developed Hindu views of caste. (Williams, 1979, 45)

Such world views did not protect the lower orders from economic exploitation and sometimes even worse predation at the hands of their "protectors." In the case of caste, for example, the principal divisions called *varnas* (Sanskrit for "colors") orginally resulted when the lighter-skinned Aryans (Ksatriyas and Brahmans) subjugated dark-skinned peoples such as the Dasas, who as Shudras were to do most menial labor not passed along to the subcaste untouchables (Thapar, 1966, 38). Yet extreme exploitation was often absent at the start of a system of social ranks. The peasants may at first have perceived a nearly equal exchange when exactions of labor service, rents in kind or cash, tithes and taxes were counterbalanced by priests' intercessions with the gods to assure good harvests and the rulers' protection against loss of *all* of their grain and even their lives to local thieves or external raiders (McNeill, 1980, 17–18, 26–28). Disintegration of this mutual sense of fair exchange may explain the Spartan turn to annual ritual murders to terrorize their helots, or the periods in China when an entire extended family could be executed for the crime of one member.

When the lower orders doubt the officially defined common good and readily turn to conflict, the Aristocrat must shift to the coercive apparatus to contain in act what could not be contained in mind. While the paradigm distrusts most innovation once a regime is constituted, agrarian societies in practice often exempted the innovation needed for effective control. Hence, traditional China was inventive in apparatuses of torture and war; after trade with Europe began, and before entering our century, it sought out the even better military technology of the West. In China, as elsewhere, many intellectuals were bent on preserving their traditional culture, but importation of Western military technology usually had the unintended consequence of undermining it. Ironically, much of the economic resources denied to the lower classes were consumed by the armed forces required to repress them or ward off external invaders who could ally with the local poor to despoil the rich.

To conserve any needed labor as well as to maintain control, the Aristocrat sometimes prohibited both internal and external migration. Having closed the possibility of exit, they also forestalled evasion: Traditional regimes required censuses of population and resources for tax purposes, and most maintained a hidden apparatus of domestic spies or police agents.

While the best Aristocratic theorists opposed the tyrannical extremes of autocracy, they traditionally lacked enthusiasm for any form of really popular government. Displaying an obvious bias in denying the title of "philosopher" to the paradigm's many contemporary critics, Allan Bloom baldly writes, "The ancient philosophers were to a man proponents of aristocratic politics" (Bloom, 1987, 284). Even in modern history, Aristocrats have rarely favored emergent institutions of liberal democracy, although the semiliberal Baron de Montesquieu did admire British liberties and favored provincial power as a counter to the centralizing French monarchy.

## Strategic Fields of Political Means and Norms of Liberal Democracy

F. G. Bailey once noted that in politics there are certain "pragmatic rules" of struggle, which may press against and possibly transform any "normative rules" such as those of constitutions and statutes as well as conventional morality (Bailey, 1969, 1–17). His pragmatic rules are those of opportunism or no-holds-barred struggle. While he did not elaborate those rules of purely expediential politics, Bailey grasped the importance of asking how pragmatic rules relate to normative ones.

Viewed as if a game, politics is unique in that part of the rules of the game (the pragmatic ones) include efforts to change the standing rules (the normative ones) to your advantage even as the game is being played. One must grasp pragmatic politics to understand the emergence or demise of certain normative rules, since opportunistic political action is continually recreating or destroying the normative limits on opportunism. While certain norms such as constitutions, statutes, and so forth may endure for centuries, these are ultimately but episodic equilibria produced by the struggles, compromises, and machinations of agents following pragmatic rules. There is even an element of opportunism when political agents keep temporarily within the bounds of norms merely because these cannot be easily changed to greater personal or partisan advantage.

Politics usually involves coalitions where agents pool resources for more effective political struggle. Preference orderings of groups (as well as individuals) arise in pragmatic action. Many group loyalties become internalized and stable, although different issues may shift the relevant frame of reference in distinguishing friends (favored groups and their close allies), neutrals (the more or less uncommitted), and rivals (disfavored groups and their allies). Relative distributions of resources among friends and rivals and any effectively sanctioned (i.e., "en-forced") normative rules shape the field of political action.

In pursuit of policy ends, the logically possible courses of action necessarily exhaust what we actually observe in history. I shall analyze political means as a set of six strategic fields encompassing all pragmatically possible responses to any claim of some to exercise authority over others. Three fields—enduring, exiting, evading—are strategies for adaptation to uncontrolled authority and are used more often by the relatively weak, as addressed in Chapter 5. More likely to be pursued by the stronger, the other three strategic fields—influencing, recruiting, restructuring—offer means to control the content of authoritative decisions. Here agents play to win in politics, but evaluate smaller wins in terms of larger ones. Winning in the largest sense is best viewed as maximization of the value of the mix of goods held by oneself and favored groups.

In *influencing*, the manipulated variable ultimately consists of the wills of the incumbent authorities. In *recruiting*, one strives to win by advantageously selecting personnel, or those who make the decisions. In *structuring*, one aims to win by pulling power away from decision-making units controlled by rivals and putting them, rather, wherever friends prevail.

All regimes attempt to constrain the field of possible political action, specifying what is mandatory, prohibited, and—usually by silence—permitted. But if all regimes restrain opportunism, not all sets of restraints are democratic. In fact, democratic rules of the game constitute a quite specific set of limitations on raw politics, as described below.

Modern or liberal democratic norms, then, place specific restraints on no-holds-barred political struggle, requiring that such struggle be confined to open, peaceable competitions informed by the root norm of equality of basic rights for those deemed to be citizens. Their consent (from French *consentir*, to feel with or together) determines provisional precedence (i.e., what wins) in the three mentioned fields of strategic action to control the contents of authoritative decisions. Meaningful majority consent must be voluntary or uncoerced, with an open contest across *all three* strategic fields. Permanent closure of any one field of contest may be enough to make liberal democracy unreal. Put otherwise, no field is sufficient and all are necessary for any meaningful and sustained popular power. In its predominant adversarial mode, the competitions of "liberal representative democracy" touch all three strategic fields as quests for consent: (1) a combat of ideas or programs (the "liberal" element, implying freedoms of speech and assembly); (2) a system of competitive elections among candidates for public office (the "representative" element, implying the rights to vote and to run for office); and (3) popular control on most other questions of constitutional design, or allocations of powers of decision among various institutional units (the "democracy" element, or the right to ultimate popular sovereignty). Modern democratic norms thus close some possible choices (e.g., to shoot the opposition) and open certain opportunities (e.g., to run your own candidates against them).

## Strategies to Maintain Hierarchy

Having recognized the three fields of pragmatic play and how liberal democratic norms have restrained them, we can better understand how the Aristocratic paradigm could conflict with those norms. Quite practical concerns shape the typically inegalitarian philosophies of the Aristocrats regarding the strategic fields for control of policy. My elaborations below should further clarify the meaning of the strategic fields sketched in brief above.

### The Influence Strategy: Private Philosophizing and Public Persuasion

The influence strategy takes as if constants both the allocations of power among offices and the persons who fill them, directly or indirectly working—as the variable—the attitudes or at least the wills of those who make decisions. The strategy has three subfields for maneuver: (1) creation of messages; (2) their communication or delivery; and (3) their reinforcement with appropriate rewards or punishments. Played pragmatically, it spawns people who are often intolerant, favoring freedom of speech only for their friends, silencing their opponents. When this field is subjected to the restraint of liberal democratic norms, the generalized rights of freedom of speech and assembly are most important, but freedom of information has auxiliary value.

Since the term "liberal" is linked to liberty, perhaps one could say that this strategic field especially concerns the word "liberal" in the phrase "liberal representative democracy." Without freedom of communication we could not speak of any majority "consent" to policies, candidates, or institutional forms. If there is no possible contest, there is no meaningful consent. Even if the majority of people were able to think differently, they could not say so against an enforced orthodoxy (cf. Spitz, 1984, 112–15).[1]

Any form of popular government involves enlarged freedom of speech, as evident in ancient Athens. Modern liberal democracy has demanded open access to public information and an unfettered public competition of ideas. However, the classic Aristocratic viewpoint was usually hostile toward both these norms. It historically favored censorship to block leakage of elite secrets as well as to stop any public criticism of the inegalitarian religious or political orthodoxy.

In the past, Aristocrats did not favor much public access to information, even regarding the content of the laws. Favoring broad discretion in judicial decisions, elites often resisted demands for published law codes with pre-established penalties. Nor did they favor public observation and public records of all official proceedings, disliking much publicity of political decision-making. It would require a long struggle before what affected the public would be available for public scrutiny.

Yet the Aristocrat accepted the need of the authorities to gather sensitive information about the people, obtained through swarms of informers such as *les mouches* under the Bourbons. Even where the people had won political rights, the Aristocrat could oppose any secret ballot. At the dusk of the Roman republic, Cicero urged repeal of secret voting, permitting ballot inspection by at least "our best and most eminent citizens" (*Laws*, III, xvii).

The paradigm handicapped popular participation in political communications. One effective barrier was use of an elite language not accessible to the mass population, such as Sanskrit of the Vedas in India, Mandarin in China, and Latin in late medieval Europe (with survivals in later legal proceedings). Another was discouragement of the enlarged public education that can aid participation in political discourse. While noble estates often hired live-in tutors, in both ancient Athens and republican Rome the nobility opposed the teaching of rhetoric on a fee basis, which would have permitted wealthier non-nobles to challenge its monopoly on the art of public speaking

(Stone, 1988, 41–43). Common people also had little to back up their arguments, even when they did manage to articulate complaints. Apart from invocation of a common moral code in the classic entreaty of the weak before the strong, bribery and rioting were just about the only other means of influence available to the lower classes.

The Aristocrats did not encourage free inquiry into the operation of society, and even contemporary Aristocrats criticize empirical research within reach of the vulgar. Thus, Leo Strauss complained, "The new political science puts a premium on observations which can be made with the utmost frequency, and therefore by people of the meanest capacities" (Strauss, 1962, 326; cf. also Voegelin, 1952). More receptive to speculation about human nature, the Aristocrat urges that priority be given to the moral question of how we ought to live our lives. It is assumed that the answer must be a matter for discovery rather than choice; and this presupposes instruction of the unwise many by the few wise, whether involving sacred texts, traditions, or philosophy.

I will say little here of the interpretation of sacred scriptures, let alone other signs such as auspices and auguries. The absence of contradiction would assure knowledge of the one true meaning of texts, for the implicit assumption of such hermeneutics was that the divine cannot be self-contradictory. But to avoid any rival readings, the few would usually interpret the divine for the whole body of the faithful, monopolizing the mysteries and unchanging rituals. Any age of prophecy was thus implicitly over, unless carefully reserved for certain high priests informed by corporate wisdom.[2]

As for tradition, the Aristocratic distrust of innovation is apparent in Cicero's law on religious observances: "These rites shall ever be preserved and continuously handed down in families, and . . . *they must be continued for ever*" (*Laws*, II, xix). But even secular institutions may be put under a sacred aura by those invoking tradition. Richard Hooker, Joseph de Maistre, Edmund Burke, Michael Oakeshott, and Russell Kirk would claim that the only valid constitutional orders are not designed like machines, but rather grow organically out of the past. What is handed down from the past and tested by time is the collective wisdom of all. Such argument speaks as if all were involved in the testing and approval, not just a narrow elite. In any event, traditionalists usually turn to the corporatist viewpoint in permitting but a few to interpret the traditions for the whole of society. Some traditionalists have distrusted philosophy, disdaining what Burke called "metaphysical speculations."

Even when, as in Plato or Aristotle, emphasis falls instead on philosophic design, the constant factor is the monopoly of a knowing elite. The classical natural-right Aristocrat's practical political episte-mology may be roughly rendered as this: (1) Ultimate value judgments can be known; (2) only a few can "know" in the sense of discovering such truths; (3) their knowledge is not transferable as such to the many who dwell in the cave of mere opinion; (4) yet a semblance of such knowledge or "true belief" (*orthe doxa*) must be disseminated to the many; and (5) no *public* expression should be permitted to undermine that orthodoxy.

Like most other hierarchies in history, Aristocratic political orders let the favored few pass judgment on the criteria of desert by which inequalities are ordered, while shielding these criteria from any public criticism. While the Aristocrats would probably argue that their epistemology drives their political evaluations, it is more plausibly argued that prior political preferences shape their epistemology. For it has the foreseeable, practical consequence of limiting access to participation in all strategic fields of politics, including the influence field.

### Philosophic Dialogue in Quest of Knowledge

A tradition of Western philosophy embraced by Plato and Aristotle emphasizes the intrinsic superiority of the contemplative life, with philosophic study—for their own sake—of things that cannot be other than they are, such as Aristotle's divine things. But the Aristocrat also believes that knowledge in matters of ultimate valuation is possible, to be sought as having practical value for living the good life.

In Asia (especially), some traditions hold that such knowledge requires apprenticeship with a seer, then an exacting course of disciplined individual thought, felicitously followed by an intuitive, integral awareness. But in the Western tradition embraced by Plato, Aristotle, Cicero, Aquinas, and many others, the seeking has generally been more collegial and the knowing less by personal awareness than by the testing of philosophic dialogue. The key test of truth is always coherence or noncontradiction. Although Aquinas and other much later scholastics conducted their dialogues in published works, these were not in vernaculars accessible to the many (which was one of the many protests of the Reformation). But earlier traditions urged yet more closure for the deepest philosophic questioning. This should be conducted in private, it was held, admitting to dialogue only the select few of good birth and known goodwill.

As Leo Strauss emphasized, the ancients believed not only that the public could be dangerous to philosophers, but also that philosophers could be a danger to public order. While one response was a turn to esoteric writing in published works, the resolution of the tension between philosophy and politics required, in any case, that responsible philosophers conduct their disputations apart from the many so that each would be safe from the other (cf. Strauss, 1952). Even without such sins against philosophy as the execution of Socrates, the demos as the greatest Sophist could corrupt even philosophic natures by the force of loud applause or censure (cf. *Republic*, 492c). Public opinion is less the creature than the creator of the Sophists and the demagogues. Both are esteemed by the many because they flatter the many, pandering to their opinions and passions of the moment. As Plato scornfully remarks, "The man who serves them most agreeably, with the regime as it is, and gratifies them by flattering them and knowing their wishes beforehand and being clever at fulfilling them, will on that account be the good man and the one wise in important things" (*Republic*, 426c). A democratic society thus permits the inflaming of popular wants, constituting a standing threat to the core of the Aristocrat's paradigm.

If what the people *want* is a flawed guide to goals, what they *believe* about the world is little help in knowing good means. Although commonly received public opinions may be taken as the starting point of dialogue, any direct public involvement is an obstacle to the discovery of truth. Hence the proper scene for dialogue is a closed setting—perhaps a private home or discussion circle as dramatically illustrated in Plato's *Republic* as well as Cicero's *De Re Publica*. Alternatively, reformed political orders could create closed settings such as the Nocturnal Council of Plato's *Laws*.

A carefully screened group is admitted to this discourse, which may critically examine even the most delicate subjects, such as the local norms or the nature of the gods.[3] Plato would debar youths under age 30, although some mature women could be invited. But dialectic is not for the lower classes. Those with "souls doubled up and spoiled as a result of being in mechanical occupations" would normally be unworthy suitors of philosophy (*Republic*, 495c–496a). If the historical Socrates really said that the unexamined life is not worth living, Plato relegates most people to exactly that.[4]

The ideals of classical dialogue assume a select company—mature, competent, and of known goodwill. Most interlocutors would have broadly shared views and aims; and agreement on ends can facilitate consensus on appropriate means, just as agreement on procedural means can sometimes facilitate consensus on ends (this latter theme is more prominent in Capitalist thought).

Most of us love the ideals of dialogue primarily for the convenience of imposing them on others. Yet those norms are prominently endorsed by any who urge a cooperative ethos: "Come, let us reason together." Just as Aristocrats do not compete with each other in the economic sphere, so those committed to the quest of truth for its own sake would not be distracted by goals of personal wealth or power. As in friendly sporting competitions, they could want personal recognition. Yet to aim at mere victory in argument (the Greek *eristic*) would be unseemly if it distracted from the search for the truth. For that is a good that can be enjoyed by each fitted by nature and nurture to receive it, without preventing the like enjoyment by all who are such.

Reasoning in the silence of base passions, such seekers of wisdom would not allow anything extraneous to the merits of the argument to influence the course of debate. Unlike vulgar public argument, there could be no place for threats and promises, pressure tactics, or appeals to "low" standards such as public opinion, save perhaps in the Aristotelian way as a starting point for deliberation. None would resort to verbal trickery to score debating points; nor would they deploy such low tactics as depreciation of the person of an opponent.

Since the ethos of dialogue is not a combative debate but a cooperative quest for truth, those who know they have nothing helpful to contribute would naturally keep silent, yielding the floor to others. Unlike immature debaters with their verbal elbowing, the ideal disputants would take pains to let all others speak and to listen very closely. If one offers a point of view, it is stated in the proper spirit of dialogue as nicely summed up by Plato:

> I think we should all be contentiously eager to know what is true and what false in the subject under discussion, for it is a common benefit that this be revealed to all alike. I will then carry the argument through in accordance with my own ideas, and if any of you believe that what I admit to myself is not the truth, you must break in upon it and refute me. For I do not speak with any pretense to knowledge, but am searching along with you, and so if there appears to be anything in what my opponent says, I shall be the first to yield to him. (*Gorgias*, 505e–506a)

Indeed, if one knows of any good objections to one's own point of view, these would be cheerfully supplied if no one else supplies them. Or one may helpfully strengthen an adversary's affirmative case, even if that should impede carrying one's own view. Every ideal debater wants to hear the strongest case for each viewpoint, never wishing to see an argument carried against a straw target.

Therefore, one never ignores or pretends to ignore a critical argument against one's case, nor would one substitute laughter for serious reply. A major norm of dialogue is absolute sincerity, although candor does not preclude devil's advocacy when helpful to the discourse. Ideal participants would aim at clarity and logicality as critical measures for discovery of truth, not the popularity of some standard of argument or set phrases expressing it.

In sum, participants in dialogue would choose only those rules for themselves that they would want all others to follow. But this means only the others admitted to dialogue. A universality that reaches beyond the elite would be alien to the Aristocrats. Expressly judging the many incapable of philosophy, they apply very different norms to *public* discourse.

### The Public Rhetoric of Orthodoxy

Philosophic dialogue, as discussed above, was regarded as suited only to those of superior aptitude and character. In Plato's words, "it's impossible that a multitude be philosophic" (*Republic*, 494a). The many not only are incapable of the dialectic that discovers knowledge (*episteme*), but cannot even receive a direct transfer of knowledge as such. Rather, on many matters, at most a semblance of knowledge—mere true opinion (*orthe doxa*)—may be conveyed to them through rhetoric.

In Plato, rhetoric can cut two ways. His *Phaedrus* distinguishes evil and good uses: by a false lover who would ruin his love, and by a true lover who would morally improve the object of his attentions. Similarly, Plato's *Gorgias* distinguishes base from noble rhetoric: Used by those who mistake their pleasure for the good, the base form aims at gratification of the rhetorician's lower passions by flattering existing tastes and passions of the audience. Practiced with skill by the Sophist, the demagogue, and the would-be tyrant, base rhetoric may bring short-term pleasures for rhetoricians but create long-term dangers even to them from a people made worse rather than better by the practice of the art.

In contrast, noble rhetoric may mean short-term dangers to rhetoricians but promote the long-term good of both the rhetoricians and the city as a whole. It does not pander to present passions of the audience but demands that these be disciplined or corrected to secure the true good of the well-ordered soul ruled by reason. True rhetoric thus becomes the ally of philosophy, as illustrated by Thrasymachus in the *Republic* (tamed from his wolfishness to become as a watchdog, a "friend" to Socrates). It becomes the authentic art of politics, which aims at moral reform: "He who is to become a rhetorician in the right way must after all be a just man with a knowledge of what is just" (*Gorgias*, 508c).

Although sharing the ultimate goal of moral improvement, the discourse that discovers truth may be quite unlike that which promotes its practice in the world. The latter may employ means inconsistent with the high ideals of dialogue. For Plato, Aristotle, and Cicero, rhetoric is on one level but a means of persuasion. As Aristotle said, it is "the faculty of discovering in the particular case what are the available means of persuasion" (*Rhetoric*, I, ii). Cicero, who by his oratory against dangerous popular reformers rose from the equestrian order to Rome's highest offices, held that some innate aptitude as well as acquired art is needed to excel in the three tasks of conciliating the audience, instructing them in the case, and moving their passions (*De Oratore*, II, xxvii; II, xxviii). The many, who are incapable of reasoning in the silence of their passions, may be led through those passions and the less exacting premises of mere belief to attain good order in their souls.

In Plato, knowledge is knowledge, but belief may be either true or false. Knowledge is more stable than belief because it can give a rational account of itself, while the holder of even true belief is likened to a blind man on the right road (*Republic*, 506c).

Paradoxically, true belief may be based on falsehoods, the noble lies delivered by rhetoric and defended by public censorship. In the *Republic*, the ruler-guardians lie even to the auxiliary-guardians regarding the matchings of the eugenic mating scheme, but all guardians will lie to the trades stratum. This appetitive class needs to embrace helpful illusions such as the myth of the metals or the religious myth of Er that have the practical consequence of rightly guiding their behavior. While true belief is also emphasized in Aristotle, he at least warns against deceptive oligarchic political practices that would strain credibility. Also, like Cicero, he cautions against philosophic conclusions that ignore the collective wisdom of assemblies and of tradition—also important in matters of practical wisdom. But the main Platonic idea of using lies to implement the truth has had a long history.

One student of Leo Strauss told me that another one taught Sunday school although privately a nonbeliever. Whether true or not, it illustrates the spirit of the Aristocrat: Hypocrisy is no vice when helping inferior others live in virtue. While the Aristocrats hold that moral nihilism is the cause of violence and other ills of our century, they do not regard personal or public dishonesty as in itself nihilistic.[5]

Note that the noble lies in Plato aim at maintenance of inequalities. Characteristically blind to inequalities as a contributing cause of conflicts, the Aristocrat must find such causes in flawed human nature or failure to cultivate an inegalitarian orthodoxy. But to seek peace through a moral or religious orthodoxy may be misguided, if only because the project of securing uniform belief in a society has long been quite unworkable. Indeed, I submit that it will remain so forever.

Even if our current problems do arise from a crisis of moral and religious disbelief, it need not follow that the view denying that ultimate ends can be known is invalid. While there is a so-called genetic fallacy in concluding the invalidity of a statement by its origins, one must also be wary of a "projective fallacy" in concluding invalidity by merely noting unpleasant consequences.[6]

Yet whenever one is enumerating the horrible consequences of disbelief, it is fair enough of us to ask what consequences might follow from the quest for uniform belief. When the maintenance of one orthodoxy is unworkable, a belief in moral or religious absolutism can

cause not unity but acute divisions. This is so whenever *rival* absolut-
isms are pursued, especially if these have a religious content.[7] Thus,
even if one were to grant the dubious proposition that moral relativ-
ism is the source of all contemporary ills, it need not follow that a
return to moral absolutism is the solution, let alone a more specific
return to Plato or Aristotle.

## Censorship

Political orthodoxies imply intolerance, even when narrowly defined as coercive repression of rival messages. In the past even most
"popular" regimes practiced some form of official censorship (cf.
Bloom, 1960, esp. xv–xxxviii). However, among the four paradigms,
the Aristocrat is the most consistent advocate of permanent censorship for the sake of moral and political order. Under autocratic
versions of Aristocratic practice, there was usually defense of an
established religion, although sometimes permitting quiet practice of
minority religions, as when Islamic rulers tolerated other People of
the Book (Jews, Christians). Only rarely, as under the Enlightenment
rule of Frederick II of Prussia or Catherine II of Russia, was a more
principled toleration practiced.

The silencing of public heresy—sometimes even fixing definitions
of words, as in Confucian "rectification of names"—is another facet
of the Aristocrat's discounting the mental potentials of the average
citizen. But a position that seemed intelligible in centuries of mass
illiteracy becomes an outrage as most acquire secondary or higher
education degrees, even if some may complain that excessive access to
higher education, or excessive attention there to the diversity of
human cultures, may undermine "excellence" (e.g., Bloom, 1987).

Prominent recent exemplars of the paradigm such as Leo Strauss
and Eric Voegelin have criticized liberal tolerance of Nazis or communists.[8] For the Aristocrat, "virtue" is a superior value to mere
"freedom"; and it follows that, to promote more virtue, one may
defend some censorship, especially against some ideology such as
communism that would undermine virtue (e.g., Berns, 1957).

Reflecting a wish for a hierarchy of the better over the worse, the
Aristocrat has little enthusiasm for an unchecked "competition of
ideas"—an early derivation from equality of basic rights in a liberal
democracy. Nothing could be more unequal than for a minority to
use state coercion to silence its critics. Indeed, liberal democrats
should not even accord that right to a majority. Even if that majority
is restricting expression to promote more equality for disadvantaged
groups, one may ask whether this is consistent with liberal norms.[9]

## The Recruitment Strategy: Installing the Best as Leaders

A parallel demand for a hierarchy of allegedly better over worse
applies to the Aristocrat's choices regarding the strategic political

field of "recruitment"—a political science term for selection of personnel.

Abstractly viewed, this field of strategic action takes as if constants both the powers of office and the wills of incumbents, manipulating the remaining variable of incumbency itself. The main pragmatic game is to put political friends into posts of authority and to get rivals out.

Recruitment politics hence focuses on screening procedures, which become most thorough for offices of highest importance. One may screen persons by both formal and informal criteria of three types: (1) ascriptive (who you are, primarily birth-dependent attributes); (2) achievement (what you can do, or some kind of performance criteria); and (3) attitudinal (where you stand, often including personal loyalties as well as policy leanings). In important policy-making positions, often ascriptive or achievement criteria first narrow the circle from which final selection occurs. But attitudinal criteria tend to eclipse the other two in the final cut, since the main game is getting friends into positions of power, getting rivals out.

To control such screening, six tactical subfields for maneuver define a recruitment system: (1) who is eligible for office, formally and informally; (2) how they are selected; (3) who does the selecting; (4) how many are chosen, as relevant to purging or packing ploys; (5) how long their tenure is; and (6) how they can be removed from office, if at all (short of resignation or natural death). By the merely pragmatic rules, just about anything goes, which in the last subfield could include ouster of rival incumbents by coup d'état or selective assassination.

But the liberal norm of equality of basic political rights restrains all these tactical subfields—a restraint that gives meaning to the "representative" in "liberal representative democracy." A peaceable and recurrent competition of candidates for the popular vote is the primary mode of recruiting leaders in modern democracy. However, democratic elitists (e.g., Joseph Schumpeter and William Riker) have been wrong to view this as if it were the whole of democracy. Such a view neglects the influence and structures games. Regarding influence, elections without any political opposition, or where "opponents" are unwilling or unable to differ really, do not assure much chance of popular power. Or if the formation of public opinion is dominated by a few, the meaningfulness of electoral consent comes into question. Nor can the strategic field of structures be ignored, since voting for distinctive candidates would be quite pointless if victors entered offices with no important powers attached to them.

### The Best as Rulers?

Lacking faith that really popular elections would be helpful, the classic Aristocrat defines the key political problem as that of bringing the best (*aristoi*) into positions of leadership or at least into key advisory posts to such leaders. The "best" are in large part defined in terms of the paradigm, meaning that kind of character which can help moderate mass desires. To judge of Pericles' leadership, one asks not about his public building projects or other irrelevancies but whether he morally improved any citizens, if only his own sons. Plato makes clear that, by the test that most matters, Pericles never rose above the demagogue to true leadership, preferring instead to dish out "dainties" to the many (*Gorgias*, 513e, 515d, 518e–519b; also *Protagoras*, 319e–320b). Only those with measure could teach others moderation, as Cicero phrased it well: "Just as the whole State is habitually corrupted by the evil desires and the vices of its prominent men, so is it improved and reformed by self-restraint on their part" (*Laws*, III, xiii).

Recognition that ruling aptitudes may not be readily inherited underlay Plato's utopian dream of recruitment by co-optation rather than either hereditary right or popular election. In his *Republic*, those born with rational characters have their potential developed through a rigorous system of education. While also assuring that the guardians will not themselves need guardians, the educational system perpetuates the co-optative system of leadership recruitment. Those already designated best select any new ones. The best are fit to rule in part by their vision of the forms illuminated by the sunlike Good Itself. Plato exalts such "expert" ruler-guardians while disparaging the capacities of ordinary people. He thinks only fellow experts can select experts, whereas in the real world ordinary people choose to make themselves clients of some expert (e.g., a doctor) or to dismiss the expert in whom they have lost confidence (Stone, 1988, 13, 169). Plato illustrates a common prejudice of intellectuals: the belief that only those who know abstractly how to define a skill can successfully practice it or even recognize it (ibid., 255–56, 72–3, 83).[10]

While many argue that the study of epistemologies can illuminate political problems, I hold, rather, that theorists' political problematics explain their political epistemologies. Once elaborated, these problematics have highly practical implications: Contents sometimes subserve argument as to what functions should or should not be performed by the state (e.g., the Aristocrat typically favors—but the Capitalist usually opposes—an extended state supervision over both economics and religion); more often they focus on allocation of participatory rights. As already noted, the Aristocrat denies that the mass population can discover knowledge or even receive it by transference. Only a narrow elite has the potential for political deliberation, as the great Anglican theologian Richard Hooker made clear: "Most requisite . . . it is that to devise laws which all men shall be forced to obey none but wise men be admitted. Laws are matters of principal consequence; men of common capacity and but ordinary judgment are not able (for how should they?) to discern what things are fittest for each kind and state of regiment" (*Ecclesiastical Polity*, I, x, 7).

### Or the Best as Counselors to Rulers?

Whatever Plato's dream of philosophic rulers—a dream revived by the nineteenth-century British eccentric Thomas Carlyle—in most historical practice the Aristocrats have acquiesced in the selection of at least the top leaders by the ascriptive criterion of hereditary right. At least in origins, often the royal family was little more than the leading family among all noble families. The belief that some are simply born to rule and others to be ruled has been central to the Aristocratic outlook, eventually sharply challenged by the Capitalist theory, which denied any hereditary talent for governance and favored election of legislators and chief executives.

In most traditionalist regimes, power normally passed along in hereditary dynasties without any screening for Platonic golden metal. Perhaps in compensation, those of the Aristocratic persuasion have often claimed that wisdom may lie not so much in the single individual who leads the state (or the church, in the case of the papacy) so much as in the corporate whole, as previously noted. In the case of a secular ruler, the wisdom lies less with the single monarch than with the monarch in council, since a panel of the wise—often mixing noble and commoner advisers—will guide most choices. The royal advisory council also insulates the secular ruler from the full weight of criticism, should decisions have bad consequences.

Given only rare opportunities for choosing among alternative successors to a throne, the Aristocratic formula was also attentive to the formation of character in whoever would become the monarch. This encouraged several thousand years of the highly moralistic "mirror for princes" writings. The primary aim was to depict an ideal model for a prince's education and later emulation once he became king. This genre—coming down through the ages to Erasmus's *Education of a Christian Prince*—may refer less to recruitment than to influence as its field for shaping policy.

### Moderating Popular Governments

In his *Laws* Plato proposed his second-best or best practicable regime, claiming to mix monarchy with democracy. But, as Aristotle said, it really mixes oligarchy (rule by the few wealthy) with democracy. As Leo Strauss saw the shared aim of both his predecessors, in place of philosopher-rulers, who view the good life as contemplation, the second-best regime would substitute gentlemen who think of the good life as public service. Although having a place for selective assemblies of the wise in guiding policy—exemplified by Plato's Nocturnal Council and Law Guardians—this practical regime accepts a hereditary right to rule by a nobility of 5,040 households. Just as Plato makes estate ownership a precondition for this citizenship, Aristotle similarly favors regimes that enfranchise only those who meet moderate property qualifications, preferring citizens with agrarian estates. Both theorists envision higher property-ownership eligibility requirements for major offices, and they disapprove of providing pay for any public office. Far from accepting the Athenian practice of subsidizing participation of the poor in the assembly or mass juries, Plato would sometimes mandate fines on members of the upper classes who failed to vote. Aiming toward Athenian practice prior to the more democratic Cleisthenic reforms, Plato's second-best regime obviously overrepresents in its council the richest of the four classes of citizens (cf. Morrow, 1960). Similarly, in the waning days of the Roman republic, Cicero nowhere objects to the vote counting by whole assemblies and the obvious overrepresentation of the upper classes that made a sham of the *comitia* as a popular element of the Roman republic (cf. Cowell, 1967, 154–64). De facto leadership by the Senate accented "the rule of an oligarchy of wealthy landed proprietors" (Wood, 1988, 27).[11]

And even if the propertyless were excluded from voting or eligibility to office, the Aristocrat would worry that open competitions for office might yet favor the newly rich. The main point of the practical political recommendations of Plato, Aristotle, Xenophon, Polybius, and Cicero is to lodge effective political power with those of older wealth, of stable family fortunes—those who would not be venal, who would have the education and leisure to appreciate great books, and who would listen to wise counsel.

### Exemplary Leadership

When urging the empowerment of old-wealth gentlemen, the Aristocrat may be right in expecting less money corruption, but that does not preclude the possibility of other corrupting motives, such as ambition for powerful office. Hence the Aristocrat emphasizes the importance of "character" in selecting individual leaders. Only those of high moral standing could be good examples for others of their class as well as the lower classes. While radicals criticize character as a wooly standard by which the upper classes can justify preferential recruitment of their own, the Aristocrat's paradigm really does require some moral restraint of greed in top leaders who set the tone for society as a whole.

The Aristocrat often insists on a distant, austere style of leadership to encourage deference in the mass public, as recalled by Charles de Gaulle in our time. If earlier monarchs functioned as judges, later

ones tended to be insulated from mass interactions and likely pressures. Political prescriptions of the Aristocrat emphasize not only
hierarchy but superiority of those placed at high rank. The emphasis
on difference sometimes went to the extreme of claiming that rulers
either have special ties to the gods or that they themselves are gods,
as with the Egyptian pharaohs, Roman emperors, and Japanese emperors.[12] At that remove, even the most humble entreaties for justice
would seem out of place. Wisdom in council increasingly supposes
some insulation from popular petitions of grievances.

In long-established regimes, heirs to hereditary office were often
dignified by elaborate ceremonial, a subject treated with light humor
by novelist Gore Vidal: "It would seem to be a rule of history that as
the actual power of a state declines, the pageantry increases. Certainly
the last days of the Byzantine empire were marked by a court protocol
so elaborate and time consuming that the arrival of the Turks must
have been a great relief to everyone."[13]

### The Aristocrat's Representation

Many past autocrats claimed to "re-present" the divine forces on
Earth, and even John Calvin conceded that kings (unlike his "magistrates of the people") were "wholly God's representatives" on Earth.
Even if watery doctrines of popular consent were expressed in Aquinas, Marsilius, and Hooker, the Aristocrat traditionally did not want
authorities understood as "re-presenting" the people in any meaningful way. Richard Hooker, for example, held that one's ancestors have
irrevocably consented on one's behalf. Representativeness could not
mean being like the people in characteristics of either birth or
rearing; and often in China, India, and Europe a ruling dynasty
could even be of foreign origin. Nor would representativeness mean
responsiveness to what the people want. Unless those wants were
carefully shaped by aristocratic leadership, responding to them would
violate the formula, which abhors the pandering of demagogues.
Leaders would be responsible, representing merely in virtue of law-
fully holding office. They must listen to a higher voice and be able to
recognize yet discount any indecorous demands from the multitude.
Far from responding to what the people *want*—especially what those
in a specific constituency may want from a representative legislator—
the representative would think only of what the people *need*, addressing the common good. As in Edmund Burke's "Speech to the Electors
of Bristol," leaders would be trustees of a high personal discretion in
judgment (on alternative models of representation, cf. Pitkin, 1967).

### Preventing Tyranny

Undue responsiveness to democratic demands could lead to tyranny. If the better does not prevail over the base, it is said, the
situation may culminate in rule by the very worst.

Denigrations of the demos often seem contradictory. Sometimes, the Aristocrat may fault the many for the uniform, low standard that they would impose on the few of excellence. This extends to the "tyranny of the majority" thesis of de Tocqueville and J. S. Mill—an Aristocratic echo in largely Capitalist theory.[14] On the other hand, the Aristocrat may criticize the people for its excess diversity of desires and refusal to distinguish the better and worse among them.

Plato would deny any contradiction, seeing a constant commitment of the many to their mistaken views that their pleasure is the good and that no one should deprive them of freedom in its gratification, whatever the proliferating and protean wants of individuals. Their master desire is freedom, but that sinks into license followed by loss of all freedom.

The devolution of regimes from monarchic or aristocratic rule of the best occurs through stages as sons repudiate the values of their fathers. In the first stage, timocracy abandons wisdom for honor and victory; but the sons of this regime see that their fathers have forgone wealth. The oligarchy shifts to money-making; but the successful accumulators neglect the rearing of their own children, who are then guided by older spendthrifts to taste of unnecessary pleasures. In turn, these children's installation of democracy sets up the immoderate pursuit of present pleasure as the good—a "many-colored" liberty that becomes near-anarchic license. They make a popular leader of an oligarch's son who has wasted his wealth in ministering to the most bestial pleasures, including forbidden desires that arise in dreams or drunken stupor. In quest of wealth for himself, the potential tyrant also lets the people taste of the honey taken from the rich, while talking of cancelling debts and redistributing the land. When the rich react, he surrounds himself with armed protectors who permit him to take total power. But the tyrant soon makes enemies among his former popular allies, turning to harsh internal repression and the diversion of foreign wars. He soon kills the best among the people to seek a power base in mercenaries, including among them aliens and emancipated slaves.[15]

One could cite real-life instances of this origin of tyranny, but perhaps more tyrants have been champions of wealth against the people than champions of the people against wealth. Or—like Argentina's Juan Perón, who borrowed a leaf from early Mussolini and Hitler—they may pretend populism and defend wealth.[16] But to at all address the question of any class nexus suggests that inequalities and not just some moral crisis may underlie political crisis.

In any case, the philosophic Aristocrat rejects autocratic tyranny as a worse regime than a weak democracy, which is incapable of doing much evil if also much good. Plato refused to support the regime of the Athenian Thirty Tyrants, which prominently involved at least two of his relatives and may have killed some 1,500 democrats (Winspear, 1940, 74). Socrates even opposed that brief tyranny by an act of civil disobedience: his refusal of an order to arrest Leon of Salamis. Cicero and Seneca paid with their lives in opposing tyranny, as did the more Saintly Thomas More.

### The Aristocrat and the Structures Strategy: Token Democracy in Service to Economic Inequality

If Aristocrats lack a commitment to competitions of ideas or of candidates for leadership, one can only expect to find a similar preference for secure rank ordering when it comes to potential decision-making units. Putting the better over the worse translates here to raising less popular institutions over any more popular ones, whether the "popular" unit is a popularly supported autocrat, an assembly, or the people guiding themselves without government at all.

By my definition, the structures field of political action considers as if constant both the incumbents and their wills, manipulating as variable the powers at their disposal. By the pragmatic rules of unfettered opportunism, the game can be simply defined: One pulls powers from decision units controlled by rivals, and puts them where friends prevail.

While operations would be reversed for a friendly decision unit, I shall define the tactical subfields as if one were trying to win against a hostile unit, in which case there are nine maneuvers to consider: (1) abolish it; (2) split it to win in at least one part rather than lose in the original whole; (3) merge it (perhaps "submerge" is the better word) to win in a whole where one would have lost in at least one part; (4) subordinate it to a friendly unit; (5) selectively strip away its powers and put them elsewhere; (6) drain its necessary operational resources to the point of incapacitation; (7) facilitate or even require that appeals of its decisions be made to friendlier units; (8) change the decision rules to give at least a blocking (veto) capacity to any minority of friends within the unit; or, finally, (9) manipulate agenda—usually by promoting obstruction or stalling—such that a losing situation may be saved by any of the other tactical maneuvers of the structures strategy, or else by tactics from the recruitment or influence fields.

The raw play of the structures strategy has no inherent bent toward democracy. Classic revolutionaries such as Cromwell, Robespierre, Lenin, and Mao were outrageously unsentimental about institutional forms, playing the mentioned tactics only to win. Counterrevolutionaries have often been just as unprincipled in shifting powers of decision from democratic institutions to military juntas and administrative agencies controlled by them.

But what happens when fair-competition and popular-consent norms are applied to the structural field? When thus focused on constitutional or other allocations of decisional authority and resources among institutional units, this field of political means is central to the somewhat elusive rights of both pluralism and popular sovereignty.

As already evident from our discussions of democratic influence and recruitment, liberalism supposes *pluralism*, which means a multiplicity of private and public institutional units enjoying considerable autonomy.

> Pluralism . . . is a vital part of democracy. It is almost a synonym for democracy, because a society organized pluralistically is inevitably constitutional and more or less democratic. . . . For democracy to be a reality, it is essential that there be competitive centers of power offsetting one another, in the framework of the state and outside it. (Wesson, 1987, 6–7)

But democracy also supposes at least ultimate *popular sovereignty*, as the pluralist Althusius strongly affirmed in the early seventeenth century. For even with free speech and free elections, democracy would be hollow if most important decisions were monopolized by decision units beyond popular control (e.g., kings, churches, military juntas, corporations, elitist single parties, expert commissions). Most analysts of "liberal representative democracy" stress the competitions of ideas and the competition of candidates for office—the "liberal" and "representative" elements. Fewer grasp the significance of competition among alternative decisional units, although such conflicts may shape the ultimate measure of "democracy." Modern democracy is most vulnerable in this least obvious field of political competition.

The popular majority must assert the ultimate right to decide questions of parity or precedence among alternative decision units. If such a final say is not located with the people, any popular rule is easily subverted. In cases of severe conflict between units, democratic majorities have historically tended to favor the more popularly controlled units over those less subject to popular control—as in favoring direct votes of the people, or perhaps parliaments, over executives or their appointees. Thanks to a venerable insight on the part of Machiavelli, Montesquieu, and others, certain social and political frictions are recognized as favorable to liberty. At least moderate rivalries of group interests expressed through contests among institutional forms maintain limits on those very forms. Given popular consent to such arrangements, there is nothing necessarily undemocratic about them. Absence of Cartesian lines of subordination of less popular units to more popular ones is undemocratic only to the extent that arrangements are not testable for popular consent. Democratic norms imply no more than *ultimate* popular sovereignty in the matter of locating decisional powers; that is, the people have the right of last word on just who will exercise the last word, even if acting on their behalf.

To deny this principle is to run the risk that they would have no word at all, that literally all decisions could be located beyond even indirect popular control. On the other hand, as the experience of ancient Athens suggests, democracy may be unworkable if the more popular units attempt too much. Pluralism runs the risk that independent power bases may be abused, and even turned against popular power, but the absence of pluralism virtually assures that there will be no popular power at all. So democrats choose to take their chances with competition among decision units, just as they do with competitions of ideas and of candidates for public office.

### Putting Power Out of Popular Reach

Traditional Aristocrats, at least, were not democrats—not favorable to much leveling of authority. Alone among my four main paradigms of social theory, only the Aristocrat almost never envisions such a successful application of the favored formula that one could wholly dispense with government. The Aristocrats explain their rejection of even a dreamed-up anarchy not only by the view that it would readily slide over into tyranny, but also by the deeply held notion of human nature as so lamentably flawed that it would make anarchy impracticable.

Rejecting the idea that inequalities as such cause conflict, the Aristocrats emphasize innate depravity (or in Christianity, original sin) as a root cause. But even if an innate inclination toward aggrandizement or aggression were conceded, such a biological constant could not by itself explain widespread historical variations in magnitudes of violence and other aggressive behavior. Shifting the focus to what *restrains* such allegedly innate aggressivity, Aristocrats find the source of variation to be in the quality of either moral training, as the first recourse, or the system of public coercive control, as the second. But such instruments of good order clearly preclude anarchy and really require quite unequal authority, whether in family, in religious organization, or in the political system.

The Aristocrats implicitly concede that inegalitarian government will always be necessary to maintain a high degree of economic inequality. Unequal fortunes can only be safeguarded by unequal power. As Cicero admitted early on, government functions not just for ethical purposes and protection of persons, but for protection of property as well (Wood, 1988, 130–32). Not surprisingly, a leading advocate of the slavery cause in America—John C. Calhoun—held that "it is a great and dangerous error to suppose that all people are equally entitled to liberty. It is a reward to be earned, not a blessing to be gratuitously lavished on all alike." Further, Calhoun believed that an anarchistic, egalitarian state of nature "never did exist, as it is inconsistent with preservation and perpetuation of the race." For him it was simply true that "government is indispensable" (Calhoun, 1953, 42, 45, 63).

If the Aristocrat imagines any self-ruled communities, they are only for select circles of the morally restrained, and are partly isolated from the larger political order—as in the Indian ashram or other communities of the wise, or perhaps Christian monks and nuns (who are the earthly sojourners of Augustine's City of God). Self-rule cannot be imagined for the many with their immoderate desires.[17]

### Simple Forms: Democracy Less Favored than Aristocracy or Monarchy

If firm government is needed to preserve order and promote morality, it must include certain religious and economic functions within its pale. Notwithstanding Aristotle's cautions at the outset of his *Politics*, the Aristocrat tends to model political authority after the patriarchal family or the paternalistic estate.

As already evident, Plato admires—above all—rule without constraint of law, by the one or the few best (the *aristoi*) in ideal regimes of either monarchy or aristocracy. But short of the ideal, Plato advances the classic sixfold typology of simple forms—that is, on one dimension, rule by the one, the few, and the many; and on the other dimension, the distinction of good forms that follow law and the common good, as opposed to the corrupted forms that do not. In ranking the three deficient forms, Plato favors—because it is too weak to do much evil—degenerated democracy over oligarchy, which is in turn preferred over tyranny. Leaving the corrupted forms aside, the Aristocrat ranks the good forms to favor the less popular regimes over the more popular: monarchy (rule of one according to law) over aristocracy (similar rule of the few), and aristocracy over law-abiding democracy.

As noted, in most historical experience those committed to the Aristocratic paradigm supported hereditary monarchs. In other cases, the Aristocrat could support political dominance by an equally hereditary aristocratic council, such as the Spartan Gerusia or the Roman republican Senate. In very rare cases, the Aristocrat could also accept a nearly theocratic regime where the ruling elite was less of noble birth than of high religious station—a caste of high priests. All of such regimes insulated leaders from popular pressures.

Democracy was historically viewed as the least acceptable of the uncorrupted simple forms, since it exalts the immoderate desires of the demos, gives rise to demagogues, and slides over into semi-anarchistic mob rule. Aristotle holds that a democracy may be relatively tolerable when the people limit their function to enactment of laws—that is, *general* rules—not encroaching on magisterial authority by also enacting *particular* decrees. The latter becomes likely when democracy shifts from more salutary plural leadership to a single demagogue who further flatters the people by bringing everything before them. Then the mass of people becomes less like a single monarch than like a tyrant as it follows its lawless fancy and abuses the best persons of the city (*Politics*, IV, iv). Perhaps that pattern does approximate some modern plebiscitary autocracies, but democrats could retort that sharp limits on *popular* power really mean empowerment of *unpopular* power through administrative or judicial units influenced by the wealthy.

While his *Politics* at least reports some common opinions in defense of democracy, Aristotle does not embrace those opinions as his own, advancing them only with accompanying criticisms. When he seriously evaluates regimes, he shares with Plato the standard of moderation or virtue; and the democratic regime does not do well by that measure. Hence when Aristotle compares various subtypes of the democratic regime, he finds more tolerable those that allow least power to the urban many. The better democracies are dominated by farmers—not urban populations, and least of all the poor among them. These democracies would have moderate property qualifications for citizenship and require even more property for higher offices. They would not subsidize attendance at assemblies or mass juries. They would have minimal changeability in their laws; and they would, as noted, only act through laws. In sum, for Aristotle the least objectionable democracies are those that are least exposed to popular control (Johnson, 1986). If forced to concede something to democracy, the Aristocrat prefers to mix it with nondemocratic political forms.

### The Mixed Regime: Token Democratic Units Subordinated to Nondemocratic Ones

Political conditions have sometimes forced a compromise with democracy, some concession to popular power. In certain commercially active cities such as ancient Athens or Rome, and then much later in some cities of Renaissance Italy or the Rhineland, one could not readily exclude freeborn male adults from politics. Often the observed fact of ready mobility across jobs would in such circumstances lead to the view that persons were rather interchangeable in roles, and hence could participate in rule as well as hold down a trade (Rogowski, 1974). Unlike scattered peasants, urban populations had ready communication among themselves and could quickly assemble to press their case, sometimes by armed might. They especially demanded participatory rights wherever military security required that they be trained combatants, as was true of the fighter-oarsmen of Athenian triremes or the infantrymen of the Roman legions.

The necessity of making a concession to popular sentiment of this nature usually elicited the tactic of permitting some unit(s) of a more or less democratic tone, carefully checked by one or more units of nondemocratic social base.

This is the theory of the "mixed regime," much later also called "balanced government." Any pure or simple form of rule—whether of the one, the few, or the many—would tend to be unstable. However, the regime could be stabilized by mixing two or more simple forms, effectively compromising the contending claims to power. Popular support could be won by conceding something to citizens' claims based on their numbers or their military role, yet one retains the support of elites by reserving special units for those who claim status by their wealth or merit. At a practical level, the sole constant in mixed-regime theories is the presence of at least one democratic unit. Theorists otherwise vary regarding which form or forms would be intermixed with it.[18]

While the classical Aristocrat would prefer the democratic element to be largely a gesture—its potential effectively nullified by one or more nondemocratic elements—some regimes had popular units that were strong enough not only to protect the people from any projects of the rich, but even to support raids on the power of the less democratic units. In ancient Athens the chief democratic bases were the Ecclesia and the dicasteries, which over time managed to pull powers from more aristocratic organs. Plato's version of the mixed regime—that of his *Laws*—obviously aimed to reverse that. It restricted suffrage to estate owners (disfranchising native-born merchants as well as manual laborers), weakened the assembly (Ecclesia), overweighted the wealthy in its council (Boule), eliminated popular courts, and placed vital powers such as the right to veto any change of law in elitist bodies such as the Law Guardians or Nocturnal Council.

Not surprisingly, Plato admired much about Sparta. In Sparta's practice of the mixed regime, neither the citizen assembly (Apella) nor the five ephors offered much really democratic weight, perhaps restraining the dual monarchy more than the powerful aristocratic council, the Gerusia. In republican Rome—aside from the assemblies (*comitia*) weighted to favor the propertied—the chief democratic element was office of the ten tribunes, who could veto measures favored by the upper classes. Popular purposes were also defeated, however, whenever the wealthy persuaded or bribed just one tribune.

In later expression, the mixed-regime theory would lodge popular power in a parliamentary body dominated by commoners, while the nobility or the wealthy would often base their power in an upper house such as the British House of Lords or a senate. The upper council or chamber was meant to check the lower, often by controlling—as in Sparta—the subordinate assembly's agenda. This was the plan for James Harrington's *Oceana*, which in its senate sought empowerment of the gentry against both the high nobility and the propertyless many.

The mixed regime amounted to a veto-model constitution, whereby those of rather modest means and those of affluence could mutually veto policy initiatives of the other.

The upper classes had a higher stake in their blocking power, since it could stop implementation of any immoderate economic demands of the lower classes, such as cancellation of debts or redistribution of the land. The nobles could also use their blocking power against a war that did not benefit the nobles but did bring them costs, as in Athens where the fighting ships were provided by special levies on the wealthy. The nobility favored neither the empire nor its ill-fated defense in the Peloponnesian Wars.[19] It would be otherwise in other contexts, such as republican Rome when senate nobles shared in land and other plunder from the expanding Roman empire.

The people had less stake in blocking projects of the affluent, although they, too, could oppose a war they did not like. And although notables could often attempt to enlarge their landholding at a weak neighbor's expense, they were less likely to advance some general policy for economic aggrandizement (such as the Corn Laws of Britain) when a popular assembly was watching. The value of the democratic element was mostly, however, for security of the lives and liberties of average citizens against any unpopular tyranny. It could also curb the petty tyranny of venality, at least that which went beyond the corruption of very minor officials. While one could easily bribe a few higher officials in a monarchy or aristocracy, there was more risk as well as cost in any attempt to bribe a popular assembly or Athenian dicastery.

Reflecting Aristotle's observation that a regime could be stable as long as all significant groups perceived their interest to be in its continuance, some mixed regimes endured for centuries, as was true of ancient Sparta and Rome. But they worked best when most were content with not being made economically worse off. The aim of the mixed regime is nicely summed up in this remark Cicero made while urging proper respect for a magisterial veto over the assemblies of the people: "It is better that a good measure should fail than that a bad one should be allowed to pass" (*De Legibus/Laws*, III, xviii).

Yet, as Rome in Cicero's lifetime showed, the veto-model constitution experiences difficulty where there are very acute discontents over economic policy. When lower orders want a major change in economic policy, either the upper classes might attempt to reduce the democratic part(s) of the constitution, or the people might attempt to pull powers from any nondemocratic part(s). A rivalry of class forces could then express itself in a rivalry of parts of the regime, often preparing the way for major shifts of relative powers. While on the one hand Rome was inflexible and fell to the popular tyrant Julius Caesar, on the other hand the constitutional balance has shifted toward more democracy in modern British history.

Some modern approximations to the mixed regime have been long lived, even where delicacy requires suppression of the idea that any parts of the regime might be less than fully republican (e.g., the separation of powers with checks and balances system of the United States). But economic discontents may arise when these governments are not helped by an advancing economy, or when a stagnating economy causes greater rivalry over the distribution of burdens and benefits. No longer content with being able to block harmful initiatives by the others, each group wants to carry certain positive policy aims of its own. But a zero-sum situation finds few of the others willing to compromise their interests, and they too may have the power to block adverse change. Then the mixed regime may almost guarantee frustration for everyone—perhaps in part expressed by the eroding American trust in the national government from the early 1960s to the 1980s.[20]

### Defending Democracy

In 1701 the philosopher Gottfried Leibniz—who was not a democrat—remarked, "The end of democracy, or polity, is to make the people themselves agree to what is good for them" (Riley, 1981, 23). So, what is good for them? My own image of the good consists in moving as many people as possible as far up as is feasible on a Maslow-like hierarchy of needs. If this aim has its ambiguities, remember that political theory is not an exercise in Euclidean deduction but a practical project of attempting to improve the human condition. Democracy taken as means would help achieve the mentioned project of climbing Maslow's ladder, the rungs consisting of physiological, safety, social, esteem, self-actualization, and higher needs.

I share Hannah Arendt's view that the forms of freedom must be valued as an end, not as a means only. But there is nothing wrong with asking how democracy may help meet such human needs. Like what was said of justice in Plato's *Republic*, democracy may be the best kind of good—worth having both for what it brings (an instrumental good) and for its own sake (an intrinsic good). Personally valuing democracy both as means and as end, I see dangers in considering it rather as only an end or as merely a means.

In regard to the thinking of Arendt and others who take democracy as *only an end*—not also regarding it as a means—some problems may be noted. To the extent that one forgets that democracy is a means toward meeting human needs such as curbing poverty or political murder, one is deprived of some good arguments for bringing democracies into being and keeping them alive. Refusal to consider democracy as a means also puts into question what could be appropriate standards for any reforms of democracy. If—in political architecture—form should follow function, then one must have some notion of appropriate functions in order to judge among alternative forms.

Yet those who look on democracy as *only a means* may sometimes ask only how it may impact the implementation of or support for their favored paradigm, making it merely a means to the end of their formula. If it seems to get in the way, democracy is then too readily confined or abandoned.

### Good Order?

The Aristocrats have only minimal appreciation for democracy as an instrumental good, seeing it primarily as a lesser evil in the face of tyranny (e.g., in our time, against fascist or communist regimes). A moderate, mixed regime employs limited democratic concessions to assure popular support, which may also be needed in case of a domestic insurrection or a foreign invasion. But the Aristocrat may not always regard democracy as better than a moderately authoritarian government of the right.

I think the Aristocrat underestimates the possible contributions of democracy to domestic security of life. Early states arose for both domestic order and security against external attack. Such threats to safety have often led peoples to acquiesce in undemocratic authority—if only in temporary and limited form—such as the constitutional dictatorship in the Roman republic or the modern chief executive's emergency powers. But when it is workable, secure people often prefer democracy, even if that aspiration is often blocked. One cannot say, however, that democracy is the "normal" kind of regime; throughout history most peoples have been ruled by autocrats (cf. Buultjens, 1978). Only 23 nations have had regular competitive elections since 1948 (Lijphart, 1984, 38–39).

Regarding domestic violence, there is no evidence that democracy curbs violent crime. A table of reported homicides per 100,000 population shows no apparent relationship to presence or absence of democracy (cf. Newman, 1979, 92). If anything, the greater toleration of guns among the population, and more restrained policing, of democracies could plausibly increase rather than decrease homicide rates. As the cliché holds, freedom is not free; it has its costs.

Increased deaths by communal rioting or civil war may also follow the instituting of democracies. Under democracy, discordant groups are free to express themselves through competitions of ideas, candidates, and decision units, with this last sometimes extending to separatist struggles even within advanced democracies. India, the world's most populous democracy, has had much communal killing since 1947, possibly more than would have existed under a tight dictatorship. Even modest loosenings of the reins in Yugoslavia, the Soviet Union, and China have been followed by rises in nationality riots and related violence. But when ethnic animosities that were merely contained or made worse during nondemocratic rule become open communal riots under democracy, is it not unfair to blame the latter for them? Perhaps democracy—by reducing social inequalities—may improve the chances for long-term reductions in such forms of strife.

The chief democratic contribution to safety lies in its checks against systematic *official* murder, which may more than compensate for any increases of unofficial violence. Well-institutionalized democratic practice seems to minimize, at least, official brutalities such as torture or condoned death-squad killings. When in 1984 a national committee in Argentina was investigating the disappearance of thousands of persons during the former military regime's 1976–82 "dirty war," it concluded that democracy was necessary for protection from government. The committee's remarks recall Locke's response to Hobbesian absolutism: "The armed forces responded to the terrorists' crimes with a terrorism infinitely worse than that which they were combating, since . . . they could operate with the power and impunity of a dictatorship, kidnapping, torturing and murdering thousands of human beings" (Simpson and Bennett, 1985, 399). Sometimes mistaking their victims—eventually murdering a young Swedish woman— the right-wing military in Argentina tortured and slaughtered nearly 9,000 listed individuals, possibly thousands more. On an even greater scale, in the mid–1970s a communist regime in Cambodia executed at least 75,000–150,000 of its people, contributing to the starvation deaths of vastly larger numbers (Kiljunen, 1984, 31).

Granted, even democracies sometimes kill alleged enemies of the people. The Athenian democrats cannot be forgiven the murder of the men of Melos who had rebelled against their empire, nor can they be pardoned for the execution of Socrates, Plato's mentor. Antidemocrats continually cite the case of Socrates, ignoring the fact that thousands of political gadflies have been executed by nondemocratic regimes. In seventeenth-century England, Algernon Sidney—soon himself cruelly executed for sedition by the restored Stuarts—argued with reference to Socrates that one should apply the same test to popular governments and absolute monarchies (*Discourses*, vol. 2, xviii). Autocracies murder critics and no one remembers; whereas when a democracy lapses, we never forget. But perhaps this is just as it should be, since an official murder of a political opponent is an anomaly in a democratic society.

A study of 55 less developed nations found a modest correlation of democracy with an index of personal integrity, or the absence of such practices as open killing, disappearances, political imprisonment, and torture. The worst records emerged in states that were once democratic but had then become autocratic, especially in nations that were less democratic than their economic potential would predict—in 1981 including Argentina, Uruguay, Chile, Bolivia, El Salvador, and Turkey (Cingranelli and Hofferbert, 1988, 15). While the authors believed that this reflects intensity of social conflict, they accepted my suggestion that during open, democratic phases it is easier to list names of future victims of murderous military regimes (a personal conversation).

No fully democratic regime has ever carried out a literally planned public policy of genocide comparable to Hitler's Holocaust or Stalin's destruction of Ukrainian farmers. True, the U.S. military practiced near-genocidal wars against Native Americans who managed to survive the whites' diseases. But the political circumstances were, in fact, not those of a full democracy. The Native Americans had been denied equality of political rights, and it was not until long after the frontier wars that reservation Indians could—in 1924—finally vote in national elections. Other liberal regimes with restrictive civic rights, such as South Africa in general or Israel in the occupied West Bank and Gaza, have been harsh in their rule of unenfranchised populations. One could similarly cite some excesses against foreign peoples, as in past British imperial repressions, the U.S. slaughter of rebel populations in the Philippines in 1901, and the carpet bombings of parts of Vietnam in very recent history.

Most such cases of violence from democratic regimes arose through glaring departures from democratic ideals, where the victimized group was outside the circle accorded equality of basic rights. This was especially clear in the history of American slavery and later segregation laws. Even in the rare cases when democracies in effect vote to extinguish themselves—as in Weimar Germany in 1933 or Czechoslovakia in 1948—nations become most despotic precisely where they cease to be democratic.

Democracy almost guarantees some citizen opposition to excesses. Fully legitimate elective national leaders have never approached the grades of evil achieved among nonelective autocrats. While democracies violate their own norms in running to excess, murderous repressions may grow out of the very principle of antidemocratic regimes: Consent is not needed when the life plans of some are intrinsically superior to those of others.

### Moral Development?

The Aristocrat's call for a return to "the ancient philosophers" is implicitly a return to inegalitarian premises that were highly critical of democracy, claiming that it could threaten not only good order but also moral development. For the Aristocrat, democracy is not favored as an *intrinsic* good. Rule of the demos means rule by the low—those least able to moderate their passions to some norm such as Aristotle's "man of high moral standards," who is the very definition of the virtuous mean between the polar vices of excess and deficiency.

As our discussion of Plato should have made clear, democracy may be spurned when it inflames popular economic demands, or when it supports demands for economic redistribution. Conservatives who talk of "the overload of demands" on modern democratic systems seem to be thinking of the demands of the middle-to-lower classes more than the many budgetary or tax-expenditure demands of the affluent. Yet, as the Aristocrat's own disdain for the newly rich tacitly concedes, immoderate consumption by the upper classes may stimulate immoderate aspirations among the lower.

Too often the Aristocrat forgets that the Aristocratic formula itself was originally instrumental—a means of protecting inequalities of wealth and stratified patterns of consumption under conditions of no growth. The moral training to be fostered clearly aimed at the curtailment of mass desires far more than the desires of the rich. But now the Aristocrat may sound quite superior in saying that living the moral life is the intrinsic good. It may now seem that they reluctantly acquiesce in economic inequalities only as the necessary means of supplying gentlemen to preserve the moral tone of the society.

While attacking egalitarian economic demagogy, the paradigm may cultivate demagogues of its own. If not pandering to economic aspirations of the lower classes, these leaders may pander to other kinds of popular wants or fears, including fear of crime, undue international-security concerns, or—at its worst—ethnocentric prejudice. As part of their divide and rule policy, Russian tsars often cultivated anti-Semitism and other ethnocentric bigotries. Such politically exploited bigotry was certainly rejected by Leo Strauss and Eric Voegelin, both of whom fled the Nazis. But the point is that this paradigm at its worst can succumb to a kind of demagogy of its own.

Most people will not hesitate to applaud the Aristocrat's praise of moral excellence when it means Socrates fighting courageously in war, refusing the order by the Thirty Tyrants to arrest Leon of

Salamis, daring to criticize Pericles, opposing an unlawful popular move to put some generals on trial en bloc, or refusing to accept silence in exchange for his life. But to the extent that the Aristocrat's moral code primarily emphasizes moderation of *mass desires*, one must recall that it was originally but a means to the end of social pacification. And if, then, this moral code is a merely instrumental good, it may have to be compromised for the sake of other goods in lifting our kind up Maslow's ladder.

Especially when many live in squalor and a few in luxury, the moderating of mass desires can be pursued to excess. Sometimes the awakening of mass desires is defensible as creating the motivation to move toward reforms that will make a better society, in part by developing the hitherto untapped potentials of the poor. The Aristocrat tends to say little about the rude exploitation of the poor that has characterized most societies known to human history.

The Aristocrat may say even less about the violence against the poor often required to maintain inequalities.[21] Only democracy may reliably force a moderation of *upper-class desires*—a moderation perhaps necessary to promote a social balance between wants and powers to satisfy. Intellectual development of the few in hierarchical societies was accompanied by pretensions of their having a different nature from the many. Democracy may promote a society where the upper class ceases to think of itself as everything, as almost more than human, and where a lower class need no longer be asked to think of itself as nothing, as if less than human.

Besides, democracy may develop character in other ways. Democratic practice may promote higher Maslowian attributes such as social, esteem, or self-actualization needs. Either the process or the results of democratic participation may ultimately bring more social trust and social feeling. While a change toward democracy sometimes permits discord before the emergence of such concord, this is better than moving from talk of fraternity to acts of fratricide, as in the French and Russian revolutions against autocracies.

The very possession of democratic rights may promote esteem, as when Mexico through revolutionary struggle ended the dictatorship and constituted a relatively democratic regime in which the native Indians were for the first time accorded dignity. Democracy, as even Plato acknowledged with deep disdain, promotes a sense in all participants that they are somebody, and that they are owed good reasons to secure their consent to authority. Part of liberal democratic culture is the idea that all must give reasons for their political preferences, neither refusing such reasons when challenged nor claiming that either they or their projects are intrinsically superior to other persons and their purposes (Ackerman, 1980).[22]

The learning associated with democratic participation promotes self-actualization, as do related policies such as expanded access to education. If democracy promotes human growth through its very practice, then democracy considered as a means merges into democracy as an end. Participation may promote certain forms of human development, as argued by de Tocqueville and J. S. Mill;[23] but just as importantly, its very practice is part of living the good life. Through the mouth of Socrates, Plato says that the unexamined life is not worth living, but his *Republic* confines most people to unexamined lives. Why even discuss how we ought to live our lives, if some minority will dictate it to us?

## Summary:
## Egalitarianism under Attack

Fully in the Aristocratic mode, Allan Bloom's best-seller *The Closing of the American Mind* (1987) critiques every excess in American democracy—especially egalitarian movements of all kinds. While many such movements deserve pointed criticism, Bloom loves to claim that militants are "anti-intellectual." Doubtless, some do deserve that epithet. But one must beware of implicitly defining "intellectuals" as those who search for new preciosity of phrase to urge the old aim of moderation of mass desires. Nowhere does Bloom show the Saint's awareness that perhaps the paramount need is moderation of the desires of elites—some of whom in his own nation and time blocked American blacks from voting in the South for a century after the Constitution made them citizens. Contemporary elites also prosecuted a war of doubtful justice that left about 1 million Indo-Chinese dead. They have recently increased luxury-goods consumption while poverty, homelessness, drug addiction, and prison populations soar. Doubtless, better character formation could help. But are the Aristocrats meeting such problems by preaching an austerity that they do not personally practice?

Successful moderation of mass desires could, in principle, pacify society. In some past societies the many have, in practice, limited their economic aspirations to what was appropriate to their social layer. But in modern practice, the formula has failed. And the failure may be forever, in the sense that never again will it be easy to persuade people to demand no more than the standard of living of their parents.

Far from accepting a paradigm that glides too readily into anti-democratic excess, I prefer to regard moderation of mass desires less as an end in itself than as a means to the end of maintaining democratic freedoms.

## Notes

1. Far from holding to the old law of *lèse majesté*, the U.S. Supreme Court has correctly understood that, by the basic norms of liberal democracy, public figures should have less protection than others from libel and slander directed against them (e.g., *New York Times v. Sullivan*, 1964). On the other hand, protection against de facto censorship or even removal by agents of the king led British members of Parliament to give themselves immunity from libel or slander actions for anything they might say in Parliament about others.

2. Especially in Roman Catholic theory—which accents the ultimately authoritative voice of the pope—assertions of wisdom in the institutional whole must not slip over to the view that all or at least a majority should speak for the whole (as urged by late-medieval conciliarists).

3. Guided by the aim of morally improving human beings, the "tolerance" of Plato's Socrates is far less permissive than "liberal tolerance," yet it is for the same reason capable of questioning received religious views or the local laws (Mara, 1988, esp. 482–83). True, but such questioning should not be in the marketplace, Plato makes quite clear.

4. The Aristocrat would say that the many lack the will—let alone the capacity—to rise very high on a hierarchy of needs. Surely there is some such limit, but democrats should not concede it too soon. We cannot know the limits as long as inequalities—both economic and political—deny many the capacity to develop the best that is in them, just as it may cripple their will to strive toward excellence. The capacity to contribute to society is largely a function of what one has got from it.

5. Although himself close to the Aristocratic paradigm in many ways, Alexander Solzhenitsyn has said that most problems in the Soviet Union could be solved if people refused to say what they do not believe. Stalinists, too, used lies to promote their "truths." Thomas Mann once said, "A harmful truth is better than a useful lie" (Koestler, 1963, 73).

6. In his *Enquiry concerning Human Understanding*, David Hume seems to have noticed the projective fallacy: "It is not certain that opinion is false, because it is of dangerous consequence" (cited in Spragens, 1981, 295).

7. Need I add that I am not identifying a merely hypothetical problem? Our time shows resurgent religious neofundamentalisms, usually focused about sexual and familial mores in Hindu, Islamic, Jewish, Christian, and other variants. But if not all members of such a society commit themselves to the same beliefs, sectarian murder may be the consequence, as recently evident in Northern Ireland (Ulster), the Punjab, Sri Lanka, the long war between Iran and Iraq, and later within Iraq itself. In Europe and Latin America, a nineteenth-century battle pitted Catholic conservatives demanding the teaching of religion even in public schools against sharply opposed anticlericals (usually under some liberal or radical party label). The victory of secularized public education now turns out to be less secure than it long seemed, for, at least within the United States, Protestant fundamentalists take their turn as challengers.

8. Eric Voegelin in 1936 argued that Austria need not tolerate expression by revolutionary forces that would overthrow the constitution (Serba, 1982, 12 n.16). Nor did he think Germany's Weimar Republic should have permitted

Nazi political participation: "Playing the freedom-of-thought game is the opposition's business; for the ruler it is suicidal" (ibid., 13). Showing kindred reservations about liberal tolerance, Leo Strauss also lamented the "weakness" of the Weimar regime, specifically complaining that the liberal heritage of a state/society distinction and the shift of religion to the private sphere had this consequence: "Just as certainly as the liberal state will not 'discriminate' against its Jewish citizens, so is it constitutionally unable and even unwilling to prevent 'discrimination' against Jews by individuals or groups. To recognize a private sphere in the sense indicated means to permit private 'discrimination,' to protect it and thus in fact to foster it" (Strauss, 1965, 6).

9. I am addressing myself here to the use of public authority not just to discourage but to *prohibit* or *punish* racist, sexist, and like stereotypy and language, which extends to group libel laws in some European nations.

If the Aristocrat manipulated public expression to maintain inequalities, some moderns would do so to promote equalities, extending to new variants of noble lying. (E.g., to depict women or blacks as corporate chief executives could help promote equality, but it distorts the empirical reality of their total absence from such posts in the Fortune 500.) Those favoring more equality as well as freedom and candor in expression must feel ambivalent on the matter.

10. The moderns are usually unsympathetic with Plato's idealistic ontology and epistemology. Thus, Jack D. Douglas complains: "If humans live in a cave where they cannot see the realities of things, but merely the shadows of those realities, and only the exercise of reason, the very thing the intellectual does, will reveal the 'really real' things, then the intellectual is the only one who can reveal the really real truths. The intellectual becomes the arbiter of reality itself and his enemies, the *hoy poloy* who scoffed at his mental legerdemain, become mere cavemen unable to see reality. He becomes the one person capable of freeing all the others from their submission to the idols of the cave. Plato's shadowy cave has been the opiate and the inspiration of centuries of intellectuals" (Douglas, 1976, 22). But a more materialistic and sensationalistic outlook can be quite as elitist, as illustrated by a line running through Bacon, Helvétius, Bentham, and many Marxists by which the superior knower (as *res cogitans*) penetrates appearances and can become the master planner over those (*res extensa*) who are passively products of their circumstances (Spragens, 1981, 79). Yet who would maintain that the world normally *is* just as it *appears* to the average person, save in certain things of familiar experience?

11. Cicero was remarkably candid in stating his class prejudices (cf. *De Officiis*, I, 50–52). While usually a defender of the patricians, he did oppose any hereditary seats in the Senate for nobles who had not served in high magistracies—which thus left room for more talented equestrians like himself.

12. By one account, the Egyptians understood that their pharaohs were yet men, but men who manifested in themselves the presence of the gods (Voegelin, 1956, vol. 1, 72–74).

13. Gore Vidal, "The Grants," *New York Review*, 22, no. 14 (September 18, 1975), p. 6.

14. De Tocqueville summed it up in an oft-cited phrase: "There is . . . a

manly and lawful passion for equality that men wish all to be powerful and honored. This passion tends to elevate the humble to the rank of the great; but there exists also in the human heart a depraved taste for equality, which impels the weak to attempt to lower the powerful to their own level and reduces men to prefer equality in slavery to inequality with freedom" (*Democracy in America*, I, iii). Adherents to the Aristocratic outlook may overlook the parallel when members of the upper classes exalt themselves by keeping or pushing down all others who have the audacity to attempt to rise above their status of birth. Zealous attention to honor, place, and the like has typified highly stratified societies in every historical context.

15. Plato's devolution sequence in his *Republic*, book 8, seems to have expressed itself through the whole career of Western political thought, at least in the shift of dominant values of some leading theorists—from Aristocratic wisdom (Plato and Aristotle), to timocratic honor and victory (Machiavelli), oligarchic money (Locke through Bentham), democratic diversity (especially Marx), and tyrannical desires such as emerge in dreams (Nietzschean transvaluation, and then Hitler or Stalin).

16. In Buenos Aires during the return of Juan Perón in 1973, I was by chance invited to ride in a jeep that was leading truckloads of Peronist youths going to see their hero at a suburban house. As we wended through the city, the well-dressed in the better neighborhoods turned their backs or gave even more vivid gestures of disapproval—as did a line of soldiers who brandished guns in our faces, seeking to delay the flow of the crowd. But triumphant smiles and V-for-victory signs were flashed everywhere in the working-class suburbs.

Yet once in power, Perón repressed leftists within Peronist unions and movement organizations, and shocked feminists by a pronatalist policy against readily available contraceptives. Many tyrants of our century have similarly adjusted ideology to their needs in taking and holding personal power—conquering power with one coalition and shifting to another to consolidate it.

17. Yet Bhikhu Parekh describes an exceptional Aristocratic tradition: "According to Hindu thinkers, each individual does his *dharma* [duties] in an ideal society. There is, therefore, no disorder, and hence no need for *danda* or force, and obviously no need for government. For some Hindu thinkers men were once in such a state; for others they have always had refractory impulses; for yet others human history is cyclical in nature and characterized by a regular and inexorable alternation of four distinct epochs representing different degrees of human corruption" (Parekh, 1986, 20).

18. Democracy could be mixed with monarchy (as in Plato's *Laws*, although said by Aristotle to really mix with oligarchy there), with oligarchy (Aristotle's "polity"), with aristocracy (John Calvin), or even with both of the other two good simple forms—thus combining democracy, aristocracy, and monarchy (Polybius, Cicero, Machiavelli, and much later Montesquieu).

19. In our world, as Max Weber noted, we are used to thinking of how investors could benefit by imperialism, but the Athenian empire differed: "The Attic *demos*—and not they alone—lived economically off war. War brought them soldier's pay and, in case of victory, tribute from the subjects. This tribute was actually distributed among the full citizens in the hardly

veiled form of attendance-fees at popular assemblies, court hearings, and public festivities. Here, every full citizen could directly grasp the interest in imperialist policy and power" (from *Wirtschaft und Gesellschaft*, in Gerth and Mills, 1946, 170).

20. Preliminary research reports suggest that trust in government slightly recovered under the Reagan administration. This may reflect a restored confidence among alienated conservative white voters—a confidence not present among African-Americans, whose policy objectives were largely ignored. The Bush administration began on a standing of better rapport with the black community.

When blacks were indignant about Daniel Moynihan's leaked advice to the Nixon administration that they could use a period of "benign neglect," it was apparent that henceforth government neglect would never again be viewed as benign. More positive expectations of government may challenge the future of the complex, veto-model constitution.

21. I am not speaking only of the ancient Spartans warring on their helots. In Brazil, rural landowners have long hired professional murderers to gun down peasants who attempt to organize unions. Between 1964 and 1988, an estimated 1,500 rural workers were murdered, and the scale continues at about 200 per year. In Guatemala, the slaughter has run far higher, but without exact accounting (reports of the International Confederation of Free Trade Unions, esp. 1989, 8).

22. Bruce Ackerman (1980) could be criticized for really assuming the intrinsic superiority of his own vista of what liberal society requires. He forgets that a key feature of liberalism is defense of the right of anyone to argue, at least, against its basic tenets. That can be dangerous, but it is democracy.

23. John Stuart Mill has paradoxical views on democratic participation as related to human development: (1) a people that has not already attained a certain threshold of development is unfit to practice democracy; (2) yet democratic participation is helpful for human development; and (3) once a well-educated people practicing democracy becomes very highly developed, the appropriate sphere for democratic decision will retreat.

# 4

# The Saint's Problematic

## or Social Conflict as a Problem of Moderating Elite Wants

Earth provides enough to satisfy every man's
need, but not for every man's greed.

Mohandas Gandhi

While the Aristocrat defends the affluent within an agrarian context
or later steady-state ecological vision, the Saint within such a horizon
of restricted supply identifies downward, with those of little or almost
no property. Whatever the contribution of sensitive temperament,
only this shift in stratal identification explains the great change in
problematic: While both the Aristocrat and the Saint demand moral
training to limit wants in order to relieve the strain between social
wants and capacities to satisfy them, the Aristocrat asks minimal
sacrifice of the upper classes and maximal sacrifice from the lower
orders. The Saint reverses that, as in Christ's words: "How hard is it
for them that trust in riches to enter into the kingdom of God! It is
easier for a camel to go through the eye of a needle, than for a rich
man to enter into the kingdom of God" (Mark 10:24–25).

The Saint concedes that the lower classes must curb their desires
somewhat for the sake of social harmony. They must purge any
green-eyed envy and any red-eyed violent impulse to attack the rich.
But exhortations to more austerity are clearly *unreasonable* when the
lower classes are already denied satisfaction of basic needs. Urging
more abstinence on the poor can be outrageous where most live at or
below the margin of subsistence, as in Tolstoy's Russia or Gandhi's
India. Even now, roughly half the world population subsists on very
little, and some literally lack enough. Exhorting the poor to limit
their wants is also *ineffectual* if the upper classes do not set an example

of restraint and the lower classes compare themselves with the upper. Aristocrats would blame democracy—rather than their own extravagances—for rising demands from the lower classes. The Saint shifts attention to the need for restraint of upper-class greeds.

The Aristocrat would deem it unseemly to question the origins of at least older landed fortunes. But the Saint—like the Socialist—not only suspects force or fraud at the beginning, but also wants to minimize the exploitation of labor that creates new wealth. In premodern India, for example, the Brahman caste was not only exempted from taxation prior to Muslim rule but was forbidden to do field labor during the semifeudal period. Yet at varying times and places, landlords exacted from lower-caste peasants anywhere from a low of one-sixth to a high of three-fourths of the value of their agricultural produce (Thapar, 1966, 77, 146, 248, 330). The poor should apply more of their labor to satisfy their own needs, the Saint says—not the greeds of upper classes. The Aristocrat as well as the less progressive Capitalists see undue force only in any projects aimed to create or sustain conditions of equality, while seeing only a general social good in state maintenance of "order" or "protection." But the Saint believes that far too much coercion sustains an order of highly unequal wealth and income. Further, large spending on the police or armed forces is always at the expense of the poor, whether directly through taxes they pay or indirectly by reductions of charitable or social welfare assistance.

Those such as Thomas Carlyle (albeit the son of a mason-farmer) who are drawn toward the Aristocrat paradigm think it adequate compensation to the landless if great estate owners practice enough present charity to forestall revolution. But the Saint demands far larger charity, as if measuring generosity less by what is given than by how much is kept, as suggested in Christ's parable of the widow's mite (Mark 12:41–44).

Opposed assumptions thus reinforce the Saints' rough reversal of the Aristocrat, putting the burden of moderating desires for social pacification maximally on the upper classes and only minimally on the poor.

Either Aristocrats or Saints may be born to affluence or come into affluence during the course of their lives, but only the Aristocrats experience no tension in urging on the poor an austerity they do not practice. Unable to evade guilt by claiming superior natures, unable to live in hypocrisy, the Saints cannot accept such a lived contradiction. Hence, when not themselves of humble station, Saints of affluent circumstances are quite unlike Aristocrats in their typical impulse toward "voluntary poverty" in their personal lives, as elaborated later in the chapter.

The Saints include the ascetic, gentle sages of all societies. China gave us Lao Tzu, Chuang Tzu, and generations of Taoists. Also, there were centuries of Buddhist monks once Buddhism took root in China with the fall of the Han dynasty in 220 A.D. In fact, Buddhism became the state religion in 379 A.D., but suffered periods of repression thereafter. Later systematizers such as Chih-i (d. 597 A.D.) helped lodge it firmly in Chinese culture.

Although Buddhism was to flourish primarily elsewhere—as in China, Sri Lanka, and Southeast Asia—Siddhartha Gautama, the Buddha, was a son of India. India has supplied a recurrent history of Saint figures. A contemporary of the Buddha—Mahavira—inspired the Jains. Much later, in the *bhakti-Sant* tradition, the brilliant poet Kabir arose from a weaver caste and became an ancestor of the Sikh religion (cf. Schomer and McLeod, 1987). Generations of gentle and usually ascetic Hindu sages precede recent historical figures such as Gandhi, Vinoba Bhave, or Sri Auribindo. Often India's Saints were critical of orthodox Hindu emphasis on caste inequalities.

In the West, the Pythagoreans and even Socrates lived rather ascetically, but their known teachings more closely fit the Aristocratic paradigm. However, there were pagan exemplars of the more egalitarian Saint, such as Diogenes the Cynic or the ex-slave Stoic philosopher Epictetus.

Among the Hebrews, some prophets such as Jeremiah and the second Isaiah as well as the later Essenes approximate the type. But the outstanding Jewish figure was Jesus Christ, whose teaching and example have inspired many imitators.

If later Christian thought was often corrupted toward the Aristocratic teaching (partly evident in St. Augustine), many thinkers kept close to the original. Within Roman Catholicism, St. Francis of Assisi and St. Dominic fit the type; beyond monks of such orders, centuries of nuns precede a current example in the person of Mother Teresa. Often in tension with the hierarchy, the "poor church" tradition sometimes approached the edge of heresy—as illustrated by Gerard Groote and Thomas à Kempis—and it touched at least the utopian side of Thomas More. Catholic mystics such as Catherine of Siena and Teresa of Avila offered another current. In recent history, one may cite Catholic intellectuals such as the "personalist" critic of capitalism Emmanuel Mounier, or semi-anarchists such as Adin Ballou, Ammon Hennacy, and the founders in the 1930s of the Catholic Worker movement, Peter Maurin and Dorothy Day.

Influenced by neo-Platonism, a lower-class dissident religiosity ran through the Gnostics, the Cathars, and the Waldensians (followers of Valdes, also called "Peter" Waldo). From this ultimately Protestant current emerged the Swiss-German mystic Paracelsus, the Bohemian Chalicky, Thomas Müntzer, and variants of Anabaptism. Kindred spirits arose throughout the Rhine Valley, including the Dutch Menno

Simons (Menius) and his Mennonites, the Austrian John Hut and his Hutterites, and similar groups of usually gentle religious communitarians. After the Reformation, these often emigrated to escape persecution from either Roman Catholic or Protestant state churches, or from the warring armies of Catholic and Protestant states. England produced the Baptist Roger Williams, who eventually emigrated to Boston and then Rhode Island, as well as George Fox and his Quakers. Albert Schweitzer, who doctored the poor in West Africa, is a more recent example of this ascetic Protestant type.

Theistic yet more this-worldly, at least the earlier Etienne de la Boétie fits the pattern. Jean-Jacques Rousseau—notwithstanding his improbable admiration for Lycurgus and Spartan warriors as well as Christ—was far less the Aristocrat than the Saint. Mary Wollstonecraft, even more than her partner William Godwin, could be mentioned as approximating our type in some respects. Henry David Thoreau, John Ruskin, and Leo Tolstoy were all inspirations to Mohandas Gandhi in his approach to both ends and means.

In practical politics, the United States saw the Saint teachings of Gandhi inspire Martin Luther King and César Chavez. Peace activists such as the ex-communist A. J. Muste and the more militant Daniel Berrigan also illustrate the model. And—perhaps against the grain of his own temperament (he began his leadership by slugging a Communist party official)—Lech Walesa of Poland has also respected Saint teachings on civilized limits in political struggle. In China's Tiananmen Square in 1989, thousands of hunger strikers and hundreds of thousands of other prodemocracy demonstrators largely followed nonviolent tactics before the military overcame its hesitations and repressed them. In one dramatic televised scene, a single unarmed individual stood down for a time a whole column of tanks.

The modern ecological spirit has created a sometimes distinctive mode emphasizing "appropriate technology" that will not destroy the Earth but gently cultivate it, living more lightly on the land. Its advocates include Albert Howard, Lewis Mumford, Ivan Illich, Theodore Roszak, E. F. Schumacher, Wendell Berry, Fritjof Capra, or Francis Moore Lappé.

The ecological Green party of Germany approximates the Saint approach to policy, influencing parallels in the Netherlands, Scandinavia, and even Britain. Especially among those close to Petra Kelly, the German Greens have been morally fervent in their environmentalist critique of the ideology of growth shared by the former Communist elites of East Germany as well as most Social Democrats and Christian Democrats of West Germany. Beyond opposition to such programs as reckless "development" that would kill the Black Forest with acid rain, the Greens have been pacifistic on national security policy, searching for nonviolent alternatives to conventional deterrence. Their "postmaterialist" political style stresses local initiatives, decentralization, and participatory democracy. Electorally, the Green party began by primarily appealing to the well-educated and affluent young, but they have broadened that base to include workers. While backing away from their earlier practice of rotating all party posts (including their elected members of the national parliament, who were not permitted to fill out their terms), they still seek to curb political professionalism. The party closely instructs its deputies in the Bundestag, who must remit to the Green party organization that part of their salaries exceeding the average of a skilled worker's wage. Yet they do not otherwise emphasize voluntary poverty (cf. Mewes, 1988).

One could cite many differences among such varied Saint figures. Yet they themselves have often acknowledged more affinity with each other than with the rival paradigms of social thought. While some— perhaps Martin Luther King or Lech Walesa—have used the Saint teachings more in a tactical mode than as a total way of life, my comments will focus on those who fully adhere to the Saint world view.

## Commitment to the Saint Formula:
## Why Moderation of Upper-class Wants?

Saints have understood their aim as pacification of human existence, ending human predation as the first step in building civilization. E. F. Schumacher illustrates their belief that limiting wants is the central imperative:

> The cultivation and expansion of needs is the antithesis of wisdom. It is also the antithesis of freedom and peace. Every increase of needs tends to increase one's dependence on outside forces over which one cannot have control, and therefore increases existential fear. Only by a reduction of needs can one promote a genuine reduction in those tensions which are the ultimate causes of strife and war. (Schumacher, 1973, 33)

While Aristocratic writings as old as the Mesopotamian Epic of Gilgamesh celebrate warrior heroes, the Saints seem driven by their revulsion against all killing, usually extending to other animals.

### The Saint's Nonviolence

Saints are singularly sensitive to the suffering and death of sentient creatures. Most of the Saints are unusually gentle, habitually kind. Often endorsing a warm personalism over the cold abstractions of other formulas, they advocate yielding to the promptings of compassion, of feeling into the suffering of the other. The way of love is that of duty, it is said.

Unlike adherents of other paradigms, the Saints are skeptical of arguments holding that compassion must often be repressed, that humane promptings could be unjust in the larger social scheme of things or even cruel to the object of solicitude.[1] Aside from sometimes subordinating feelings toward kith and kin to help others in any greater need, the Saint recognizes no good reason to be hardhearted. The first act of civilization is in not raising one's hand in anger to injure or kill others; the second is in extending a helping hand to those in need.

Surely, part of the Saint's aversion for violence comes from an identification with the weak, who are often targets of the brute force used to maintain the position of the dominant. Perhaps throughout history, women have been especially drawn toward the Saint formula; and beginning with the Buddhist acceptance of nuns, male Saints have opened their ranks to them. Women would be even more prominent on the roster of its great theorists but for their debarment from advanced education in the West until the seventeenth century. Pope Paul VI has awarded posthumous doctorates to St. Catherine and St. Teresa. While many of the outstanding women among the Saint model were celibate—including many Roman Catholic saints as well as others such as Dorothy Day—there is apparently no evidence of unusual sexuality.[2]

But male Saint figures often manifest an unusual prominence of what Taoists would call yin relative to yang. Many display outstanding courage in their personal lives, especially in letting themselves be wronged rather than do the wrong of violence. But in their low aggressivity, and in their conscious effort to subdue machismo even further, they seem more receptive than other men to the feminine side of the somewhat bisexual human nature shared by us all.

The acceptance of the feminine by many male Saints has in part been expressed through their happiness when performing nurturant roles. Christ welcomed children about him. Thoreau liked cookery and knitted booties for Louisa Alcott's kittens. While many Saints themselves had sickly or delicate constitutions, Gautama, Pascal, and Gandhi loved to nurse the sick.

While many Saint exemplars have displayed quite normal sexuality (e.g., Rousseau, Martin Luther King, Scott Nearing, Lech Walesa, Wendell Berry), for the sake of understanding we must note that many have not. They recoiled from the normal measure of sexual initiative. But if many Saint males have revealed a troubled sexuality, their frequent celibacy may mean no great renunciation. It is difficult to say whether the trouble was due to nature or their nurture, the latter linked to a fairly common biography of early close association with a warm mother and distance from a harsher father.

Whatever the cause, the cases are clear enough. The prophet Jeremiah, who delighted in denouncing "backsliding" among the high and mighty, especially excoriated the whoring and adultery among all of his people: "They were as fed horses in the morning: every one neighed after his neighbour's wife" (Jeremiah 5:2). He believed that God personally instructed him, "Thou shalt not take thee a wife, neither shalt thou have sons or daughters in this place" (Jeremiah 16:2). Many Saint figures never marry, as illustrated by most of the Essene sect as well as Jesus Christ. Perhaps temperamentally closer to the Saint than to the Aristocrat, St. Augustine had a son by a mistress, who appropriately enough deserted him when he stated his intention to marry another woman; but at age 33 he chose instead religious conversion and celibacy. Also avoiding matrimony were St. Francis of Assisi and other Roman Catholic monastics, the semi-Aristocratic Blaise Pascal, the mystic physician Paracelsus, and Henry David Thoreau (who once unsuccessfully proposed marriage). Some Saints seemed to have a sense of guilt at any sexual temptation: St. Francis penitently hurled himself *naked* into a thorny hedge. Other Saint figures who married seemed to regret it: Siddhartha Gautama and Peter Waldo abandoned their wives and children. The Roman emperor Marcus Aurelius married; and Faustina, his notoriously unfaithful wife, had 14 children before dying in her mid-forties. But even if Marcus may possibly have then taken a mistress of unknown name, he offered the revolting description of the sex act as a "friction of innards and convulsive ejaculation of mucus" (Birley, 1987, 225). At age 45, George Fox finally married; but most biographers doubt that there was anything carnal in his relationship with the widowed Margaret Fell, who was ten years his senior and the coordinator of Quaker correspondence. John Ruskin was to be married for six years, but probably did not consummate the marriage and hence lost his wife to a friend (McLaughlin, 1974, 127–29). Another observer notes, "Ruskin, who seems to have been incapable of normal relations with a grown-up woman, had a passion for little girls" (Clark, 1964, 8). Leo Tolstoy, by contrast, was as lusty as a goat during much of his life, although at age 60 he decided to commit himself to celibacy and thereafter felt intense guilt at occasional backsliding to Sonja's charms. Their marriage became a torture, and the nearly mad Sonja eventually drove old Tolstoy to flee their home at Yasnaya Polyana to die of pneumonia elsewhere (Troyat, 1967).

All biographers elaborate on Gandhi's troubled marriage with Kasturbai, his sense of guilt surrounding the sexual act, and his eventual commitment to total abstinence (*brahmacharya*). If sexual abstinence accords with the broader renunciation of desire advocated by the Saint, it bears a heavier freight of guilt—an association of sin with the sex act. Erik Erikson thought Gandhi associated sex with aggression, for "as you would not attack an inimical person with weapons, you would not attack a loved one with phallic desire" (Erikson, 1969, 237, and also see 249–50).[3]

Whether or not an inborn femininity may in part explain why the Saints abhor aggression, they are nonviolent in principle and practice. Yet, in India, the conquering Mauryan emperor Ashoka (d. 232 B.C.) only belatedly turned against gore; and although he then became a dedicated Buddhist, he could not avoid some defensive war and recourse to capital punishment. Similarly, Emperor Marcus Aurelius—stoically confronting his duty—found himself forced to coordinate defenses of the frontiers of the Roman empire, but he looked for peaceful resolutions through diplomacy and meanwhile ordered substitution of blunted weapons to stop bloodshed in gladiatorial combats (Birley, 1987, 148). St. Francis was once briefly in combat, and the younger Leo Tolstoy saw major action in his military profession; but their sensibilities turned both into sharp critics of all violence.

The Saints pen the great treatises against the moral outrage of wars. While theorists of the other paradigms may argue the justice of at least some wars, Saints normally repudiate all warring even when they see justice as favoring one side. If the gentleness of their characters may in part explain such pacifism, the Saints also recognize that most of the suffering and dying occur among those of humble stations in life. Yet while Catherine of Siena worked in the fourteenth century to end warring among European Christian nations, she urged a new crusade to oust the Muslims from Jerusalem.

If Saints rarely accept a "just war," Saints also repudiate domestic political violence, especially when the authorities apply force to maintain a system of great economic inequality. While an Aristocrat such as de Maistre defends the executioner as the bulwark of civilization, and if the younger Carlyle had a morbid fascination with public hangings, the Saint typically rejects capital punishment. Thus, when the Russian authorities were about to execute some peasant trespassers, Tolstoy wrote to those authorities that they were not going to hang them in *his* name, even volunteering to substitute his own neck. He shared the impulse to confess personal failings common to many Saints, and his novel *Resurrection* argues that we are all too guilty to punish anyone. The Saints especially abhor mass repressions by official violence, rarely even then accepting any defensive violence.

If opposing violence by the rulers, the Saint also normally opposes any initiated by the ruled. Again, there are a few lapses. Thomas Müntzer urged his peasant followers to take up the sword in 1525, leading to their slaughter and his own beheading. An aberrant wing of Anabaptism turned Maccabean, employing violence in a hopeless defense of communistic and polygamous Münster in 1534–35. The defenders were led by "King" John Beukels of Leiden, who even beheaded and trampled one of his wives for questioning his title to rule. Captured, Beukels was eventually tortured to death by hot irons, with his body publicly displayed in a cage.

The gentle Thoreau quit teaching rather than cane his students; but in "A Plea for Captain John Brown" (Thoreau, 1950, 683–707), he saw an analogy with Christ's crucifixion in the imminent hanging of a man who had raised arms against slavery. Perhaps our century's liberation theology (a bridge from Saint toward Socialist) is anticipated in Thoreau's acknowledgment that he could understand why killing and dying may be "unavoidable" in a world where unacknowledged evils are supported "by deeds of petty violence very day." But most Saints reject any turn to violence as a political means to throw off a system of injustice, although often accepting or even encouraging nonviolent forms of resistance.

### Vegetarianism

The Saint usually repudiates even violence toward the other animals. Few go to the extreme of India's Jains, who so carefully avoid killing even insects that they postpone journeys when many bugs are crawling, refuse to engage in agriculture because it entails intentional or unintentional killing of pests, and even wear muslin masks to avoid inhaling small insects. But concern for larger creatures has caused many other Saints to embrace vegetarianism. Tolstoy's renunciation of war brought with it an abandonment of not only hunting but also the eating of domestic animals. (He never knew that Sonja sometimes slipped meat broth into his diet in order to "strengthen" him in old age.)

Vegetarianism unites several commitments of the Saint, including to avoid bloodshed and to live simply. Today there are additional arguments best articulated by Frances Moore Lappé and associates: Meat eating is a wasteful production of protein, directly or indirectly displacing grains that could improve the nutrition of the world's malnourished. Although Gandhi often talked of health benefits from his vegetarian and goat-cheese diet, our modern knowledge regarding the healthiness of vegetarianism was historically not an important motive compared to simple living and avoiding violence toward any kind of sentient being. The Saint is alien to the Aristocrat's gradation of forms of being by relative intellect and so forth—perhaps, rather, identifying the higher animals as does Tolstoy in his *Resurrection*, by capacity to transcend self-interest and to look to the happiness of others. "Blessed are the meek," taught Christ; and this means total renunciation of violence—a teaching of the apparently vegetarian Essenes who preceded him.

### The Saint's Asceticism as Voluntary Poverty

If their unique natures may incline Saints toward nonviolence— seeking an outward peace to reinforce the inward form—their own recognition of their common nature with others encourages them to practice "voluntary poverty." The Saint emphasizes what is shared rather than distinctive in our natures, unlike the Aristocrat (the Confucian partially excepted). No Saint could accept such common Aristocratic beliefs as that certain classes or even peoples are innately superior to others and thus deserve costly cultivation of "the finer things." Nor would any Saint tolerate the claim that ruder natures do not feel the hardships of their condition. The Saint's sympathy with the humble leads to rejection of such rationalizations for inequality.

That sense of fully shared nature with the lower classes makes it impossible for the Saints to live in the high style of many Aristocrats. Lacking immunizing illusions of their innate superiority, they could not live that way without the deepest guilt. Thoroughly committed Saints feel compelled to live simply while teaching others to live so. As Rousseau's motto held, "I live life as a test of truth." To live in luxury would mean complicity in causing both the economic suffering of the poor and the official violence that preserves inequality.

Hence a Saint born to wealth might repudiate it. One may walk away from wealth into a life of mendicancy (Buddha, St. Francis); another may try to give it away (Peter Waldo, John Ruskin, Leo Tolstoy). The clumsy incompleteness of the efforts made by Ruskin and Tolstoy could be cited by critics as proving their hypocrisy, but there is no denying their impulse to live in voluntary poverty or that they actually *did* give much away. Many Saints long to live as mendicants, in simple communes, or perhaps in relative isolation on minimal properties worked by their own hand (Thoreau at Walden Pond, the later Scott Nearing on a New England farm, or the contemporary Kentucky farm of writer Wendell Berry). Rousseau sought to be twice born, getting rid of his watch, wig, and lace-ruffle shirts. While always drawn like a moth toward the corrupting flame of Paris, he recurrently embraced life in a small country cottage where he could raise some of his own food and keep close to nature.

While critics might charge them with conspicuous nonconsumption—seeing only a vain self-advertisement in it all—the Saints *do* simplify their lives. In fact, this is often so much the case that to the Aristocrats it may seem to be a reproach, or perhaps even a threat that an "involuntary" poverty might be imposed on them (as the militant Socialists would want to do).

The Saints are further very unlike the Aristocrats in that Saints want to live like the poor not only in style of consumption but also in the practice of labor. One must note the exception of some mendicants who endure the even greater humility of begging, as with the classical Buddhist monks of India who were not only forbidden to grow their own food but even to cook uncooked food given as alms (Thapar, 1978, 63–104). But usually Saints not only teach the dignity of useful manual labor but also perform some. Tolstoy, who chopped wood and made boots, criticized the unequal ownership of property that made it possible for some to do no labor, thus taking for themselves without toil: "In political Economy and Sociology there is only one question to solve; 'Why do some people work and others do nothing?'" (Green, 1983, 220). Gandhi was to recall his great fulfillment when he was at Tolstoy Farm in South Africa, for "he made himself his own farmer, carpenter, cook, laundryman, doctor, sandalmaker, just like Robinson Crusoe" (Green, 1983, 123).

Any charity of the Aristocrats consists only in opening a purse, arguably filled by prior exploitation of the labor of others. The Aristocrats do not give personal labor as charity. They would be uncomfortable if the lower classes "took familiarities" with them, perhaps addressing them as if equals or even touching them. By contrast, Christ's faith healing as described in the gospel of Mark characteristically involved his touching or being touched. The Saint may become physically engaged even at risk to health, as when Gandhi, Schweitzer, Clara Barton, Florence Nightingale, or Mother Teresa directly ministers to the sick.

Pained by the suffering of the Russian famine of 1891–92, Tolstoy not only opened his purse (to spend more, even borrowing back money he had given to Sonja) but gave of his own energies, going to the scene of misery to manage food distributions. Nothing more reveals the contrast of the Saint and the militant Socialist than how Tolstoy and Lenin differed regarding that famine. Lenin opposed giving help, saying that the misery of the peasants would undermine their faith in God and tsar and thus drive them into the cities and revolution. He sneeringly spoke of Tolstoy's teaching as "the sermon of the saintly idiot" (Rapoport, 1960, 270).[4] As noted, the Saint deplores such arguments against compassion, being inclined to yield to the unsophisticated promptings of the heart. That—more than some abstract philosophy—undergirds the golden rule.

## The Economy of the Saint: Small Is Beautiful

Having addressed some background attitudes affecting the economic arrangements favored by the Saint, I return to the framework used to analyze the Aristocrat's economic order, looking at productive property, the division of labor, and the distribution of the product.

### Private Property in Means of Production

Like the Aristocrat, the Saint works with the assumption of a steady-state economy, whether imposed by preindustrial limitations or postindustrial recognition of ecological limits to growth (cf. Elgin, 1981; Berry, 1986).

It sometimes seems as if the Saint dreams of a prehistoric economy of sharing—that of our millennia of hunting and gathering preceding both pastoralism and the more recent onset of settled, field agriculture. The latter began some 10,000 years ago; it was followed within some 5,000 years by writing, to coordinate such an economy. Although the varied forms of hunting-gathering societies had always had some inequalities of age or gender, it was the emergence of private property in herds and lands that really permitted great economic inequalities to set in.

Although usually offering no solution except preventive policies and voluntary redistribution (involuntary redistribution could require unacceptable violence), the Saint disapproves of great inequalities of property. Those drawn at all toward the Aristocratic paradigm may explain property as does St. Augustine, seeing it as a consequence of Adam's fall, or original sin, and yet also in part a corrective, since settled rules of mine and thine minimize conflicts among the depraved. While many Saints also acknowledge flaws in our common human nature, not even those who concede innate selfishness accept the Augustinian view as justifying great inequalities. Rousseau frontally denies original sin or innate depravity, defending the idea of "natural goodness" in its limited, largely negative sense of denying that viciousness is innate rather than learned. The Saints in either case tend to believe that unequal holdings of private property (like some forms of unequal authority) constitute not a cure but the *cause* of human conflict.[5]

Rousseau argued that inequality is the origin of most human corruption. In the economic sphere, this is especially so when some are so rich that they can buy the labor of others, who are so poor that they must sell themselves. Some use others as mere instruments for gratification of their own wants. Such inequality corrupts both the victimizer (greeds grow with the prospect of satisfaction without personal labor) and the victims (hostility develops when people are unable to employ their own powers toward satisfaction of their own needs) (cf. Cook, 1975).

Other Saints offer similar critiques of property or its inequalities. St. Francis of Assisi prohibited individual property among his monks and even warned against their holding property collectively: "From property come disputes and lawsuits; it makes obstacles to the love of God and one's neighbor. So we won't possess any temporal goods in this world" (in Bishop, 1974, 58). Or again, while Gandhi conceded some flaws in human nature, he is forthright on the primary cause of human conflict: "Violence is bred by inequality, non-violence by equality" (in Fischer, 1950, 425; also, Pantham, 1986, 327–28). Gandhi repudiated the inequalities of the smaller caste divisions (the *jati*), and he accepted the larger categories (the *varnas*) with this stipulation: "All Varnas are equal, for the community depends no less on one than on the other" (Béteille, 1983, 13, 51–52). The Buddha had similarly said that the varnas were equal in purity, which the Brahmans and Ksatriyas did not believe.

The Marxist critique of alienated labor also sees corruption in the capacity of some to take without toil, but it seeks a solution in social ownership rather than small-holder ownership. Although Müntzer had preached *omnia sunt communia*—meaning that a semi-Socialist sharing is appropriate for Christians—the Saint usually does not advocate social ownership of the means of production unless in the Franciscan sense of voluntary community of goods. Quite typically the Saints endorse small-scale private property in the means of production, such as peasant proprietorships or the shops of artisans owning the tools of their trade. In ancient India, lower-caste artisans and small merchants apparently were prominent among both Buddhists and Jains (Thapar, 1978, 58, 71). Critical of both Hindu and Islamic orthodoxies, the later bhakti-Sants were also of Vaisya or Shudra ritual caste divisions, being mostly artisanal in their occupations (Schomer and McLeod, 1987). In the West, Fox, Winstanley, Rousseau, Thoreau, Tolstoy, Ruskin, Gandhi, Schumacher, and Berry think of a society of small owners more than one of social ownership only. Marxists would see a "petty-bourgeois" outlook behind the economics of the Saint as reflected in the economic theories of Jean Baptiste Say or John Ruskin. But even if this were so, it would not refute the Saint proposition that few could be exploited if most had some means of production owned and worked by themselves. Yeoman farming could also counter political tyranny, as Thomas Jefferson and John Taylor would argue in writings intermixing a few themes from the Aristocrat and many from the Whig anchorage of Capitalist theory. Wendell Berry laments that the "get big or get out" pressure of the Capitalist market has had much the same effect as communist collectivization in eliminating small farmers with diverse products: "As a social or economic goal, bigness is totalitarian; it establishes an inevitable tendency toward the *one* that will be the biggest of all. Many who got big to stay in are now being driven out by those who got bigger. The aim of bigness implies not one aim that is not socially and culturally destructive" (Berry, 1986, 41).

As the classic critics of the Aristocrat, the Saints disliked the great landed estate, even if Rousseau's epistolary novel *La Nouvelle Héloïse* imagines a well-run estate with a more egalitarian spirit as a plausible reform for France. But if the Saints of that era opposed what was then central to the Aristocrat, they opposed no less the emergent signs of the industrial revolution. Each time Rousseau names another cause of corruption, he hits another needed element of the large-scale, industrialized Capitalist economy. He indicts not only unequal wealth and income but also an excessive division of labor, urbanization, commercial interactions with other peoples, excessive national scale, and so forth (Cook, 1975).

The Saint doubts the value of large-scale machine production. In his typical excess, Rousseau wrote, "In everything that depends on human industry, one should forbid with care any machine and any invention that can shorten labor, spare manpower, and produce the same effect with less difficulty" (in Vaughan, 1915, vol. 1, 320). Some raised in the Saint tradition, typified by the Amish and Mennonite communities, believe God wants them to avoid forever most fruits of mechanical progress, using teams of horses rather than tractors while earning their bread by the sweat of their brows.

Yet most Saints are open to improvements in tools that would not control the workers but be controlled directly by them. They accept what is now called "soft" or "appropriate" technology. Driven by his ecological sensibility to abandon Marxism, André Gorz offers a typical statement:

> *The inversion of tools is a fundamental condition of the transformation of society.*
> The development of voluntary cooperation, the self-determination and freedom of communities and individuals, requires the development of technologies and methods of production which:
> * can be used and controlled at the level of the neighborhood or community;
> * are capable of generating increased economic autonomy for local and regional collectivities;
> * are not harmful to the environment; and
> * are compatible with the exercise of joint control by producers and consumers over products and production processes (Gorz, 1980, 19).

Most modern Saints would endorse this account, fearing that industrial giantism goes with overspecialization of labor, exploitative inequalities, ecological ruin, and congested, corrupting cities.

This spirit is clear in Thoreau, Ruskin, Tolstoy, and Gandhi. It is symbolized by Gandhi's advocacy of revival of the spinning wheel as the means toward economic self-sufficiency for household, village, and even nation, offering freedom from Britain's empire and emergent world capitalism. Recent statements by E. F. Schumacher and Wendell Berry have critiqued the capitalization of agriculture, symbolized by agro-industry's massive monoculture fields, mechanization, irrigation, and use of artificial fertilizers, herbicides, and pesticides. Productivity measures should not ignore what happens to people or to the quality of the environments within which they live (Schumacher, 1973; Berry, 1986).

Unlike the pro-urban orientations of the Capitalist or the Socialist, the Saint distrusts large cities, preferring decentralized economies of farming and artisanry. Paul and Percival Goodman in their *Communitas* (1947) also accept light manufacturing powered by electricity rather than the outsized factories built in the past around drive shafts linked to steam engines. But Saints emphasize agrarian development over industrialization, or village over city, as especially important for the Third World (cf. Lappé and Collins, 1979).

While Wendell Berry sees production controls as necessary to preserve family farms, most Saints accept much freedom of trade. Yet most distrust the intensified commerce that creates overlarge cities and then spans the globe to sustain them. Thoreau's "Life without Principle" (Thoreau, 1950, 711–32) looks skeptically on world trade, saying that "there are those who style themselves statesmen and philosophers who are so blind as to think that progress and civilization depend on precisely this kind of interchange and activity—the activity of flies about a molasses hogshead."

### The Division of Labor: Critique of Specialization as an Obstacle to Mental and Moral Development

The typical Saint is a critic of any extensive division of labor. It is not that they are opposed to the idea of the acquired skills of the crafts, whether that of Rousseau's watchmaker father, Thoreau's pencil-maker father, Tolstoy's service as a bootmaker for his friends, or Gandhi's regular work at the spinning wheel. Scott Nearing turned wooden bowls, collected maple sap, and made mulch. Even now, Wendell Berry skillfully uses draft horses on his Kentucky farm.

Rather, they criticize an exploitative division of labor that represents not the interdependency envisioned by Plato so much as simple inequality. More self-sufficiency would be salutary, argued Rousseau: "As long as men were occupied in work they each could do by themselves, and practiced arts that did not require the collaboration of many hands, they lived a free, healthy, good, and happy life" (*Oeuvres Complètes*, vol. 3, 171). There are eloquent warnings in the writings of Wollstonecraft, Thoreau, Tolstoy, Ruskin, and Gandhi that the manufacturing division of labor could cretinize workers, stunting their intellectual, moral, and physical development. Thus argued John Ruskin:

> It is not, truly speaking, the labor that is divided; but the men—divided into mere segments of men—broken into small fragments and crumbs of life; so that all the little piece of intelligence that is left in a man is not enough to make a pin, or a nail, but exhausts itself in making the point of a pin or the head of a nail (*Stones of Venice*, vol. 2, vi, 16).

Adam Smith and Karl Marx said as much, too, but while the Capitalist defends the division of labor as necessary for productive efficiency, the Socialist joins the Saint as critic, spurning the false god of mere productive efficiency. As Wendell Berry describes what he calls "the disease of modern character," specialization makes us pay dearly "for a calamitous disintegration and scattering-out of the various functions of character: workmanship, care, conscience, responsibility" (Berry, 1986, 19). Beyond damage to specialists themselves, too many modern "experts" serve predation.

### *Distribution of the Social Product: Toward More Equality of Results*

Plato, Aristotle, and Cicero claimed to assign persons to roles according to innate capacity, and the capacity to give to society governs what is gotten. In their inegalitarian version of distributive justice, A's reward surpasses B's reward as A's merit in the way of contribution to society surpasses B's merit. The Aristocrat would define merit in such a way that it leaves much to the gentlemen, further permitting small differences of such merit to yield large differences in rewards. The Capitalist only adds an insistence on at least a formal equality of opportunity, while defending the unequal distribution less by arguments regarding charity and cultivation of finer things than by its encouragement of self-improvement, innovation, investment risk, and other spurs to efficient growth.

To the Saint the capacity to give to society is not only a product of personal effort at self-development, risk taking, and so on, but largely a function of what one has got, first, from nature in the way of wholly uncontrolled genetic endowment and, second, from society as largely uncontrolled advantages or disadvantages of inheritance and station passed on from parents. To the extent that capacities are thus unearned, the Saint decouples contributions and allocations of the economic product.

The Saint in any case differs from the Aristocrat in regarding useful manual labor as the primary contribution to society, rather than anything performed by those who do no such labor. But even conceding that contributions to society may be unequal, the question of what people get should emphasize their natural similarity of needs. The Saint at least leans toward this idea of substantive equality as a concept of just distribution.

The Saint understands with the Marxist Socialist that unequal distribution of ownership of the means of production dominates unequal distribution of the burden of labor, which in turn dominates unequal enjoyment of the product. But the Saint sees more flexibility than does the Socialist, favoring certain reforms to increase the share of the peasants, the artisans, and even the industrial workers. Occasionally the Saint may even try to organize them to improve their lot (e.g., Gandhi at Ahmedabad). But for the most part, the Saint rather relies on personal example and persuasion to encourage more equal sharing, even if public policy limits on inequality would be ideal. Gandhi once recommended a uniform wage for all occupations, the time of one person to be equated in value to the time of another (McLaughlin, 1974, 86). In a more modest proposal, he urged that at least one should set a ceiling on the income of a mill owner in India at no more than 20:1 ratio to the wage of the average worker in it (Gupta, 1971, 434).

The Saints are skeptical of most arguments for highly unequal consumption. Rousseau saw luxury as one more cause of corruption, and he expressly rejected the argument that the production of luxury goods for the rich creates jobs for the poor, seeing luxury consumptions as, rather, taking necessities from the poor. This zero-sum view of luxury or subsistence consumptions abounds in the writings of Saints, as typified by Thoreau's statement on "economy" in opening *Walden*: "The luxury of one class is counterbalanced by the indigence of another. On the one side is the palace, on the other are the almshouse and 'silent poor.' " Or Ruskin: "Luxuries . . . must be paid for by labor withdrawn from useful things; and no nation has a right to indulge in them until all its poor are comfortably housed and fed" (in McLaughlin, 1974, 86). At least in the realm of material production, this collides with the Aristocrat's defense of inequality as the means for promoting the finer things.

If the Aristocrat and the rightist variants of the Capitalist put the burden of argument on those urging more equality, for the Saint as well as the Socialist the presumption in economic distributions instead favors equality. The burden of argument belongs on those who would espouse much inequality—which is also the stand taken by the contemporary liberal philosopher of justice John Rawls (Rawls, 1971).

## Does Anyone Really Love Leveling?
## The Religion of the People

Both the Capitalist and Socialist paradigms may dismiss the economic teachings of the Saint as irrelevant anachronisms—a dream of a lost world that cannot and will not be restored. While rustic simplicity of consumption may always be a minority passion, a world where "less is more" is not likely to win stable majority support. If only because women constitute a majority, we can expect no enthusiasm for one Saint's suggestion that male unemployment be solved by returning women to the home (Schumacher, 1973, 57).

### Do Majorities Want Economic Equality?

While the Saint, like the Socialist, is often accused of excessive leveling, perhaps majorities rarely support even the modest shift toward economic equality that Saints demand. It may be a mistake to think that only a small, affluent elite is fond of economic inequalities. I earlier cited John Adams's observation that most people like equality when looking up the social ranks, inequality when looking down.

Thus, majorities who are looking down may really defend inequalities. Perhaps that is what happens when income distribution shifts from the classic pyramid to a more diamond shape. If an enlarged middle class is intent on defending its standard of living against welfare spending and similar leveling devices, not even the Saint's degree of egalitarianism would be favored.

But John Adams's view that most of us like more equality when we look up the social ranks may need qualification. Majorities may not want equality of results but only the hope of doing better for themselves or their children, immediately comparing themselves only with those near their own condition. Many people can accept that higher wealth or income is held by others, provided they can at least imagine that either they or their children will some day enjoy the same advantage. In many hierarchies, those in lower ranks accept the fact of high pay in the ranks above them if they expect a future promotion to like rewards. Similarly, publics accept the legacy or lottery millionaire—if conceivably they too can be so lucky! Far from agonizing in their envy, mass publics even seem to take vicarious pleasure from the affluent life-styles of the rich and famous.

If the above statements have some validity, then perhaps any majority egalitarianism lies elsewhere, focused less about economic circumstances than equality of respect, which brings us to religious or other symbolic experience.

### Religion and Symbolic Equality

Cultural contrasts limit generalization about the religion of the Saint type, but it usually leans toward more equality of status in this life as well as any future life. Against the Aristocrat's tendency to order all grades of being in proper hierarchies, the Saint neither imagines celestial hierarchy among divine beings nor likes priestly hierarchy among human beings.

True Saints cannot really approve of a high priesthood living in luxury. Simple living was favored by such founders of religions as Buddha and Christ. However, as observers have often noted, maturing religions tend to slough off simplicity as they fatten on worldly possessions and enter into partnership with the protective secular authorities. In China, even Taoism and Buddhism at times were to become more closely tied up with the emperors than founders of the religions would have liked, as illustrated by the cult of Lao Tzu under some T'ang emperors or the use of both religions by the Sung (cf. Chappell, 1987). The Theravada Buddhism of Thailand in modern times has also tended toward hierarchical organization. Many observers of India's past have spoken of cycles whereby ascetic sages found a religion or sect, the followers eventually corrupt the teaching, and then new sages arise who in part point back to the teachings of the original sages.

Among the Hebrews, the Essenes disdained the Sadducees and the Pharisees who had corrupted the faith. Christ's teaching was obviously also critical of the corruption, and both Sadducees and Pharisees wanted him crucified. But Christianity shared the pattern, evolving from humble early churches to the arrogant heights of the regal church in the late medieval era. As the Roman Catholic hierarchy imitated secular elites in luxury and titles, some Saints sought penance in monastic life. While he avoided challenging the Catholic hierarchy, St. Francis wanted both his order and its association with a similar group of nuns to be egalitarian. But the very credibility of Franciscans brought them many posthumous bequests, which only hastened their own corruption.

Successive waves of reformers sought to raze the ecclesiastical hierarchy, purge the luxury, and return to the spirit of the early church. The main religious bent of the Saint emerged in the more egalitarian forms of such repudiation, such as the early Waldensians, the Anabaptists, and the Society of Friends (Quakers). The Quakers gave up not only cathedrals but even parish church buildings for plain rooms, and they abolished all icons and ritual trappings within them. They dispensed with bishops and for the most part any clergy at all, refusing in an egalitarian spirit to doff their hats for any human authority. The somewhat similar Russian Dukhobors were helped by Tolstoy when they were forced to emigrate, many of them to Canada.[6]

Even with religious consolations, the Saint's renunciations can be hard. St. Francis was said to be a blithe spirit in his personal life, often given to the kind of laughter that Plato deemed unseemly for his guardians. Gandhi, too, was said to be normally cheerful. Apparently not every Saint is such, since the later years of Ruskin and Tolstoy were quite somber. Often the Saint figures claim more happiness than is apparent in their lives, touched by the sorrow they would succor. The *Catholic Worker* newspaper shows a disparity between earnest protestations of happiness and involuntary signs of sadness among those who are deeply involved with the damaged lives of our contemporary urban poor. It requires an unusual temperament to preserve good cheer in choosing abstinence, hard labor, and exposure to poverty, sickness, and death.

Recapitulating, the Saint shares with the Aristocrat a stronger religiosity than is typically found in the Capitalist or the Socialist, but it is a very distinctive religious outlook—one that reflects the Saint's identification with the lower strata rather than the higher. The main practical teaching is egalitarian: "Thou shalt love thy neighbor as thyself" (Mark 12:31).

Religious views that begin with a spirit of equality and repudiation of the violence required to maintain inequality can degenerate into justification of both inequalities and the violence that defends them. When the heresy of the humble becomes the orthodoxy of the great, a teaching aimed against predation is warped into its defense. Hierarchy, rules and rituals, and collaboration with secular authorities ensue. Opposing sects may clash.[7] Rival sects of Christians go to war, each claiming the name of the teacher of peace from Galilee. And in 1987 in Sri Lanka, Sinhalese Buddhist monks joined mobs calling for the repression of the Hindu Tamils. As in Alexander Pope's famous line, "The worst of all madmen is a saint run wild." But this turns us toward the Saint's solutions for the political problem.

## Notes

1. Among pre-Christian variants of the Aristocrat in the West, compassion was not even recognized as a cardinal virtue. Arguments *against* yielding to compassion abound in the writings of the Aristocrat (e.g., on the need for order), the Capitalist (e.g., nature teaches the survival of the fittest, or the market knows best), and even the Socialist (e.g., only class struggle, which is often violent, engenders historical progress).

2. Yet one study of Roman Catholic saints found that, while only 19 percent of 713 male saints were recorded as having had some form of sexual conflict, 42 percent of 151 female saints had such conflict. That could suggest prejudice on the part of biographers but also something of social reality when women were given in marriage as if a kind of property. Later saints were more likely to be female, usually either virgins (more likely to be famous) or widows choosing celibacy (Weinstein and Bell, 1982, 97–99). Most studies of the stories of the saints of either gender find disproportionate upper-class origins, an unlikely birth (as from long-barren parents), claims of unusual

precocity in piety and self-denial, some hint of rebellion against parents in later saints, and entry to a religious order (ibid.; cf. also Brown, 1981).

3. My comments are by no means meant in criticism but only for the sake of understanding. I do not know of any empirical studies of correlations of, say, hormone balances with political predispositions, aside from the common report of less observed aggressivity in female children.

4. Another modern, Chekhov, remarked that "there is more love in electricity and steam than there is in chastity and the refusal to eat meat" (Troyat, 1967, 512). Note that here it is not moderation of desire and sharing but expansion of powers that is considered central in human progress. That will be the teaching of the Capitalist as well as the Socialist.

5. Perhaps these views only seem to be mutually exclusive. Parents can appreciate Augustine's point in minimizing conflict by clearly designating what things belong to whom within the family setting. Any ambiguity of children's property titles threatens to bring on the full terror of sibling rivalry. And when the political right similarly argues that inequalities of power can minimize conflict (e.g., unambiguous "dominance-ordering" in the theory of Konrad Lorenz and other ethologists), this too becomes a standing temptation to parents in relation to their children. But the Saint is no less correct in saying that these very identifications of personal property as well as excessive inequalities of either property or power can engender conflicts.

6. Tolstoy's *Confession* denounces how the hypocrisy of his class had corrupted religion: "The teachings of faith are left to some other realm, separated from life and independent of it." The landed gentlemen "did not live according to the principles they professed . . . , they were deceiving themselves . . . , they had no sense of life's meaning than to live while they lived and to lay their hands on everything they could." They ran into self-contradictions because they were unable to admit that they were parasites, that the lower classes lived better and more meaningful lives (Tolstoy, 1983, 18, 65, 76–77). Tolstoy was excommunicated by the Russian Orthodoxy in 1901.

7. Sometimes new sects arise that understand themselves as synthesizing two or more previous faiths, but—although they may see themselves as thus agents of peace—they may find themselves under attack by the very religions they would unite. To some extent this has been the experience of the Sikhs of the Punjab, and it is even more vividly clear in the harsh repression recently visited on the Baha'is by the Islamic revolutionary regime of Iran. Perhaps a safer course is merely to express openness to other religious views, as was true of the Hindu sages Ramakrishna (d. 1886) and Vivekananda (d. 1902) in the late nineteenth century (cf. Ross, 1966, 13–27). But a kindred teaching in Gandhi, who liked to say that one's religion is the whole of one's thoughts, brought his assassination at the hands of a Hindu fanatic.

# 5

# The Saint and Democracy

Resolve to serve no more, and you are at once
freed. I do not ask that you place hands upon
the tyrant to topple him over, but simply that
you support him no longer; then you will be-
hold him, like a great Colossus whose pedestal
has been pulled away, fall of his own weight.

Etienne de la Boétie,
*The Discourse of Voluntary Servitude*

Near the end of the 1980s, we witnessed such a collapse as Boétie
describes of autocratic rule, in the Philippines as well as much of
Eastern Europe. But while nonviolent civil disobedience can sometimes work quickly in practice, nonviolent means may more often
require great patience. As Gandhi expressed it, "I personally would
wait, if need be for ages, rather than seek to attain the freedom of
my country through bloody means" (Fischer, 1950, 283). With time,
one may persuade and train the many who are needed to join
courageously in the practice of nonviolence. With more time, one
may turn the wills of adversaries, or even lead them toward a change
of heart, such that they freely abandon tyrannical practices. Even
apart from any nonviolence campaign, time could change conditions
to remove the original motives for repression.

During the interval, tyrants can do great damage to bodies, if not
to souls. Most Saints counseling such restraint are religious. They find
solace in assuming that, should their nonviolent resistance result in
death, some kind of afterlife exists for gentle souls. Less patient Saints
such as Henry David Thoreau and William Lloyd Garrison may
condone others' use of violence in a just cause, if unable to practice it
themselves.

By our definition, the Saints accent moderation of desires among

113

the upper classes as the main strategy against scarcity and the conflicts
it engenders. While on the one hand this could promote the material
well-being of the lower classes, on the other hand the Saints' nonviolence in means may require of followers risk of the ultimate sacrifice.
Whether persuading their own followers or the powers that be, the
common theme is subordination of the body's claims to the needs of
the soul. The Saints expect others to practice ascetic denial, even
should others fall short of their own capacity for voluntary poverty or
martyrdom.

Many Saints tend to a mystic's world view, which often doubts that
any solution of our troubles is available through politics as such. No
political solution is likely, anyway, without prior discipline of the
raging desires that cause strife and predation. Even more than the
Aristocrat, the Saint is always the moralist, warning against expecting
too much and too soon from any political practice. Teaching the
Taoist principle of "nonaction" (*wu wei*), Lao Tzu suggested that, even
in seeking justice, we should think of soft water gradually wearing
away hard rock. One does not set a hard edge against the hard edge.
Quite alien to the Saints is Lenin's promotion of class animosities, his
political metaphor of a military march, or talk of "smashing" institutions. Making war as the means to the end of peace—as often urged
by the other paradigms—seems to the Saint a simple contradiction.
As ex-Marxist A. J. Muste put it, "There is no way to peace: peace is
the way" (in Yoder, 1971, 70).

If rejection of even defensive violence is ultimately premised on
denial of the body—especially the bodies of Saints themselves—the
Saints' identification with those who have little in the way of political
resources almost defines the selection of appropriate means in relation to politics. Hence we must scan the strategies of the relatively
weak before addressing how the Saint would use the more demanding
strategic fields aimed at control over decisions. For when any attempt
to improve things would surely make things worse, the Saints may
counsel avoidance of any active politics.

## Using the Strategies of the Weak:
## Enduring, Exiting, Evading

Like other strategic fields, the strategies of the weak are analytically
distinctive yet not exclusive in practice: They can be pursued either
simultaneously or sequentially, often to promote more active strategies. Hence such fields of choice may not always constitute defeat, but
rather strategic retreat for later advances. In *enduring*, if only to avoid
even worse results, one practices such variants as identification with

the dominant, assimilation, nondeferential resignation, or sullen submission watching for better options. Leaving suicide aside, in *exiting* one turns to internal or external migration. In *evading*, one eludes adverse authority by concealment of one's identity or activities (cf. Cook, 1983b).

Such fields of choice are affected by the liberal democratic norm of equality of basic rights. The individual's rights to be let alone in privacy, to migrate freely, or to keep silence could curb potential harm from uncontrollable authority. Even without the constitutional guarantees of a popular government, the pursuit of such options becomes especially important, for people who are unable to control public policy make much of these variants of self-control. Thus, in Hellenistic Greece and imperial Rome, many powerless ex-citizens joined resident aliens in the politically quiescent strategies of most Stoics, Cynics, Epicureans and early Christians.

No one should ever disparage the rights of privacy. U.S. Supreme Court Justice Louis Brandeis spoke of "the right to be let alone—the most comprehensive of rights and the right most valued by civilized men" (dissent in *Olmstead v. United States*, 1928). Yet privacy rights, like those of migration and holding one's tongue also, become most important *politically* when sheltering civic rights that relate to the strategies of the strong, as in private organization for public action.

When urging relatively passive strategies, the voice of the Saint may sometimes converge with that of the Aristocrat, who normally counsels that change is not identical to progress, that any quest for reform runs an often greater risk of making things worse. Because of the almost inevitable unintended and unwanted consequences, both paradigms say, it is often best to tolerate some of the lesser imperfections of society. Hence the strategies for adaptation to uncontrolled official decisions are important to the Saints.

### Enduring

The Saint may sometimes urge acquiescence in nonaction. This may be forced by circumstances. The exploited peasant of history, for instance, had little choice but to submit to onerous rents and taxes that supported the landlords, whenever there was no possibility of finding sufficient food elsewhere and rebellion was hopeless. But often there were also religious consolations. Effacement of the ego and its material claims is basic to the often mystical Saint vision of spiritual serenity. The *Bhagavad Gita* is clear: "Renounce reward—at once there is peace." Usually the teaching stresses the greater importance of attaining an inward peace, harmony, or freedom more than any outward gain: "When an inquirer asked Sri Ramakrishna, 'When shall I be free?' the saint replied, 'When the "I" shall cease to be' "

(Burtt, 1965, 267). Or hear the philosophic slave, Epictetus: "My will is simply that which comes to pass." Even Seneca, a Stoic raised to better circumstances, taught that what one cannot alter one must accept. The this-worldly price of such resignation may be high, as the semi-Aristocratic Nietzsche sneers: "Stoicism is self-tyranny" (Nietzsche, 1968, 205–6). Yet such a spirit of stoic resignation coursed through early Christianity, for Christ himself said, "My kingdom is not of this world" (John 18:36). Quaker founder George Fox also urged quiescence: "Meddle not with the powers of the earth" (Wildes, 1965, 246).

Yet often the powers of the Earth meddle with Saints, as in the forced suicide of Seneca, the crucifixion of Christ, and the recurrent jailings of Fox. Rulers have never been fond of those who claim to interpret an inner voice or other standard deemed higher than the ruler's commands. But often those counseling quiescence are left alone, especially when the Saint's message becomes not only like that of the Aristocrat but often like that of the tyrant as well. Perhaps in part because most humans have lived under despotisms since the beginning of recorded history, quiescent forms of religiosity have been widespread. Although this may be more a consequence than a cause of tyranny, it does feed back to the support of tyranny. Rousseau reluctantly conceded that true religion and political freedom were in conflict:

> Christianity preaches only servitude and dependence. Its spirit is so favorable to tyranny that tyranny always profits from it. True Christians are made to be slaves. They know it and hardly care. In their eyes, this short life has too little worth. (*Social Contract*, IV, viii)

Saints make a virtue of "humility"—a word etymologically tied to "humus," suggesting a bowing down to the soil. Keeping this-worldly aspirations modest may give the individual outward as well as inward peace. Yet even that is often doubtful, as in the Russian proverb, "Make yourself into a sheep and you will soon meet a wolf nearby." While the Saint could respond that at least it helps attain *social* peace, both the Capitalist and Socialist in revolutionary mode would sneer, "A peace of the graveyard." But from the Saint's point of view, the choice of enduring over violence would at least save one's soul, given the imperative of most great religions to avoid killing. If one must choose, it is better to suffer wrong than to do wrong.

Although a few exceptional Saint-like figures were secular (such as the older Bertrand Russell), almost all Saint theorists have been religious believers. Belief in an afterlife seems almost necessary to induce many not only to forgo pleasures but even to endure suffering or death rather than turn to violent resistance. This often means hardships and dangers in the short run; and as the cliché goes, the long run is but a succession of short runs. The Holocaust showed that a strategy of merely enduring may risk even extinction.

Advocates of nonviolence respond that pacifism need not mean passivity. There are many ways of resisting without causing physical harm to an adversary (Lakey, 1973; Sharp, 1970; 1979; 1985). But even nonviolent resistance may at some point require the courage of religious convictions, as in Gandhi's assurance that death constitutes no great evil. Without communicable experience from beyond the grave to warrant that belief, it must be taken on faith. For some of those lacking religious assurance (such as Marxist-Leninist revolutionaries), it may seem better to kill for a cause than to die for one.

### Exiting

A more active strategy of the weak is physical removal from repressive authorities. Sometimes resorted to by those otherwise likely to be forced to do evil, suicide is an extreme form of exiting. Although rejected by Saints of Roman Catholic persuasion, that extreme measure was accepted by many Stoics as well as adherents of Pure Land Buddhism and Shinto in Japan.

The more hopeful mode of exit is migration, whether as a shift of residence within the same political system or as exile abroad. While either course supposes that moving is possible (often banned in past empires), a moving *from* is pointless without a better place for moving *to*.

Internal migration only helps if there is some diversity of political subsystems or else certain zones of lax enforcement of authority. Saints of ermitic tradition would relocate to wilderness retreats, in part revering nature but perhaps also hoping to be tolerated at such a safe remove. Roman Catholicism in its religious orders offered places for such retreat, perhaps attaining its institutional longevity by finding special niches for its various kinds of adherents.

Other Saints choose migration abroad, as was true of the Mennonites, the Amish, and the Dukhobors whom Tolstoy sought to help. After the Stuart Restoration brought harsher persecution of Quakers, George Fox considered mass emigration to some enclave in the New World, as eventually pursued by William Penn. For people no less than other animals, flight is one immediate alternative to fight. But if neither a physical nor propaganda return is contemplated, flight also forecloses any fight, even of the nonviolent kind.

### Evading

Another option for those despairing of change in official decisions is evasion, meaning concealment of either membership in a repressed group or concealment of punishable behaviors. Christians in the earlier Roman empire usually hid their heretical beliefs as well as their practice of Christian worship in secret places. After any confrontation and confession, a refusal to recant and worship pagan gods would bring death by beheading (for Roman citizens) or by wild beasts (for noncitizens).

Sometimes evasion is but a tactical move to prepare for a turn to the influence strategy, as when it protects communications among one's own while preparing to reach out to others. Such outreach may include self-revelation and death to witness for a faith (*martyr* is Greek for "witness"). Saints may have enough confidence in their truths to die for them, but perhaps not enough to kill for them. As Gandhi said, truth "excludes the use of violence because man is not capable of knowing the absolute truth and therefore is not competent to punish" (in Erikson, 1969, 241).

## Strategies to Bend Authority

Their stand that martyrdom is better than murder constrains any Saint recourse to more active political strategies. Violent means are unacceptable in any efforts to influence authorities, to put friends into authoritative positions, or to bring decisional authority under more popular control.

### The Influence Strategy: Moral Regeneration and Civil Disobedience

In contrast to the Aristocrat, the Saint favors those flows of information and persuasive messages that relatively advantage those of modest station.

Excepting the Confucians, the Aristocrats stress differences more than similarities of class natures, at least where helpful in defending unequal levels of economic consumption or access to political power. The Saints instead teach what is common to our kind—which may partly explain their confessional impulse. We are not only similar in our basic needs for physical and spiritual health, but in large degree even in our cognitive capacities.

Hence the Saints typically favor more public information about how the secular and religious authorities make their decisions.[1] As for the rulers' monitoring of subjects, the Saints in political quiescence may resent domestic spying. But if engaged in civil disobedience, the Saints sometimes choose the posture of having nothing to hide. Gandhi's planning of civil disobedience campaigns was routinely open; he would go out of his way to inform the authorities what he and his followers were about to do. This would sacrifice any advantage of strategic surprise, but it could minimize likely violence. It also fits with Gandhi's wish to keep open lines of communication with adversaries, with whom one wants ultimate restoration of community. Such reconciliation is easier for those who employ nonviolent rather than violent means, for one is not cut off by either warlike secrecy in organizations or by vindictiveness.

Shifting to management of persuasive messages, the Saint never assumes with the Marxist Socialist that ruling elites are beyond persuasion. Nonviolent campaigns aim to touch the common human conscience. Humane means of struggle elicit the latent humanity of the opponent, while any turn to violence would stifle it. Violence raises fear, and the more irrational fear brings mental closure. Hence, Gandhi's campaigns went through recurrent rounds: quiet entreaty with the authorities; if rebuffed, a turn to a demonstration; renewed entreaty if they would hear him; and around again. This was often accompanied by fasting, which threatened harm or even death to himself rather than to the adversary.

While the soft voice "turneth away wrath," one can only persuade the powerful if one does not fear to address them forthrightly. "Speak truth to power," urged George Fox, in what must be one of the noblest maxims in the English language. As my friend John Donnelly has added, those who refuse to speak truth to power always end up lying to themselves. While the Taoists taught the wisdom of living unobtrusively for self-protection, even they spoke critically of power; and they would not have sought self-protection by giving undeserved praise to the powerful.

If the Aristocrat denounces demagogy, understood as pandering to the wants of the many, the Saint sees much greater evils in sycophancy, or pandering to the few rich and powerful. If Plato reserves his greatest contempt for those seeking personal advantage by flattering the many, the Saint most despises those who do so by flattering the few.

Surely, these obsequious flatteries have been by far the more damaging of the two, over the centuries. Through most of recorded history, people have been governed not by powerful popular assemblies but by narrow oligarchies or autocrats. While the Aristocrats hold that the false rhetoric of flattering the people can be corrupting for both rhetorician and the people, should one not expect parallel corruption of the sycophant and superior? Such ubiquitous toadying to those on top has often led to spirals of corruption among both subordinates and superiors. As with countless tyrants before them, sycophancy fed the megalomaniacal tendencies in both Hitler and Stalin.

Within any kind of regime, a similar damage in smaller scale arises in panderings to the petty tyrants of everyday lives, especially in places of work. Too often, the fastest way to rise through either public or private hierarchies is through loud flattery of superiors. This often goes along with efforts to persuade others to accept this particular authority—a tactic that typically advances the self-interest of sycophants at the expense of their groups of origin, and usually without benefit for any larger community.

Quite in contrast, speaking truth to power often brings punitive consequences to those who do so. In private life this means losing some petty reward of pay or promotion, but in political life it can sometimes cost life itself. Yet Saints will not be obsequious to obtain some personal benefit or grovel to avoid some personal harm.[2]

Saints want plain talk, whether to the powerful or to the people. Thus urged the emperor of Rome, Marcus Aurelius: "Speak both in the Senate and to every man, whoever he may be, appropriately, not with any affectation: use plain discourse" (*Meditations*, VIII, 30). Sometimes the same message reaches both the powerful and the people. Quaker founder George Fox followed up Anglican church sermons by standing up to give a countersermon. He would go on preaching in a loud voice even when strapped across a saddle as the authorities carried him off under arrest (Wildes, 1965). Less formidable as a speaker, the abolitionist William Lloyd Garrison penned a relentless reply to those who said he was too harsh: "I *will* be as harsh as truth, and as uncompromising as justice. . . . I am in earnest—I will not equivocate—I will not excuse—I will not retreat a single inch—AND I WILL BE HEARD" (in Grimke, 1891, 117).

But normally Saints tend to more feminine modes of action, and loud public speaking is less typical than quiet persuasion used to address both elites and ordinary people. Persuasion is not a "combat of ideas" as in the Capitalist model of discourse, but a meeting of the minds made possible by our common nature and our common good—peaceable resolution of any social tensions.

If the Aristocrats confine philosophizing to the few, the Saints open dialogue to the many. This is partly manifested in the deep, often personal commitment of many Saint figures to the education of the poor, as when even Tolstoy set up a school to teach literacy. But in persuasion, the many would be reached less through print or formal address at mass meetings than through quieter, face-to-face discussion circles. Recall that the economics of the Saint tends to favor the small, and tends to downsize things to the human scale of, say, the peasant village or perhaps the craft guild. Gandhi would sometimes engage village assemblies or groups of workers, and Saint discourse tends to favor even smaller units, where interpersonal relations are close.

In almost any society, the dominant flow of persuasive political messages is down rather than up the stratification system. That is, on a per-capita basis the upper classes deliver vastly more persuasive messages to the lower classes than vice versa. Hence, regarding flows of messages crossing class lines, lower-class individuals receive far more messages than they send.

But people can and do resist indoctrination by the powerful by increasing the horizontal flow of communications among themselves. While such interchange of experiences and evaluations spontaneously occurs in any case—limiting the penetration of any dominant class ideology—it can be deliberately encouraged, as best described in Paulo Freire's *Pedagogy of the Oppressed* (Freire, 1970). Any participants of higher class origins are but catalysts to the interchange among the lower class of their experiences and interpretations of their everyday life world. The contemporary Latin American Roman Catholic "base communities" (*grupos del fundo*) typify the style of communication urged by the Saint.

In the Protestant world, similar egalitarian exchanges typify Quaker meetings. These occur in a common dwelling, normally array participants in a circle with no physically designable leader, and seek a sense of the meeting without any formal vote at all. This is reminiscent of the classical Buddhist monastic style, where all monks were equal and where unanimity was the ideal.

If liberal democracy includes an open competition of ideas followed by majority-vote resolutions, there is another style of democracy that avoids competitive quests for votes as suggesting and even encouraging division. What is wanted in this style of democracy is a meeting of the minds. This quest for consensus and even perfect unanimity may again require great patience. Unlike "adversary democracy" where the scent of victory would encourage the majority to force a vote to cut off minority voices, in this "nonadversary" or "unitary" mode one must value others enough to take the time to persuade them. Certain situations and certain kinds of people make this mode attractive (cf. Pennock, 1979; Mansbridge, 1980).

As observed with regard to Rousseau's conception of the general will, the belief that consensus is possible suggests again the Saint's belief in our common human nature. We are so much more alike than we are different that the same information and arguments would tend to bring us to agreement because of the similar way we would form valuations and judgments (cf. Canovan, 1983). One might argue that a face-to-face meeting style can indeed encourage the sense of common rather than conflicting interests, although it can also court the risk of a pseudoconsensus by intimidation (Mansbridge, 1980, 33; and Popkin, 1979).

The Saint usually rejects an elitist theory of knowledge, for the experience of each would have value in any deliberation. Indeed, the mass population may have in some ways a *superior* capacity to know, as learned through their own suffering; and such knowledge is not easily transferred to an elite. As the Leveller Richard Overton put it, the common people know where "the shoe pinches." This need not prevent the Saint from criticizing public opinion—for it may have been shaped by elites and, then too (it might be said), most people have not yet been awakened to thought. But at least as potentiality, Saints believe in a broad comparability in cognitive competence. They dismiss most assertions of innate class superiority and often denigrate pretensions of higher learning.[3] Praise of practical wisdom is extended to the nameless woodcutter in Thoreau's *Walden* and to the peasant appropriately named Platon in Tolstoy's *War and Peace*.

For the Saints of the West, there has normally been a rejection of the arrogant claims of university-trained figures to know what is right by a monopoly on interpretation of the Word, tradition, or philosophic right reason. Knowledge of God's will is to be found, the Saint says, through direct readings of vernacular scriptures without any hierarchy to impose an authoritative interpretation. Among Quakers, even Scripture must be interpreted through our shared and divinely endowed "inner light," recalling again that belief in the common conscience which seems to be basic to most variants of the Saint. Unlike many adherents of the Capitalist and Socialist formulas, the Saint still believes in the common good, known by a conjunction of conscience and information largely accessible through everyday life experience.

Rousseau did concede that the greater genius of the lawgiver may be needed to discover and propose the framework of the ideal regime, but the philosopher's knowledge is then transferable through institutional forms. Plato's "the Good," accessible to the ruler-guardian, is replaced by the general will as declared by the popular assembly, which is sovereign.[4] Ordinary people make any further adjustments of laws and policy. Rousseau tells us that long debates and dissensions would suggest that the general will is dead. When properly educated prior to the vote, citizens who find themselves in the minority would assume that they had been mistaken and that the majority position is correct. The principles of the general will are those of conscience, requiring the subordination of the particular to the general in two senses. First, the less inclusive interest is to be subordinated to the more inclusive one; and second, none are to exempt themselves from a rule of action that they would impose on others.

If the Saint would have people speak truth to power, only the truth would be spoken to and among the people as well. There is no place for a rhetoric of noble lies to encourage "true belief" in a mass population incapable of knowledge. Aside from Rousseau's concession regarding the lawgiver's design of the regime, the Saint believes that, in the things that matter, ordinary people have *at least* as much capacity as social elites to know.

Many Saints distrust coercive censorship that shields from criticism inegalitarian practices and supporting arguments. This censorship would normally be controlled by the powerful, not the weak and poor; and most Saints would recognize it as an admission that those who resort to it really lack good arguments. When the truth has its own force, there is no reason to add force to truth. However, as if illustrating George Orwell's warning that in any anarchist society a tyranny of public opinion could replace public force, some religious communitarians such as the ancient Essenes, the Mennonites, the Amish, and the later Jehovah's Witnesses have made extensive use of "shunning" to discourage heterodoxy among themselves. Rousseau would similarly banish from the state those refusing to embrace his minimal civil profession of religious faith, or even go beyond the Saint to administer capital punishment to any hypocrite in the matter (*Social Contract*, IV, viii).

### Reinforcing Arguments

In the usual case, no threats of force would bolster any of the Saints own persuasive messages aimed at egalitarian change. Abhorring the violence that protects great inequalities, the Saints usually spurn as well any use of violence to overthrow them. Unlike the Zealot sect that drew knives against the Romans and their collaborators, Christ's message was clear: "Put up thy sword," he said when arrested in Jerusalem. Later works extended the teaching of Christian nonviolence, as in Chalicky's *Drawnet of Faith* and Ballou's *Catechism of Christian Non-resistance*. Yet skeptics may argue that nonviolence is a dangerous self-limitation whenever murderous elites are in fact beyond persuasion and are yet convinced that they can dominate through main force.

Writing his *Discourse of Voluntary Servitude* as a young man, Etienne de la Boétie (d. 1563) analyzed tyranny as not really just an imposition by force that can only be overthrown by force. Even if a regime initially established itself through fear, it persists less by fear than by unthinking habituation, the distractions of bread and circuses, and ideological illusions.[5] While in his *Power/Knowledge* (1980) our contemporary Michel Foucault urged that despotism depends on intermediate ranks of specialists sharing in what is plundered from the people, de la Boétie first emphasized that despots ultimately depend on *popular* cooperation, which should be withdrawn.

Influenced by Thoreau, Tolstoy, and varied religious teachings, Gandhi perfected the theory and practice of civil disobedience. It is a unique form of political communication in its close union of message, delivery, and reinforcement. The very act of openly disobeying authority is part of the message of a moral condemnation, manifesting the Saint's abhorrence of any inconsistency in words and deeds. The public fact of such disobedience means that its message is delivered not only to the powerful, but also to the largest possible audience. Acceptance of a subsequent punishment such as jail then acts as a further witness to the moral wrong. Finally, when well orchestrated, the very disobedience may become its reinforcer, a strong dissuasive from the practice it condemns.

There are many kinds of nonviolent reinforcers for persuasive messages, including demonstrations that awaken moral sensibilities, strikes or economic boycotts, and various other kinds of disruptions of the routines of life (cf. Sharp, 1970; 1979). Such forms of action can often obtain the same objectives with less gore and without the Lenin-like command structures, class hatreds, and so forth, that make a poor climate for any viable democracy (Lakey, 1973). As Tolstoy commented in 1881: "Revolutionaries are specialists. They exercise a profession like any other, like the military profession. . . . It is a mistake to believe their profession nobler than any other" (Green, 1983, 188).

The strategy of nonviolence has often won gains for democracy. Notable successes include Gandhi's quest for India's self-government, Martin Luther King's gains in civil rights, Cory Aquino's restoration of democracy in the Philippines, and like emancipations of Poland, Hungary, Czechoslovakia, East Germany, and Bulgaria. For the defense of democracies, such thinking now seeks alternatives to the unacceptable risks of nuclear war (Sharp, 1985).

### Need Only Armed Prophets Succeed?

Yet, has nonviolence been oversold as a means of countering tyranny? The teaching of nonviolence supposes the paramountcy of human love; but perhaps compassion can after all conflict with justice, as the Aristocratic Confucius held: Enmity should be given justice, saving the reward of virtue for virtue.

In any case, it may often be the immoderation of militants that permits the gains attributed to the moderates. Activities of those committed to violent means may encourage the authorities to negotiate with the lesser evil: their gentler opponents. Without Bose or Jinnah threatening guns, would Gandhi have won? Without the Black Panthers and ghetto rioters, would King have succeeded? Aquino's victory in the Philippines involved not only the background threat of communist guerrillas but the foreground fact of major defections from the Filipino armed forces, although these allies were protected from counterattacks by a human shield of civilians armed only with flowers and songs. In Eastern Europe, too, the armed forces largely deserted regimes no longer able to count on Soviet interventions, although the division of armed elements in Romania and Albania brought violence. Perhaps unarmed prophets succeed best when they have well-armed allies, even when not acknowledged as such.

There may be other limiting conditions for successful nonviolence. It seems to suppose enough freedom of the press to publicize campaigns. (Note that the denial of press freedom from 1981 to 1989 delayed the victory of Poland's Solidarity.) It also requires at least some civilization in the adversaries, for Gandhian demonstrators would have been taken care of in short shrift before Hitler, Stalin, or modern Latin American death squads. What if, as Sigmund Freud argued, the conscience is not innate, but merely the residual "dread of the community" inculcated by parents? The record of recent history does not support the Saint's notion of an innate inhibition against harming others (Rapoport, 1989, 446).

While I think most conquests of popular government from determined adversaries have required some use or threat of force, the Saint is correct to urge that we should first explore any nonviolent alternatives. Especially when aided by outsiders who are not under threat of retaliation, nonviolent actions can often be enough. Imagine, for example, a world consumer boycott of nations that fail to give their peoples democratic freedoms.

### The Recruitment Strategy: The Status of Electoral Politics

Aside from often urging noncooperation with extreme tyrants, the Saints seem more attentive to persuasion of adversaries than to getting them out of office.[6] At least for the larger political system, getting friends into office is rarely feasible.

When living under hereditary monarchies, the Saints had even less opportunity than did the Aristocrats to affect the question of who rules. If they were themselves from the ruling strata, their turn to voluntary poverty and removal from the scene of palace intrigues would have cut them off from any projects to change the succession or the dynasty. In any event, they would not want any complicity in what could turn to violence, and they often had personal ties with people in high places, which precluded such projects.

In fact, one cause of the Saint's restraint in the face of autocratic government may be that often they themselves have kith and kin in high places. Many Saint figures had prominent protectors. St. Francis had his friend Ugolino, who was bishop, then cardinal, and eventually—after St. Francis's death—pope. Fox was sometimes released from jail because of his friendships with Oliver Cromwell and Esquire Marsh. Tolstoy's cousin Alexandra was a lady-in-waiting at the court of Nicholas II, from whom he hoped to elicit a grant of constitutional government. Gandhi was close to Mountbatten. His admirer Martin Luther King had fairly good relations with Democratic presidents Kennedy and Johnson. In default of such protection by notables, a modern functional equivalent may be close media attention, as enjoyed by Lech Walesa in Poland or Alan Boesak and Desmond Tutu in South Africa.

Like the Aristocrats, the Saints of the past often drew up portraits of exemplary rulers. But while the Aristocrats' ideal monarchs—such as the Confucian sage kings—would rule with firm correctness and hierarchy, those of the Saint would have a spirit of equality. Thus Lao Tzu: "World sovereignty can be committed to that man who loves all people as he loves himself." But the *Tao Te Ching* also says that the ideal ruler would pretty much leave the people alone: "Rule a large country as small fish are cooked" (Lao Tzu, 1955, 65, 113). Implicitly, too much poking would cause its disintegration. When the Saints envision the best monarchs, they would—like John Ruskin—imagine kings who gave more and took less than any actual monarchs; such kings would be both wise and gently good, perhaps familiar rather than distant (Ruskin, 1978, 5–6; see also Earland, 1971, 163, 318). Beyond hoping to persuade rulers to self-moderation through such portraits, the Saints could also hope to influence their selection of good counselors.

But usually Saints have democratic instincts. It is not surprising that both Buddha and Mahavira—implicitly sharp critics of the Brahmanic caste arrangements—emerged from relatively republican territories where any chiefs had very limited powers (Thapar, 1966, 52–53). The Essenes—the ascetic and communal Hebrew sect at the time of Christ—are described by Josephus as practicing democracy among themselves: "Men to supervise the community's affairs are elected by show of hands" (*Jewish War*, II, 125, ch. 7).

As for any larger government, Saints normally distrust Aristocratic notions that nonelective kings could really represent the people or that elective leaders could—by virtue of being legally responsible— freely represent others, as with Burkean "trustees." Closer to the Saint model than to any of the others, Rousseau said that any claims made of freely representing another are "fiction," saying the English are "free only during the election of members of parliament. As soon as they are elected, slavery overtakes it and they are nothing" (*Social Contract*, III, xv).[7] If his ideal of direct democracy was not to prevail, in his *Constitution for Poland* Rousseau proposed the theoretical alternative of instructing deputies, making them bound delegates. In fact, such close control as he envisioned was the late-eighteenth-century practice of many American colonies and then states. Other radical democrats of yesterday and today also want more surety of responsiveness to popular majorities, sometimes insisting that the only means to that goal is to have parliaments or other assemblies reflect the group attributes of society as a whole, as if a cross-section (cf. Pitkin, 1967).

As to who selects any elective leaders, Wollstonecraft, Gandhi, and King all worked to expand suffrage. Mary Wollstonecraft, like later suffragettes, sought voting and other rights for women. When in South Africa, Gandhi worked against substitution of a racial for a property qualification, which threatened to disfranchise many Indian voters. His acceptance then of steep property qualifications suggests that his campaign was motivated more by status concerns than any political aim (Green, 1983, 75). In India, Gandhi sought votes for the Harijan ("untouchables"), although he opposed putting them on a separate electoral roll for selecting who among them would occupy reserved seats.

Martin Luther King followed civil disobedience teachings to promote black voting in the South as well as other civil rights. César Chavez used the same tactics to secure fair union votes for U.S. field laborers. Lech Walesa followed civil disobedience in quest of full civil rights for Poles, culminating in Solidarity's defeat of communists in nearly all contested seats in 1989. Alan Boesak and Desmond Tutu in South Africa have also worked to secure votes for the excluded. In sum, whenever the Saints find themselves under popular governments and become involved with the question, they consistently favor enlarged voting rights, more equality in the key political action in the electing of leaders.

If the Saints have democratic souls, however, they are not always enthusiastic practitioners of democracy. Their frequent semi-anarchism could turn them away from electoral politics. Thoreau—alienated by the political parties' positions on slavery—sneered at the "cackling political conventions." Gandhi, who worked to enlarge suffrage, did not himself register or vote. The originators of the Catholic Workers such as Ammon Hennacy, Peter Maurin, and Dorothy Day did not vote in U.S. elections. Never quite convinced of the legitimacy of government at all, or if espousing popular government not trusting representation, the Saints could at most show contingent support for democracy, subordinating it to moral principles such as personal integrity and nonviolence. As the poet W. H. Auden said, let us give two cheers for democracy, saving three for love.

Precisely because they so austerely rule themselves, Saints can be notoriously hard on family and followers in their immediate circle, often becoming unelected despots over their entourage. The Saints put a high value on their autonomy, which is understood as requiring that they impose firm rules against their own passions. They cannot let themselves go, not at least in more vulgar enjoyments. They seem to imagine themselves as unconditioned self-conditioners, forgetting that rigid rule-following can itself be quite despotic. As George Ainslie has suggested, some people are so eager to avoid yielding to *impulse* that they soon become *compulsive* adherents to rules (Elster, 1983, 21).

Rousseau, whose theory of the general will shaped the Kantian categorical imperative, was very much like Kant in rigidity of rule-following. To be wholly consistent in thought, word, and deed, he had to follow a law that he gave to himself. An acquaintance of Rousseau's family reported that he would attach "the most solemn importance to the resolutions which he once adopted. However trifling their object, he always regarded them as covenants made with himself, which he ought no more to fail in performing, than if made with others. This seemed to me to have been regarded in his family as a prominent feature of his character" (Corancez, 1798, 34). Among the Quakers a similar teaching inspired a theory minimizing external, physical, and especially capital punishment in favor of that which is internalized, rehabilitative:

> Individual autonomy was synonymous with the establishment of internal discipline for the Quakers and was the project to which they increasingly devoted their time, especially once they renounced political action. Such internal discipline, necessary for the reception of Inner Light, could be achieved through prayer and silent meditation. (Dumm, 1985, 392)

Gandhi, who on one occasion thought it unseemly to permit majority rule to dictate that people take an oath—properly a moral commitment—held that "a man who deliberately and knowingly takes a pledge and breaks it forfeits his manhood" (Fischer, 1950, 75).

Those who so tyrannize over themselves often slip into tyranny over others. It is one thing when a loner such as Thoreau follows a different drummer, but it is quite another when a Saint would extend personal rules onto those of lesser clay in their entourage, especially when these would prefer otherwise.

Christ, it seems, simply commanded his disciples. And St. Francis, at least when in vigorous health, was unchallenged in making key decisions for his order, although when his health began to fail he shifted power to a minister general. Francis's last testament claims divine inspiration for its directive that after his death his followers were to give total obedience to any future minister general, as well as to the bishop and the pope. A biographer says of the founder of the Quakers: "Fox was a domineering man, direct in method, unyielding in his principles" (Wildes, 1965, 214). Another biographer reports of William Lloyd Garrison: "Garrison ill brooked opposition, came it from friends or foes. He was so confident in his own positions that he could not but distrust their opposites" (Grimke, 1891, 326). Although originally intending to hold an election eventually, John Ruskin simply assumed the title "Master" of his utopian communal experiment, St. George's Guild. Tolstoy, as the articulate Sonja has told us in detail, was a stern patriarch at Yasnaya Polyana.

We do not know whether the less articulate Kasturbai shared Gandhi's wish to practice total celibacy (*brahmacharya*) from 1906 until his death in 1948, but we do know that his sons found his ascetic style a bit too much. Understandably enough, they resented his effort to convert sons into disciples, and disciples into sons. If Gandhi—with some justification—claimed to be an "anarchist" and also a "born democrat," nothing like majority rule was ever practiced at his ashrams (cf. Fischer, 1950, 136, 329). And if St. Francis's followers called him "Mother," it is revealing that Gandhi's followers called him "Father," for Gandhi was paternalistic (or was it also maternalistic?) toward his followers. He remained the dominant guru even after 1925, when he ceased his presidencies of the All-India Home Rule League and the Indian Congress.

The Saints do not abuse their authority for personal economic advantage, since they live in the same simplicity as their family members or followers; but a Nietzschean will to *power* may be there nevertheless. Their quest for more autonomy can mean less autonomy for those around them. They might argue that it is not that they are seeking more power for themselves but that they want rather to elevate principle, and part of principle is to put more general interests above more particular ones.[8] But short of some indefinable threshold, a refusal to grant at least some preferential consideration for family and friends is not moral but monstrous. One must beware of becoming inhumane in reaching toward all humanity.

Yet, despite usually being authority figures, the Saints also usually avoid formal public officeholding. (Marcus Aurelius was pained in his role of emperor.) Also, it seems that the Saints are least likely of any adherents of the four great paradigms to be drawn to the idea of rule by experts. After all—especially when they themselves come from a higher class and turn to voluntary poverty—who could be more expert than themselves in how to moderate desires of the upper class?[9]

### The Structures Strategy: The Impulse of the Saint toward Decentralization

As described in Chapter 3, the structures game is control of policy by pulling decisional authority from units controlled by rivals, and locating it with those controlled by friends. Although the Saints may acquiesce in various forms of rule, they normally tend to make the most of any possibilities for urging devolution, decentralization, or shift of power to downsized units (cf. Sharp, 1980).

Leaving aside inconsistency in their own relations with followers, most Saints resist hierarchy almost as much as Aristocrats embrace it, whether in religious or political organizations. If Saints emerge in association with a well-established religious hierarchy, they can be expected to seek out or to create enclaves with considerable autonomy from that authority. Thus, religious communitarians sought de facto autonomy in primitivist retreats or in separatist religious colonies of coreligionists. St. Francis and St. Dominic founded their monastic orders within the hierarchically ordered church. Many later Saint figures, among them the Baptist Roger Williams as well as Quakers such as George Fox and William Penn preferred the razing of religious hierarchies, leaving full autonomy of local congregations.

As for secular authority, if most Aristocrats abhor the thought of anarchy, many Saints calmly contemplate the advantages of having no government at all. People then could voluntarily coordinate themselves in their household, village, or guild life. In the above-mentioned Taoist ideal of Lao Tzu, a good autocrat would rule the center such that it would seem like anarchism at the periphery. It is a commonplace that the Taoist philosophy of withdrawal had a sour grapes appeal for scholars blocked from power, but its larger appeal seems linked to periods of disorder.[10]

In the West, not all Saint figures aspired to democracy. Living when Alexander the Great eclipsed the polis in any case, Diogenes the Cynic would have been quite content to be left alone, living in his tub. But whenever Saints turn toward politics, they usually show an egalitarian bent.

Most seventeenth-century Levellers were more a left variant of Capitalist than Saint, for they did not stress asceticism and were mostly not pacifistic, with key leaders emerging from Cromwell's army. Yet their economic and political preferences were typical of the outlooks of artisans and smaller traders and were shared with Baptists and Quakers of the day. Beyond calling for religious freedom and votes for all men but servants and beggars, they wanted to pull power from Britain's king and lords, locate all valid central representative authority in a popularly controlled house of commons, yet keep much power at the level of local government or even as individual rights (Dow, 1985, 30–56).

In the nineteenth century, John Ruskin seems not to have expected central government to do very much, showing a typically localistic orientation of life as symbolized by his St. George's Guild. And Thoreau—although owning that he himself was not quite a "no-government man"—nonetheless pushed this hands-off mood further in his "Civil Disobedience" when he said, "That government is best which governs not at all."

In our century, Gandhi quipped that one of the more tolerable things about British rule of India was that the British governed very little, since he too believed "that government is best which governs least" (Fischer, 1950, 127). While Gandhi may have conceived of any central government as an elite of the few wise and good, for him real democracy would emphasize the decentralized village communities (*panchayati*) with their elective boards (McLaughlin, 1974, 63–65).

Leaning toward local autonomy, the Saints sometimes also tend to favor national self-determination of peoples. One of Tolstoy's complaints against the tsarist rule of Russia was its domination over the minority nationalities. In thinking of national government, most often the Saints believe that any larger government should be like the smaller in being maximally democratic, linked to the grass roots. Rousseau's *Constitution for Poland* imagines a pyramidal regime whereby local direct-democracy assemblies send strictly instructed deputies to the next higher level, with those sending like deputies upward to the national or all-Polish Diet.

Rousseau emphasized popular sovereignty more than any liberal individual rights apart from equality in voting and equality before the law, but this need not imply totalitarian centralism. He had a "positive" definition of freedom, emphasizing freedom *to* vote for all laws. He was so committed to popular sovereignty that, as long as it followed principles of the general will (e.g., no exclusion of particular citizens from the vote, no particularity in the content of law), it is conceivable that one could be free under such a system even if everything not legally mandatory were legally prohibited. But Rousseau saw the general will as self-limited by generality itself: "Under this system, each necessarily submits to the conditions he imposes on others" (*Social Contract*, II, iv). Thus, almost none of us would vote for a law requiring all to brush their teeth at exactly 6:45 A.M., or for a law abolishing all political subsystems.

But classical liberals (our Capitalist paradigm), rather, emphasized pluralism and individual rights relative to popular sovereignty. Those who wanted more "negative" freedom—that is, freedom *from* government—limited government not by mere formal generality but by substantive natural rights. Also, they favored institutional frictions that foster such freedom (cf. Berlin, 1969, esp. 118–72).

Both traditions recognize some equality of basic political rights for the citizenry, but the former view that accents popular sovereignty is more protective of majority rule, while the latter, which accents pluralism, is more solicitous of minority rights. Perhaps the two concepts are only really rivals when either is pressed too far, for within limits the one kind of freedom may be necessary for meaningful enjoyment of the other.

Strikingly unlike most Aristocratic and some Capitalistic theorists, the Saints give little or no attention to mixed-regime theory. Constitutional chicanery to give the appearance of democracy to protect inequality better would not impress them. In view of their predominant egalitarianism, however, it is quite unusual to find Saints who become critics of democracy itself.

## The Saint as Critic of Democracy

Whatever their failings regarding their immediate followings, most Saints have been democratic in inclination. Yet, as Rousseau understood, Saints can be unintentional enemies of democracy, as when their attitude of otherworldliness and pacifism effectively means acquiescence in despotism. It may even extend the sway of despotism, as when gentle Franciscan missionaries among the native Americans only furthered imperial penetration.[11]

Even when counseling resistance to despots, the Saint's insistence on nonviolence may often be ineffectual in implementing or protecting democracy. If raising a knife with the cry "*Sic semper tyrannis!*" may also fail, there are circumstances when principled nonviolence becomes the worst kind of masochism, especially if accompanied by Gandhian fasting. While pacifistic restraints on *means* may sound reasonable, this almost implies a self-limitation on *ends*, forcing effective abandonment of any egalitarian economic and political objectives that would require violence. To insist that political action be preceded by the moral regeneration of all actors can mean no action at all.

If they have ruled out recourse to force, and if they cannot launch an equally effective nonviolent struggle, then Saints must often compromise with inequalities. But there is no symmetry here. Although the Saints renounce violence in the effort to overthrow a set of inequalities, the rulers will not renounce violence in their preservation. Before eventually releasing him, the South African government insisted that Nelson Mandela renounce the use of violence against apartheid, without themselves renouncing the use of force to sustain it.

Far from themselves espousing violence, both Tolstoy and Gandhi practiced social peacemaking, becoming involved in peasant–landowner rent disputes or worker–owner pay disputes. The Capitalist with reference to landowners, or the Socialist with reference to the bourgeoisie, could complain that such a blunting of class conflict advantages the wealthy, doing a disservice to the laborers exploited by them. One eighteenth-century Japanese, Ando Shōeki, wrote a double-barrelled criticism of both the Aristocrat and the Saint: "The Way of the Sages functioned to make excuses for thieves. . . . [A]ll the sages, saints, and Buddhas down through the generations in Japan

. . . violated the Way of Heaven by robbing the common people" (Ooms, 1985, 296).

In politics, too, the Saint often compromises with political inequalities, even if trying to modify undemocratic forms of rule toward a more decentralized-democratic mode. But even acceptance of democracy is a compromise when some Saints would really prefer no government at all. They may imagine that the formula of moderating desires—especially those of the upper classes—could be so successful that coercive social control would be unnecessary. But aside from certain preliterate peoples, peaceful stateless societies remain an idle dream. Armed forces really governed at Kronstadt, in Makhno's Ukraine, and in the "anarchist" regions of Spain during that nation's civil war.

### Democracy Taken as an Instrumental Good

Like the Aristocrat, the Saint will often tend to regard democracy as a merely instrumental good to be abandoned should it impede the intrinsic good (i.e., the favored formula). The core of the Aristocrat's objection to democracy is that it allegedly inflates rather than moderates mass desires, and then gives those desires authority. But the core of the Saint's objection has to do with when democracy seems to pander to certain upper-class desires. In other words, the Aristocrat rejects democracy if it awakens demands that threaten the propertied few, whereas the Saint denounces democracy when it supports property's predation on the poor and weak. Thus, even should the Aristocrat and the Saint sometimes utter similar phrases in depreciation of democracy, they do not *mean* the same thing.

Quite unlike the many Aristocrats who sometimes endorsed even slavery or serfdom, the Saint believes democracy to be an instrumental good if it contributes to the awakening of a repressed human longing for freedom and equality. And this awakening should in turn compel the upper classes to restrain any greed to use public force in the maintenance of near-feudal conditions in the countryside, the practice of slavery, or even segregation.

Yet, once voting rights are broadly extended, democracies are better at protecting majorities from rich and powerful minorities than they are at protecting poor and weak minorities from majorities. If the Aristocrat becomes antidemocratic out of concern for the *privileged* minority, the Saint may become so out of concern for the *underprivileged* minority. Rousseau may have said that the general will is always right, but this applies only when each individual submits to the conditions imposed on others; it is a violation of political right to order any particular will in the political system. Such an injustice to only one person, Rousseau held, suspends even a republic's claim to citizens' obedience.

While Saints can often compromise with an undemocratic regime that supports socioeconomic inequalities, some Saints are uncompromising with a democratic regime that fails to remove unjust inequalities. Antislavery agitators Henry David Thoreau and William Lloyd Garrison are two cases in point.

In his essay "Life without Principle," Thoreau states, "Do we call this the land of the free? What is it to be free from King George and continue the slavery of King Prejudice? . . . What is the value of any political freedom, but as a means to moral freedom?" Note well his language: Political freedom has value "but as a means" to implement "moral freedom." This in part means removing the desire of the upper classes to maintain an immoral inequality. While regarding political freedoms as a merely instrumental good, Thoreau fails to consider that moral codes were also instrumental at their origins. Perhaps such a recognition would have blocked his unduly high expectations of democracy, permitting him to understand that sometimes even present right may be compromised for the sake of preserving a system where the many may judge what is "right" and all may contest its definition.

Thoreau's "Civil Disobedience" critiques public opinion, democratic practice, and even the Constitution for its tolerance of slavery. He denounces the war with Mexico, understood as initiated by the few to enlarge the South's slave territory by injustice to Mexicans. Even democratic government may only be a clumsy instrument for expediency. Should the majority, if only by indifference, support what is wrong by the higher standard of the individual conscience, it is not then enough to express an opposed conviction, or even to have cast a vote for the better candidates. If one goes on paying taxes that support the evil, then one becomes an accomplice in it. While lesser injustices may be a necessary part of the friction of government and may thus be tolerated, "if it is of such a nature that it requires you to be the agent of injustice to another, then, I say, break the law. Let your life be a counter friction to stop the machine." Thoreau makes clear that he would not wait to persuade the majority through mere words, for that could take too long, and "any man more right than his neighbors constitutes a majority of one already." Making the state put in jail its most just citizens would be the most rapid means of persuasion in any case. While Thoreau seems to judge democracy more severely than any other regime, he says, "The progress from an absolute to a limited monarchy, from a limited monarchy to a democracy, is a progress toward a true respect for the individual." He can imagine a yet higher stage of justice and respect for individual conscience, and does not seem to consider that the two could come into conflict.

The Saint can value democracy when it works *against* predation by the affluent but not when it rather *serves* such predation, as in helping slave owners. Thoreau's more radical essay "A Plea for Captain John Brown" praises a man about to be executed for choosing even with violence "to step between the oppressor and the oppressed." Not even Ethan Allen and his like showed so much courage: "They could bravely face their country's foes, but he had the courage to face his country herself when she was in the wrong." When the democratic majority is wrong, Thoreau sees himself "represented" only by an opposing moral minority, such as the vigilant committee that was operating within the Underground Railroad to frustrate the Fugitive Slave Law:

> The only government that I recognize—and it matters not how few are at the head of it, or how small its army—is that power that establishes justice in the land, never that which establishes injustice. What shall we think of a government to which all the truly brave and just men in the land are enemies, standing between it and those whom it oppresses?

The irony is that he denigrates the freedoms of those who do not *use* their freedoms on behalf of the morally right emancipation of others. He himself is unable to persuade either slave owners or those who would return fugitive slaves to them. As with the war with Mexico, inability to have the Fugitive Slave Law expunged is another failure to carry the American public—which, in Thoreau's eyes, reflects poorly on democracy itself.

Abolitionist William Lloyd Garrison's trajectory was similar. He even recommended disunion, splitting the United States into North and South to avoid his complicity with slavery: "Why not have the union dissolved in form as it is in fact, especially if the form gives ample protection to the slave system, by securing for it all the physical force of the North." The union, he said in 1853, was "but another name for the iron reign of the slave power" (Grimke, 1891, 308, 351). The Liberty party, Garrison thought, was wrong to claim that the Constitution was hostile to slavery. Garrison concluded in a Biblical phrase that it was, rather, a "covenant with death and agreement with hell." After repeal of the Missouri Compromise, he burned both the Fugitive Slave Law and the Constitution. Himself a religious perfectionist and pacifist, Garrison judged John Brown's act as "misguided, wild, and apparently insane, though disinterested and well-intended" (Grimke, 1891, 366). While initially inclined to let the seceding South depart in peace, he warmed to Lincoln when the president vanquished slavery—even if by the use of force, which Garrison himself could not practice. He found no inconsistency in favoring the just side when violent struggle engaged others. Like the Socialist, the Saint often does not evaluate violence in the cause of equality by the same measure as violence that instead protects inequality.

### Defense of Democracy

Thoreau and Garrison both despised a democracy that permitted unjust inequalities.[12] But even conceding that the American republic did permit slavery for nearly a century (and then let African-Americans be blocked from voting in the South for another century), they did not see that democratic regimes can at least offer more protection for such weak minorities than most nondemocratic regimes. Democracies often have largely autonomous subsystems where what is a minority in the system as a whole may be a local majority (even if one must as quickly grant that sometimes the subsystems can be more tyrannical than the larger system, as illustrated by both slavery and later segregation in the United States). In the larger whole, when some persecuted minority may be denied freedom of expression or a right to vote, others enjoying both may speak to the needs of the group, perhaps even urging that they be brought into the democratic process. The very democratic process itself will tempt some who already enjoy full rights to extend rights to expected coalition partners among the voteless. That has been at least as important as pressure from below in many expansions of political rights.

True, sometimes democratic majorities may oppress disadvantaged minorities (or even a politically weak majority, as was historically true of women). Yet, with the occasional exception of an ethnic minority looking to some outside protector, most disadvantaged minorities would prefer to take their chances with democracy rather than autocracy. As earlier noted, democracy at least minimizes the chances of official mass murders.

Regarding domestic security of life, democracy may also minimize dangers from environmental hazards, whether natural or humanly caused. In the former case, no democracy could conceal a great natural disaster, such as when Emperor Haile Selassie—trying to avoid embarrassment—blocked reportage of a major famine in Ethiopia, causing a catastrophic delay in bringing in outside aid.

Democracy also elicits loud protests against humanly caused hazards, such as unsafe workplaces and environmental pollution. As Daniel Moynihan once quipped, travelers can always tell if they are in a democracy by whether or not the newspapers print bad news. Much of the bad news repressed by nondemocratic regimes has concerned environmental hazards. Communist autocracies have cynically instructed their reporters to repress such information, as illustrated in sordid detail by the Polish Communist party's secret (but leaked) directives for press censorship (Curry, 1984). Enforced silence often feeds into scandal, as attested by recent revelations of the environmental disasters in the former communist states of Europe.

In short, the Saint understates the instrumental values of democracy, failing as well to emphasize adequately the intrinsic goods of the democratic way of life. In democracies it is usually safer (than in nondemocratic regimes) to speak truth to power, and doing so may eventually bring that power around toward justice and environmental sanity.

Turning to international security, if both Thoreau and Garrison faulted American democracy for its war with Mexico, democratic regimes at least prevent *some* wars. While Immanuel Kant and other liberals argued that "republican" regimes are less inclined to initiate any aggressive warfare, we can at most affirm this striking fact: "Even though liberal states have become involved in numerous wars with nonliberal states, constitutionally secure liberal states have yet to engage in war with one another" (Doyle, 1983, 213). That at least helps.

## Summary:
## Saintliness Not a Majority Pursuit

The teaching of the Saint shares some problems with that of the Aristocrat. For one thing, moderation of this-worldly wants seems easier when there is belief in some kind of afterlife, which becomes difficult wherever either religious skepticism or practical indifference becomes widespread.

Another problem is that, even if all persons were to moderate their wants, aggregate demand would still increase merely from growth of population. The slow increase of population in the past has been accelerated by improved nutrition, sanitation, and—belatedly—medical care. Both the Saint and the Aristocrat would quite characteristically recommend population limitation by moderation of desire, by sexual abstinence. Sometimes strong cultural controls have been effective in encouraging such renunciation of sexual gratifications. But in larger societies, it has not been enough, and the growth of the human population as a whole has vastly expanded aggregate demand. This may partly explain why modernity has shifted its attention to enlargement of powers as an alternative strategy against scarcity and conflict.

If human reconciliation seems an end worth seeking, does this require the extreme sacrifices demanded by the Saints? Perhaps they make too much of both ascetic renunciation and nonviolence as if ends in themselves. As for the first, invitations to rusticity do not impress majorities. Regarding the second, while life is an end, absolute nonviolence may not always minimize mayhem. The other paradigms concur that deterrence of aggression usually supposes a credible will to fight back. The main threat of the Saints to democracy was aptly identified by Rousseau: Caring less for democracy than for the other world with its call for kindness in this one, they cannot turn to violence to fight for it. But is that the only way to fight?

## Notes

1. This may not apply when mass apoliticism is counseled, as in Lao Tzu's recommendation of minimal publicity of governmental affairs: "The more the folk know what is going on / The harder it becomes to govern them" (Lao Tzu, 1955, 118).

2. The Socialists, too, denounce servility. But given the suggested femininity of many male Saint figures, one is not surprised to find Gandhi worried about whether authorities are "prostituting" the people (cf. Erikson, 1969, 219 ff.). I leave it to the Freudians to explain why Socialists, rather, seem inclined to speak of authorities who are "castrating" those they rule, as in Marxist denunciations of "eunuchs" surrounding the authorities.

3. This may extend to technical knowledge. Thus a founder of antiseptic surgery—Paracelsus—complained that the fixation of medicine on the old books of Galen and Avicenna blocked reading from the book of nature. He said that the wise physician would "consult old women, gypsies, magicians, wayfarers, and all manner of peasant folk and random people, and learn from them; for these have more knowledge about such things than all the high colleges" (in Jacobi, 1951, 131).

4. Rousseau understands himself as responding to the *philosophes* much as Plato had responded to the Sophists, but Rousseau also built his thought in large part as a populist corrective of Plato. The Rousseauean hierarchy of the sovereign general will above the corporate will of government above the will of the prince above the will of the individual subject seems meant to match the line metaphor of Plato's *Republic*, book 6. The levels describe degrees of removal regarding participation in the "luminous principle" of right.

5. "He has indeed nothing more than the power that you confer upon him to destroy you. Where has he acquired enough eyes to spy upon you, if you do not provide them yourselves? How can he have so many arms to beat you with, if he does not borrow them from you? The feet that trample down your cities, where does he get them if they are not your own? How does he have any power over you except through you? How would he dare assail you if he had no cooperation from you?" (Boétie, 1975, 51–52).

6. Often a Saint assumes that God handles dethronements of bad kings, as in Isaiah's image of an all-powerful God who takes delight in pulling down "haughty" human rulers or others who would "grind the poor" from wicked

cities: "He bringeth down them that dwell on high; the lofty city, he layeth it low; . . . even to the ground; he grindeth it even to the dust. The foot shall tread it down, even the feet of the poor, and the steps of the needy" (Isaiah 26:5–6).

7. Either extreme of tenure can raise problems. Short terms and rotation, such as Tito required of Yugoslav officeholders, may impede development of their autonomy and competence. The U.S. House of Representatives has a two-year term of office, but—in part due to massively financed mass media campaigns and other advantages of incumbency—98 percent of members seeking reelection are returned.

There are disturbing questions for democrats in the opposite extreme of long tenure such as "good behavior" (i.e., for life unless removed by impeachment and conviction) for members of the judiciaries, whatever the defense in terms of the claimed necessity for an independent judiciary (the original purpose being that the House of Commons wanted to render British judges less the creatures of the king).

8. The gospel of Mark depicts Christ as letting his mother and brothers wait, saying that his real "family" was his following. A possibly testy relationship was also suggested when Christ says that a prophet may be regarded without honor "among his own kin, and in his own house." Further, he praises those who would subordinate ties of kinship to follow him (Mark 3:32–35, 6:4, 10: 29–30).

9. Not only the Saint but also the Socialist may attain charisma by heroic self-denial (Mazlish, 1976). But perhaps the key is merely being different from ordinary mortals, since other leaders sometimes astound an unsophisticated following by heroic self-indulgence, as in sexual athleticism or opulent living.

10. "Opposing Confucianism, it [Taoism] stood something like a party out of power with respect to the party in power. In times of great prosperity and peace, or in times verging on decline but not yet fallen into disorder, Confucianism always waxed strong and Taoism waned. But when social order disintegrated and the people suffered hardship, ideas of inaction and anarchism rose to prominence in response to such conditions." Taoism "was the enduring source of protest in times of national degeneration and harsh government" (Hsiao, 1979, 22, 60).

11. Thus one historian of American Roman Catholic experience notes that the Spanish conquest of the New World favored a policy called "reduction," which stopped nomadism among the natives by using missions to concentrate and "civilize" them (Dolan, 1985, 25).

12. Gandhi, too, believed that one could neither attain a democracy that would surpass the inadequate level of yet-exploitative liberal democracy nor attain nonviolence "so long as the wide gulf between the rich and the hungry millions persists" (Pantham, 1986, 327, see also 328).

# 6

## The Capitalist's Problematic

*or Social Conflict as a Problem of Enlarging*
*Productive Powers with Private Property, Division of*
*Labor, Income Differentials, and Markets*

> The natural effort of every individual to better
> his own condition, when suffered to exert itself
> with freedom and security, is so powerful a
> principle, that it is alone, and without any assis-
> tance, not only capable of carrying on the
> society to wealth and prosperity, but of sur-
> mounting a hundred impertinent obstructions
> with which the folly of human laws too often
> encumbers its operations.
>
> Adam Smith,
> *The Wealth of Nations*

Both primarily modern paradigms—those of the Capitalist and the Socialist—urge application of science and technology to conquer nature and thereby transcend scarcity. They both envision great advances in the productivity of labor, for labor was regarded as the paramount source of value by the early Capitalist as well as the Socialist. As John Locke put it, "if we will rightly estimate things as they come to our use and cast up the several expenses about them, what in them is purely owing to nature, and what to labour, we shall find that in most of them ninety-nine hundredths are wholly to be put on the account of labour" (*Second Treatise of Civil Government*, V, 40, cf. also V, 43).

But Adam Smith's remark above suggests one difference: Only the Capitalist formula holds it commendable for the individual "to better his own condition," even striving to become rich. Beyond new technologies, the Capitalist expects extra production gains by shifting from traditional sociocentric motives to the energizing incentive of self-interest. The main idea is *harnessing* rather than *repressing* self-interest, at least in its economic mode (Hirschman, 1977, 16; also, Vaughan, 1982).

Such harnessing is done through alienable private property in means of production, extensive division of labor, unequal rewards for unequal performance, and free-market mechanisms to coordinate exchange. This system is so familiar that we must strive to regard it as strange, for only detached comparisons with rival paradigms of social thought can permit critical analysis.

While I eventually address practical difficulties such as evasion of market risks, economic problems that cannot be simultaneously solved, and continued social conflict, I will first consider what sorts of people developed the paradigm and then explore the core assumptions of classical liberalism that even now undergird capitalist economics.

## Commitment to the Capitalist Formula: Why Expansion of Private Production?

Some aspects of the Capitalist formula are visible even among premodern urban merchants and professionals, as among ancient Hebrew Pharisees or Greek Sophists. But I will emphasize the more robust developments of modern history.

I broadly define the Capitalist paradigm to include all variants of the "liberal tradition" of political thought. Etymologically linked to the Latin root *liber* (free), liberalism championed individual freedom of choice. Adam Smith defended what he called the "system of liberty" before the term "capitalism" came into common use (Berger, 1986, 18). As Harold Laski put it, "The movement from feudalism to capitalism is a movement from a world in which individual well-being is regarded as the outcome of action socially controlled to one in which social well-being is regarded as the outcome of action individually controlled" (Laski, 1936, 21).

### The Middling Classes

This individualism was primarily an urban product. Both the Aristocrat and the Saint typically distrust the city, unlike adherents of the Capitalist paradigm. As an old German maxim maintained, "City air makes one free." A runaway serf became literally free after a year's stay in a "free city"—a trading center that had either bought or fought its way to autonomy from surrounding feudal institutions.

Associated with the entrepreneurial bustle of business life, modern adherents of the Capitalist formula soon displayed the optimism typical of groups that sense themselves rising in the status quo. Against the more typical pessimism of both the Aristocrat and the Saint, they believed that the real and the desirable were destined to converge. At least until recent doubts, they increasingly tended to put their utopias in the future rather than in some past golden age. The idea of progress not only supposed cumulative gains in science, technology, and mastery of nature but the accelerations of a new economic order and the exploration and settlement of the New World (cf. Bury, 1924; Ophuls, 1977).

Earliest Capitalist theorists spoke primarily for the interests of those associated with more extensive and freer trade—especially propertied mercantile or professional urban dwellers, the burghers or bourgeoisie. James Mill called them "the middling classes." His use of the plural suggests that they did not initially regard themselves as a single class, perhaps because of the great diversity in both sources and levels of their livelihoods. But the appeal was less to the petty bourgeois shopkeepers or artisans than to somewhat greater bour-geois—those associated with major trade transactions. Often involving cultural outsiders debarred from the land, mercantile interests had prospered earlier in other great trading cities. These often arose on intersecting routes of travel linking contrasting civilizations, as illus-trated by cities of Renaissance Italy or the Reformation Rhineland. But mercantile interests were to especially flourish in seventeenth-century Amsterdam and London—the cities that gave us bigger ships able to carry bigger guns, the great Indies or India trading compa-nies, and liberalism's first great philosophers, Baruch (or Benedict) Spinoza (d. 1677) and John Locke (d. 1704).

Most leading theorists of classical liberalism were personally in-volved in commercial life.

Born into the trading community of Amsterdam Jewry, son of an owner of a prospering import-export house, Spinoza worked in it from about age 13 to its sale when he was 24. Yet he personally disdained commercial money-making. As much for his frictions with some great trading company merchants as for his denial that the Jews were a chosen people, he was excommunicated from the synagogue as a heretic. He took up his lifelong artisan's trade of lens-grinder when he entered a more Saint-like phase of association with the Mennonites, which lasted until he was about 30. Then repudiating Mennonite political withdrawal, Spinoza became an active secularist republican, until disillusioned when in 1672 Calvinist religious zealots panicked by military invasion viciously murdered the republican leaders (Feuer, 1958, esp. 17–18, 40–47).

John Locke was patronized by the Earl of Shaftesbury (Lord Ashley), who led Whig forces favoring market agriculture, opposing royal monopolies, denouncing lack of competition in London banking, and supporting free trade. When Shaftesbury became president of the Council of Trade, Locke in 1673–74 was its secretary. Locke also served with the Board of Plantations and held investments with trading companies, some of which dealt in African slaves.

Similarly, the pioneering capitalist economist William Petty (d. 1687) was actively linked with trade matters and improved productivity, for "Labour is the Father and active principle of Wealth, as Lands are the Mother." Against the waste of productive labor potential in overuse of capital punishment and idle imprisonment, he favored punishments as "pecuniary mulcts, which will encrease labour and publick wealth" ("Treatise on Taxes and Contributions," X, x). Scotsman Adam Smith (d. 1790) was a close student of trade and industry and eventually served as customs inspector in Edinburgh. His *Wealth of Nations* (1776) was condemned as false economic philosophy by the Roman Catholic Inquisition. Like Spinoza in his Portuguese-Dutch Jewish ancestry, the economist David Ricardo (d. 1823) was the third generation of his family to prosper in financial investments, and he specialized at the London Stock Exchange in brokerage of government bonds. Utilitarian Jeremy Bentham (d. 1832) was also an active business investor, for a time holding shares in Robert Owen's reform mill at New Lanarck; he also hoped to get rich by privately warehousing either public prisoners or paupers in his building designed for easy monitoring of inmates, Panopticon. Bentham's close companions James Mill (d. 1836) and John Stuart Mill (d. 1873) were examiners with the East India Company, handling correspondence about varied trade matters.

Thus it would only impede understanding to deny that classical liberalism was "the philosophy of a business civilization" (Laski, 1936). Indeed, many of liberalism's political concepts were transparently transfers from business practice and business law ("contract," "agent" or "fiduciary," "accountability," etc.). Bentham's absurd "calculus of felicity" betrays an obvious parallel of pleasures and pains with credits and debits. He conceded that the former had to be given monetary expression to permit a science of ethics (Sahlins, 1976).

Commercial capital was central, and the great joint-stock trading companies emerged at the outset of the seventeenth century. Yet the putting of capital at risk for future gain also concerned market-oriented agriculture before it began to transform manufacturing to exploit new technologies in the late-eighteenth-century industrial revolution.

While the French nobles were debarred by royal proclamations in 1561 and 1583 (until 1701) from most forms of commerce and industry on penalty of losing noble status, British landowners had no such restriction. Further, a century and a half of inflation had by the mid-seventeenth century so eroded their cash incomes from tenants that many landowners had turned to enclosures and improvements as well as trade as means to sustain their incomes (Jacobs, 1989; Goldstone, 1986). Influenced by Francis Bacon's scientific method and William Petty's economic speculations, John Locke reflected this rise of agrarian capitalism among some landowner groups. Personally interested in horticulture, watchful for the most productive apple trees, Locke was committed to scientific agricultural investment as a spur to higher production for larger markets. Also supportive of manufacturing, Locke favored a more decentralized and competitive credit system, and was critical of London bankers for charging oligopoly interest rates (Wood, 1984).[1]

Every generalization is overgeneralized in the eyes of historians. Their often localized studies describe complex alignments during the English Civil War of the 1640s, including a not surprising tendency of people of all classes to drift with the dominant leaning of their local county, whether what came to be called Tory (for the King) or Whig (pro-Parliament). In passing, the word "Tory" was originally an anti-Catholic epithet; it derived from a Gaelic term for fugitives, applied to Roman Catholic bog-trotter bandits in Ireland. Also originally an epithet but then adopted with pride, the term "Whig" probably derived from whigg, a whiskey-flavored whey drink of Scot Presbyterian farmers (Drucker, 1974, 108). The Whigs—eventually renamed "liberals" in what was orginally meant as another slur—sought a political alliance of a few progressive nobles and many gentry, independent merchants and professionals, and even lower-middle-class supporters. They understood themselves as opposing any Stuart threat of restored Roman Catholicism and royal absolutism, believing the two went together, as in Shaftesbury's quip that "popery and slavery, like two sisters, go hand-in-hand" (Wood, 1984; Ashcraft, 1986, esp. 228–85). The coalition of agrarian progressives and urban mercantile forces first successfully opposed King Charles I and the higher nobility in the English Civil War, then much later recombined with heightened anti-Catholic fervor to oust the restored Stuarts during events leading up to the Glorious Revolution of 1688–89.

Aside from a few republicans such as Algernon Sidney (executed for treason in 1683), most British Whigs or liberals were constitutional monarchists. But Whig and later neo-Whig theories characteristically favored parliamentary power more than that of the king. Their economics as well as politics deeply resonated among American founders such as Washington, Madison, and Jefferson, who were also much interested in improved productivity of their land and securing better world market prices for tobacco, and so forth.

Those thoroughly committed to the Capitalist paradigm with its individualistic competition express it not only in their economics but also in their politics and religion. Locke neither said it first nor last, but in his time his *Two Treatises* said it best. Beyond Britain, the later French Enlightenment parallels included the liberal side of Montesquieu but especially leading *philosophes* such as Voltaire, Diderot, Grimm, d'Alembert, and Helvétius.

In the eighteenth and early nineteenth centuries, the Capitalist economic model was elaborated in the great names of capitalist "political economy"—especially Adam Smith and David Ricardo. Ricardo's antiprotectionist (opposed to the Corn Laws) economics were largely espoused by utilitarians Jeremy Bentham, James Mill, John Stuart Mill, and John Austin. Much the same basic economic theory was expressed by the social Darwinists, dominated by Herbert Spencer and William Graham Sumner. In the twentieth century, the uncompromised Capitalist credo has continued in neoclassical schools of economics, as championed by Ludwig Von Mises and Friedrich Hayek (both of the Austrian school) as well as Milton Friedman and his student Robert Lucas (monetarist theory, rational expectations theory). Confidence in the free market is pushed to a new extreme by libertarians such as the economist Murray Rothbard.

But the liberal tradition has two great wings—one leaning right and the other more leftward, the first more defensive of business demands and the second more critical. The libertarians, the mainstream "conservatives" of liberal origin, the religious fundamentalist "social conservatives," and the disillusioned academic liberals called "neoconservatives" are all variants of the rightward side of the Capitalist model.

The second main wing of the Capitalist paradigm contains the more progressive variants. Anticipated in the seventeenth-century Levellers, whose political aspirations were opposed by Oliver Cromwell, it seemed more sympathetic to either farmers or shopkeepers. In the earlier agrarian mode of progressive liberalism, plantation owners Thomas Jefferson and John Taylor were vigorous advocates for yeoman farmers and homestead policies. More aligned with urban artisans, Thomas Paine advocated a variety of policy measures to favor them, notwithstanding his expressed belief in minimal government.

Reform liberalism has evolved to defend progressive taxation and social program expenditures, often with John Maynard Keynes's emphasis on induced demand to curb troughs in the business cycle.

Making somewhat less of freedom and more of social justice in its rhetoric, this wing has been more critical of big business and more sympathetic to those of modest income. After the onset of industrialization, the later progressive variants of the Capitalist outlook sought coalitions with the then rising labor unions and increasingly tended to favor more "positive" or active government, in part as a "counterweight" to big business. This was expressed in the United States by populism, progressivism, the New Deal, and later heirs to such reform traditions. Only the accident of Franklin Delano Roosevelt's monopolization of the "liberal" label (which Herbert Hoover as well as Friedrich Hayek viewed as a usurpation) has caused Americans in everyday politics to confine that term to center-to-left variants of the liberal tradition in its larger sense (Rotunda, 1968). Those nearest the midpoint of the left–right continuum, especially the current "neo-liberals," now combine the idea of counterweight with the concept of "government–business partnerships," as if blocking and boosting business were wholly compatible. At the other, leftward edge of reform liberalism, the laborite (e.g., Canada's New Democrats) and social democratic (e.g., West Germany's SPD) parties that have abandoned advocacy of social ownership also largely belong here, whatever any lingering influence of the Socialist alternative.

### Continuity and Change in Rhetorics of Liberalism

As noted early in the chapter, the term "liberalism" is linked to liberty. Freedom in part meant a drive toward national autonomy (part of Protestant animosity against papal authority from Rome) as a companion to national unification. Within a nation the kind of liberty originally sought was usually that of individuals against government, at least if government went beyond its properly limited sphere of protecting rights of life and property. The Lockean liberal wanted no invasion of natural rights, whether by improper exercise of unlimited government, by private persons, or by foreign enemies. To Herbert Spencer as well as Friedrich Hayek, the state becomes the "enemy" when it acts through other than general laws, as when robbing Peter to pay Paul.

As evident in Hayek (who regards himself as the authentic classical liberal), the rightist wing of liberalism has especially tended to understand "freedom" negatively. It finds freedom less in the presence of participatory rights than in the absence of coercive governmental constraint. As Hobbes put it, freedom is located in the silence of the laws. This definition holds that, beyond the minimal threshold of governance needed for security of life and property, bigger government entails smaller freedom (Hayek, 1972). This is so even if the government were attempting to regulate corporations or other private entities that constrain human choice by other than coercive means.

Aside from continuity of the negative understanding of liberty or freedom, the substantive core of the Capitalist paradigm is often obscured because of its changing justificatory languages (cf. Cook, 1980). Since the sixteenth century, liberal economics and politics has been defended by a rough succession of dominant rhetorics:

1. dissident Protestant invocations of Scripture, especially in the Zwinglian and Calvinist currents of Reformed, Presbyterian, and Congregational churches;
2. the civic humanist tradition that dreamed of the ancient Roman republic;
3. natural rights/social contract;
4. utilitarianism;
5. social Darwinism; and
6. the presently ascendant instrumental rationality or scientific selection of means, working such rubrics as productivity, efficiency, and cost–benefit analysis.

Arguably, a rhetoric tends to be abandoned by leading liberal theorists—especially those toward the right—once it has been taken up on behalf of the lower classes or other excluded groups such as women. Nevertheless, there was considerable continuity in substantive goals of economic policy as well as in procedural preferences for certain political forms.

Beyond changing rhetorics, another problem in seeing the unity of the Capitalist paradigm is that it shifts its main adversary from the Aristocrat to the Socialist.

Largely ignoring the apparently unthreatening Saints, the Capitalists first took aim against the Aristocratic paradigm. In that phase, running up to about the mid-nineteenth century, they often opposed the royal family, accepting royalty only when and where they could find a dynasty or individual heir who seemed more amenable to their aims (the British replace the Stuarts with the House of Orange; Japanese reformers secure the Meiji Restoration). More consistently, they set themselves against the aristocracy and the associated higher clergy, at least in Western Europe. This was vividly clear in the polemics of Tom Paine, a corset maker's son who dreamed of enriching himself through his invention of a steel bridge. In France, Destutt de Tracy established a science of ideas called *idéalogie* to expose the self-interested prejudices of nobles and Catholic hierarchs. In his *Handbook of Political Fallacies*, Bentham's "sinister interests" included idle aristocracy, military officers, Anglican bishops, and the lawyers who served them. Bentham's friend James Mill, the son of a small-owner farmer and cobbler, identifies "the powerful classes" and "the clergy" as being most resistant to accepting "evidence" inconsistent with their self-interested "affections" (Mill, 1971, 22).

By the later nineteenth century, the paradigm retargets against Socialists, especially in the Marxist variant. This modifies some aspects of the teaching. The early Capitalists routinely said that government arose to protect property and its unequal holdings—a message that is muted once the Socialists concurred but held it undesirable (Parenti, 1988, 5). Or again, thinking of great landowners, early liberals often urged that *excessive* inequalities of wealth and income endanger popular government. But that message of James Harrington, Thomas Jefferson, John Taylor, and Tom Paine almost vanishes in at least the more rightist side of the Capitalist view. The right also ignores Alexis de Tocqueville's worries about great industrial fortunes and accent rather his warnings about tensions between democratic egalitarianism and liberty.

While one could dwell on substantive or rhetorical variations in liberal theories, I am defining our primary paradigms by core commitments shared by many, looking for what is common to the Capitalist variants. If anything, I accent those who are most enthusiastically committed to capitalist economics in order to sharpen contrasts with the other paradigms. Anticipating discussions, I have identified ten core propositions of classical liberalism that define the basics of the paradigm, as shown in Figure 6.1. The first five do double duty in that they are central to the political as well as the economic theory of classical liberalism. But the last five primarily give form to Capitalist economics, even now generating many right economists' statements about the world.

## The Economy of the Capitalist:
## The Market Knows Best

The theory demands that we allow self-owned persons to pursue their own self-interested wants to make voluntary exchanges of equivalents. It is claimed that this will maximize human productive powers, conquer scarcity, pacify our existence, and bring us happiness. As has been said of some capitalist ads, if that sounds too good to be true it probably is. In practice the Capitalist paradigm often fails to deliver consistently, especially as we move down the list of premises.

Now that many communist nations are moving toward market economics, we must beware of accepting a false dichotomy: If Socialist economics is false, then Capitalist economics is true. The fallacy is a dual one. First, it forgets other alternatives, including the very distinc-

**Figure 6.1   The Core Premises of Classical Liberalism**

1. All persons wholly own their bodies, and by derivation they also have a claim on the value of their capacity to labor. Neither any other particular human being nor any collectivity has any claims on the powers of adults without their consent.

2. All persons are more self-interested than sociocentric, and they know best their own minds. Mature, mentally competent individuals are the supreme judges of what they want, including anything sought through exchange with others.

3. All exchange transactions not dominated by force or fraud are "voluntary." At least where there is no coercively maintained monopoly (i.e., where there is free commercial competition), any economic constraints do not detract from such voluntariness.

4. All such voluntary exchange transactions tend to be exchanges of equivalents. That is, they are symmetrical or balanced in the giving and the getting.

5. All symmetrical exchange transactions are Pareto optimal for participants involved in them. Most willingly make exchanges that make them better off, but almost none willingly make choices that make them worse off.

6. All Pareto-optimal exchanges will also tend to be productively efficient, both from the standpoint of the parties to the exchange and from the vantage of any third parties (or the public at large).

7. All productively efficient arrangements engender economic growth.

8. All growth tends of its own accord toward eventual equity—that is, toward flattening of income inequalities and advancement of equal opportunity to the extent feasible without invasion of the afore-mentioned liberties.

9. All such progress toward growth-with-equity engenders social happiness.

10. All happy peoples will tend to enjoy domestic peace, or absence of any severe social conflicts that could lead to the predatory behaviors of crime, civil strife, or externalized aggression.

tive economics of the Aristocrat and of the Saint. Second, it fails to consider not only that Socialist economics may be at least partly right, but also that Capitalist economics may even be largely wrong, especially as delineated by its more extreme theoreticians.

In approaching the practical problems it must address, I will apply to this formula the same analytical categories applied to the other paradigms, looking for typical positions regarding property in means of production, division of labor, and distribution of the economic product.

### The Forces of Production: Alienable Property, Competition and Contract

The essence of liberal economics as well as politics is to free things and persons from traditional bonds, expose them to an arena of competition, and then recombine them only through voluntary consentings or formalized contracts, which add enforcement to the reluctant reciprocity of this vision.

While sharing the Aristocrat's strong endorsement of private property and unequal holdings of it, the Capitalist paradigm endorses distinctive kinds of property claims in our bodies, in the labor of our hands, and even in the labor of our brains.

The individualistic idea of self-ownership is the bedrock assumption of classical liberalism, whether of its relatively leftist or rightist wings. This proposition was forthrightly stated in seventeenth-century Britain by both the Levellers and Locke. Thus the Leveller Richard Overton in 1647: "Every individuall in nature, is given an individual propriety by nature, not to be invaded or usurped by any" (in Wolfe, 1967, 162). Or Locke a generation later: "Every man has a property in his own person; this nobody has any right to but himself" (*Second Treatise*, V, 27).

The current libertarian variant of rightist liberalism shares the Leveller view of self-ownership as implying that persons cannot be exposed to the risks of military combat without their consent. But libertarians make an absolute of property in one's body, extending to a full right to sell one's services as a prostitute, sell oneself into slavery, sell off one's transplantable body parts, or even commit suicide if one so pleases (cf. Nozick, 1974). This departs from classical liberalism, which understood the right of self-ownership as being given to us by God to promote our self-preservation and well-being. Both the Levellers and Locke opposed suicide on the ground that we belong *also* to God (cf. Wolfe, 1967, 125, 177; Locke, *Second Treatise*, IV, 23; and Locke, 1965, 173).

With reference to God, then, our bodies are co-owned. But to concede that other *persons* can also share ownership in bodies would defeat the liberal aim of opposing serfdom and slavery as defended by many past Aristocrats. Vestiges of slavery continued into our century in the Middle East, and feudalism continued in parts of Ethiopia until the overthrow of Haile Selassie in 1974. Nor could the Capitalist concede any sense of co-ownership by the community or collective, as recognized by the Saint or Socialist. God's claim aside, the liberal may set up what some would regard as a false dichotomy: *Either* one wholly owns one's body *or* one wholly belongs to some other person or group (contrast Plato, Letter IX, 358a–b).

If we owned (with God) our bodies, the early liberals maintained, then we also owned the labor of our hands. But this proposition did not lead them to the Saint or Socialist critique of the alienation of labor, since Capitalist liberty includes a right to sell or rather lease one's labor power to another by the hour, day, week, month, or year.

Finally, at least one wing of early liberalism also assumed that we have a right to make property claims on the products of our brains. Unlike the wary Aristocrat or Saint, the Capitalist welcomes the endless innovation of new technology to raise the productivity of labor in both fields and workshops. One argument holds that, after Britain's first patent act of 1624, strong rights in "intellectual property" (patents, royalties, copyrights) constituted a decisive factor in explaining why capitalism took root first in Britain and Holland rather than elsewhere (North and Thomas, 1973; North, 1981). If this argument is plausible, the irony of it is that a type of monopoly or market corner gave rise to the competitive Capitalist economy. The Levellers, however, denounced the issuance of patents on inventions, recognizing that Charles I abused them to raise revenue by issuing royal monopolies even on products such as soap, which nearly everyone then knew how to make out of lard and lye.

The Aristocrat in feudal contexts could assume that ownership of land gave virtual ownership of its attached serf laborers, with Russian landowners even in the nineteenth century speaking all in one breath of their ownership of so many versts of land with so many "souls" on that land. A Capitalist such as Locke turns this assumption around: Ownership of labor gives first proper title to the ownership of land worked by that labor. However acquired, land as well as labor shall be freely exchangeable on markets, ending entailments, primogeniture, and other feudal restrictions on transfers of acreage and natural resources.

Money capital must also be subject to easy transfer among persons. The market in capital had been hindered by medieval usury laws that permitted Jewish lending (usually for military exigencies or luxury consumptions) but blocked Roman Catholic Christians from anything but charitable lending without interest. The Capitalist needed high returns on capital for the high risks of productive investment. Although nowadays the productive aim is often ignored in generalizing it to all appreciated investment, this element of risk remains a standard argument for lower tax rates on capital gains.

So far, we have labor, land, and capital subject to sale in the free market. To use the later language that Marx would apply to capitalism, early Capitalist theorists saw feudal relations of production as "fetters" holding back their mighty steed. New forces of production needed new economic forms for maximal development. Liberalism wanted to make way for *choice*. It was imperative to unlock all productive resources for more efficient recombination through voluntary contracts among mutually self-interested parties who know best what they want.

### Competition and Contract

Entrepreneurs need room for maneuver, which is impossible if state-enforced rules and regulations block flexible recombination of resources for more efficient production. The Capitalist understands the self-regulating market as a victory against the state—an assertion of the autonomy of the economic sphere from feudal encumbrances or mercantilist regulation (which misunderstood wealth as national accumulation of precious metals rather than in more production of consumable commodities). The quest for the relative detachment of polity and economy was radically new. As Karl Polanyi puts it, "A self-regulating market demands nothing less than the institutional separation of society into an economic and political sphere" (Polanyi, 1957, 71). Beyond freeing those spheres from domination by each other, liberalism sought added autonomies of their subsystems, culminating with abstract individuals (etymologically "not divisible"). What has been thus torn asunder within each realm may be reconstituted through contracts or, later, new consentings.

Yet, self-interested market behavior had historically been either marginal or subordinated to social purposes. All past markets had been thus regulated, and the new notion of a purely self-regulating market was to prove utopian, engendering forces to check its scope (Polanyi, 1957).

Actually, it takes much regulation to make a "self-regulating" market. While the Capitalist could conceive of markets—no less than property—as spontaneous occurrences of nature, real-world markets normally suppose the artifice of state-enforced norms. At least a few restrictions were obviously needed from the start.

### No Force, No Fraud in Contractual Exchange

Beyond removing feudal encumbrances on exchange, the new system at least needed rules against distortions of market transactions by fraud or force.

As for fraud, market activity involves considerable mild deception acceptable under the maxim "Let the buyer beware" (*caveat emptor*), which only became prominent under capitalism; earlier, the guilds themselves policed their product quality. But a Capitalist economy could not exist with Plato's anticommercial recommendation that all who make contracts should largely do so only at their own risk

(*Republic*, 556b, cf. also 425d–e and 426e). To retain *some* predictability before hazarding what is unpredictable in markets, Capitalists needed to have nonfraudulent contracts enforced, sometimes even abroad.

But a contract between private parties is also invalid if one party used or threatened force against the other to set its terms. Also, early liberals regarded royal monopolies as another such forceful interference with a free market, just as contemporary liberal advocates of "privatization" view any public competition with private enterprise as unfair competition because it involves taxpayer-subsidized space, capital, and so forth.[2]

To plan ahead at all, the business contract becomes indispensable in all arrangements of the means of production (for borrowing capital, for renting land, for securing delivery of raw materials, for hiring labor, for marketing or other contracted services, etc.). Within liberal horizons, any contractual arrangement that is neither fraudulent nor forced is necessarily free, since at least adults of sound mind form their own wants and know what they want.[3]

Distortions of force or fraud would disturb the Capitalist view of free-market transactions as voluntary exchanges of equivalents. But while either fear or misinformation could cause an involuntary and unequal exchange, economic duress need not, since to admit otherwise would raise troublesome questions about the capital–labor relationship.[4]

### Market Exchange as Efficient

With characteristic refusal to concede that structural distributions of economic resources severely constrain real-world choices, often leading to unequal exchanges out of economic duress, the Capitalist assumes that free-market choices allocate land, labor, and capital not only voluntarily, but also fairly and efficiently.

The "fairness" arises from the idea that exchange must involve equivalents if any exchange is to occur at all.

Economists use two concepts of "efficiency" that must be distinguished. The first of these—*Pareto-optimal consumptive efficiency*—is defined as making any transaction where some (at least one) are better off and none are worse off. Now if there were no force or fraud in a market transaction, liberals hold, no rational person would give more value than they got in exchange. Equilibria arise in markets either where the asking and the offer do not converge (no exchange occurs because at least one party expects to be made worse off) or where sellers and buyers both find their advantage in an exchange (the market clears). Since market transactions thus require unanimity, they would normally be Pareto efficient, at least for those immediately engaged in the transaction. If all possible Pareto-optimal exchanges were made (cattle for corn, labor for a wage, etc.) and no other exchanges occurred, the society as a whole would attain a Pareto optimal efficiency.

Turning to the second meaning, *productive efficiency* equals units of output divided by units of input. As Arthur Okun put it, "To an economist, as to the engineer, efficiency means getting the most out of a given input" (Okun, 1975, 2). Getting the most product for labor inputs or the most profit on capital invested would be cases in point. Free-market transactions are said to be not only Pareto efficient but productively efficient in that the price system offers the best signal regarding states of demand and supply, guiding allocation of resources for best return.

Perhaps most exchanges that are Pareto efficient for private parties are at least productively efficient for the larger society as well. Regarding side consequences for third parties, any positive externalities of most market transactions usually exceed any negative externalities.

But not all productively efficient allocations would be Pareto-optimal efficient. Certain allocations that might be productively efficient for society as a whole could make some worse off and thus by definition not be Pareto-consumptive efficient. Perhaps a land reform or a breakup of a monopoly would lead to more output per units of input, but it would be opposed by any adversely affected.

Pareto optimality offers an implicit veto to anyone affected adversely by a change from the status quo. It is often said to be distributionally neutral in that in a *hypothetical* condition of perfect equality it would be impossible to move toward any inequality, since anyone who anticipated being made worse off could veto the change. But in *real* conditions of inequality, Pareto optimality is a very conservative standard, biased against redistribution of wealth or income.[5] Further, while the rich usually wield an effective veto against redistribution favoring the poor, the poor are often unable to block redistribution of some of their meager income to those of higher income. This is apparently what happened via the Thatcher and Reagan programs in Britain and the United States, in part through shifts of tax burden, as when Reagan's cuts in progressive federal income and inheritance taxes led to compensatory increases in regressive state and local taxes (cf. Piven and Cloward, 1982).

It was clear to the early Capitalists that continued royal monopolies, feudal land laws, or the protectionist British Corn Laws could be favored by the nobility without being productively efficient for society. If only productive efficiency is likely to yield the growth that brings supply into line with demand, then the public interest requires a competitive market, for—as William Graham Sumner put it—competition "develops all powers that exist according to their measure and degree" (Hofstadter, 1959, 59).

*Bigness in Productive Operations and Markets*

If little of the Capitalist project for change is Pareto optimal from the point of view of the Aristocrat, even less of it is so for the Saint, who is identified with small producers such as peasants and artisans. The early Capitalists sought these groups as political allies against the landowners, but Capitalist economics in practice undermines such small producers. Critiques by such figures as John Ruskin have been either ignored or viewed by Capitalists (as well as Socialists) as quaintly irrelevant, being against the grain of economic "growth" (perhaps naively equated with "progress").

The focus of modern economies has shifted sectors—from primary (extractive) to secondary (manufacturing, etc.), and then from secondary to tertiary (services). Adam Smith thought this the natural order of development, frustrated or even inverted by mercantilism. In each phase, capitalism seems initially to proliferate the number of competing units, only to shift eventually to increasing concentration. If this has been so for numbers of family farms and competitive manufacturing family firms within the modern nations, perhaps it will become so for the presently proliferating service enterprises (cleaning, clerical, computer related, etc.). If so, we may again expect long-term decline of the self-employed who directly own their enterprises as well as their bodies and consumer goods.

## The Division of Labor: Elaboration and Transformation

Ownership of the means of production constitutes a power over nonowners, who are largely subject to owners' decisions as to who gets employed, who does what, as well as who gets what.

As many observers in the nineteenth century were already complaining, people at work would take on the properties of machines, eventually to be replaced by machines. This lament so typical of the Saint is echoed by the Socialist. Marx noted both that workers were becoming appendages of the machine and that they were often being displaced from any employment by automation. Against the theory of compensation, which holds that building machines creates as many jobs as are destroyed, Marxists say this would imply the unlikely assumption that it takes as much or more labor time (and hence cost) to make machines as the capitalist using them saves in labor time over the life of the machine.[6]

Being replaced by a machine is not Pareto optimal to the fired worker, who has no voice in the matter—especially if nonunionized. No one would ever argue that dismissed workers "voluntarily" leave the place of employment, since police can be brought in to remove any recalcitrants.

As for workers remaining unemployed, recall that liberal theory assumes choices not dominated by force or fraud are necessarily free. Hence a currently respected economist argues that unemployment is a free choice, since the unemployed could always *choose* to migrate elsewhere in quest of work or else lower their price enough to find work almost anywhere (Lucas, 1983). Indeed, he says, their obstinacy causes the business cycle! Viewed not from a conservative professor's chair but from the standpoint of the many workers who are tied to place, mortgage, and family, these may not be viable options at all.

As a percentage of the labor force in the private sector, union membership is steeply declining in most advanced capitalist nations. Especially when collective bargaining rights are weak, the ownership of capital also empowers its owners to decide what any employed workers do. Although early capital formation was largely focused on the internal market, widened zones for commerce—whether through free trade, empire, or the British use of both—are needed for high-volume production and efficient use of modern machinery. Larger production scale also permits more specialization of function.

The Capitalist endorses Plato's view that specialization of function can make production easier and yield higher quality and quantity in products. David Hume spoke optimistically about the advantages of the division of labor once a person enters society: "His wants multiply every moment upon him, yet his abilities are still more augmented and leave him in every respect more satisfied and happy, than 'tis possible for him, in his savage and solitary condition, ever to become" (*Treatise on Human Nature*, III, ii). Hume's fellow Scot, Adam Smith, also emphasized increased productivity arising from a division of labor. Apart from the advantage of repetition, specialization promotes innovation in tools, Smith said, since a worker who is intimately familiar with doing one task will recognize contrivances that would make the job easier. But whatever the advantages in productivity, even Smith conceded that industrial specialization may have the side consequence of stupefying workers.

While the Aristocrat often wanted a castelike layering in the social division of labor to help assure limited economic comparisons with those in higher social ranks, the Capitalist wants, rather, an ambitious striving in the worker "to better his own condition." And while Plato simplifies and freezes task specializations, the Capitalist supposes an ever more elaborate and changeable division of labor, except in the unusual case where a reversal through job enlargement may boost productivity as well as morale. This continual adaptive transformation of roles may require the reeducation of workers throughout their lifetimes.

Thus, while Protestant theology requires literacy such that each can read the Bible, the Capitalists need literate workers, able to read instructions and to be retrained for new tasks as productive efficiency requires. Moreover, beyond its function in training workers, expanded access to public education was also helpful in the dissemination of the myth of equality of opportunity, as if the school—like the six-gun of the Wild West—were the "great equalizer."[7]

As noted, the Capitalist cannot regard economic constraint as—in reality—often causing an involuntary and unbalanced exchange, as when some must sell their labor power to others who employ it with much profit. Sometimes work with a specific employer is the only game in town, and bargaining leverage is then by no means equal. More attentive to such constraint, Marx saw not only a background of force but a foreground of fraud in the slogan of "a fair day's pay for a fair day's work."[8]

### Distribution of the Social Product: The Capitalist's Justifications of Economic Inequality

The Aristocrat openly defended inequality of results, if sometimes using the rhetoric of "proportional equality." With allowance for some upward mobility through at least the lower ranks of the military or clergy, the Aristocrat envisioned permanently stratified consumption. The Capitalist, rather, makes individual places merely provisional.

Many premodern arguments for inequality are recycled by the Capitalist, but often with more elliptic statement. Thus, instead of praising inequality, one may either dispraise egalitarianism or praise rewards for "excellence." If these approaches sound very up to date, some past arguments for inequality become less relevant.

The Aristocrat held that wealth permitted patronage of the arts, but the Capitalist can have a philistine disdain for art. The son of a Puritan, Locke wanted to convert the sons of landowners not into soldiers or poets, but into capitalist farmers of enlightened self-interest with a work ethic.[9] Concern for productive efficiency leaves no role for poetry: "It is very seldom seen that anyone discovers mines of gold or silver in Parnassus. 'Tis a pleasant air but a barren soil; and there are few instances of those who have added to their patrimony by anything they have reaped from thence" (*Some Thoughts Concerning Education*, IX, c).

The Aristocrat's argument that wealth permits charity looks pointless if the Capitalist thinks profit-motivated productive investment is virtual charity, aiding those who share in the growing social wealth. Locke says that one should engage in charity to the extent that it does not diminish one's estate, which would be self-contradictory without the assumption of personal capital accumulation. As for any more giving, those who become rich by being uncharitable will rarely become charitable. Yet some real cases such as Andrew Carnegie would not surprise early liberals such as Adam Smith, who assumed that our selfish instinct is counterbalanced by a "sympathetic" one. Smith himself was generous in his charity once financially secure. But Capitalist literature, especially in its social Darwinist mode, includes frequent cautions against charity to the undeserving, such as the slothful or drunkard.

The distinctively Capitalist defenses of economic inequality stress the growth of socially available supply, for individual material incentives alone can stimulate harder work, savings rather than frivolous consumption, and risky productive investments. Only the aspiration to accumulate property will promote harder work, invention, saving, and investment risk. While Adam Smith thought Bernard de Mandeville overstated the idea that private vice could be public virtue, Smith did believe that neither (temporarily) ascetic saving nor the larger risks of entrepreneurial investment would occur without appropriate larger rewards. While enlarging their powers to satisfy their own wants, entrepreneurs would be the famous "hidden hand" that would enlarge productive capacity and gratifications for the whole society, even the humblest day laborers. This had been already stated clearly in Locke's *Second Treatise* chapter "Of Property." Locke also thought that the more "industrious and rational" workers would save some of their earnings so that they, too, could become investors. Later restated as William Graham Sumner's "Forgotten Man," this is the mythos of rugged individualism, now so strangely juxtaposed with corporate global giantism. Advertising nostalgically depicts the origins of such corporate giants in backyard or garage tinkerings of the founders, and indeed this is sometimes yet a reality in certain lines of high-tech manufacturing (e.g., the founding of Apple Computer).

Liberalism questioned the pedigrees of landowner fortunes, but not the accumulation of wealth by Capitalist investments. The latter, from Marx's point of view, involved not only much obvious force and fraud in "primitive accumulation" but also more subtle equivalents in nonprimitive accumulation, where surplus value is created in the sphere of production (when commodities are manufactured) but seems to arise mysteriously where merely realized in money form, in the sphere of circulation (when things are sold at market).

Liberal economics also disguises the coercive nature of the Capitalist property system and its dependent inequalities (cf. Lindblom, 1977, 26, 46). The right-liberal assumes that the "natural" tendency is for individual differences (of talent, ambition, etc.) to express themselves in unequal acquisitions of wealth and income. In contrast, only "unnatural" coercive intervention by the state could even temporarily sustain any equality. Further, any forced egalitarianism would necessarily result in less liberty, productive efficiency, and social amity.

Yet—by what is called the "Kuznets curve"—while growth initially tends to *increase* inequalities (with some exceptions such as recently in South Korea and Taiwan), further growth will itself tend to boost social mobility and to flatten somewhat such inequalities before settling into a pattern. This is visible even in communist systems, and in capitalist nations it works its effects even before any added redistributions of public policy interventions, which the right holds may slow the growth that had moderated inequalities (cf. Berger, 1986, 43–47, 59–60, 136–39, 150–51). Conceding the descriptive validity of the Kuznets pattern, one may question the "self-correctiveness" that capitalist defenders assume for most of its evils. It implicitly discounts any mediating struggles of, say, labor unions to *make* accumulated national wealth "trickle down."

Shifting to the reform wing of liberalism, even a progressive economist may concede that, while Capitalist inequalities of income cannot be ethically justified, one should acquiesce in them for the sake of productive efficiencies: "Any insistence on carving the pie into equal slices would shrink the size of the pie" (Okun, 1975, 48). Yet many reform liberals see no good evidence that a nation needs to have very high levels of inequality to elicit high savings, investment, and growth. They point to contrary cases. Booming Japan, like Sweden also, has had less income inequality than the United States (cf. Kuttner, 1984).

The reform liberal accepts some public redistributive policy, believing that the state has sufficient autonomy to act thusly. In the nineteenth century, Marx had argued that ownership of the means of production "determines" not only the division of labor but associated unequal rewards—monetary claims on the social product. John Stuart Mill then denied that the relation was rigidly deterministic. Reformers correctly foresaw that labor union action or progressive state legislation could make income distribution less inegalitarian than property ownership, as is now manifestly so in the most advanced Capitalist democracies.

Thus, if Marx argued that capitalism generates the proletariat that will destroy it, the Capitalist in either variant argues, rather, that it generates forces that moderate inequalities of income. Yet if inequalities eventually lessen somewhat with growth, reversals can occur. Also, standing inequalities of income provide a de facto rationing of access to the beckoning array of consumer goods and services that business enterprises invent and advertise.

The phrase "The market knows best" dodges both explanatory and moral questions of income distribution by dwelling on present procedures of market exchange. It takes for granted both prior resource distributions and presently existing prices and preferences of agents.

Recall that, in the absence of visible coercion and fraud, all transactions are taken to be voluntary exchanges of equivalents. Any result from such fair transactions must be perfectly fair, or reflect "entitlements" in the language of Robert Nozick.

Within this sphere of circulation occurs what Marx called "fetishization" of commodities. It seems as if free-market prices are simply natural, reflecting a "consumer sovereignty" that governs how much labor is put into each product and even how labor is remunerated.[10] Arguments against labor union activities, and against affirmative action, often take market procedures as the oracle of natural pricing, even for wages and salaries. To the Capitalist the market and its operations constitute the presumptive criterion of "fair." It is improper to consider what comes before or after, such as how inherited productive property is mediated by market procedures into consequent and usually greater inequalities. If inheritance makes one a millionaire, it is easier to become a billionaire. Further, many political "interventions" in markets may increase rather than decrease such social inequalities.

## Does Anyone Really Love the Market?
## It Is a Jungle Out There!

Whatever its clear achievements, the capitalist market often seems a Moloch—a depraved god demanding sacrifice of children. If *homo economicus* really did "maximize" anything, it would be wealth and income rather than the free market as such. While Capitalist theoreticians may love the market in the abstract, in their personal lives they may instead work to break or bend markets through either private collusion or public policy. Perhaps most of us would want to exempt ourselves from the risks of free-market competition, while imposing the risks of losing on others. Although the players are by no means equal, virtually everyone gets into this game, whether as owners, workers, or consumers.

Let us first look at *producer interests*. Suppliers of a good or service who are in a *weak* market position want to shelter themselves from its bracing gales (e.g., restrict market entry, coordinate pricing, and perhaps even ask state assistance in such projects).

As Joseph Schumpeter observed, those who are in a *strong* market position may not really love markets either. When praising free-market competition, they really want opportunities to destroy their competitors, thus moving through markets toward monopoly (cf. Thurow, 1981, 153; Lieberman, 1979, 137). Suppliers of goods and services do not really want to expose themselves to the hazards of markets, yet they can enhance profits by exposing others to market risks, including their own employees.

When bending the market proves unavailing, producer interests will often seek to shape tax and budget policies in order to maximize their income. Capitalist and Socialist economics agree that gross profits arise in the spread between cost prices and selling prices. But the Socialist claims that the spread is attained in the productive process by paying less than the full value of labor. Capitalist theory, in contrast, often emphasizes sheer cleverness of marketing in yielding the spread. For my part, I think any realistic economic theory must recognize that firms bolster the spread either by distorting markets (e.g., licit or illicit debarments of competitors, practical barriers of tariff protection, and the like) or by securing some kind of public subsidy.

In other words, arguably already exploited as *workers*, people are further exploited as *consumers* and often also as *taxpayers*. While a few firms may be triple-dipping in making their profit margins, more often a firm weak in one source will turn to one or both of those remaining to create the favorable bottom line.

In tapping consumers, suppliers of goods or services often want to set *minimal* prices for whatever it is they sell, above the lower prices that a really competitive market would likely yield. They may also, on the other hand, overprice their products through public policies such as patent or proprietary information protection, price supports, or tariffs and quotas. If necessary, they may turn to illegal price fixing or implicit follow-the-leader pricing, which is easier in oligopoly sectors. While they defend their own mergers and cartels as aiding competitiveness, most firms will oppose such collusions among *their* competitors.

Various subsidies—often regressively financed from taxes paid by ordinary workers—offer the third shot at maintenance of a spread between costs and selling prices. Even the newly industrializing English manufacturers pushed not only protective tariffs but such measures as indirect wage subsidies and export bounties (Polanyi, 1957, 135–50, esp. 139). Today, some subsidies seem inescapable, as in public involvement in training workers or promoting relatively basic rather than applied science and technological research. But other subsidies are most questionable. In 1983, for instance, the combined net earnings for all American farms was $15–17 billion, while federal subsidies alone amounted to more than $43 billion.[11] In 1981–84, ingenious American tax policies gave massive "rebates" of tens and even hundreds of millions to many leading corporations, which thus paid no taxes at all. Massive subsidies were normally present in the now diminishing military procurements, whether legally (e.g., taxpayers built the plant) or illegally (e.g., misallocating costs from civilian projects to military cost-plus contracts). Footloose manufacturing firms bargain one political jurisdiction against another to secure all kinds of subsidies, euphemistically called "development incentives" (cf. Goodman, 1979; Cook, 1983a). Even reformers speak of "government–industry partnership" when the immediate effect is to privatize the profits and socialize the costs—for taxpayers pick up the bill before any possible return through enhanced tax revenues.

While the reality is arguably a flow of value from labor, consumer, and taxpayer to the capitalist, the paradigm has always claimed a predominant flow of value to them from the capitalist (who takes risks, creates jobs, meets payrolls, pays taxes, makes charitable contributions). Although long ago abandoning the labor theory of value, Capitalist theory has not quite abandoned the question of the source of real value. Nowadays, it is regarded unabashedly as coming from owners and entrepreneurs.

Let us shift from the interests of *producers* to those of *consumers*, who at first glance may seem consistently to favor competitive markets. Aaron Wildavsky has written: "No one likes competition (after all you can lose) except the consumer whose life is made predictable by the uncertainties imposed on others" (Wildavsky, 1980, 16).

However, consumers do not like competition on their own side as potential purchasers. Consumers in *strong* market positions want to make themselves even stronger, tending toward monopsony. The only consumer in town is certainly king. Only rarely would it be advantageous to have more fellow consumers than already exist, as when a few more patrons could sustain two or more local restaurants or movie theaters for price competition, or when more countries purchasing a sophisticated weapon of a certain type would lower its per-unit cost.

Consumers in *weak* market positions may often favor measures to increase competition among producers or merchants, as in favoring the creation of alternative suppliers, possibly including the state as a rival to the private sector (or vice versa). But weak consumers again want no competition among themselves, perhaps asking that the state set *maximal* prices, well below what a competitive market would offer. Or they may want a subsidy of their consumption, provided taxes to pay for the subsidy will burden others more than themselves. But consumer interests are usually less easily coordinated for political action than are producer interests, since expenditures go out in many streamlets while income tends to come as one main stream.

To corrupt a phrase from Rousseau, those who would study economics and politics separately will never understand either. Whatever the enthusiasm of intellectuals for the capitalist competitive market, almost everyone is trying to evade its burdens and risks, while exposing others to them. Business firms and professionals have long been successful players, and increased democratization lets others get into the game, most successfully by alliances of producer interests (uniting owners and workers) against consumers or taxpayers.

In either great wing of liberalism, economists will lament that resultant policy "distorts" and "rigidifies" markets and stifles growth (e.g., Thurow, 1981; or Olson, 1982). Often dogmatically assuming that free-market solutions are invariably in the best public interest, they almost concede that democracy is in tension with their formula. But one may question whether majorities really do dominate, in the marketplace ("consumer sovereignty") or in democratic interventions in markets ("citizen sovereignty").

When people accept the intrinsic fairness of procedures, they may be more willing to accept as also fair the results of such procedures. But the players in the Capitalist game are not equal. Those on the losing end of capitalism may realize that past property distributions simply register themselves through market procedures to unequal outcomes. Beyond challenging the fairness of inherited inequalities, they may also question the fairness of present procedures, especially if the political procedures merely reinforce the result. Just as antecedent inequalities largely shape what follows in free-market transactions, so also prior inequalities may dominate what emerges from the alternative of political interventions in markets. It is at least plausible that the sum of all government interventions may on balance increase rather than decrease socioeconomic inequalities. Whether facing or fighting a market, it is nicer to be affluent.

## Does Capitalism Increase Supply More than It Bolsters Wants?

Although practice is often far from Capitalist theory, the Capitalist formula has brought great achievements, as even Marx and Engels acknowledged in the *Communist Manifesto*. Capitalism has historically accounted for some of the greatest increments of human productive powers, even if these are directly owned by relatively few. But the great strides of capitalist productivity are to be chiefly found among nations that developed early on: Western Europe, the United States, Canada, Australia, New Zealand, and Japan. One must add the recent surge of the newly industrializing nations of South Korea, Taiwan, Hong Kong, and Singapore—the so-called Little Tigers or Little Dragons of Pacific Rim prosperity. Regarding those stars, however, it is misleading to celebrate five successes and ignore, say, 50 cases of capitalist stagnation elsewhere.

The roster of "economic miracle" nations of capitalism can change, as the Brazilians could remind us. Perhaps, in the underdeveloped world, boom in a few nations may be at the price of bust elsewhere. If a handful of nations develop because of practices that either could not or would not be implemented everywhere, one must critically examine the special conditions for rare success in late development.[12]

In many primarily market economies—especially in Latin America where only drug-exporting Colombia gained in per-capita income in the 1980s—capitalism has not yielded cornucopia. Far from being the goose that lays golden eggs, it has plundered the garden, fouled the yard, then winged away as flight capital to foreign investment havens.[13]

Often better at explaining the past than predicting the future, the classical Marxists prematurely forecast the exhaustion of the Capitalist formula, especially where it first emerged. The powerful motive of harnessing self-interest to stimulate economic activity is by no means extinct, as conceded by recent economic liberalizations in China and the Soviet Union and the wholesale repudiation of centrally planned socialism in Eastern Europe.

### Fatal Contradictions or Fated Frustrations?

But capitalism does not deliver on all of its promises. Both within and across nations, it tends to produce the social dislocations of uneven development that are currently a major problem in Great Britain. Also, to choose a market economy is to accept the business cycle. If public policy can at best advance or retard its swings, we are nearly as much prisoners of this humanly created cycle as preindustrial peoples were subject to the cycles of nature. Even if capitalism creates great productive powers, the downsides of the business cycle waste them. Plant and equipment are then idled, as when the United States used about 60 percent of capacity in the severe 1981–82 recession. Although economists of the right will say that it would be more wasteful to keep open obsolete plant, many firms may close forever, leaving empty factory buildings and equipment sold off as scrap. The material waste sometimes extends to the ruin of whole cities, regions, or even smaller nations. Business cannot claim credit for externalized benefits (the multiplier effect, etc.) and then duck blame for any externalized costs (the reverse multiplier in disinvestment).

Great losses are imposed on many not involved in the corporate investment decisions, especially where business acts without any collaboration with government or labor. Yet the economies of nations such as Sweden and West Germany that have followed the "corporatist" style of having business–labor–government collaboration on such decisions have outperformed those lacking it (Schmitter, 1981; Wilensky and Turner, 1987).

A slump exacerbates socially damaging unemployment, disproportionately concentrated in groups such as ethnic minorities, youths,
older people, and women. If developed capitalist economies may show
figures up to about 15 percent unemployed in serious recessions short
of the Great Depression, many underdeveloped nations with already
chronically high unemployment may find up to half the labor force
either unemployed or severely underemployed. Capitalist economics
began by worrying that there was not enough available labor, but its
more common problem now has been a glut of labor, perhaps
temporarily relieved by the birth decline in the United States and
Japan.

Capitalist purists routinely blame such slumps on some "socialistic"
specific of government policy, which is usually implausible in that
such cycles of boom and bust long antedated whatever policy may be
the current target of blame.[14] The swings arise from the dynamics of
capitalism itself, which tends toward recurrent overproduction of
commodities that remain unsold because of the lack of consumer cash
and confidence when workers are either unemployed or fearing it. In
noting one of Marx's instances of a "contradiction" of capitalism, two
contemporary Marxists put it like this: "People are forced to live on
too little because they produce too much" (Ollman and Vernoff, 1984,
xiv).

The contemporary capitalist economy has an apparently endemic
set of interdependent problems, and policy-makers veer from one
priority to another as the numbers change: stagnation and its unemployment, inflation, budget deficits, balance-of-payments deficits, in-
equity, workplace health and safety hazards, or environmental deg-
radation.

For each mentioned problem there are many suggested "solutions,"
but implementing any solution almost invariably exacerbates one and
usually more of the remaining problems. While one must not preclude occasional serendipitous side effects, the more sinister unintended consequences seem more pronounced. In any case, almost
every proposed solution to a problem calls not for any sacrifice from
business but for yet another sacrifice on the part of labor, consumers,
or ordinary taxpayers (cf. Dolbeare, 1984).

I do not mean to be misread as implying great expectations of some
rival paradigm such as Socialism, which obviously ran into even more
intractable problems. But when communist countries turn in desper-
ation toward market solutions, they merely shift part of their problem
set.

### What Capitalism Does to Human Wants

Against stagnation, some left-liberals were long insistent "demand-
siders," adopting the neo-Keynesian view that the problem has to do

with deficient or unstable levels of consumption. But it is ironic that, when capitalist growth slackens and sociopolitical tensions rise in what is called the "zero-sum society," even the reform wing of the Capitalist theory turns toward a premodernist emphasis on the need of all to moderate their demands (Thurow, 1981). Especially as rising demands press on the political process, many who are further right may speak of an "overload" of demands (cf. critical comments by Piven and Cloward, 1982, 122–23).

Others bravely return to the formula, especially in the "supply-sider" response that we must accept even greater inequalities to get more savings and investment, as in cutting progressive taxation, diminishing social welfare expenditure, and taking risks in deregulation—risks such as those that now underlay the U.S. savings-and-loan debacle, which may end up costing taxpayers up to half a trillion dollars.

With considerable boldness (brashness?), the Capitalist formula once assumed that it would actually be safe to raise human aspirations, on the cheerful projection that increased social wants would be more than exceeded by consequently increased powers to satisfy them. Thus, Herbert Croly in 1909 offered this explanation as to why American growth was outpacing Europe's: "The mass of mankind must be aroused to still greater activity by a still more abundant satisfaction of their needs, and by a consequent increase of their aggressive discontent" (Croly, 1963, 15). But if "aggressive discontent" is not directed at self-improvement but rather at others as obstacles to one's progress, this readily becomes an acute political problem. People *see* what others *hold*, but that has never caused much social envy when people limited their comparisons to their parents or to those in their own station. Promising opportunities for upward mobility, capitalism needs to pose standing examples of higher consumption as a spur to (salutary) ambition, but always at the risk of (unsalutary) envy. However, when modern scarcities are less absolute and material than socially relative and "positional" (e.g., having the expensive house near the trees or being leader of the organization), almost all the people in such a society are frustrated in trying to show that they are ahead or getting ahead. The very success of capitalism in meeting basic material needs only exacerbates the striving to escape the "congestions" that go with growth (Hirsch, 1976).

Attention then shifts from more production to redistribution. Here, class hatred is not the only possible outcome. The Great Depression unleashed ethnic scapegoating that became a genocidal rage in Europe. Recent "stagflations" have rekindled xenophobic bigotries in North America, later in Western Europe, and now in decommunizing Eastern Europe. In hard times, many people are more likely to turn against new immigrants and new alliances, than against capitalism. Put into rat races, people become ratlike.

True, there should be no danger if social powers grow even more than the comparison-induced enlargement of wants that both bolster such powers and use what they yield.[15] If the formula argument for inequality under capitalism is that it promotes growth, this argument is less than compelling when and where growth is not occurring (Ophuls, 1977, 186).

Even under conditions of growth, certain groups may be left in stagnation or become yet worse off (true in Brazil and Mexico in their past boom years). This pattern is even more likely during national stagnation and contraction, when some groups bear a disproportionate brunt of unemployment.

One argument for inequality under capitalism is that the set of inequalities of *results* is defensible because the system provides equality of *opportunity* in their pursuit. But unless one assumes without good evidence that whole categories of people such as women and racial minorities are innately inferior in either aptitude or motivation as related to most social roles, equality of opportunity for individuals would imply a kind of equality of results for groups. Allocations of roles and rewards should increasingly be observed as if randomly distributed across social groups, with women and minorities being found in top rewarding roles in rough proportion to their presence in the population. Since this is not the case, equality of opportunity is unreal, whether or not that default is the product of intentional discrimination. The losing groups know it has been unreal, and they have often rebelled against the inequality.

Welfare programs may palliate things, but these are often shaved back when growth falters. Sluggish growth may strain tax revenues for such programs, or raise the burden on resistant taxpayers (cf. O'Connor, 1973). Middle-income taxpayers who had been uncomplaining as long as they enjoyed ever higher real incomes become recalcitrant. While the lower-income groups feel *held down*, the middle groups now feel *held back*; and the social strain rises. As income distribution patterns have gone from the classic pyramid to a diamond, it becomes easier to form voting pluralities or even majorities that leave out the poor, especially when the poor population is disproportionately made up of ethnic minorities. This seems to have been the case with the periods of Thatcher in Britain and Reagan in the United States.

Margaret Thatcher, Britain's Conservative former prime minister, imposed a program of harsh austerity that eventually found renewed growth, but at the cost of worsened ethnic discontents and uneven development of regions. In efforts to discourage high levels of social program expenditure and undermine Labor party incumbents who would back them, Thatcher even dared to have Parliament shift local taxes from a progressive property tax to an extremely regressive capitation tax whereby the owner of a great estate would pay the same as someone owning virtually nothing. Riots ensued in 1990 and unpopularity forced her resignation.

In the United States, inflation was beaten down by the severe 1981–82 recession, triggered by a Federal Reserve tight money policy that helped creditors with higher interest incomes and hurt debtors or would-be borrowers. Yet in the Reagan–Bush period, what a journalistic incantation calls "one of the longest peacetime growths on record" actually may be due to wartime levels of deficit spending (a near tripling of the national debt in the 1980s).

## Systematic Expansion of Wants

Capitalist success seems recurrently to threaten the conditions for such success. Uncertain or fitful increases in powers to satisfy will be of little help to the formula if human wants grow even faster because of the nature of the system. C. B. Macpherson states it well: "Moral and political philosophers had from the earliest times recognized in mankind a strain of unlimited desire, but most of them deplored it as avarice and believed that it could, and judged that it should, be fought down" (Macpherson, 1967, 98). As if in confirmation, consider Pope Gregory's 600 A.D. list of the seven deadly sins: anger, envy, lust, gluttony, pride, sloth, and avarice.[16] Most of these sinful motives are exploited by advertisers to make us want to buy what we do not have.

The Capitalist originally assumed two kinds of moderation of wants: (1) the aspiring capitalist's wish to save for future productive investment; and (2) the worker's lack of much left over after covering subsistence needs. However, by Veblen's day, many capitalists were indulging in "conspicuous consumption"; nowadays, even the workers lose restraint. As Daniel Bell puts it, "The greatest single engine in destruction of the Protestant ethic was the invention of the installment plan, or instant credit. Previously one had to save in order to buy, but with credit cards one could indulge instant gratification" (Bell, 1976, 21). Actually, this may have a modest impact relative to the demonstration of high consumption in live models all around us or experienced through the beautiful people in multimedia advertisements. Partly because capitalism recurrently invents new things that can be wanted, the advertising industry cultivates ever higher wants, which may turn into a dangerous social envy more than a satiable ambition.

The problems of capitalism are especially apparent to those who bear its burdens (e.g., unemployment) without enjoying its benefits (access to consumer goods). Both within and across nations, those who fall to the rear of modern rat racing may develop an explosive rage, which can defeat the paradigm's promise of peace as well as abundance and happiness for all (Apter, 1987). Defenders of capitalism often cite the communist world's frustration of people having money but being unable to buy goods because the queues are too long or the shelves are empty. But another formula for frustration would be a world that has well-stocked stores with display windows, and endlessly advertised invitations to buy—but whose people are hit with the constraint of having insufficient money to buy, perhaps because they are unemployed. Such a situation becomes an almost open invitation to crime, or perhaps to instant gratification through drugs that constitute another insatiable want—which causes yet more crime. Some cocaine addicts "need" to steal abundantly to sustain their daily habit. The United States consumes 60–80 percent of the world's illicit drugs, although it has only 6 percent of the world's population. And there is a national tragedy written in the widely cited report of 1990 that 23 percent of American black males of age 20–29 were in the corrections system (in prison, on parole, or under probation), which was nearly four times the rate for white males of that age. As Jon Elster has written, "Much of the gain from economic progress can be absorbed by the costs of rescuing or policing the losers" (Elster, 1989, 162).[17] If true within a nation, it may also apply internationally.

The other paradigms would see the inflaming of demand via advertising as a mad social practice. While defenders speak of the informational function, often "misinformational" would be more accurate. While the more modest advertisers may claim that they are merely shifting an already existing consumer demand among possible product lines, they also create some wants that would not otherwise exist (Galbraith, 1958, 158). Overcommitment of resources to advertising is in itself consumption of social productive power. As Veblen once argued, "Expenditure on salesmanship is nearly pure waste, as rated in terms of serviceability to the material welfare of the community at large" (Veblen, 1915, 122–23). Ironically, the modern project is supposed to have involved new techniques to get more productivity from land and labor.

Leaving aside already visible ecological limits, the Capitalist formula may be criticized from its own point of view. Even where capitalism expands human powers to satisfy through awakening self-interested ambitions, it may fail to pacify society because it raises aggregate wants even more than it enlarges social powers to satisfy them. This can encourage not only every form of predation, but severe political problems. In the past, many with wants unsatisfied would substitute or do without. Now more of them turn to politics, expecting government to intervene in the marketplace. But as Capitalist theorists have always said, such intervention can impair the efficiency of markets.

The Capitalist formula culminates in asking moral restraint on demands that capitalism itself raises without stint.

In a much discussed paper, Francis Fukuyama has argued that history—at least the history of ideas, rather than mere events—is over, in that both economic and political liberalism are clearly triumphant. Earlier theories depended on religious foundations, but could not reach agreement and therefore could not engender peace. Recent rivals such as fascism or communism have been left behind as historical relics, and all other societies must "end their ideological pretensions of representing different and higher forms of society" (Fukuyama, 1989).

But such crowing like Chanticleer has recurrently arisen in history, only to be proven wrong. The kinds of problems reviewed above suggest that reports concerning the deaths of history and its rival systems of ideas have been greatly exaggerated. Perhaps anyone who is now feeling a sense of smug superiority should rather recall that the ancient Romans could have prophesied in the fifth century great things ahead for themselves, yet within just a century "goats were grazing in the forum" (Amalrik, 1970, 67). In saying that, Andrei Amalrik was prophesying the disintegration of the Soviet Union due to nationality conflicts exacerbated by a war with China. So far, Amalrik's pessimistic outlook has proved at least half right. In any case, we who live in the more prosperous capitalist nations cannot really know our future until we get there.

## Notes

1. While Thomas Hobbes embraced much of economic liberalism, he distrusted "the great number of corporations; which are as it were many lesser commonwealths in the bowels of a greater, like worms in the entrails of a natural man" (*Leviathan*, II, xxix). Apart from his emphasis on at least the one natural right of self-preservation and his contractual and prudential style of argument, Hobbes's fear of pluralism caused him to reject political liberalism.

2. While often a good case can be made for competitive private or public supply, there is an ideological bias in one-sidedness: Anything in the private sector is forever immune from any new public service competition, whereas anything in the public sector is up for grabs—as if it were a new commons to be privately appropriated.

3. This underlies the principle of "nonperversity" in rational choice theory, which assumes that agents really prefer what they actually choose. Or it arises in the libertarian's "entitlement" theory: Beginning with hypothetical communal ownership before labor creates any initial private property, all subsequent distributions are just if attained through transactions not involv-

ing force or fraud—that is, through inheritance, gift, or free exchange (Nozick, 1974).

4. Recall that a libertarian accepts even the sale of prostitute services. According to an AP dispatch, in just one city of India—Bombay—100,000 young girls and women wear gaudy clothing to market themselves as prostitutes in order to prevent starvation, but—because patrons refuse condoms— up to 35 percent of them may have contracted the presently fatal AIDS or its preinfection (*Spokesman Review*, January 4, 1990, p. A–10). Does it not violate language to say that such tragic exchanges are really "voluntary" for the women, let alone also "fair"?

5. While I have addressed Pareto *consumptive* efficiency, which is loaded against any change, there is another measure called Pareto *productive* efficiency, which could—on the contrary—require much change. An allocation of productive resources is Pareto productive efficient if no alternative allocation could yield more of at least one good without producing less of another good.

6. But a national economy could gain jobs if many of the new machines were exported at more than favorable terms of trade—which, in the past, was true of most U.S. exports of production machinery. Yet eventually, by the use of such new machines together with their cheaper labor, sharp competitors may arise against future exports, often including machinery. The Japanese and Europeans are now competitively selling machinery in the United States. Globalization of the market has countered domestic oligopoly, but one wonders if this is but a respite before the onslaught of world oligopoly in many product lines.

7. While education does permit upward mobility for individuals, it largely just mediates family advantages. Even expanded access to education leaves the larger pattern of social inequalities unchanged (cf. Jencks et al., 1972).

8. As Marx saw it, the capitalist does pay the full *value of labor power*—that required to produce the worker at the socially acceptable standard of living— but the capitalist does not pay for the full *value of labor*, which when embodied in products yields a larger value—a "surplus value"—over what is paid in wages. Put otherwise, labor gets less in wages than the value of its product: "The capitalist's profit is derived from the fact that he has something to sell for which he has paid nothing" (*Capital*, vol. 3, ii).

9. While Max Weber saw the elective affinity of Calvinist religion with the work ethic, perhaps life situations created both. If they lacked connections at the court and were unwilling to turn to crime, the ambitious could advance in the world *only* by hard work, frugality, abstention from drink, and so on. They would then fault both the aristocrats above them and the poor below them for lacking their bourgeois ethics. But the successful inculcation of such liberal virtues in subsequent generations could be in tension with liberal "tolerance" of varied opinions and life-styles (cf. Galston, 1988).

10. To Marx this was upside down: Differences in average socially necessary labor time create the normal ratios of any barter exchange and at least roughly the differences in prices of any freely reproducible commodities (i.e., all things sold in a K-Mart, but not rare collectibles).

11. The figure includes $28.3 billion in direct price supports; payment in kind or other income supports; $10.0 billion worth of credit programs; $3.6

billion of agriculturally targeted tax expenditures; and $1.2 billion of federally funded research (from *Alternatives '85*, p. 4, published by the National Agricultural Forum, Washington, D.C.). Government supports as a share of prices received by farmers rose in 1980–88 from under 15 percent to 35 percent in the United States, and from 35 percent to 47 percent in the European Economic Community. "Farming the government" is obviously vital.

12. While the Crown Colony of Hong Kong needs distinctive attention, South Korea, Taiwan, and Singapore have had certain favorable conditions: (1) cheap labor, long kept cheap by the repression of autonomous unions; (2) docile politics, long kept so by authoritarian governments that repressed any leftist unions or parties; and (3) populations that are anticommunist in any case because of proximity to the uninspiring example of backward China.

13. Many on the right argue that capitalism "fails" only because insufficiently practiced, or perhaps because of some flaw in the local culture.

The Socialist typically counters that underdevelopment does not spontaneously arise but is rather a product of international stratification and unequal terms of trade. Even without force or fraud, some are structurally constrained to give far more than they get. Note the parallel: This can apply in either the domestic relationship of labor to capital or in the international relationship of underdeveloped nations to advanced capitalist nations.

14. Corporate-funded think tanks such as the American Enterprise Institute or the libertarian Cato Institute churn out books and other publications that blame left-liberal programs for almost any problem of the contemporary capitalist economies, even when the problem preceded the program and the program was aimed at its correction. If sincere, such criticisms are only intelligible by the right-liberal assumption of ultimate self-correctiveness in pure capitalism (as in this chapter's epigraph from Adam Smith). Right-liberal economics assumes that markets tend toward stable equilibria—with growth and all good things—but for blundering government interventions.

Left-liberal economics (Keynesian, neo-Keynesian) assumes that markets tend to disequilibria—with nongrowth and all bad things—unless prevented by government planning (cf. Alt and Chrystal, 1983, 71). This economics assumes that wise government programs may promote efficiencies rather than block them (cf. Kuttner, 1984). After all, it would seem odd to assume that every liberal program just happened to have the opposite effects from those intended (cf. Hirschman, 1989).

15. Thus, Friedrich Hayek cheerfully concedes that "the ambitions of the many will always be determined by what is as yet accessible only to the few." But far from viewing this as an argument against inequality, he sees only the incentive for innovation: "The rapid economic advance that we have come to expect seems in a large measure to be the result of this inequality and to be impossible without it. Progress at such a fast rate cannot proceed on a uniform front but must take place in echelon fashion, with some far ahead of the rest" (Hayek, 1972, 42). A vanguard of the bourgeoisie?

16. Note that now, for many of these sins, not moderation of desire but just another gratification is prescribed. Anger? Try Valium. Lust? In lieu of abstinence, the birth control pill. Gluttony? All sorts of over-the-counter nostrums promise that you can become less fat not by cutting down on eating but by consuming some special formula food. And so on.

17. Many Capitalists echo the Aristocrat's denial that inequality could possibly be the cause of criminality or social strife. Thus, Milton and Rose Friedman offer a tortuous argument that, on the contrary, *egalitarianism* and its product in overly high taxation and tax evasion caused the rise of general lawbreaking in Britain: "When people start to break one set of laws, the lack of respect for the law inevitably spreads to all laws, even those that everyone regards as moral and proper—laws against violence, theft, vandalism. Hard as it may be to believe, the growth of crude criminality in Britain in recent decades may well be one consequence of the drive for equality" (Friedman and Friedman, 1980, 145).

Hard indeed. Those less imprisoned by the paradigm could suspect that standing inequalities and perhaps personal experience of discrimination could cause social discontent—especially if not palliated by social welfare programs, which stand in for insufficient charity in societies with weakened family and community bonds.

# 7

# The Capitalist and Democracy

The security of property and the freedom of
speech always go together; and in those
wretched countries where a man cannot call his
tongue his own, he can scarce call anything
else his own.

John Trenchard and Thomas Gordon,
*Cato's Letters*, February 4, 1720

While no less insistent that property rights sustained the freedoms
constitutive of liberal democracy, early liberals knew that these freedoms had instrumental value. Competitions of ideas, of candidates,
and of institutional forms were *means* to protect property as well as
life itself. Later liberals increasingly emphasized that democratic
freedoms were *also ends* in themselves, as instanced by Seymour
Martin Lipset: "Democracy is not only or even primarily a means
through which different groups can attain their ends or seek the
good society; it is the good society itself in operation" (Lipset, 1963,
403). Especially after World War II, others such as Hannah Arendt
went further (too far, I think), insisting that the forms of freedom
were *only an end*. They feared that to concede any use of freedom as
a means risked its sacrifice for some other end, such as attaining
economic justice (Arendt, 1963).

Emphases may thus run full circle, with liberal political forms
regarded in one of these four modes: (1) as primarily means, but in a
sense favorable to moderately "popular" government; (2) as both
means and end (the view I recommend); (3) as primarily end only;
and (4) sometimes as mere means once again, but this time in an
antidemocratic mood. The purely instrumental view dominates at the
birth or death of popular government. It is a useful means to

implement capitalism in place of feudalism (or now socialism), but it is a discardable instrument if a democracy rather votes for socialism.

Recapitulating, classical liberalism sought autonomy of the religious, political, and economic realms, then sought added autonomy for subsystems down to the level of individuals. The recurrent pattern in each realm was to cut units free from traditional ties or subordinations, let them then compete for precedence, and reconstitute liaisons through consent, often formalized in contracts. Below I will comment on the evolution of liberal representative democracy as both ideal and practice. I will also ask how the economic system of capitalism affects the liberal political competitions of ideas, of candidates, and of rival decision units. Finally, I warn that some Capitalists may retreat to being only economically liberal, abandoning political liberalism as a threat to capitalism. This succumbs to a pattern already observed in the Aristocrat and the Saint—namely, putting a special strategy against scarcity above freedom. That, I think, is unwise.

## The Rise of Liberal Political Theory:
## Freedom Shifting from an Instrumental to Intrinsic Good

There has been a strong correlation between market economies and political freedom, understood in its negative or liberal sense (Hayek, 1972; Lindblom, 1977, 116). In explaining the correlation, it would be implausible to argue that an abstract love of freedom caused emergence of both its economic and political actualizations. With slightly more plausibility, some seventeenth-century liberals, such as Baruch Spinoza or Roger Williams, argued that political freedoms stimulated emergence of prospering market economies such as Holland's (cf. Feuer, 1958, esp. 66–69). Similarly, de Tocqueville argued that politically egalitarian peoples tend to form a rich associational life, and that this fosters the production of wealth (*Democracy in America*, II, xiv). But historical sequences rather suggest that the main causal direction was chiefly from the rise of market economies to political freedom. Under favorable cultural and other conditions, quickening of commerce seemed to encourage the search for political freedoms. As primarily urban groups acquired property, they sought to sway political power to protect or enlarge it. When yet weak under autocracy, business interests used bribes to that end, as they may still do in Third World dictatorships. But more confident commercial interests in Holland and Britain demanded a stake in political power, whether allied with friendly kings (the House of Orange) or opposed to hostile ones (the House of Stuart).

Not all capitalist nations have been liberal democratic, for many nations with primarily free markets have been ruled by monarchs or dictators. Yet *all* stable liberal democratic systems have had primarily capitalist economies, if measured by the predominance of private productive property within a market framework (which includes Sweden, notwithstanding its extensive welfare state). Hence Capitalists justifiably scoff at Socialist assertions that capitalism is incompatible with the existence of liberal democracy. While they may more plausibly identify some tensions, Socialists must concede that no primarily socialist economy has as such evolved to stable liberal democracy, although several semisocialist systems have sought to do that.[1]

Just why has there been no instance of a fully socialist liberal democracy? Friedrich Hayek and other anti-socialists have claimed that centrally planned socialism is simply incompatible with democracy (e.g., Berger, 1986, 76–81). The irony is that this endorses a variant of the Marxist claim that the economic base "determines" the political superstructure. But an alternative explanation is more contingent and political: Leaderships of both communist and capitalist nations have heretofore *chosen* to keep democracy and socialism separated.

It may be less anything intrinsic to socialism than fear of losing control that caused most past communist leaders to crush democratic strivings that seemed to threaten their power, their privileges, or the Socialist formula. Aside from the evidence of early Soviet history, some ugly cases include Hungary in 1956, Czechoslovakia in 1968, Poland in 1981, or China in 1989. But since Gorbachev's 1985 ascendancy in the Soviet Union, most Eastern European regimes have rejected the communist monopoly of power and have moved at varying speeds toward competitive economics as well as politics.

Fearful communist leaderships constitute just half the story. When elites within capitalist nations have feared expropriation or even major redistribution of income because of socialist wins at the ballot box, they have recurrently sabotaged liberal democracy, as instanced by Spain in 1936, Greece in 1967, or Uruguay and Chile in 1973.

As if a joint product of both communist and capitalist efforts to keep them asunder, the absence of even one example of a fully socialist democracy is thus not clear evidence that they are *intrinsically* incompatible. Yet if a match of socialism and democracy seems possible, I think it would have at least as many tensions—if not always the same ones—as the marriage of capitalism and democracy as reviewed below.

While Aristocrats distrusted liberal political institutions from their origins in the sixteenth and seventeenth centuries, most early liberals were confident that an element of "popular" government could only favor their formula, especially where voting rights were largely limited to the propertied. After all, as Adam Smith wrote, the Tories were "the calm and contented folks of no great spirit, and abundant fortunes which they want to enjoy at their ease," while the Whigs were "the bustling, spirited, active folks, who can't brook opposition and are constantly endeavoring to advance themselves" (Winch, 1978, 52). Capitalist doubts only arise when overextended democracy threatens opposition from the lowest classes.

Both the Aristocrat and the Capitalist normally defend not only inequality of *property* but a state with enough inequality of *power* to protect it, for as Adam Smith said, the poor "if not hindered by government, would soon reduce the others to an equality with themselves by open violence" (Winch, 1978, 58). But the Aristocrat in quest of "order" may sometimes so emphasize inequality of power that titles to property may be weakened another way (e.g., Sir Robert Filmer makes his absolute monarch virtual owner of all property). The Capitalist, in contrast, may often so elevate property rights and individual autonomy that the state may be weakened (e.g., among social Darwinists, libertarians, and individualist anarchists). Although the Capitalist may sometimes veer to the opposite extreme of favoring a coup d'état to protect property, under normal conditions the paradigm has historically leaned toward liberal political forms.

### Popular Government as Means: The Businesslike Instrumentality of Early Liberal Politics

The rising Western European bourgeois usually first found themselves under autocratic rule. Usually a monarch was in close alliance with the nobility and the higher clergy of the state church, initially Roman Catholic everywhere. Kings and commoners sometimes found areas of common interests, as when the personal ambitions of monarchs accorded well with merchant interests in consolidation of nation-states or protection of trade lanes for more extended markets. Conflicts of interest arose, however, over the major domains of public economic policy, where feudal and capitalist preferences often clashed in issues of regulation, taxation, and budget expenditure.

While seeking legalization of opposition, early British liberals often went into illegal, conspiratorial opposition, risking their lives as well as their estates. During the Restoration, Algernon Sidney was arrested, tried, convicted, and in 1683 executed for sedition. To be merely "hanged by the neck until dead" was a kindness when compared to the cruel death sentence imposed on a rebel such as Sidney (see Sydney, 1805, vol. 1, 243–44). John Locke also feared for his life, but he slipped into exile when it seemed he would be arrested by Stuart authorities. As he argued, the use of force without right (by his definition, a "state of war") by tyrants was worse than that of private persons within an ungoverned state of nature, since tyrants claimed legitimacy in it and had the state coercive apparatus at their disposal. Whigs, neo-Whigs, and American patriots influenced by them saw unlimited government as a grave threat to human life (cf. Bailyn, 1967). As the tyrannies of our own century attest, they were certainly right.

Nevertheless, primarily economic objectives—amplified by status and religious concerns—first cast British liberals into the illicit opposition roles that endangered their lives. Personal physical insecurity was less cause than consequence of their political activities. Once they themselves took power, liberals in their turn brought insecurity of life for those who threatened *their* property or political order, as shown by extensive use of hanging for even petty theft.[2]

When the existing regime seemed to be the instrument of the nobility and high clergy, the Capitalists groped toward an understanding of what form of government would be a better instrument for their own purposes. Some were initially drawn toward enlightened despotism, but this was not destined to be the dominant direction (cf. Lentin, 1985). Its problem was unpredictability, since heirs to the throne could lack the will or capacity to safeguard property. They needed some reliable model of limited or constitutional government.

Where does one find models of authority? Whereas the Aristocrat often looked to the extended family, the manor, and sometimes the aristocratic brotherhood (e.g., Plato's camp of guardians), the Saint took inspiration from the craft guild (e.g., Ruskin's St. George's Guild) or peasant village council (e.g., Gandhi's *panchayati*). While the Socialist may often look to the industrial labor union or syndicate, the Capitalist drew inspiration from the structures of urban business, the merchant guild as well as the joint stock companies, including the great London and Dutch East India companies launched near the start of the seventeenth century. As I have already suggested, the very categories and relationships of business law or practice pervade classical liberal thought.

### The Importance of Contracts

In a classic dictum, Henry Maine stated that "the movement of the progressive societies has hitherto been a movement *from Status to Contract*" (Maine, 1888, 165). The Old Testament offered abundant imagery of "covenants" of the Jewish people with their God; but even when bound by religious oath, the new contracts were primarily among those deemed formally equal. Unlike a barter economy where most in-kind transactions were immediate, capitalist economics needed confidence in future performance of present agreements. One must be as good as one's word. Business needed at least some zone of predictability in transactions before more unpredictable markets.

For example, a typical joint stock company was a contract to pool funds to finance a shipment, with subscribers of stock hoping to recover their original capital along with a proportional share of any profit, but risking the like share of any loss. Before entry, investors were in full possession of their preferences, their resources, and their rights. Their engagement was with an organization of strictly limited purposes, usually not really including winning glory or saving souls.

Similarly, in seventeenth-century political thought one may begin with a "state of nature" where none are subject to the authority of others. In a time when even marriage becomes less a sacred and irrevocable bond guided by parents than a more conditional contract between two individuals, the liberals assume that one owes in act virtually no positive duties toward others before a "social contract" constitutes political authority.

Of our four paradigms of social theory, the Capitalist is ever more impressed with the strength of self-interested motives relative to social ones. If beyond the narrowest circles of kith and kin there are only watery social motives, then self-interested motives dominate engagement in either business or political contracts. Formation of social institutions is highly instrumental, limited to the more or less express purposes of contractees at the origin and at any later revision, although perhaps implying certain necessary and proper means to any listed objectives (as Hamilton and Marshall would argue of the U.S. Constitution).

Yet none could unilaterally withdraw for self-interested reasons except as the terms allowed. Just as in business life, political contracts aimed at predictable performance by others. Unlike feudal oaths of fealty to *persons* where friendship as well as honor could assure the tie, contractual promises were to impersonal *projects* and hence more vulnerable. This is why early liberals feared or would even censor any teaching implying that promises need not be kept. Religiomoral reinforcement was viewed as an important auxiliary to coercive enforcement in preventing violation of agreements.

The wrong religious views may undermine the credibility of promise-keeping, as when anarchistic, atheist, or authoritarian.

In the former case, as early as 1523, Huldreich Zwingli—a major Reformation theologian aligned with the guildsmen burghers of Zurich—attacks the Anabaptist (also called Catabaptist) rejection of religious oaths: "Take away the oath and you have dissolved all order. . . . [All] order is overthrown when the oath is done away. . . . Give up the oath in any state then according to the Catabaptists' desire, and at once the magistracy is removed and all things follow as *they* would have them. Good gods! What a confusion and upturning of everything!" ("Refutation of Baptist Tricks," in Jackson, 1901, 208–9). The Zurchers hence made Anabaptist rebaptizings of adults or even attendance at Anabaptist meetings capital offenses! (See Williams, 1962, 142–44). In seventeenth-century Holland, Spinoza favored religious toleration, yet even he would repress doctrines "which by their very nature nullify the compact by which the right of free action was ceded. For instance a man who holds that the supreme power has no rights over him, or that promises ought not to be kept, or that everyone should live as he pleases" (*Theologico-Political Treatise*, XX).

Locke's *Letter concerning Toleration* would not accord toleration to an atheist: "Promises, covenants, and oaths, which are the bonds of human society, can have no hold upon an atheist." Autocratic religion is also a threat. Locke in the same essay implicitly rejected tolerance for Roman Catholics, elsewhere explaining that their "blind obedience to an infallible pope" implies that they may "dispense with all their oaths, promises, and the obligations they have to their prince" (Ashcraft, 1986, 99, n. 95).

### Shareholders

Excepting the more radical Levellers, many early liberals assumed that among adult males, the subset of the propertied class and the political class should be identical. Accustomed to enter civil contracts in their private capacity, in their political capacity they would form political ones. The former were particular-purpose economic associations, while the latter involved general purposes, to use the 1603 language of Rhineland burgher Johannes Althusius in his *Politics* (1964).

The private world had contracts between the owners and their workers, and only force or fraud—not economic duress—could invalidate them. Economic pressures do not make choices involuntary. But when liberals turn to the political sphere, they often inconsistently argued that the propertyless could have no autonomy of will, since they were subject to the economic pressure of estate owners and others with property. Perhaps in part because of their lack of property, women too were judged incapable of full political consent. Yet once one posits abstractly isolated individuals, one then needs to justify authority both in the horizontal bond that creates a society and in the vertical bond that constitutes government. Those who are not parties to the original contract must also be bonded by some sort of consenting (cf. Pateman, 1979). Later accessions may be permitted in either a business contract or a political contract, but only the latter must somehow oblige even those never made full partners.

While apparently denying votes to women on the Biblical dictum that "he shall be your master," one solution involved a religious screening. While the doctrine of election has some Biblical bases, its austere Calvinist version may concern a very practical problem concerning even church voting rights. Given their wish to abolish episcopacy and replace it with consent of congregations, how could Calvinists admit almost everyone to the ordinary worship, require them to adhere to rules, and yet reserve voting rights, and so forth only to the propertied? The theological doctrine of a sharp dichotomy between "unregenerate" and "regenerate" served this practical purpose. Thus in early Puritan Massachusetts Bay only the elect of God could be electors on Earth, in both church and state affairs.

Another resolution was more secular. Although Locke welcomed the nonpropertied as allies in resistance to the Stuarts, he seemed reluctant to welcome them as voters. While maintaining that either royal prerogative or parliamentary legislation could change the electoral system, he nowhere committed himself to an expansion of the suffrage to the nonpropertied (cf. Ashcraft, 1986, 238–39 and n. 47, also 270 n. 173).[3] Locke in the *Two Treatises* resolves his problem by a distinction between express consent (overt political commitments limited to propertied citizens) and tacit consent (effected by mere residence or even a temporary visit of foreigners). The latter would obligate obedience to the laws by noncitizen members of society, those denied votes but yet accorded some minimal rights of speech, legal equality, and so on.

In some nations well into our own century, the "stake in society" argument was used to deny an equal franchise to the propertyless. As if almost forgetting that liberal forms were also meant to protect everyone's life from tyrannical caprice, that theory assumed that the main purpose of the government was protection of property. While it is true that the seventeenth century had a larger sense of "property"—which extended to everything that properly belongs to one, including life and freedom—the main concern linked to voting or officeholding rights was what Locke called the "outward things, such as money, lands, houses, furniture, and the like" (*Letter concerning Toleration*).

Even Herbert Spencer's *Social Statics* frankly spoke of "our joint-stock protection-society" (Spencer, 1910a, 122). As in the joint stock company, even full citizens have few duties beyond paying their share and otherwise obeying the general rules.

Parliaments had medieval antecedents and annual elections had classic Greco-Roman models, but the annual shareholders' meeting may have suggested ideas for reforming parliament, which James Harrington and others said should be annually elected to prevent tyranny. Shareholders' meetings weighted voting by numbers of shares owned (cf. Philips, 1961, 1–22). But there was by contrast formal equality among the largely propertied minority of male adults holding the suffrage in Britain in the seventeenth and eighteenth centuries. But in Britain and elsewhere in the nineteenth century, once the elites conceded the vote to the propertyless, they introduced something comparable to shareholders' weightings: The propertied and educated gave themselves plural voting rights to counterbalance the single votes accorded workers.

### Trustees and Enforcement

As in a business, so in politics, one needs some surety that the interests of those with a stake in the enterprise are protected by enforcement of contracts. Semiliberal Thomas Hobbes finds what he calls "the fountain and original of justice" in "that men perform their covenants made" (Leviathan, I, 15). But as he added, "covenants, without the swords, are but words, and of no strength to secure a man at all" (Leviathan, II, xvii). Commitments must transcend any personal nexus—for, as the lawyer's maxim runs, good friends make bad contracts. Liberal theorists such Harrington and Hume maintained that the design of constitutions should be with an eye to the worst rather than the average or the best among us.

Against Hobbes, a good political executive must be constitutionally limited, described after the language of business law as "agent," "fiduciary," "trustee," or the like, as if comparable to the shipboard agent of investors in a joint stock agreement. Against the royalist thesis but close to the business practice, the chief executive was subject to removal if violating the trust, even if not a tyrant but simply incompetent—as argued in John Milton's Tenure of Kings and Magistrates (Milton, 1957, 750–80). Close stipulation of powers, periodicity of election, and exposure to the equivalent of shareholders' revolts become central.

In time a king's ministers would come to be viewed as representing the parliamentary majority, which would constitute cabinets as a kind of board of directors to oversee the real chief executive: the prime minister. Whether executives were parliamentary or presidential, it was a commonplace eighteenth-century idea that higher officials should also be men of substantial wealth. John Jay remarked, "The people who own the country ought to govern it" (Parenti, 1988, 5). Yet the constitutional convention did not adopt Pinckney's recommendation of a high property qualification ($100,000 net worth) for the U.S. presidency, since most expected wealthy George Washington to be the first president in any case.

Whether royal or not, the executive was expected to seem class neutral, as typified by John Adam's concept of the "Impartial Mediator" who had to "balance" the rich and those of more modest means. Yet beyond assuring impartial execution of the law, the classical liberal executive was not intended to be impartial in policy decisions between the propertied and the propertyless who would covet their property.

Even policy legislation becomes businesslike. When Jeremy Bentham developed his utilitarian system on the business accounting model, he admitted that, for practical measurement of pleasures and pains, all values had to be put on a common monetary yardstick. To be weighed at all, everything had to be given its price—a pattern that continues in modern "cost–benefit analysis," which one economist conceded "is an act of imperialism by economists" (Okun, 1975, 13n.).

If liberal politics was largely created by and for the needs of trade, it was in thought and language influenced by business practices. Close study of merchant guilds and joint stock companies could deepen our understanding of classical liberal political ideas. Even now, business metaphors rival sports in talk about politics, as in market analogies of competitions of ideas, candidates, or institutional forms.

## Democracy as End Only: Liberalism in the Proceduralist Mode

Many later liberals enlarged their view of the purposes of liberal freedoms, speaking of ends of freedom as human dignity or development, if not wholly denying instrumentality.

In the father and son James Mill and John Stuart Mill, one may distinguish "protective" versus "developmental" liberalism. The former used utilitarian argument to emphasize protection of rights of life and property, whereas the latter (influenced by de Tocqueville) emphasized human growth or maturation through the process of participation—something more than human development useful for economic productivity (cf. Macpherson, 1977; also, Held, 1987). Thereafter, arguments for democratic participation could be framed in terms of either better decisions or better human beings, the latter instanced by John Dewey and participatory democrats (Cook and Morgan, 1971, 1–40). If figures from the reform wing of liberalism as well as moderate social democrats remain attentive to instrumental objectives of democracy, they no longer stress protection of property so much as the welfare needs of those lacking it, and they also give more attention to self-actualization needs.

### Proceduralist Presentism

Once the poor begin to press their own demands through democracy, many begin to deny that the liberal state had any economic purpose. In fact some liberal theorists distrust the view of democracy as being a means to anything, maintaining only that it is an end in itself. Hannah Arendt thus viewed the forms of freedom as at most a vehicle for immediate, expressive rewards: In public spaces, political actors properly enjoy their liberty and strive for personal distinction, but leave aside "the social question."

To the extent that it takes democracy as end only, liberal thought typically focuses on present procedures, bracketing them from what comes before or after. Leszek Kolakowski somewhere spoke of a "dawn to dusk" quality of liberal thought, its fixation on the present to the neglect of both past and future. In parallel with the Capitalist theory of the market as previously discussed, there is closure to how the past works through present structures to shape the future.

Proceduralist liberalism dwells on the procedures while losing the larger process. It avoids scrutiny of what goes into the procedures— namely, the origins of the procedures themselves, states of preferences, and distributions of the resources needed to manipulate the procedures to attain those preferences. It also avoids scrutiny of what comes out of the procedures—namely, maintained or even deepened economic inequalities. These closures function to block the criticism that antecedent economic inequalities are passed through the procedures to consequent inequalities, often amplified when the wealthy shape policy to increase their wealth. Marx's central criticism of liberalism arises here: that bourgeois democracy's formal equality of rights masks substantive inequality (cf. Macpherson, 1966).

In reply, liberalism claims that its competitive procedures are self-corrective, whether in its economics, its politics, or even its culture. Viewed in the liberal way, the self-corrective nature of the economic as well as political procedures will arrest any undue deepening of inequalities. In the political sphere, there are ever-renewed beginnings and fair resolutions through the procedures of marketlike peaceable competitions not only of ideas, but also of candidates and institutional units. Provided that force and fraud are absent, the fairness of such procedures promises at least a long-run fairness tout court, regardless of what may have come before or after. Contests are subject to more or less neutral rules of the game and resolved by recurrent soundings of consent.

In either the economic or the political marketplaces, the standing competitive procedures displace moral evaluation of results. Avoidance of questions of "value" or "power" contribute to such proceduralist presentism. It is usually easier to attain a social consensus on the fairness (i.e., formal generality) of present procedures than to attain consensus on the outcomes of such procedures. But at some level of dissatisfaction, the procedures themselves may be brought into question, as already noted of markets.

### The Givenness of Preferences

Taking a closer look at what comes before the present play of liberal democratic political procedures, liberalism in its politics as well as its economics tends to take preferences or demands as a given. No explanation is desirable, if possible at all.

Liberal social science dwells more on current states of public opinion than on inquiry into its sources. As Robert Heilbroner once noted, "It is often said that people get what they want, but that statement is rarely followed by the question, 'Why do they want what they want' " (Heilbroner, 1966, 42–43). While early researchers believed in the great efficacy of mass media in shaping opinion, there followed a phase stressing rather quite limited effects. Only recently have many returned to recognition of the media's role in agenda-setting or cognitive structuring of the world. But they may see this as perhaps a function of the limited time and attention of the audience or else as something shaped by reporters—not as linked to questions of ownership of the mass media (contrast McCombs and Shaw, 1972; and Gitlin, 1980). Within liberal horizons, minds seem to be self-formed, at least when they acquiesce in or actively support liberal economics and politics. But any contrary preferences would have little impact for lack of resources to push them.

### The Givenness of Resource Distributions

A liberal theory of "political systems" such as David Easton's took mental states like "demands" and "supports" as the "inputs." While mental states are relevant, minds are always embedded in bodies linked to unequal tangible resources of political influence. Even if articulated with the tongues of angels, political demands have little weight in political persuasion without reinforcing signals of mobilizations of resources to back them up, rewarding the compliant or punishing the resistant.

While some may argue that expert testimony also has some autonomous weight, the chief reinforcements of messages within functioning liberal democracies are votes and economic favors. Ineligibles and nonvoters aside, the distribution of votes could roughly mirror the distribution of preferences in a population. However, this is not true of the capacity to give or withhold campaign contributions or other kinds of economic inducements.

### The Givenness of the Procedures Themselves

Finally, proceduralist liberalism may resist critical inquiry into the origins of a set of procedures, which may have been projects of the propertied more than of "the people" in any large sense. When Charles Beard critically reviewed economic interests behind the U.S. Constitution of 1787, it elicited many conservative rejoinders; but even Forrest McDonald—the most thorough critic—did not deny likely economic influences on the Constitution so much as challenge Beard's specific version of it (Beard, 1914; McDonald, 1958).

The point of all this is that distributions of preferences, political resources, and even institutional power must be viewed as variables rather than constants to understand limitations of Capitalist politics, however much we may cherish the freedoms it has bequeathed to us.

## Strategies to Shape Policy

While capitalism historically promoted the formal equality of rights behind liberal democratic procedures, it also frustrates effective citizen equality in their operation. This becomes apparent as we look at the strategic fields of influence, recruitment, and structures.

### The Influence Strategy: The Capitalist's Public Combat of Ideas

To enhance productivity through technological advance and enlightened self-interested activity, the Capitalist paradigm required enriched information flows. With added impetus from Protestant religious ideas, support for public education as well as encouragement of public libraries were practical consequences. Benjamin Franklin reflects this in his activities in publishing, founding the University of Pennsylvania, and starting the Philadelphia public library. Only extreme free marketeers such as Herbert Spencer or the libertarians question the value of public libraries. Liberalism also encouraged enlarged public information about the activities of public officials, if sometimes limited regarding external security, internal security, or what could impact forthcoming markets.

But let us shift to flows of persuasive messages. This story began with the Reformation's challenge to public enforcement of Catholic orthodoxy. Beginning with the individualist currents of the Reformation, this paradigm is more likely than the other three to espouse one's right to silence: No one should be forced to publicly profess beliefs not privately held. Believing rather that each should profess only the truths that they find in the Bible, Lutheran, Calvinist, and other Reformation protestants wanted to end the Roman Catholic monopoly on public discourse. To them, that church was in collusion with secular authorities in maintaining a distorted reading of the Word. It even blocked translation of Scripture into modern languages, although the printing press and growing literacy made it possible for many to read God's Word for themselves, as in Luther's vision of a "priesthood of all believers."

While opposing Roman Catholic censorship of themselves, most early reformers did not oppose censorship as such, even if Luther in his last years grew more tolerant of rival views such as those of peaceable Anabaptists. But Calvin's sixteenth-century Geneva was severely intolerant, executing heretics such as Servetus. But by the seventeenth century—against other Calvinists (mostly Presbyterians) who wanted prior licensing of books—John Milton's *Areopagitica* broadens toleration to at least fellow-Protestant "neighboring differences." Milton would yet silence Catholics, atheists, and whatever else was judged superstitious or seditious (Milton, 1957, 716–49). Locke's *Letter concerning Toleration* made similar exceptions, for reasons noted earlier. Lacking the Whigs' great fear of Catholicism, Benedict Spinoza in Holland and Roger Williams in Rhode Island enlarged their tolerance to most forms of religious expression, provided that no sect preached anarchism. Most early advocates of toleration not only had diverged from the orthodoxy of their context but could reasonably anticipate that their own expression could be censored unless they secured like freedom for others. When they did not expect their own views to be officially established, they often turned toward separation of church and state (Baptists, Quakers, and later deists such as Jefferson).

Toleration often emerged less from principle than from practical stalemate. Machiavelli had held that patrician–plebeian frictions of Rome had fostered freedom; and the same would be true of frictions among contending religious groups, if no side could dominate by main force. In Holland and England, nasty civil wars encouraged eventual acquiescence in mutual religious toleration, readily extending to politics because of the close nexus at that time. John Neville Figgis sums it up: "Political liberty is the residuary legatee of ecclesiastical animosities" (Figgis, 1916, 118). In Britain, however, even the Restoration Stuarts were resistant, deeming seditious any publication of parliamentary debates and briefly in 1675 even trying to close down coffeehouses when their opponents gathered in them (Ashcraft, 1986, 141–42, 144).

Beyond quest for public peace, advocates of separation of church and state argued that state religious establishments block discovery of religious truth. In *The Bloudy Tenent of Persecution*, Roger Williams thus warned of the censors' fallibility, which could block the way to Heaven for the few he expected to be ultimately saved. Imposed religion also fostered hypocrisy and hindered commerce.

Like Spinoza or Locke, a more secular figure such as Jefferson was much more concerned about how religious censorship could block the discovery and implementation of *political* truth.[4] Divergent aims yet converged on the need for the new political procedure of public competition of ideas. By the eighteenth century, increasingly secularized liberals almost everywhere sought to take their new philosophy fully public, as if illuminating the Platonic cave. In France, Diderot, d'Alembert, Grimm, and others pushed projects of educational reform as well as the *Encyclopédie*, aiming at popular dissemination of the most advanced views of the age.

Aside from the lonely voice of Rousseau, there were few vestiges of the Aristocrat's teaching that only a few could be exposed to philosophic knowledge while the many could at best attain true belief dependent on salutary myths.[5] Voltaire—otherwise a defender of enlarged tolerance—still believed that the people needed their Biblical religion.[6] Rousseau claimed that philosophes of his acquaintance held a secret doctrine, concealing their materialism and disbelief in the Bible. By contrast, Thomas Paine's *Age of Reason* frontally denied the authenticity of the Bible. But when he asked an endorsement from his friend and fellow deist, Jefferson demurred on the ground that Paine's polemic was excessive.

### Trial by Combat?

Any such hesitations aside, the Capitalist increasingly saw no need to distinguish philosophic and popular audiences. Fully public debate implies rejection of the Aristocratic dichotomy of procedures for discovery of philosophic truth (dialectic among the few) and for implementing it in the world (rhetoric for the many). All that was needed was a fair fight—an end of the censorship that permitted only one-sided defense of feudal institutions. A public competition of ideas would certainly bring progress (Thomas Paine) or at least the best chance at it (J. S. Mill). Without censorship, public opinion would not be an obstacle to discovery of truth but rather register its progress in the world.

The competitive motif dominates some of the most famous liberal statements, whether working the metaphor of trial by combat or that of the capitalist marketplace:

> Though all the winds of doctrine were let loose to play upon the earth, so Truth be in the field, we do injuriously by licensing and prohibiting to misdoubt her strength. Let her and Falsehood grapple; who ever knew Truth put to the worse, in a free and open encounter. (John Milton, *Areopagitica*, 1644)

> Truth is great and will prevail if left to herself; . . . she is the proper and sufficient antagonist to error, and has nothing to fear from the conflict unless by human interposition disarmed of her natural weapons, free argument and debate; errors ceasing to be dangerous when it is permitted freely to contradict them. (Thomas Jefferson, preamble to his bill for Religious Freedom in Virginia, 1779 [adopted 1786])

> If the lists are kept open, we may hope that if there be a better truth, it will be found when the human mind is capable of receiving it. (John Stuart Mill, *On Liberty*, 1859)

When men have realized that time has upset many fighting faiths, they may come to believe even more than they believe the very foundations of their own conduct that the ultimate good desired is better reached by free trade in ideas—that the best test of truth is the power of the thought to get itself accepted in the competition of the market, and that truth is the only ground upon which their wishes safely can be carried out. That at any rate is the theory of our Constitution. (Oliver Wendell Holmes, Jr., dissent in *Abrams v. United States*, 1919)

When ideas compete in the market for acceptance, full and free discussion exposes the false and they gain few adherents. . . . Some nations less resilient than the United States, where illiteracy is high and where democratic traditions are only budding, might have to take drastic steps and jail these men [Communists] for merely speaking their creed. But in America they are miserable merchants of unwanted ideas; their wares remain unsold. (William O. Douglas, dissent in *Dennis v. United States*, 1951)

The public competition that promotes discovery of truth coincides with its widespread dissemination. For there were certain acceptable passions common to all and intensely felt (roughly synonymous with natural rights), which encouraged the view that the public could recognize truth regarding appropriate ends. Displacing the older concept of the "common good," which worked more from the good of the whole toward what is fitting for the parts, the seventeenth century's "public interest" could only be an aggregation of private interests, at least those that do not mutually cancel out (cf. Gunn, 1969). While the Aristocrat would test truth claims by looking for intellectual coherence, the Capitalist assumes that some truths are almost *felt*. The people need only hear the truth in order to recognize it (Locke's "self-evidence" was "ready assent upon hearing"). Once the consensus on truth emerged, many early liberals optimistically assumed what Rousseau denied—namely that to know the good was automatically to love it and to act on it. Prior moral training becomes less vital.

Uncensored public discourse would also test merely prudential value judgments and the empirical statements that support them. For the most, liberal philosophy of science sees cooperation risky, and competition healthy, engendering "growth" in knowledge as well as in economies.[7]

Whatever the special rules for science, in opening persuasive discourse to the many, the rules of Aristocratic dialogue would not really be followed. It is now enough to cultivate the seeming rather than the being of candor, logicality, and the like. When the game is played to win in adversary court proceedings, policy debates, or election campaigns, it is difficult to be generous to the opponent's case. Overlooking that one at least applies the additional test of *who* wins, the New

Dealer Thurman Arnold crassly put it like this: "The only realistic test of a political speech is its vote-getting effect. This is recognized by the tradesmen of politics but denied by political scholars and high-minded persons generally" (Arnold, 1935, 27).

A questionable idea of progress underlies the Capitalist's confidence in the marketplace of ideas. This recalls O. W. Holmes's language, as cited above: As a social Darwinist he believed in the survival of the fittest after a fair fight, whether it be a question of firms and their competing products or, rather, groups and their competing ideas.[8]

If *caveat emptor* applies in either case, poor products such as ineffective patent medicines may prevail at markets just as bad programs may prevail in politics. These last range from useless panaceas to the most vicious predations (the Nazi "truths" disseminated in Weimar Germany). It would be countered that the risks are less with the competitive procedure, which promotes learning, and that some self-correctiveness would hold of both economic and political markets. Yet, often the education comes too late to be of much use, and errors can be damaging. Even ancients such as Aristotle conceded some natural advantage of the truth over falsehood, at least in a court trial; but the Aristocrat recognized that, because it may be poorly argued or influenced by irrational popular opinion, the truth would not always prevail. Seeing only demagogic pandering to the many, Plato even said that *untruth* tended to prevail in the Athenian Ecclesia. I can hear his response to the new doctrine: Those who claim truth always prevails in an uncensored public combat of ideas merely *define* truth as whatever prevails. Some modern conservatives have also voiced their objections. Hobbes—argued de Jouvenel—held that, in matters where truth is evasive, the "combat" would merely proliferate sects and their conflicts (in Brittan, 1975, 150–51). In his *Liberty, Equality, Fraternity*, James Fitzjames Stephen argued that such combat could foster skepticism rather than agreement on the truth.

The Saint would wonder whether combat brings any good in any sphere of life, unless it is against our own egoistic passions. Yet other objections arise from the Socialist left, as sketched below.

### Unequal Combat
Along with certain other civil rights such as moving about or changing jobs, workers acquired the right of freedom of speech long before obtaining a right to vote (about two centuries earlier in Britain). Yet it is arguable that the right of freedom of speech may have been more substantively equal at its origin than now, for wealth tends to dominate the creation, dissemination, and reinforcement of ideas.

In the creation of political messages, capital has a major presence in control of universities, publishing firms, and both print and electronic mass media. While it screens top management of such institutions, it has less control over the professors, writers of books, and journalists—who can be much more critical of capital. But proliferating capitalist think tanks sponsor a flood of books and editorials of the proper point of view. Further, the few wealthy business leaders who get into politics in a major way hire public relations experts to write and even think for them.

### Delivery of Messages

Wealth also dominates the dissemination of messages. In stable liberal democracies coercive censorship becomes vestigial, yet an indirect censorship may arise in the screening system for the upper tips of hierarchies.[9]

Another subtle form of de facto censorship involves use of economic or symbolic pressures to muzzle opponents, as when conservatives threatened defunding of the U.S. National Public Radio, which has since been docile (like the BBC). Or the merely verbal pressure of jawbonings by prominent people may try to silence a certain point of view.

The most formidable "censor" in a capitalist system consists of restricted resources. In either markets or politics, the adversary proceeding assumes the existence of many small sellers who are competing, not in collusion with each other. The reality, however, has massive concentrations of corporate power that may shape public consumption of either commodities or political ideas.

Elimination of dissident media can occur by market forces alone, and this may defeat the really more popular ideas. In nineteenth-century Britain, the social democratic *Daily Herald* was read by 5 million people—twice the combined readerships of the bourgeois *Times, Financial Times*, and the *Guardian*. Obviously not for want of readers, the paper nevertheless failed. It could shake off other harassments (libel suits, predatory taxation, and requirements of posting bonds), but it succumbed to market forces. Not out of ideological bias against the radical newspapers but because of readers' lower purchasing power, businesses preferred to put advertising with the bourgeois papers, which then were able to sell papers for below production cost and undermine the salability of working-class newspapers. Only a few radical newspapers survived, whether by keeping to a small audience, by securing union or Liberal party subsidy, or often by ceasing to be radical and thus drawing more affluent readers of interest to advertisers (Curran, 1979).

Thus, in lieu of the state censor, the market has became the de facto censor, selectively boosting dissemination of some ideas and blocking others. In the absence of censorship, the boosting largely replaces intentional blocking, but an overwhelming boosting of pro-

Capitalist messages effectively crowds out any non-Capitalist perspective (the economic views of the Aristocrat and the Saint, as well as of the Socialist).

Yet the pattern is porous. When media are genuinely competitive and controversy boosts circulation, market competition may bring attention to unorthodox demonstrations and sometimes even the ideas of demonstrators. Also, people have personal experience of the world, and mass media cannot wholly predispose perceptions. Nor can capital control word-of-mouth communication among workers, consumers, and so forth—which can be critical of the corporations. Such uncontrollable communication joins market competition in keeping some diversity in the capitalist nation's "marketplace of ideas," even outside the more abstruse world of scholarly books.

### Reinforcement of Messages

Capital also dominates the reinforcement of persuasive messages, whether these are threats/promises or arguments invoking a range of possible standards. The former immediately involve punishment for noncompliance and rewards for compliance, while the latter may at least signal likely mobilizations of reinforcers.

Votes constitute one key reinforcer in liberal politics, but the obvious rival consists of money or the economic favors it can buy. As Amitai Etzioni puts it,

> The essence of politics in a mass society is the ability to amass the support of a large number of individuals. Although there are several ways to gain such aggregation, under most circumstances money is by far the most effective. Volunteers help, but they are fickle and unreliable, and they themselves require organizing. They cannot be aggregated in large numbers, stored, shifted around, readily shipped across the country. Money obviously can. It is highly liquid, convertible, and nonperishable. (Etzioni, 1984, 11–12)

The more outrageous forms of what Etzioni calls "capital corruption" consist in illicit bribes, kickbacks, secret business deals, open business favors, exorbitant "speakers' fees" for appearances at interest-group conventions, and the like. These have variously appeared in most liberal democratic nations, often corrupting top national leaders. Even legal campaign contributions must be viewed as often really but a tactic for influencing incumbent officials, as quite obvious when the money flows to politicians having power to influence matters of special concern. In the United States, incumbent members of Congress are massively favored over challengers even when they have no significant opposition. Consider also that, when producer-interest contributors find they have backed losing candidates, they may cynically make amends with postelection contributions to the winners, as in 150 instances after the 1986 U.S. Senate race (Sabato, 1989, 17–18). Politically invested money can often yield unusually high returns, as in one estimate that in the 1980 U.S. elections $30 *million* in political action committee (PAC) contributions returned $250 *billion* in tax reductions (Hansen, 1983, 121).

## The Recruitment Strategy: Capitalism and Electoral Competitions

The recruitment strategy aims at control of policy through control over what persons are put into position to make policy, so the main game is to get friends into such vital offices and get rivals out.

When high property qualifications for office can no longer be defended, informal screenings have much the same effect, under normal conditions limiting highest offices to those who are of the wealthy or have supportive wealthy friends. In both primary and general elections, most recent candidates for the U.S. presidency have been millionaires, as have many candidates for the Senate.

As for the mode of recruitment, the Aristocrat's hereditary and lifetime right tends in the Capitalist paradigm to elective and accountable incumbency, since wisdom is not hereditary. An undercurrent of liberal theory—visible in Paine, Jefferson, and others—even argued that royalty and nobility are innately *inferior*, becoming flat chested, short winded, or even feeble minded due to inbreeding. While the liberal tradition often left room for increasingly ceremonial constitutional monarchs, there could be no hereditary birthright to leadership, nor any claim to life tenure—aside from unusual cases such as the "good behavior" incumbency of U.S. federal judges. Any further appointments would be political at the top layers but increasingly meritocratic (civil service) in lower bureaucratic levels, accenting criteria of education, examinations, experience, and effectiveness. But our primary concern is with elective recruitment, which opened key policy-making offices to nonlandowner interests.

### Voting Rights: The Stake in Society

In the cradle of liberalism, aside from local offices, votes determined who would be elected to the British House of Commons. This body was from the late seventeenth century up to the nineteenth century often subject to royal manipulation through posts, pensions, bribes, and so forth, to the great indignation of most liberals (except Hume), although some of their ideological progeny would use money corruption in their turn. The House of Commons was also exposed until 1911 to an absolute veto on all but money bills by the nonelective House of Lords.

Adding to our prior discussion of suffrage, while voters in seventeenth-century England were largely propertied, in some localities the suffrage reached down to servants and paupers. The Levellers wanted universal manhood suffrage in the 1650s, rather than Oliver Cromwell's compromise that excluded household servants and beggars. While the property qualification rule (the "40-shilling-freehold") applied during the Restoration, more could meet it because of inflation, growing real wealth, and permissive rulings by parliamentary Whigs who wanted to enlarge an electorate favorable to themselves. But if possibly as many as 40 percent of male adults could vote in the mid-seventeenth century, this shrank to perhaps 10 percent a century later; yet it climbed again by installments in the nineteenth century (Ashcraft, 1986, 145–72). While in 1832 only landowners could vote, from 1832 to 1867 this expanded to nonlandowner men of substance such as leaseholders. From 1867 workers could vote, effected by Tory Prime Minister Disraeli to preempt any Liberal move; but plural voting gave an edge to the propertied and well educated.

Despite hesitations of his father, John Stuart Mill and later reformers accepted extension of the vote to workers. But Mill did not accept an equal suffrage, weighting his ideal of plural voting as much to education or presumptive intellectual capacity as to property alone. In national elections he would still exclude paupers on relief and also illiterates, and even in local government he would accept limitations of voting to taxpayers and allow plural voting (*Considerations on Representative Government*, VIII, XV).[10] As late as 1948, in Britain a minority of historically privileged persons could enjoy votes for their constituency of residence, their place of any business, and even their university constituency (Oxford or Cambridge).

Thus, even when attempting to make government more popular, early liberals could be reluctant to make government too popular, too soon. Classical liberals loved equality when thinking of the pretensions of the nobles—just as the American patriots loved equality when thinking of the British Parliament in which they had no representation, but many yet loved inequality when thinking of the propertyless, of women, or of the American slaves. However, the suffrage would generally expand to new groups over time, relentlessly moving toward universal adult suffrage in a pattern described by de Tocqueville in *Democracy in America* (I, iii). Most expansions involved some conjunction of pressure from below and pull from above, the latter meaning sponsorship by some already enfranchised group eager to broaden the franchise in confidence that new voters would favor themselves more than rivals.

Such moves as shifting from a landowning to a taxpaying qualification enlarged the suffrage to the urban lower-middle class. Suffrage extended to most adult white males in the United States much earlier than in Britain, largely by the 1820s. While Democratic-Republicans and the later Jacksonian Democrats favored enlarged suffrage, Federalists such as John Adams or the later Whig Daniel Webster opposed removal of property rights for voting in Massachusetts. Until such restrictions were abolished or simply atrophied, the "stake in society" argument reigned.

The older practice of open voting gave plausibility to the stock argument that those without property should not have the ballot. It was assumed that, since they were dependent for their livelihoods on those who employed them, rural laborers, servants, and the like would follow choices of their landlords. This assumption, along with the further assumption that urban labor would oppose the men of business, encouraged conservatives Disraeli and Bismarck to support working-class votes (Bowles and Gintis, 1986, 42). A comparable argument of dependency was used to delay women's votes. Once the secret ballot was adopted—pushed by Britain's philosophical radicals (utilitarians)—it neutralized this argument, although some persisted in denying that women could conceal their vote from their husbands. However, if secrecy in voting removed likely pressure from above, it also removed possible peer pressure to vote a group interest.

As voting rights enlarge to new groups (especially when compounded by population growth), an individual vote becomes less likely to make or break a tie, especially in large national legislative constituencies (particularly when following single-member district plurality rule). But if votes may be less important to the voters themselves, harvesting those votes remains very important to candidates. Political parties thus became necessary to mobilize or coordinate the enlarged voting populations, putting forth candidates under a common label.[11]

Where political parties remain strong, they still mobilize amateurs; but the game becomes increasingly professionalized when candidates work the mass media—the primary vehicle of modern marketing. The campaign experts know they are engaged in capitalist marketing. Pollsters closely study the voter-consumers—including the delimitation of various segments, some of whom are to be ignored as beyond persuasion and others singled out for specialized messages.

While this maximization of sales may be called "improved democratic responsiveness," perhaps in real responsiveness the candidates would actually reshape themselves to what voters want, not just *seem* to do so by cultivating an image (or images) to suit electorates. In politics no less than in ordinary markets, what people want is not independent of the media sell in any case.

Hiring professionals and pumping the mass media (especially TV) with messages costs big money. To the extent that elections are not publicly funded—and especially if campaigns are protracted as in the United States, rather than brief as in Britain—wealth goes into the procedures of electoral contests, and it shapes what comes out of them. This may be less by controlling who wins than by prescreening who can seriously run at all. In effect, the game is half over before the voters vote.

When candidates for office become a commodity to be manufactured and marketed, the need for much money brings much potential power to the minority of the wealthy who get into the game.[12] In the United States, limitations on individuals' donations to specific federal candidates have been enacted, but there is no limit on noncollusive or independent expenditure on behalf of a candidate or a candidate's causes. Nor is there any limit on what affluent candidates may spend on their own campaigns. In such rulings on campaign legislation, the irony is that the U.S. Supreme Court strives to keep open one political game ("freedom of speech") while bringing some closure to another (cf. especially *Buckley v. Valeo*, 1976).

The inequality of campaign contributions tends to negate formal equality of voting rights, whether considered as an instrument of recruitment or rather as a means of influence. While a voter controls but one vote, the contributor of large sums to election media campaigns may indirectly guide many votes. While a voter votes in one constituency, campaign contributions may effectively "vote" in many. Money crosses over congressional district or state boundaries and may illicitly corrupt foreign elections as well.[13]

Are liberal democratic elections but the means whereby the minority that controls our lives through control over the means of production gives the majority the illusion of popular control?

Electoral contests deflect discontents from the capitalist system and its leading corporate actors. When the whole system moves into a recession or even depression, it is blamed on some specific set of politicians and their policies. In reality, politicians can do no more than marginally affect the timing of a recession, advancing or retarding it to suit the electoral cycle. At least that is more than King Canute could do with tides. But when incumbents insist on claiming credit for any ups in the business cycle, there is a certain justice in blaming them for any downs that happen on their watch. In the 1970s and 1980s, economic difficulties in many nations tended to undermine the electoral chances of whatever hapless set of politicians held national leadership, unless saved by some highly popular action in another domain (e.g., Thatcher in the Falkland Islands). Such erosion of popularity caused by economic forces beyond control affects both left and right civilian parties. Fortunately, it also plagues military dictatorships in the Third World. This may in part account for the long swings of alternating predominance of democracies and military juntas in Latin America. There the tragedy is that neither the "ins" nor the "outs" can be expected to have much control of the local economy, dependent rather on world capitalist dynamics, whether unplanned (business cycles) or effectively planned by those not elected (imposed International Monetary Fund austerity programs).

When election contests are effectively limited to procapitalist parties, the results could only elicit probusiness policy, especially when guided by campaign contributions or less respectable forms of venality.

Yet capital seems to have only a few unifying, core interests—namely, preserving private property against expropriation (compensated "nationalizations" can be acceptable, especially if at or above book value), and preserving the inequalities of income often linked to such wealth.

Beyond that core, the business world divides against itself on many aspects of regulatory, revenue or budgetary policy. That business firms are inconsistently impacted makes room for labor and consumer interests, in part expressed through meaningful struggle in electoral contests. Elections also give weight to citizens on a broad range of issues that leave business inattentive or indifferent.

Apart from the marginal case of Greece in 1967, in the postindustrial democracies, elections become less threatening to property and more threatening to those with no property and little income. For in the past pyramid-shaped income distribution there was always a chance that the lower to lower-middle classes could coalesce, while in a diamond-shaped distribution the coalition would more likely be in the middle class alone or even middle with the relatively small upper-class apex, as was arguably so in the Reagan and Thatcher victories. The poor (about a tenth of the U.S. population) have neither campaign contributions nor many votes, especially where they have low voter turnouts. The middle group has at least collectively much campaign-finance potential as well as many votes. The upper class has a campaign-finance capacity that far outruns any direct voting potential. These facts predict typical economic policy outcomes.

Normal elections in the economically advanced democracies may be little more than a nuisance to capitalism. Yet Friedrich Hayek, the leading theoretician of classical liberalism in our time, has sought to curb the traditionally popular branch of government—the legislature. Its job is to enact only general law—not policy that would advantage specific economic interests. To further insulate the market from politics, Hayek proposes that each citizen vote for a legislative representative but once in a lifetime, say, at age 40 or 45, choosing only from among that same age cohort. With staggered terms, these legislators would serve much longer tenures of single 15-year terms—at from 40–45 to 55–60—after which they would retire to become lay judges (Hayek, 1978, 95–96, 105–10). Hayek adds, "Since there would be no parties, there would of course be no nonsense about proportional representation" (ibid., 161). This plan to disfranchise everyone not in the single privileged year is, I think, an outrageous attack on democratic responsiveness—an attack that seems oddly inconsistent with the rightist liberal claim that the political system is already far less responsive than the market. Hayek's plan is loaded in favor of the haves against the have-nots.[14]

In underdeveloped nations, income distributions remain more pyramidal, so elections there can be more threatening to capital. Defenders of property may go to greater extremes. In his 1895 essay, "Tactics of Social Democracy," Friedrich Engels forecast that, should socialists win or threaten to win elections, the bourgeoisie can be expected to "break the contract," shutting down their own electoral game (in Tucker, 1978, 556–73). Nearly a century has recurrently validated that prophecy.

## The Structures Strategy: The Capitalist Formula and the Slithering Away of the State

Recall that the structures strategy seeks to control policy decisions by pulling powers from units where rivals prevail, putting those powers where friends prevail.

### Limited Government: Putting Some Powers with Social Units

Prior discussions noted that classical liberalism sought to separate the spheres of politics, economics, and religion. Separation of the religious sphere was pursued in part because early European liberals faced orthodoxies (either Roman Catholic or Stuart Anglican) that were then allied with the nobility and royalty. They sought a shift of religious decisions toward individuals, and through them to institutional forms more subject to control from below rather than control from above—or what James Harrington somewhere called "a showing of hands" rather than "a laying on of hands." Like other voluntary associations churches are formed by contracts (or "covenants") of members.

As for the economic sphere, the Capitalist could not wholly remove state powers, requiring at least the so-called night watchman functions of protection and minimal regulation against fraud, as in enforcement of contracts. Still, a major shift of powers of economic decision carved out an autonomous economic realm of the free market, curtailing any remaining prescriptive rights of feudal lords over labor or trade. Another struggle—especially clear in Adam Smith—was to beat back state mercantilism, thus promoting both domestic and international free trade.

By the nineteenth century, these aims were clear to all. Herbert Spencer's essay, "Representative Government—What Is It Good For?" argues that, although the "primary duty" of the state is security of persons against violence and theft whether originating at home or abroad, its secondary function is to promote "equity" or "justice." But Spencer has no redistribution or welfare state in mind, only the dismantling of unjust laws favored by landlords, such as the tax laws of prerevolutionary France or the later Corn Laws of Britain. While representative government promotes equity, the essay also warns, it threatens "efficiency." It is worse than monarchy in its tendency to elect politicians who ineptly attempt regulation of the economy.

Although one may speak of either "politicizing" or "depoliticizing" decisional matters (left and right switch sides on distinctive issues), the decision to remove a function from the public to the private sector is quite as "political" as to move it from the private to the public. Powers of decision removed from one locus are effectively relocated somewhere else. Even when that new locus is a nongovernmental unit, there is indirect and often direct state enforcement of the legitimacy of decisions made.

It is one thing to shift economic decisions to individuals or to very small firms and quite another to put them with the boards or managements of our present giant corporations. Charles Lindblom concluded, "The large private corporation fits oddly into democratic theory and vision. Indeed, it does not fit" (Lindblom, 1977, 356). Vast decisional powers having great consequences on human lives are left beyond the reach of democratic institutions. While one may speak of decisions left to the private sector, a small minority holds major ownership in corporations, and even smaller managerial groups elected by them make the actual decisions.[15] We may turn to government for some minimal social planning; but much real planning depends on the corporate boardrooms that determine which manufacturing operations shall start or stop, and where these may be located within the nation or about the globe (cf. Goodman, 1979, 102).

If Americans leave plant locational decisions unregulated, most Western European democracies have legislated some restraints. But even there, vast powers are enjoyed by corporate leaders with few bounding conditions. Corporations may be legally prohibited from engaging in certain hazardous practices; but they can still decide what they will produce, how much of it, and at what quality. They may be prohibited from certain forms of employment discrimination; but they are otherwise free in hiring, promotions, dismissals. While some bounds may be set by regulations concerning nondiscrimination, minimum wage, or overtime, corporations choose what they will pay for what kinds of work. Thus, private authorities largely control not only human livelihoods but even small details of our working lives.[16]

### Locating Powers among Territorial Units

Turning to the governmental sphere, it was early apparent that Capitalist interests favored creation of wider, unimpeded markets. Hence, they promoted the nation-state—just as the same dynamic now works to establish even wider zones, including common markets such as the European Economic Community or free trade zones such as the U.S.–Canadian Free Trade Pact.

To Marx and Engels, it seemed that capitalism was averse to local government. Indeed, Alexander Hamilton was hostile to the U.S. state governments, saying in the closed-door constitutional convention that if it were politically feasible he would prefer to convert them into mere administrative units. In Western Europe the early Capitalist was nationalist in part because feudal principalities interfered with enlarged free trade zones, just as in the United States under the Articles of Confederation the problem consisted in state and local governments' being responsive to their parochial electorates. As even James Madison complained, the lack of unity in U.S. foreign trade policy made it possible for Britain in trade negotiations to play off one port state against the others (letter to Jefferson, March 18, 1786).

Yet by our century some right variants of the Capitalist viewpoint began to speak well of state and local autonomy, while the reformer wing (Teddy Roosevelt Progressives, Franklin Roosevelt's New Deal, and its heirs) instead championed unified national economic policy. The explanation seems obvious. In Hamilton's time, state and local governments were dominated by farmer and artisan interests—an economically independent nine-tenths of the population that did not fear to offend manufacturing or banking interests, which were made targets of taxes or debt moratoria. But by our century, such small-holdings of self-employment began to disappear, eventually leaving as little as one-tenth of the U.S. labor force regularly self-employed. Whether private employees of large corporations or public employees dependent on tax revenues generated by corporate local investment, voters are now vulnerable to corporate investment/disinvestment decisions in their locality.

Also, advances in transport and communication, growing numbers of plant sites (Hewlett-Packard has more than two dozen), and product downsizing have made some manufacturing operations easily relocatable. Hence, states and localities are unlikely to enact regulatory, tax, or budget policies that offend the corporations. On the contrary, even reform Capitalist politicians accommodate the corporations, offering lax regulation, tax incentives, and outright subsidies touching most categories of business costs. Much more than firms, governmental units have become "the last entrepreneurs," easily played off against each other both within a nation and cross-nationally (cf. Goodman, 1979; Cook, 1983a).[17] Lee Iacocca, the flamboyant chair of Chrysler Corporation, was forthright about this:

> Ford, when I was there, GM, Chrysler, all over the world, we would pit Ohio against Michigan. We'd pit Canada versus the U.S. We'd get outright grants and subsidies in Spain, in Mexico, in Brazil—all kinds of grants. . . . I have played Spain versus France and England so long I'm tired of it, and I have played the states against each other over here. (Bachelor, 1982, 36)

If even Adam Smith conceded that—unlike landowners—merchants have loose ties to their countries, this applies as well to current manufacturing corporations. As the game goes international, capitalism wants all territories to enter and remain in this world market, as when the World Bank speaks well of *cultural* autonomy for indigenous peoples but not of their *economic* autonomy.

### Functional Allocations of Powers: From Parliamentary Supremacy to Executive Dominance

At the national level of government, another allocation of powers concerns the functional divisions, as in demarcation of the legislative, executive, and judicial. Some near-liberals used to espouse enlightened despotism—or perhaps even an unenlightened one—as the alternative to Thomas Hobbes's fear that division of "sovereignty" would cause civil war. But many British liberals, wanting to make way for the House of Commons, embraced their version of mixed-regime theory, previously reviewed (Chapter 3) in its Aristocratic variants. A key summation was Baron de Montesquieu's *Spirit of the Laws* (1748). Though he was mistaken in believing that a mix of the three simple forms had been perfected in British application, Montesquieu's arguments were much cited through the rest of the eighteenth century, especially by the U.S. founders. However, living within a republican climate, they could not admit that their complex model contained elements of the aristocratic and monarchic.

That early inhibition eventually fell away, and many came to say that the aristocratic aspects of the Supreme Court (and possibly the Senate) joined the monarchic aspects of the presidency to check the more democratic House of Representatives. The framers of the Constitution had expected the House to be radical (it turned out tame), yet had to accept it as a necessary popular concession. But the directly elected House was exposed to the fail-safe check of a *triple* veto, any one of which would work (Senate, the president, the Supreme Court). The system has admittedly checked other branches, and some of the framers sincerely distrusted all governmental power. But it distorts the historical record (convention debates, private correspondence, and so forth) to ignore their primary fear of popular power—power then evident at the state legislative level and anticipated in the federal House of Representatives.

Capitalist mixed-regime theory faces two problems not faced by the Aristocratic version. First, the Capitalist formula threatens its success by raising the level of economic demand, especially when linked to possible public intervention in the economy. The mixed regime historically worked best when most groups wanted only to block adverse change—not secure some positive good for themselves through government. Second, as noted of the U.S. founders, the Capitalist usually avoids loud talk of diluting democracy with non-democratic forms. As Jack Lively notes,

> Instead of saying that democracy should be limited in the interests of other ends which cannot be achieved or might be harmed by democratic procedures, it has bowed to the popularity of the term and insisted that democracy *means* mixed government. The redefinition becomes a means of escaping the unwelcome charge of being undemocratic. (Lively, 1975, 80; cf. also Bachrach, 1967)

### Who Represents the People? From Parliaments to Chief Executives to Bureaucrats

In part because executive authority under mercantilism gave privileged standing to certain favored monopoly merchants, and then later to financial interests, classical British liberals successfully sought to pull power from the monarchy (and the House of Lords) into the more popularly chosen House of Commons. Old Whig and especially New Whig theory rejected pretensions of the king to "re-present" the people, claiming that only parliaments could do so. While prime ministers or premiers of parliamentary systems were but leaders of parliamentary majorities, they and their cabinets would increasingly dominate most decisions that did not slip away into the burgeoning bureaucracies.[18]

The pattern of the U.S. presidential system was similar. Despite the protests of Daniel Webster, who embraced the revived "Whig Party" label, the Democrat Andrew Jackson claimed in his 1834 Protest to the Senate that "the President is a direct representative of the American people." Later U.S. presidents have routinely claimed the like.

Going further, in recent decades public administration scholars have claimed "representativeness" even for the civil service, although bureaucrats are unknown, unelected, and unaccountable with reference to those they claim to represent. Power has gravitated to the president and the administrative apparatus.

Without undue exaggeration of the autonomy of the state, the modern liberal state yet remains pluralistic, and much of the political contest concerns favorable location of decisions among the alternative units. Structuralist Marxist Nicos Poulantzas correctly described the liberal state as not a monolith but a strategic field, where classes or fractions of classes (I would add nonclass groupings) compete to locate powers where they will win.

> Even when a Left government manages to gain control of the hitherto dominant apparatus, the state institutional structure enables the bourgeoisie to transpose the role of dominance from one apparatus to another. . . . Thus, institutional apparatuses that normally have an altogether secondary, or purely decorative function may suddenly take on a decisive role. (Poulantzas, 1978, 138–39)

While everyone plays the structures game, in normal politics it seems that business interests have the edge. One critical analyst argues that presidential power relative to that of Congress may depend on which is at the moment more probusiness (Parenti, 1988, 251). In Britain, when Labour controlled the Commons, the Conservatives resisted nationalizations from the House of Lords. But when Thatcher's Conservatives came to control the Commons, they used it to abolish the Greater London Council because it was dominated by Labourites who were too generous with welfare spending.

### The Slithering Away of the State

A troubling recent development is the shift of public power to expert administrative apparatuses beyond even indirect popular control, often with rhetorics of scientific neutrality and efficiency. In the United States, capitalism sought relative "autonomy" for independent regulatory commissions, which then became captives of the regulated industries. And it has put much power with the Federal Reserve Board. (In each case, presidential appointees serve for fixed terms.)

Now reversing itself because it is shifting manufacturing to low-wage areas abroad, business in the past joined labor and government representatives to develop public policy before its ratification by parliaments in the corporatist nations of Western Europe (from the Rhineland through Scandinavia). Internationalization seems to be the new turn in the game of putting powers beyond the reach of ordinary voters or their parliamentary representatives. True, there exists the European Parliament for the European Economic Community, although voters remain quite ignorant and apathetic toward it, notwithstanding talk of moving toward greater political unity there in 1992.

But I am thinking more about the "Eurocrats" of Brussels. I am also thinking of the powers of multinational credit agencies such as the World Bank or International Monetary Fund. These agencies are dominated by the leading capitalist nations, with voting rights weighted roughly to reflect national wealth and hence contributions.[19] (Remember the "stake in society" theory?)

Other transnational institutions must also be watched. The Reagan administration sought recourse to the council of the General Agreement on Tariffs and Trade to end national agricultural price supports—a topic also under discussion by the Group of Seven chief executive summit in 1990. If there were no need for implementing funds, this could wholly bypass national legislatures, which the Whigs had so valued. While the Capitalist aims remain a relative constant, Capitalist political philosophy proves to be much more plastic.

Illicit relocations of power are also a possibility, especially when the executive is frustrated by recalcitrant parliamentary or judicial bodies. When the U.S. Congress enacted that government agencies were not to send aid to the anti-Sandinista Contras in Nicaragua, some executive-branch officials—allegedly including the CIA director, William Casey, as well as the national security adviser, John Poindexter—turned in secret to an entity called "The Enterprise." Headed by a retired general, this was a private corporation that not only had its own air force but even elements of foreign policy. It bought weapons for one price from the U.S. government and then resold them to Iran at a much higher price—secretly diverting some profits (about $18 million) to the Contra rebels fighting Marxist Nicaragua, although Congress had debarred such aid. Unused profits were parked in a Swiss bank account. According to Oliver North, who was an aide to the National Security Council, CIA Director Casey wanted to make it an "off the shelf, self-sustaining stand alone entity." Such a self-financing entity could carry out more secretive operations without the bother of securing any statutory or budgetary support from Congress, let alone the president. (Reagan was not informed of the fund diversion, according to Poindexter.)

Where is classical liberalism's vision of open government limited to the express purposes of those who created it? Where is its view that the parliamentary body is the primary vehicle for representation of the popular will? Clearly, democracy must involve popular control over where powers are put—not just free elections and free speech.

## Summary:
## The Capitalist against Democracy?

Much evidence suggests that successful economic growth promotes the conditions for stable democracy. When people come of age in personal economic security, they tend to demand more freedoms, largely keeping that priority despite any later economic difficulties (Inglehart, 1977). With even a modest margin of economic well-being, large numbers may actively demand political liberalization, as in many communist and rightist authoritarian nations in very recent years.

There is no strong evidence suggesting that democracy in itself has helped economic growth. Yet one could plausibly argue that democratic freedoms become important for further growth of information-rich postindustrial or service economies.

Be that as it may, one must challenge assertions that democracy is to blame for *blocking* economic growth, as often argued by those turning to nondemocratic authority on grounds of supposed economic imperatives. Thus although democracy may flatten income distribution, as discussed in Chapter 9, there is no evidence among at least the developed capitalist nations that democracy is the cause of economic stagnations, as commonly argued by the right (e.g., Brittan, 1975).

Yet, good times favor democracy, while hard times can disfavor it. When the Capitalist formula is generating growth, it may sustain both the form and substance of democracy. The substance runs stronger when leading business interests are either uncommitted or divided and when nonbusiness groupings do not fear for their livelihoods in mounting political challenges. But where "free enterprise" fails and generates enemies, capitalists may blame democracy and become antidemocratic.

Those who believe capitalist markets generate only good things argue correctly that capitalist development tends to create pressures for democratization (Berger, 1986, 83). But in wanting to deny that capitalist markets can produce any evils, they forget that capitalist stagnation or collapse can encourage autocracy, as attested by 1930s fascism or recurrent waves of military coups in Latin America.

Once the Capitalist formula is made an end in itself, its adherents may regard democracy as an expendable means. The proceduralist theory aside, the Capitalist favored some "popular government" early on when it undermined feudalism, and favors it now when it undermines communism. But Capitalist enthusiasm flags if democracy threatens capitalism itself.

While the postindustrial democracies experience little more than tensions between democracy and capitalism, democracy is more likely to turn socialist in the Third World where popular majorities can yet be economically radical, seeking redistribution among classes rather than mere redistribution among cross-class producer interests. The latent instrumentality of democracy for Capitalist purposes then becomes manifest, as when prominent political figures at least temporarily back a military junta that overthrows democracy. While the social democrats or the reform wing of capitalism usually oppose this, some among the rightist variants of capitalism do not hesitate at all.

Private ownership and free-market economics have uses in promoting development within certain locations and within certain limits, but capitalism should itself be regarded as if a mere means—not an end in itself. As such, it should be compromised in part to the needs of democracy, even conceding that democracy may make implementation of pure capitalism practically impossible. To make capitalism an end in itself while viewing democracy only as a means can make one antidemocratic, in both domestic and foreign policy. In this, the Capitalist and Socialist zealots look similar. But even a right-wing authoritarian government can become a pack of thieves sandbagging capitalist development, with extreme illustrations in Marcos's Philippines or Somoza's Nicaragua.[20]

The Capitalist formula gave rise to liberal democracy—a gift worth preserving in part as an end in itself rather than as a mere means to protect life and property. While the paradigm began by seeking to protect its kind of property from absolute government, it leaves us the task of protecting democracy from corporate pressures in ordinary times, or from corporate attack in desperate times. The multinational corporations are themselves evolving into something like governments. But they are not democratic ones.

## Notes

1. Among communist nations, Yugoslavia from the 1950s was the earliest to permit some political liberalization, although resisting acceptance of party oppositions after that recently became a reality elsewhere in Eastern Europe, with Albania last. Currently suffering with severe inflation, unemployment, and foreign indebtedness, Yugoslavia's "self-management" economy intermixes mandated workers' control and some central controls with market mechanisms and considerable private ownership (especially in real estate).

2. Perhaps because the dislocations of early industrialization tended to influence crime rates, the severity of punishment was often increased. Michel Foucault notes, "In England, out of the 223 capital crimes in force at the beginning of the nineteenth century, 156 had been introduced during the preceding hundred years" (1979, 76).

Yet the paradigms of social theory tend to emphasize distinctive theories of punishment: For the Aristocrat, it is *retribution*; for the Saint, *rehabilitation*; for the Capitalist, *deterrence*; and for the Socialist, at most a temporary *protection* of society.

3. While Locke moderated his politics under Shaftesbury's influence, in an early authoritarian work that he left unpublished—*Two Tracts on Government* (1967)—Locke made it quite clear that "the multitude" was a storm-tossed

sea or many-headed beast relative to "the people," the latter consisting only of the propertied.

4. The contrast with Roger Williams was clear: "He was a libertarian because he condemned the world, and he wanted to separate church and state so that the church would not be contaminated by the state; Thomas Jefferson loved the world and was dubious about the spirit, and he sought to separate church and state so that the state would not be contaminated by the church" (Miller and Johnson, 1938, 186). Yet Williams's toleration extended to most political discourse, short of teaching anarchism. In his religion, something not forbidden by Scripture was probably forbidden by God; but in his politics, whatever was not forbidden by Scripture was probably authorized.

5. Not in my view a liberal, Rousseau rationalized writing some articles for the *Encyclopédie* on the ground that France was hopelessly corrupted in any case. A yet uncorrupted people should not be exposed to such critical ideas: "It is good that there are Philosophers, provided that the people do not dabble at it" (Rousseau, 1964, 78). He viewed himself as "a safeguard of the authority" of Plato, and he repeated Plato's view that it is impossible to make a people philosophic, adding that the very effort could corrupt them (ibid., 93). As Plato was to the Sophists, so Rousseau viewed his own role vis-à-vis the philosophes. His *Letter to D'Alembert on the Theater* even argues the case for republican censorship (cf. Bloom, 1960).

6. Perhaps such figures were protecting themselves more than the public. The noblest "Voltairean" phrase seems apocryphal: "I may disagree with what you say, but I will defend to the death your right to say it." Even conceding Voltaire's abstract commitment to free speech as well as his moments of courage on particular occasions, he was no Socrates. During most of his life, he was extremely cautious, either concealing authorship or changing residence rather than defending to the death his own opinions.

7. For Karl Popper, the very measure of science consists in the procedures of an open public testing of claims. In parallel with liberal proceduralism in markets and politics, he insists that what comes before (the origins of the hypothesis) or what comes after (who can use the theory) is irrelevant to science (cf. Popper, 1957, 135; 1968; 1979). One could challenge this artificially narrowed definition of the scientific mission.

8. In his 1918 essay "Natural Law," Holmes wrote, "I used to say, when I was young, that truth was the majority vote of that nation that could lick all the others. . . . I think that statement was correct in so far as it implied that our test of truth is a reference to either a present or an imagined future majority in favor of our view" (Holmes, 1955, 118).

9. Clumsy demonstrations of intolerance are rare. Quite recently, the moderate Marxist Bertell Ollman was chosen by normal academic procedures to chair the department of political science at the University of Maryland. His appointment was challenged by some regents, the governor, and then the university's president, who rescinded the appointment in 1978, brazenly claiming that he resisted all pressure on the matter. The incident was a gross invasion of normal conventions of academic freedom, and Ollman was to find no judicial remedy for it.

10. Mill often gave with one hand and took back with the other. Although

his *Subjection of Women* favors suffrage for women, his plural voting schedule would obviously overweight male votes. Similarly, while he holds political participation to be an effective means for human development, he makes prior development a precondition for participation, as when he favors a literacy test in Britain or accepts an indefinite period of nondemocratic tutelary rule over colonial natives. He is at least consistent in wishing voters and officeholders were very like himself (cf. esp. *Considerations on Representative Government*, XII).

11. Under most conditions of proportional voting, a multiparty system tends to thrive, whereas single-member district plurality voting leads to either one-party dominant or two-party systems, save for conditions such as Canada where lesser parties can remain viable because of unusual local concentrations and because the federal system permits provincial minor-party control.

12. Campaign contributions belong to the recruitment strategy if they could plausibly make a difference in electoral results. This would be likely if any of these three conditions apply: (1) donors try to get money to candidates very early, when it is especially vital to set up staffing and strategies for further fund-raising activities; (2) donors give more money to very close races, as is often true when there are open seats (no incumbent running); or (3) donors contribute to only one side (as most donors do) and obviously aim to support a close friend to the interest concerned or to oust a dangerous opponent.

13. Both U.S. corporate and CIA funds were marshalled to intervene in Chile's elections in 1970 and later efforts to bribe members of Chile's Congress to block Allende's ascension to the presidency. Agents of the ITT Corporation offered up to "seven figures" of cash to corrupt Chile's democracy, which was already being attempted by the CIA with U.S. taxpayer funds (cf. Secretaría General de Gobierno, 1972).

14. Friedrich Hayek believes it "immoral" to categorize people for different treatment according to their levels of economic means: "Agreement by the majority on sharing the booty gained by overwhelming a minority of fellow citizens, or deciding how much is to be taken from them is not a democracy. At least it is not that ideal of democracy which has any moral justification" (Hayek, 1978, 157).

15. To hold, as does William Riker, that government should be kept minimal because there is always some arbitrariness in the decision procedures of collective or public choice seems odd (Riker, 1982). This forgets that such problems as the paradox of voting *also* apply to corporate boards' decision procedures, although their decisions impact millions who never had a chance to vote on who makes those decisions.

16. The Capitalist tends to see threats to freedom only from *coercive* constraint—primarily governmental—which may exhibit an inattention to the near-totalitarianism emerging within some corporate workplaces. Workers have been subject to rigid dress codes, rules regarding modes of address and other speech, and yet more rules on frequency and timing of washroom visits. While the U.S. government has legislated limits on employers' use of polygraphs, Big Brother still emerges in electronic monitoring of behavior at work stations or when making phone calls. Moreover, even without any special reason for such testing, randomized or generalized drug-use testing has

made a nationwide appearance. This extreme of monitored urine sample collections reminds us that early liberals never valued the privacy of those needing control. Jeremy Bentham's Panopticon—a building designed so a few could centrally monitor many—was meant not only for prisons but also for schools and workplaces.

17. While the right now claims a principled, Jeffersonian commitment to keeping any government functions at the lowest feasible level of government, this seems to be belied when it turns to higher-level units whenever necessary to curtail some reform project voted at a lower level (e.g., overrides of any local rent control, state or local regulation of nuclear plants, unfavorable taxation of business, and the like).

18. The *Communist Manifesto*'s assertion that the executive of the modern state is but the "executive committee of the ruling class" is not so bizarre when we recall that this was written nearly two decades before workers could vote in Britain. In any event, analysts have noted that the passage refers only to the executive branch, not prejudging parliamentary bodies (Burnheim, 1985, 35).

19. "The IMF uncompromisingly pursues a free market economy ideology which forces Third World governments to restrict public borrowing substantially, cut subsidies for basic goods, social services, transport and state enterprises, increase prices for state services, raise indirect taxes; to dismiss workers in the public sector; to limit public investment in favor of (hoped-for) private initiative and to pull down protective barriers aimed to protect national industries, especially manufacturing industries, from overpowerful foreign competitors." Further, "the IMF tends to favor conservative and authoritarian regimes; indeed it sometimes even brings them to power, when governments are reluctant to apply IMF remedies and the military then take over 'to save the country from economic chaos' " (Korner et al., 1986, 133, 139). Comparable economic pressures face communist nations now seeking integration into the world economy.

20. "After the revolution, it was learned that the Somozas and their associates owned over 25 percent of the agricultural land in the country and 147 commercial entities, ranging from the Mercedes Benz dealership to a cement factory" (Colburn, 1986, 31).

# 8

# The Socialist's Problematic

*or Social Conflict as a Problem of Enlarging
Productive Powers through Social Ownership,
Role Rotation, Egalitarian Distribution,
and Central Planning*

> All emancipation carried through hitherto has
> been based . . . on restricted productive forces.
> The production which these productive forces
> could provide was insufficient for the whole of
> society and made development possible only if
> some persons satisfied their needs at the ex-
> pense of others, and therefore some—the mi-
> nority—obtained the monopoly of development.
>
> Karl Marx,
> *The German Ideology*

While Marx also believed that capitalist relations of production after
some threshold impeded further *economic* development, his larger
concern was that they blocked maximal *human* development, exploit-
ing workers left undeveloped but for some narrowly specialized task.
The Aristocrat holds that unequal property ownership is good in
permitting cultivation of the finer things by the few. Turning that
about, Marx complains that it rather means that *only* a few can develop
their higher potentialities. The ultimate aim of revolutionary transformation through class struggle is to remove that limitation.

We have been seeing a shift of relative emphases in defining the
problem of social theory, already evident when the early Capitalist
moved beyond mere self-preservation to propertied comfort as well,

although sometimes denying any economic aim of democracy whenever the lower classes would demand economic justice. While the Saint
wants more economic equality without any violence to get it, the
Socialist in effect responds that everyday exploitation thrives in the
absence of open class struggle. While Marx believes that socialism will
eventually bring an end to most crime, domestic group violence, and
international wars, such pacification would first require a period of
intensified class struggle. Even when in power, Stalin and Mao urged
that building socialism requires intensified class struggle, although
their successors have recently disavowed that. In his original advocacy
of class struggle Marx diverges from both the Aristocrat (who wants
the "order" of disciplined hierarchy) and the Saint (who wants the
"love" of nonviolent persuasion). But Marx only repeats a view found
often in early Capitalist theory, as when militant Puritans spoke of
the concord that could only arise after discord.

If immediate peace must be sacrificed toward long-run pacification
of human existence, the ultimate aim of Marx was not just peace, nor
even peace with plenty; it was the eventual condition where "the free
development of each is the condition for the free development of all"
(*Communist Manifesto*, II).

My model for the Socialist paradigm primarily dwells on Karl Marx
(d. 1883), his frequent coauthor Friedrich Engels (d. 1895), and the
later Marxists. But I will now and then note where some other variant
of socialism touches the themes developed.[1] Some early versions
include Christian socialism, tacking closer to the Saint ideal of both
social justice and peace, but unlike current liberation theologies in
not accepting possibly violent class struggle. One of the most elaborate
statements of Christian socialism was *Voyage en Icarie* by Etienne Cabet
(d. 1856). French secret police records show that the "Icarians" were
highly feared by the government of Louis Bonaparte, when Marxists
were relatively unnoticed.

The more secular variants included anarchism, which insists on
avoidance of all political means such as electoral activity in seeking to
abolish the present state, without any transitional state following.
Anarchism cannot be easily summed up because its continuum ranges
from models fully committed to private property and markets (anar-
cho-capitalists) to those closer to Marxist views (anarcho-communists).
At an intermediate stop was the "mutualist anarchism" of Pierre
Proudhon (d. 1865). Marx had nasty conflicts with the Proudhonists
in the First International, thereafter opposing as well the "collectivist
anarchism" of Michael Bakunin (d. 1876). While the "communist
anarchism" of Peter Kropotkin (d. 1921) was economically convergent, it rejected Marxist-Leninist politics.

Other important Socialist forerunners were the three so-called
utopian socialists: Henri de Saint-Simon (d. 1825), Charles Fourier

(d. 1837), and Robert Owen (d. 1858). These also left traces in Marx's theory, which Lenin correctly described as arising from three stems: (1) German idealism and especially Hegel; (2) predominantly French Socialist forerunners; and (3) the British political economists, especially Adam Smith and David Ricardo. Marx was absorbed in study of those sources in roughly that sequence, and he incorporated aspects of their thought as he fought free of their influence.

## Commitment to the Socialist Formula: Why Expansion of Social Production?

As noted, Marx's ultimate concern was a generalization of free human development, and Socialist relations of production were originally viewed as but means to that end. Attempting to understand just why he expected the new relations of production to be superior to Capitalist relations in promoting that end, I will address salient elements of his view of human nature. Then I will apply the analysis to Marx's aims of social ownership of the forces of production, the ultimate abolition of the Capitalist division of labor, new maxims for distribution of the product, and substitution of central planning for the Capitalist market.

Why did Marx expect such new relations of production to yield an abundance that experience since denies? Capitalism yields abundance only in certain times and places, and even then gags on recurrent gluts; but the communist version of socialism has yielded abundance nowhere. The sluggish growth and consumer-goods shortages have led to popular repudiations of communism. Such problems have also frustrated Marx's aim of maximal human development.

Like the other paradigms that shield their cores by assuming *ideal* conditions, Marxists following the emphasis of Leon Trotsky (d. 1940) have countered that the proper testing places should have been the highly developed capitalist economies of Western Europe or North America, where the workers were expected to win socialist electoral majorities. But without belaboring the obvious failures of prophecy, we may ask whether there were any good reasons to have expected success even there, whether by Marx's premises or critical revisions of them.

### Socialism and Human Development: Human Nature and Alienation

While they may be more consequence than cause of Marx's social class, policy, and institutional alignments, his assumptions about human nature so sharply oppose those of Capitalist cultures such as Britain, the United States, and Canada that one must directly address them.

Marx believed that conditions of existence largely determine consciousness. If so, we could ask how his own social situation created his personal needs and social thought. He was the son of a Prussian state lawyer who had converted from Judaism to Christianity for career advancement. Although the family was well off, young Marx resented the higher-status Prussian nobility. He nevertheless married the daughter of a noble state official of higher rank than his father. Upon finishing his higher education, Karl eventually found his aspirations to teach at the University of Bonn blocked because of his religious and political radicalism (which, as in Engels, preceded his economic radicalism). Then he met further political obstacles in his brief career in Cologne as editor of the eventually suppressed progressive bourgeois newspaper *Rheinische Zeitung*.

After such frustrations, he went to France and then Belgium, turning to a career of radical political journalism which eventually led him to London. By self-avowal, he had come to identify with the proletariat, said to be the instrument for human liberation. While surely authentic, Marx's identification was plausibly less out of any love for the working class—with whom he had associated very little—than out of hatred for the rich (Schwarzchild, 1947, 74). Friedrich Engels, by contrast, loved a working-class woman, Mary Burns; he lived with her until her death, then found consolation with her sister. Engels, who liked fine wines and fox hunting, was the son of a prosperous German industrialist, and eventually became a partner in Manchester's Ermen and Engels.

As with Engels, the causes of Marx's identification with those below his own class are less clear than the consequences in the structure of his thought. The identification with the propertyless dominated his economic policy preferences, political commitments, and justificatory arguments, including those framed in terms of human nature as well as others purporting to constitute a science of history and political economy.

### Our Historically Changing Nature

Marx believed in biological evolution of our species, so admiring Charles Darwin's *Origin of Species* that he would have liked to dedicate *Das Kapital* to Darwin (who declined the honor). In *The Poverty of Philosophy*, Marx wrote, "The whole of history is nothing but a continual transformation of human nature." Although often misconstrued as a denial of any human nature, he surely meant only that, aside from longer-term evolutionary change, the course of recorded history shows radical shifts in the *manifestations* of our nature. That is, our leading motives vary with changing modes of production, or the systems of production relations defined by the condition of labor. For "the human essence is no abstraction inherent in each single individual. In its reality it is the ensemble of the social relations" (*Theses on Feuerbach*, VI). Marx's beliefs of human nature are largely consistent through his texts from the 1840s to his death in 1883.

In Marx's image of human nature, beneath what historically changes are some elements that are relatively constant, and these permit contrasts with dominant Capitalist views. I will attempt to clarify those more stable elements, adding to the work of prior analysts (esp. Venable, 1966; Fromm, 1961).

### Parallel Elements of Marx's Thought: Aristotelian Four Causes?

Marx developed several aspects of his thought in recognizable parallel. Knowing that he closely studied Aristotle and expressly appreciated his "genius," the implicit core conception may well be an inversion of the order of primacy of Aristotle's "four causes." Expressed in Marx's ascending levels of a social order—each conditioning the levels above it—we have thus: (1) material causes (forces of production, or the material wherewithal together with productive technology); (2) efficient causes (relations of production, or how humans interact in economic life); (3) formal causes (the forms of state and law favoring the class dominant in that economy); and (4) final causes (the ruling class ideology, which usually includes mystified purposes). Speculation on an Aristotelian inspiration aside, one can see that Marx's dimensions of human nature and corresponding forms of alienation have affinities to those listed elements of his model of a socioeconomic formation.

Once again like Aristotle, Marx defined our human nature by progressing inward through increasingly specific circles of kinds of being. Our being has four aspects: (1) living, and animal; (2) social; (3) productive; and (4) instinct-free or conscious in that productivity. The switch of the second and third items best parallel the above four levels of a social order. I will briefly comment on each aspect of our nature, showing how it relates to a level of the social order as well as to a form of alienation—the objective and subjective experience of separation and estrangement.

1. *Our animal nature: alienation from product, means of production, and nature.* Locating our kind among other forms of being, we are in the first place living and animal, necessarily engaged in metabolic interchange with the rest of nature. Our needs of animality—of production and reproduction of the conditions of existence—obviously relate to forces of production, which include raw materials, material infrastructure, machines and tools, production technology, and human

labor power. Separation therefrom constitutes *alienation from the means of production and the product, and hence from nature as the object of our labor.* Propertyless human beings are more estranged from nature than are other kinds of animals, even if the property of the capitalist may have been originally created by alienated labor. One's labor power is useless if unemployed—a condition that entails a complete separation from the forces of production. At its worst, this could block satisfaction of the merely animal wants of eating, sheltered sleeping, and procreating. At least under nineteenth-century conditions (or even current conditions in underdeveloped nations), such needs may be but barely attained even with employment, since conditions of contract may be dominated by owners. In the *Communist Manifesto*, Marx and Engels claim that private property in the means of production "is already done away with for nine-tenths of the population." Whatever its validity in 1848, the statement has become roughly valid now, if one discounts insignificant small shareholding or indirect ownership through pension funds. Unlike most liberals, Marxists see a major problem in such separation from the means of production, which exposes workers to either denial of vital needs when unemployed or vulnerable to easy exploitation when employed in wage labor.[2]

Another kind of animal need is safety, or security from aggression (which liberal theory characteristically addressed in terms of "self-preservation"). Marx concurs that the danger arises less from other animals than from our own kind, but he rejects the Aristocratic assumption of innate aggressivity, which was also shared by many liberals from Locke to Freud. Rather, he and Engels followed Rousseau's view in the *Discourse on the Origins of Inequality*. Human nastiness, they believed, comes not from nature but from the root cause of artificial inequalities; so an account of historical emergence of inequalities can explain how a species that began so well could turn out so badly. Marxists view economic inequality as the root cause of both ordinary criminal violence and violence of the state, as well as domestic and international wars. Much illegal as well as legal violence is needed to defend unequal holdings of property (cf. Herman, 1982). But liberal theorists (especially of the right) look for causes of violence almost anywhere else. They may turn about to claim that *socialist* economies have an inherently aggressive bent—and not only in their installation, since only force can prevent skilled, energetic persons from accumulating more than others.

2. *Our social nature: alienation from other human beings.* We are also social animals, so much so that Marx thought solitary confinement of prisoners was wholly inhumane. Marx, who often laughed at the Robinson Crusoe approach to economics, meant our social nature in

a sense much stronger than wanting to be together in order to use each other in what Thomas Carlyle had called the "cash-nexus" mode. He also meant much more than the addition of a thin "sympathetic" or "benevolent" impulse of early liberal theory. In Hutcheson, Smith, Hume, and Bentham, this suggests a picture of the good bourgeois sharing bounty with kith and kin, or perhaps taking postprandial pleasure in giving small coins to beggars. This involved no real sacrifice in any case because of the assumption of accumulation. More than originally acknowledged, liberal theory then as now understood social life in terms of using each other merely as instruments of economic advantage, even if Kant held it ethically wrong to regard others as "means only."

Alone among our four paradigms, the Capitalist tradition has contained many who have doubted our basically social nature. Even now some liberal theorists have wondered whether any "altruistic" behavior is possible. If apparent sacrifice for others must be acknowledged, these liberal theorists ferret out some underlying self-interestedness, such as the rational decision theorist's expectation of ultimate reciprocity (Becker, 1976; Axelrod, 1984). Or it may be ascribed to some hidden extension of the ego, such as getting shared genes into future generations, as in the inclusive-fitness sociobiological theories (Wilson, 1975; Freedman, 1979). So strong is the self-interest assumption that many liberal theorists wonder how any sacrifice for others is possible, at least beyond the narrowest circles of kith and kin.

With but slight exaggeration, Marx sees us as so much social that the problem, rather, is explaining how predominantly egoistic action is possible. He ascribes it to historically bounded structural causes, with the selfishness most pronounced under modern Capitalist relations of production, when even many families may have few real bonds but the cash nexus.

Marx and Engels comment often on "sentimental veils" over often exploitative relations, such as idealizations of the bourgeois family or patriotic identification with the bourgeois state.[3] For Marx the state is not Hegel's institutional expression of universality, but rather an expression of the *alienation from other human beings* that arises from economic class divisions. Like the bourgeois family ideal or the religious heaven, the state as symbol offers an illusory unity that veils our divisions. Yet the state as ultimate force also helps contain the consequences of our antagonisms.

Private property in means of production is viewed by Marx as the root cause of almost all our varied lines of conflict, for divided access to such property (who owns what) shapes the division of labor (who does what), the consequent division of social product (who gets what), and hence the class-divided society. Thus, while many liberal theorists ascribe aggressivity to our animal natures, Marx sees aggression as a consequence of maintenance of major economic inequalities in denial of our social nature.

Yet one wonders how Marx would explain why levels of violence vary widely among capitalist nations, even when of comparable inequality of wealth or income. As I similarly remarked against innate-aggressivity theory in the previous section, constants cannot of themselves explain variation. Among many possible sources of variation, perhaps inequalities of power are another source of corruption and conflict, as Rousseau and the anarchists understood.

3. *Our productive nature: alienation from the process of production and our own productive activity.* Since many nonhuman animals (e.g., zebra herds) are also social but merely "collect" from nature, Marx further differentiates our kind as productive beings. For Marx, we literally need productive activity, so much so that exclusion from all work (even for prisoners or for schoolchildren, who should do token labor for learning) is literally viewed as injurious to human well-being. Marx needed his own scholarly work in the reading rooms of the British Museum: "He was perfectly serious when he declared that incapacity to work was a death sentence on any human being not really an animal" (Mehring, 1962, 227).

In contrast, the Capitalist paradigm typically has assumed that human nature shirks work. Work is considered but a present sacrifice of the good of leisure, undertaken only for more leisure and consumption later. Even when imbued with the Protestant ethic, work is present pain for future pleasure. Giving little and getting much is regarded as what most people naturally want out of economic life. As Marx complains of Adam Smith, "he has a presentiment, that labour, so far as it manifests itself in the value of commodities, counts only as expenditure of labour-power, but he treats this expenditure as the mere sacrifice of rest, freedom, and happiness, not as at the same time the normal activity of living beings" (*Capital*, I, i, 1, 2 n.1). Ironically, later Capitalist theory claims it is, rather, Marx who could not grasp that "man does not live by bread alone."

Marx not only assumed a will to work, but also a will to work at varied tasks that fit our varied individual tastes and talents. He recognized that there would always be "a realm of necessity," of necessary labor to produce and reproduce the conditions of human life. While he therefore disavows Fourier's dream that all future labor may be so much play, he shares Fourier's view that we need to express our individual productive potentialities, including *all* of our individually unique constellations of naturally endowed aptitudes and inclinations. We naturally should enjoy producing more than accumulating and consuming, especially with the added pleasure of social interaction.

So what has blocked the joys of cooperative social labor? As long as only a few own the means of production, most must involuntarily sell long hours of their labor power, which is to put their own laboring activity under control of others. Marx saw an innate need for freedom or self-direction in labor—active involvement in controlling its time, conditions, and bodily rhythms. Denial of this brings *alienation from the process of labor* as a problem to be surmounted, especially if we are constrained to one narrow task: "Constant labour of one uniform kind disturbs the intensity and flow of a man's animal spirits, which find recreation and delight in mere change of activity" (*Capital*, I, iv, 14, 2).

4. *Our instinct-free or self-consciously creative nature.* Since there are yet other animals that are social and productive (e.g., beavers, bees, and ants), Marx adds the final and species-specific attribute. This is not Aristotle's contemplative rationality but rather our capacity for instinct-free or imaginatively flexible, planned creativity. We alone are capable of imitating or surpassing what is made by other animals. As Marx put it in his *Economic and Philosophical Manuscripts*, "Conscious life-activity directly distinguishes man from animal life activity. It is just because of this that he is a species being."

Marx's ontology was by him called "naturalism" or "humanism," neither mechanistically materialist nor idealist but a negation of the negation (a synthesis) of both. In this dialectic of "praxis," while our conditions of existence determine our consciousness (our environments shape us), our consciousness through practical activity has always changed those conditions of existence (we act to reshape our environments), if not in the past with self-conscious, collective control.

With certain structural changes and a more scientific understanding of the world, our species may self-consciously shape and reshape itself through socially planned alteration of our world. Part of the new consciousness would be Ludwig Feuerbach's insight of *The Essence of Christianity*: To reverse the Biblical phrase, man created God in his own image. We are the creator and God our creature, rather than vice versa. We are in *alienation from our own nature*—our highest, specifically human possibilities—if we accept ideologies of reification, which is the confusion of humanly produced and alterable social relations with inalterable laws of nature or gods. We have alienated to the imaginary gods our own ideal possibilities—including power, wisdom, and goodness; and these should be retrieved to our kind.[4]

### Socialism and Economic Development: The Expectation of Enlarged Productive Powers

It is clear how Marx could relate socialist relations of production to more "natural" human development. But it is not yet obvious how socialism could be expected to bring great development of productive forces to minimize "the realm of necessity" as a restraint on human development. Why did Marx think socialism would eclipse capitalism in their otherwise shared Baconian project of pushing science and technology to conquer nature to yield abundance?

Marx believed that Capitalist relations of production had led within its first century to great advances in the forces of production; the bourgeoisie "has created more massive and more colossal productive forces than have all preceding generations together" (*Communist Manifesto*, I). Yet at some ill-defined threshold, those relations switch from facilitating to frustrating such development, from "harnessing" the great workhorse to "fettering" it. Thus Marx's famous preface to *A Contribution to the Critique of Political Economy*:

> At a certain stage of their development, the material productive forces of society come in conflict with the existing relations of production, or— what is but a legal expression for the same thing—with the property relations within which they have been at work hitherto. From forms of development of the productive forces these relations turn into their fetters. (in Tucker, 1978, 3–4)

Replacement with Socialist relations of production would unfetter the productive forces, permitting the Baconian project to lead again toward more abundance.[5]

Having in Chapter 6 criticized the more inflated claims of Capitalist economics, I will now critique the Socialist alternative, bypassing hybrid possibilities that attempt to inherit the best features of each parent but may often get the worst. Over a century past the death of Marx, few now believe that socialism guarantees abundance. We witness the desperate reforms of communist systems that are moving toward some Capitalist relations of production. Soviet President Mikhail Gorbachev in 1991 wanted billions in Western aid to bail out an economy made worse—even chaotic—by the dislocations of transition. Yet he blamed the economic failings not on socialism as such, but on Stalinist legacies of excessive central bureaucracy and ruinous military expenditure.

If by five-year plans Stalin's centrally planned socialism was able to force at least high industrial growth, it was largely by sacrificing Marx's aims for human development, while employing the threat and use of murder on an extended scale. But this growth in any case stagnated once it used up past capitalist technology. In part because so many good farmers were shot during collectivization, but even more because of poor incentives for collective farm workers, agricultural production has always been sluggish in communist systems. The Soviet tertiary sector of services has many glaring failures, ranging from surly restaurant employees to failure to get into the computer age.

## The Economy of the Socialist:
## Collective Coordination

Why did Marx expect better things of socialist relations of production? Let us look at social ownership, role rotation, new distributional maxims, and central planning.

### Social Ownership of the Forces of Production and Productivity

Always distinguishing means of *consumption* such as furniture, clothing, and so forth—which would continue to be private—Marx advocated social ownership of the means of *production*, including the land and its resources, factories, and so on. Since unequal wealth as a source for unequal incomes was part of the individual production incentives of the Capitalist program, why did Marx think social ownership would better advance the technology of production or the scale of its development?

Marx was fascinated with technological change, especially in the development of new tools and machines. While he saw only the germ of tool use among the other animals, our capacity for such innovation was part of our specifically human nature of instinct-free or conscious productive development. But it was "characteristic of Yankeedom" for Ben Franklin to stress our tool-making and overlook that we have also innovated most conditions of our economic life. Darwin had covered evolution of our physical organs, and Marx envisaged a history of the evolution of our "productive organs"—our tools and machines: "Technology discloses man's mode of dealing with Nature, the process of production by which he sustains his life, and thereby also lays bare the mode of formation of his social relations, and of the mental conceptions that flow from them" (*Capital*, I, iv, 15, n. 3).

While advances of production technology could seem to make social ownership more feasible, it is difficult to see how Marx believed social ownership could assist further development. Perhaps he mistakenly expected almost indefinite economies of scale through integrated production operations, sharing Henri de Saint-Simon's fascination with industrial giantism. Although this may change as the Soviets attempt to lease much farmland to private operators, *Sovfoto* used to offer us pictures of grain harvests with long rows of combines on boundless fields, as if symbolizing this faith—not at all shared by the Saint paradigm—in large size as maximizing productive technology.

Or perhaps Marx envisaged gains from the eclipse of business trade secrets, which were later much denounced by Lenin and Trotsky. At least it is clear that Marx was impressed with the disjuncture between highly "socialized" or well-coordinated operations *within* each firm in contrast with the planless chaos *among* competing firms.

He perhaps also expected that any Ludditist resistance to new technology by labor—even in his time expressed in certain currents of anarchism—would become pointless once labor-saving technology was not a threat to livelihoods.

But communist systems have not excelled in technological development, perhaps in part because of retrenchment of the private property incentive of patents and royalties as well as even larger incentives for entrepreneurial risk. Although a secular Socialist society would have no religious interferences with science, political constraints on communications have been a serious obstacle to Soviet technological advance, as in Stalinist restrictions on foreign travel and access to publications.[6] Pro-Capitalist writers may exaggerate the point, but communist economies have really been parasitical on Western technology, even to the extreme wastage of resources on "reverse engineering," or trying to ferret out technology by dismantling Western prototypes (cf. Parrott, 1983). Also, they almost missed the computer age, although only the very latest advances in information processing (electronic data interchange between firms to handle billing, etc.) could perhaps have made central planning feasible.

But perhaps Marx expected not so much more innovation of productive technology than better use of it. With social ownership, workers would know that the means of production are now their own. Not alienated from the means of production, they would no longer neglect maintenance or abuse machinery. But much impressionistic evidence makes doubtful any such claim. Indeed, workers in communist systems may abuse the means of production even more because they are not checked by vigilant private owners, and also because it expresses dissatisfaction with jobs, wage rates, and so on.

Aristotle once observed that "what is common to the greatest number gets the least amount of care. Men pay most attention to what is their own; they care less for what is common" (*Politics*, II, iii, 4). If Marx perceived the tragedy of the commons as privatization by landlord enclosures in violation of peasant rights, the Capitalists see the tragedy rather when too many peasants pasture too many cows on the green and ruin it for everybody. Most of us have enough experience of life (is it *only* capitalist life?) to recognize the tendency to "care less for what is common."

The Socialist could retort that the demise of proprietary farmers and artisans has caused most people to work amid corporate means of production that are neither their own nor owned in common. Wage workers also seem careless of corporate property—as witnessed by pervasive petty theft, neglect of maintenance, and so on—unless workers are closely monitored. But Soviet experience suggests even more abuses have occurred there. Even socialist managers have been poor stewards of social property, as witnessed by ecological irresponsibility in pursuit of maximal production.[7]

## The Division of Labor: Role Rotation and Productivity

Marx envisioned abolition of the capitalist division of labor, under which—first of all—not everyone worked, and—second—those working were full-time specialists in some increasingly narrowed task.

### All Who Are Able Work

Both distributional maxims—that of the lower phase of socialism and that of the higher—begin thusly: "From each according to his ability . . . " The *Manifesto* speaks of a postrevolution "equal liability of all to labor," and this is one way in which Marx believed replacement of Capitalist with Socialist relations of production could lead to bolstered production. Rentiers, redundant lawyers, moneylenders, and the like had added nothing to production of value yet had lived by sharing in surplus value—the unpaid labor of productive workers. Also, Marx and Engels expect most women to cease being homemakers and pursue liberating work outside the home. The added workers would presumably offset any further shortening of the working day beyond that stipulated by the British Ten Hours Bill, which Marx supported.

Like most of the early Capitalists, the Marxists did not foresee any problem using all available labor. As late as 1949, Mao said, "Even if China's population multiplied many times she is fully capable of finding a solution; the solution is production" (in Fan, 1972, 70). But by Mao's death in 1976 supporters of Deng Xiaoping saw problems in excess production of population as well as deficient production of goods.

Leaving this aside, perhaps Marx expected that having all persons work—when combined with free, varying selection of tasks—would improve morale among the work force and that this would boost overall productivity. Admitting that even under capitalism large-scale cooperation means the whole of labor can be more than the sum of its parts, Marx refers to our social nature in saying, "Mere social contact begets in most industries an emulation and a stimulation of the animal spirits that heighten the efficiency of each individual workman" (*Capital*, I, iv, 13).

For Marx, labor was not to be but a means to satisfaction of wants, but part of want satisfaction itself, since people by nature want to be productive. They want to work in human conditions, and Marx looked forward to rapid automation of tasks which are dull, dirty, or dangerous. In practice, there has been little evidence of such improvements in communist systems, which have usually disguised underemployment of labor with featherbedding and have been slow in adopting labor-saving devices, even in conspicuous manual street sweeping.[8]

*Variety in Tasks*

Marx believed people want to express all sides of their individual natures, but not through any retrograde return to maximal self-sufficiency as envisaged by the Saint. For the other aspect of a Socialist division of labor was to be role rotation. Individuals would change their tasks even within a single day, as in the image of one who could "hunt in the morning, fish in the afternoon, rear cattle in the evening, criticize after dinner, just as I have a mind, without ever becoming hunter, fisherman, shepherd or critic" (*German Ideology*, I, A, 1). This would not wholly exclude specialists—including professions such as the architect or the doctor—but only the *full-time* specialist. As Engels put it, to have a full-time architect at construction sites condemns another person to being a full-time hod-carrier—the toter of bricks and mortar.

Role rotation could presumably promote fellow feeling as well as human development. Capitalism tends to develop but a part of an individual and destroy other possibilities. Adam Smith expressly concedes this but accepts it for efficiency, proposing schooling as a partial remedy. But Marx finds the Capitalist division of labor unacceptable: "It converts the labourer into a crippled monstrosity, by forcing his detail dexterity at the expense of a world of productive capabilities and instincts; just as in the States of La Plata they butcher a whole beast for the sake of his hide or tallow" (*Capital*, I, iv, 14, 5). Beyond any gains by using the whole potential of the individual, Marx could possibly have believed that more diversity in tasks could stimulate more technological innovation, since most invention is but an unfamiliar combination of familiar things. If automation and involvement of more people in the labor force permitted shortening of the working day, the increased leisure could also make room for more invention.

But while job-enlargement experiments may show enhanced job satisfaction because of task diversity, they rarely improve productivity. That is not surprising, since the whole point of the division of labor is to boost productivity through routinization and repetition of tasks. The shift from private to social ownership would not change that reality, and the Marxist commitment to giantism in production operations would if anything favor more rather than less specialization of function.

In part to that end, the Bolsheviks even in Lenin's time quickly turned to capitalist-style management rather than the workers' self-management that had been envisioned by the left-wing Marxists. Whatever the more plausible claims for human development as well as democracy, abolition of task specialization would have hindered production. Aside from some token arrangements such as urban worker or student involvements in rural harvests, communist systems have reestablished and deepened the division of labor. Under Stalin in 1932, Yezhov proudly announced, "Our higher educational institutions have been transformed into a form of factory, fulfilling the orders of the economy for the preparation of those specialists necessary to it" (Bailes, 1978, 182).

Role rotation seems less promising for economic development than for human development, in part through improved human relations. The division of labor, said Engels, "divides men." If Plato's utopia was a celebration of the divison of labor, Marx's is its condemnation. Most of the cleavages to be overcome by final communist society suppose full-time differentiation of functions: owners versus workers, one kind of workers versus another kind as in men's work versus women's work, hand labor versus mind labor, town versus country, and so on. Distinctive functions are also expressed in ethnic, regional, and other cleavages, as well as in India's caste and subcaste groupings. Some specializations are not wholly arbitrary, such as those arising from locational comparative advantages. But just as private property is the precondition for the capitalist division of labor, this in turn seems to be a precondition for human alienation from not only the process of labor but from other human beings.

Fourier envisaged that each could be the "butterfly" and flit from one activity to another throughout a day, and Marx was cited to similar effect. Yet in his *On Authority*, at least Engels recognized that modern factories would require discipline even if put under workers' control: "If man, by dint of his knowledge and inventive genius, has subdued the forces of nature, the latter avenge themselves upon him by subjecting him, insofar as he employs them, to a veritable despotism independent of all social organization."

If anything, Engels underestimated the degree to which communist nations would subordinate human development objectives to the search for economic efficiency. After all, the Socialist paradigm is like the Capitalist one in *requiring* growing productive capacity as the means of minimizing social conflict, but early imitation of Capitalist specialization of function was not enough for growth and social harmony in the Soviet Union.

### *Distribution According to Work, Ultimately According to Need, and Productivity*

Still asking why Marx thought socialism would yield abundance, we may turn to his vision of distributions of the social product. Recall that liberal theorists see questions of who owns what as separable from who gets what. Beginning with J. S. Mill, who was accused by Marx of "shallow syncretism," they argue that the distribution of the social product is independent of the distribution of productive wealth; so, melioration of income distribution is possible under capitalism. In contrast, Marx assumed that labor unions would be largely defensive, and that the bourgeois political system would not respond to worker demands. Neither could be said to be wholly wrong.

Marx envisaged no immediate moderation of wants, save for when leaders and their followers postpone gratifications for the sake of the revolution (cf. Mazlish, 1976). But Marx expected the first Socialist societies to arise in economically advanced nations, where capitalism had already created the conditions for abundance. If Parvus, Trotsky, and eventually Lenin were willing to attempt a revolution in the backward land of the Soviet Union, it was in expectation that it would spark wildfire revolutions spreading across Western Europe and the United States. Trotsky, in his 1936 *Revolution Betrayed*, explained Stalinism and other failures of the Russian Revolution by the failure to expand to sites of abundance. To adhere to Stalin's line of "socialism in one country" in conditions of scarcity—trying to use the state as substitute capitalist—would mire them in what Marx called "all the old crap" of political contests over the distribution of the social product. But every paradigm demands for itself ideal conditions that are practically impossible.

That said, there seems to be little in Socialist ideas of distribution of the social product that could offer hope of bolstered productivity. In the "lower phase" of socialism—perhaps expected to extend beyond the supposedly ephemeral phase of the dictatorship of the proletariat—the distributional maxim would be "from each according to his ability, to each according to his work." Marx saw this as but a restatement of the bourgeois *principle*, belied however in its *practice*. Under capitalism there are many able-bodied persons who give little or no labor, yet claim a large share of the social product as if they had done much. The maxim in question also conflicts with the practice of permitting gifts or inheritances whereby parents assure easy lives for their children. The practice impedes maximal productivity if only because the progeny of industrious and rational capitalists may be lazy and stupid (although pro-Capitalists would counter that the motive of doing well by their children stimulates much hard work in parents).[9] When the idle rich take without toil, it may arguably impede economic growth by dissipating the social surplus on luxury consumptions rather than productive reinvestment. Whatever the practices of the pre-Capitalist ruling classes, however, even Marx affirmed that the bourgeoisie tended to reduce luxury consumption in favor of productive reinvestment. If that offers another defense of Capitalist accumulation not tied to personal labor, even communist systems have failed to allocate strictly according to work, being pervaded by notorious nepotism, cronyism, and the like.

Even further from attainment is the distributional maxim for the "higher phase" of socialism. Marx's passage from his *Critique of the Gotha Programme* is so central to all themes of this chapter that we may state it at length:

> In a higher phase of communist society, after the enslaving subordination of the individual to the division of labor, and therewith also the antithesis between mental and physical labor, has vanished; after labor has become not only a means of life but life's prime want; after the productive forces have also increased with the all-round development of the individual, and all the springs of cooperative wealth flow more abundantly—only then can the narrow horizon of bourgeois right be crossed in its entirety and society inscribe on its banner: From each according to his ability, to each according to his needs! (in Tucker, 1978, 531)

The new maxim yet asks each to give what their innate and acquired abilities permit, but it removes any connection between what one gives and what one gets. Unlike the "equality of opportunity" maxim of the Capitalist, it does not suppose any desert arising from an inborn talent. Like the nineteenth-century anarchist Bakunin (as well as the twentieth-century liberal John Rawls), Marx diverged from the Capitalist premise of complete self-ownership in viewing gifts of natural aptitude as if belonging to society, not individual persons. Those with the highest natural talents owe the most but would be expected to take relatively little. Those given least by nature—such as a severe birth-defective person much in need of special medical care—would give least and take most. This roughly inverts the theory as well as practice of capitalism, at least short of the extreme where advanced Capitalist nations also help those unable to help themselves (the "safety net" concept).

Marx does not think it implausible that those who are best endowed by natural aptitudes would willingly give more but take less than most, especially relative to those with physical or mental disabilities. Remember that he thinks of our nature as productive—not as acquisitive—expressing itself in what it creates rather than in what it may collect. Also, such generosity of the talented would be an expression of our social nature.

The matter of getting raises the most serious difficulties from the point of view of the Capitalist paradigm. This formula supposes that the *only* sure incentive for persons to develop their talents, to apply them energetically in labor, or to save some earnings for investment is the prospect of being eventually more than repaid in enhanced income, leisure, and ultimate consumption. What could replace such incentives in socialism?

Marx's acceptance of distribution according to *work* in the *lower* phase of socialism obviously conceded much of the Capitalist argument; but in his higher phase of socialism he put a heavy burden on universal consciousness, or the eclipse of self-interested particularism. This conquest of selfishness would in his view be effortlessly attained by transformed conditions of existence—not by the kind of moral preaching urged by the Aristocrat or the Saint. As noted above, persons with high inborn as well as acquired talents would give much, receiving the immediate rewards of expressing their shared, productive nature as well as their individual natures. There will be the further incentives of social approval or even applause, which touch our social nature. (Beyond some basic mutual respect, Marx does not require that these be allocated equally.) There would thus be high pleasure in giving of ourselves—not the hypocritical giving of charity, which Marx understood as merely returning a part of what had been earlier taken as surplus value from the lower classes, asking deference and gaining power for it. Given his inclination even within *Capital* to use bloodletting metaphors when speaking of the capitalists ("werewolves," "vampires," "generals"), it is not surprising that Marx once called charities "organized amusements for the rich" (cf. also Engels, 1973, 314–15).

Part of the appeal to our social nature, too, would be the cooperative nature of social productive activity, which could involve sporting competitions among internally cooperative groups, attempted in modern communist systems under the label of "socialist emulation." This is illustrated in a remark in *Capital* which revealingly returns to the word "fetters" cited earlier in the chapter: "When the laborer cooperates systematically with others, he strips off the fetters of his individuality and develops the capabilities of his species" (cited in Pennock, 1979, 111).

Critically viewed, if the Capitalist errs the other way, Marx, I think, underestimated human self-interestedness expressed in individualistic economic acquisitiveness. Far more optimistic than Rousseau, Marx saw freely given productivity as but an expression of universality in Socialist consciousness.[10] Perhaps social motives for cooperative production that work in smaller, more intimate groups (families, monasteries, hunting-gathering bands) may not work on an extensive and hence impersonal social scale. True, just as the discipline of a large army depends on subunit peer pressures at the level of a company or patrol, work-team pressures could offer partial compensation, but it may not be enough. In any case, communist emphases on moral production incentives have routinely failed, giving way to individualistic material incentives not long after the founding of a communist regime.

Not even bolstered wages or salaries for more productive workers within communist systems have matched the incentive effects of even wider differentials of capitalist systems. Recognizing that relative equality amid scarcity is not winning popular plaudits, reforming communist systems are now increasing the differentials, in part by allowing private entrepreneurship. While not compromising Socialist traditions for the sake of democratization, Deng Xiaoping was willing to do so for the sake of economic growth, as in his famous statement that it does not matter whether a cat be black or white as long as it catches mice. If many Chinese (as well as Soviets) resent the newly rich among them, those who work harder than others express discontent over what they regard as yet excessive egalitarianism. Aristotle would have expected this.

## Does Anyone Really Love Central Planning?
## It Is a Jungle in There

Marx believed that capitalism had in his time already "socialized" the means of production by integrating production for a single firm. A shift to social ownership of all firms coordinated by central planning would merely complete the task of rational integration, with ordinary working people involved in planning.

While I would not discount some future role for central planning, I will address two of its paradoxes. First, the adverse consequences of self-interested choices that seem to make central planning desirable also tend to make it politically unworkable. Second, in displacing the market and its prices, central planning seems to destroy the kind of information needed to make it work with any efficiency.

### Central Planning and Productivity

If the unintended consequences of self-interested behavior seem to make central planning attractive, continuation of self-interested behavior tends to make it unworkable. Like the Capitalist's ideal market, the Socialist's rational central plan faces "interventions" or "distortions" by particular interests, including those of bureaucratic planners themselves. Both having turned away from the moralizing of the Aristocrat and the Saint, the Capitalist and Socialist paradigms yet need morality for their own viability. To work well, each system requires the austere morality of Kant's categorical imperative, whereby individuals choose for themselves only what they would want done by all. Preoccupied with getting ahead in their material circumstances, real people do not cheerfully live by universal rules; and if very many grab far more than they give, it can lead any social organization into decline.

One need not share Reinhold Niebuhr's belief in original sin to accept his critique of Marx's excessively optimistic view of human nature. While I would add that it may uneasily coexist with a social or cooperative element, Niebuhr argues that some element of particularism or self-interestedness may be in our natures. With a companion tendency toward ideological rationalizations of self-interested goals, it may be that this "defect in human life is too constitutional to be eliminated by a reorganization of society; a fact which constitutes the basic refutation of the utopian dreams of Marxism" (Niebuhr, 1941, 35).

I earlier showed that the marvelous universality of the Capitalist free marketeer succumbs to the particularity of agents who, less as individuals than as organized producer ("special") interests, attempt to expose others to the bracing winds of market risks and losses but shield themselves from them. Much the same problem besets the ideal of rational central planning: Many who would seek their benefits by imposing the burdens of a plan on others will do everything they can to avoid being themselves constrained to a plan for the benefit of others.

Stalinist fear could sacrifice a generation or two to get at least rapid industrial growth through five-year plans, but the slightest relaxation of controls quickly finds agents maneuvering to bend the "rationality" of the plan to suit their particular situations, whether as all-U.S.S.R. producer interests or as some regional ethnic self-interest. Some argue with Trotsky that self-interested motives would be less likely to hinder socialism if it were applied in the economically developed rather than the backward lands. But, doubtful that wants would be self-limiting, I think much the same problems would occur: Everyone would strive for exemption from any general constraints of an ideal central plan.

Producer interests—or suppliers of goods and services—do not really love central planning. One may distinguish them as being strong or weak, with reference to their success in influencing the planners. Communist party members in general, and those in elite roles in particular, have tended to have greater success in either shaping the content of the plan or making administrative adjustments for themselves.

Strong producer interests had an edge in lawful adjustment of the plan as well as in illicit evasions of what they failed to adjust. In Soviet experience, strong interests have historically included those of management, especially in the heavy industrial sector (more so if "metal-eaters" in defense industry). Let us consider the heavy industrial plant manager as a case in point. Soviet managers (like managers everywhere) lack any really plausible direct measure of their own "productivity." This is at best indirectly measured by the more measurable productivity of their subordinates. If they succeed in getting more output from subordinates while keeping constant or even diminishing inputs, they tend—like capitalist managers—to claim higher rewards for their managerial skill (rather than raising rewards for their workers who more surely made the difference).

While the central plan demands them, great productivity gains are rare. To look good, managers submit false information to the planners, concealing any real capacity to do more with less. They conceal existing overstocks of raw materials, overstate their need for new inputs, and understate their capacity to produce a higher quantity of output. Given a tendency of planners to look only at quantitative production targets, managers have not worried much about wasting inputs or about lowering product quality in order to boost its quantity. If planners know about such typical patterns of distortion, their forecasts may allow for its likely directions, although probably missing magnitudes of error. If they dismissed all managers who played such games, they would probably have only dullards in such slots.

Weaker producer interests include labor in all sectors but especially in consumer-goods manufacturing and the agricultural sector. Such interests less able to influence the central planning apparatus have even greater incentives to evade the plan.

Some may be professionals or skilled workers. Planners in the Soviet Union and Eastern Europe planned to demand much from doctors, engineers, and highly skilled workers, while often paying them little more than wage workers. Against the plan these professionals were soon emigrating to the West for higher pay as well as freedom, forcing the planners to plan the Berlin Wall, now torn down again as East Germany joined West Germany.

Workers in any industry will want to conceal from both planners and their managers that they could perhaps do as much and probably more with less. Those who are being administered know that the price of honesty would be greater demands on them, which is why Stalinist managers readily turned to piecework. Soviet and Eastern European workers have long quipped, "As long as they pretend to pay us, we should only pretend to work." The central plan did not allow for any autonomous labor union such as Poland's Solidarity; but with any relaxation of fear, demands for such autonomy arise. But planning for really autonomous entities—whether unions or newly allowed private firms—can be inherently contradictory, as is well known by Capitalist indicator planners.

Agricultural workers have had least influence with central planners, not only in communist systems but also in nationalistic Socialist systems of the Third World. When much farmland is left in private hands—as in the 1921–28 Soviet New Economic Policy or later in such communist nations as Poland, Yugoslavia, and Vietnam—farmers have many conflicts with the central plan. It may stint access to needed inputs such as tools or fertilizers, overprice such things, and then may require that much or all produce be sold to the state at artificially low prices.

Collectivization of agriculture—a compulsory incorporation in the central plan—was usually effected at great loss of life. Stalin's 1929–33 drive cost millions of lives, especially in the Ukraine (Conquest, 1986). Collective farmers then tended to be severely underpaid for their labor, while being denied (like feudal serfs) opportunities to migrate to the cities for better life chances, let alone go abroad. There were some allowances for private plots and sale of produce, and that was long a very important sphere of food production in communist systems. But often, to evade any price ceilings, those with produce to offer turned to black markets for better prices.

Turning now to consumer interests, strong ones such as persons in the Soviet *nomenklatura* may speak well of central planning, but exempt themselves from its burdens. Even during the Russian Revolution's civil war, Lenin authorized special restaurants to assure good nutrition of Bolshevik party cadres. Since then, what Leon Trotsky called a privileged "stratum" or what Milovan Djilas called "the new class" has had exclusive access to stores where higher quality foreign goods can be bought. If the central planners block certain luxury imports, no matter, since even top Soviet leaders have pestered their diplomats and other nationals traveling abroad to bring back for them certain kinds of shirts, ties, and the like. Even at home they may wink at certain black markets that supply themselves or their children with Western commodities not available to ordinary citizens. In Eastern Europe and the Soviet Union, the press has recently been permitted to explore the luxurious vacation homes reserved for elites. The hypocrisy of such luxury-loving leaders as Brezhnev, Tito, or Mao's wife Chiang Ching is well known, but the fall of Eastern European leaders has brought shocking revelations about the luxuries of East Germany's detained Honecker, Romania's executed Ceaucescu, and others. East German communist leaders allegedly put some of their take in numbered Swiss bank accounts.

Urban consumer populations distort the plan to secure subsidies of their food purchases at the expense of the farmers, often getting produce at far below a free-market price. Communist leaders have known that they must raise certain food prices, but especially in Eastern Europe workers rioted at most attempts, reminiscent of comparable riots of medieval workers against increases of regulated prices of staples. Such food-price riots were severe in East Germany in 1956 and recurrently in Poland, where it was a central motive in Solidarity. As one pro-Capitalist observer notes, in Poland meats and other produce were vastly cheaper than in Sweden, and prices—with good reason—should have been raised (Rydenfelt, 1984). Once itself raised to power by electoral victories over the communists (in 1989), Solidarity had to increase food prices to the detriment of its popularity. In 1988 Yugoslavia also faced severe popular discontent when it raised controlled consumer prices (sparing only staples such as flour and cooking oil) even while cutting wages. In the Soviet Union, the price of bread went unchanged for some three decades, and even Gorbachev remarked on the absurdity of seeing children using a loaf of bread as a football. The related deficiency in rewards for agricultural labor contributed to stagnation of that sector in most Socialist nations, quite apart from any natural handicaps of soils, climate, and so on. This brought on an irregular and deficient supply of fresh vegetables and other farm produce, and hence the waste of consumer time in long queues, where even price-advantaged urban consumers carp about the market-day inconveniences. Often consumers have turned to parallel (by definition, permitted) or black (illegitimate) markets to buy needed vegetables, eggs or meat at somewhat higher prices.[11]

As for weaker consumer interests, most Soviet consumers have suffered regarding both quantity and quality of many manufactured goods or provision of certain services. Or they have faced the recurrent problem of irregular or inadequate supply—a problem that only deepened when *perestroika* (restructuring) reforms further dislocated production and encouraged hoarding. To get scarce goods, they often turned to evasive solutions, adding their petty corruption to the often grand corruption of the nomenklatura. Gorbachev tried to curb drinking by cutting the hours when vodka shops would be open and by raising prices, but this spawned a thriving moonshine industry in the Soviet shadows. Like the Capitalist pure market, the central plan becomes an alien ruling to be humanized by evasion when policy change is unavailing. Western media have loved to print stories of plucky capitalist entrepreneurs maneuvering between the requirements of the official plan.

Like the Capitalist market, the central plan is a universal to be imposed on the other guy, while those who can do it further their particular interests by bending or breaking its rules. Loving neither the market nor the plan for themselves, people love rather a privileged flow of income and perhaps the power that assures it.

Whatever my skepticism regarding Trotsky's prescriptions, surely his diagnosis in *Revolution Betrayed* with regard to the rise of Stalinist tyranny was largely correct. In a climate of scarcity, apparatchiks supported Stalin in exchange for his giving them their higher incomes, special stores, cars, vacation homes, and the like, quite independently of their fear of the Black Marias. These perhaps had already picked up many of their friends or associates, often because the apparatchiks had denounced them to bolster their own reputation for loyalty to Stalin. Under a tyranny, the earnest quest by each for comfort and security makes attainment of these ends ultimately unlikely for all. Due to complicity in the Stalinist tyranny, many apparatchiks both feared Stalin's power and feared his fall. Even now top Soviet bureaucrats are often edgy about reforms. Unlike a society with heritable wealth and options for self-employment, there is nothing to fall back on: If you lose your post, you lose all privileges (Moore, 1987, 62–63, 114).

### Can Anyone Know Enough to Plan?

Marx expected far too much of central planning in boosting productivity. The bleak Soviet experience says little for centrally planned innovation. The Soviets long resisted new advances in science, including Einstein's physics as well as modern genetics (the disaster of Lysenkoism). But more plausibly, central planning could permit less disuse or waste of production potential, if not offset by ineptitude in the planning itself.

Marx viewed the worsening crises of the business cycle as the clearest evidence that capitalism was blocking productive potential. Thus the *Communist Manifesto*: "In these crises a great part not only of the existing products, but also of the previously created productive forces, are periodically destroyed." Such wasted productive potential of both machines and people was not expected under central planning, and communist systems largely evaded the dives of the Western business cycle (especially the Great Depression).

But one paradox of planning is this: The informational problems that seem to make central planning desirable also make it difficult. Communist economies have escaped the wild swings of the business cycle, but the solution of central planning has raised the new problem of economically disastrous swings in the initiatives of the chief central planner—Lenin or Stalin, Mao or Castro. Such vicissitudes can be less predictable and at least as damaging as the Capitalist's business cycle or the whims of nature of agrarian societies (cf. Berger, 1976).

Central planning proved highly cumbersome. Marx had conceded that it would require much paperwork, but apparently envisioned efficiencies of scale: "The costs of book-keeping drop as production becomes concentrated and book-keeping becomes social" (*Capital*, II, vi, I, 2). Yet just before Tito turned to self-management socialism— making more use of markets—the central plan of Yugoslavia was reportedly printed on no less than one and a half *tons* of paper (Riddel, 1968, 52). Even with modern computing—yet underdeveloped in the Soviet Union—sheer misinformation due to absence of market pricing causes great wastage of material and human resources. Production operations are impeded by lack of raw materials or needed parts. Goods are produced that no one wants to buy. Human time is squandered in queues for products produced in deficient supply.

One kind of wasted production potential of capitalism is the scrapping or simple abandonment of major production facilities and equipment because of shifted profitability in market economics. Where Capitalist economics sees necessary transitions toward improved efficiency, the Socialist sees grotesque inefficiency as well as harm to workers. But if planners err in pouring more capital into obsolete plant and equipment, that can also waste production potential.

## Contradictions in Socialist Economics?

The post-Stalinist Soviet Union relaxed the terror by fits and starts; and Mikhail Gorbachev's leadership since 1985 has sought further liberalizations, recognizing the need for reforms in all three social spheres: (1) the economic (*perestroika* or restructuring); (2) the political (*democratizatsiya* or democratization); and (3) the cultural or ideological (*glasnost* or openness). But will such changes last?

### Wants and Powers

Soviet economics has some parallel problems with that of capitalism. I concluded in Chapter 6 that the Capitalist's formula may be ultimately self-defeating not only in ecological limits, but also because it increases wants even more than it bolsters social capacities to satisfy such wants—to some extent even in the economic miracle nations where capitalism is thriving for the time being.

The communist planned economy deploys less advertising and allows less publicity of income differentials, which may moderate demand; but it has done less well in increasing the social capacity to meet demand. Along with problems of increasingly sluggish growth, communist systems have found that acquisitive desires have not been self-limiting in accord with universal consciousness. Marx recognized that needs are socially relative, able to grow with increased social capacity to satisfy them: "As his development advances, the realm of necessity grows along with his needs; but at the same time the forces of production that satisfy his needs grow too." But if wants grow at all faster than productive powers under socialism as well as capitalism, and if Socialist relations of production do less well in boosting productive powers, this is a dagger into the heart of the Socialist formula.

The turn of reforming communist systems toward more openness only heightens economic aspirations. It increases exposure to visible examples of higher living standards in capitalist nations, sometimes in embarrassing juxtapositions with more prosperous capitalist economies (Eastern Europe v. Western Europe; North Korea v. South Korea; China v. Taiwan or Hong Kong, etc.). Consumer anger also rises with revelations of higher consumption among the communist elites, especially after they were toppled from power.

### Interactive Problems

I said that a typical capitalist economy faces a complex of problems, such that any proposed solution to one—even if successful regarding the aim—tends to exacerbate one or more of the remaining problems. But this is also the practical problem of socialist economies. They, too, want economies of high growth, low unemployment, minimal inflation, low budgetary deficits, minimal balance-of-payments deficits, less foreign indebtedness or other dependency, publicly acceptable levels of equity, and improving regularity in supply of better quality goods and services (especially these last).

Especially now during economic transition, even an omnipotent and omniscient central planner would find solutions difficult. To get more growth, one could reduce featherbedding in employment, but with the cost of creating a visible unemployment that has been absent in the centrally planned communist economies. Or one might import Western factory equipment, usually with the consequence of greater foreign indebtedness and balance-of-payments problems. The Soviet decision to join the world economy leads to the need to move in phases toward a convertible ruble (which has been steeply overvalued), but it will force many other changes, such as in domestic pricing (inflation) and exposure to a world business cycle. The Chinese elite found that opening to Western trade and tourism tended to stimulate democratic demands, which in 1989 they chose to repress. Any choice to rely increasingly on market mechanisms in the domestic economy may have the possible result of Yugoslavia's severe inflation and high unemployment. One could boost growth with higher wage incentives for workers, but this would bust the budget, especially in view of yet high military demands in the Soviet Union. The Soviets have admitted that they were incurring budget deficits in the 1980s. Then again, is the problem one of improving the quality of goods and services? For this one may punish workers or whole firms for shoddy merchandise or surly service, but then perhaps any improvements in quality will bring reduced quantity of production. Dislocations may cause hoarding, which further empties shelves at markets. One could restrict exports, but at the loss of vitally needed foreign exchange, now that oil revenue is a declining resource. Permitting both native and foreign private-enterprise competition could increase supplies of consumer goods, but this could also threaten more unemployment—if not the system as a whole—while foreign access could exacerbate trade deficits.[12] Can one plan the end of planning?

In practice, socialism brings no exemption from standard economic problems. At most it slightly shifts the problem set, bringing at least one new kind of problem for every problem of capitalism that is improved upon.

It has been said that this is "the century of revolution"—a phenomenon that has reached 30 percent of the world's land area and 35 percent of its population (Sweezy, 1980, 9). Implementing socialism has often required ruinous civil and international wars, involving much decapitalization, destruction of existing forces of production, and the deaths, imprisonment, or emigration of the productive resource of people. Even with victory, it often takes decades merely to restore the antecedent level of productive forces. While one must be critical of those who would tote up "the costs of revolution" without a fair estimate of possible benefits, much mayhem may be required to implement the Socialist paradigm against strong resistance. It normally takes far more violence to effect great change in a society than merely to preserve or reform existing institutions.

Marx and Engels expected far too much of their alternative technique of organizing our economic life. Socialism must no longer pretend to be an end in itself but should be restored to its proper status as a mere means that can be judiciously used, compromised as necessary to engender economic growth and even more so to foster the democracy that Socialists wrongly tend to regard as mere means. Once again, a paradigm has promised far more than it can deliver, and democracy would keep it in its proper place.

## Notes

1. The term "socialism," which first emerged in an Owenite journal, did not in use always entail major social ownership of the means of production.

As Marx and Engels argued in the *Communist Manifesto*, by the mid-nineteenth century every class had produced some version of what purported to be "socialism." In addition to authentically proletarian socialism, there were aristocratic, bourgeois, and petty-bourgeois versions of "socialism"—most of which protected some form of property rather than really promoting full social ownership of the means of production. This was later true of the Nazis, who claimed themselves to be "socialist" but eventually purged those who took this claim seriously—and confiscated only Jewish property.

2. If liberals do address the problem, it is recast in terms of a kind of private property existing in the means of state coercion within communist nations, which has a result similar to capitalism's in that relatively few control the access of many to the means of livelihood and can consequently by exploitation live off the labor of others. I think there is much validity in the view.

3. As especially developed by Engels in *The Origin of the Family, Private Property, and the State* (in Tucker, 1978, 734–59), the bourgeois family is viewed as a three-cornered web of mutual economic exploitation of husband, wife, and children, with women being the most severely exploited because of their historical separation from the means of production once private property in herds and lands arose.

4. The concept of alienation appeared in various forms before Marx (cf. Schact, 1971). Marx's forms of alienation have certain correspondences to pre-Marxist uses: (1) alienation from product, means of production, and hence nature to pre-Marxist alienation as giving over or selling property; (2) alienation from the process of labor to pre-Marxist alienation as *alienatio mentis*, as having lost one's mental faculties; (3) alienation from other human beings, expressed in state or family tied only by mutual economic exploitation, to pre-Marxist alienation of affection; and (4) alienation from our species-specific nature to the medieval alienation from God. (Marx, as noted, follows Feuerbach in viewing the anthropomorphic concept of a god as, rather, human self-alienation—denial of our own potential powers.)

5. Fourier similarly believed that improved Socialist techniques of organizing production would boost abundance, thinking his phalanstery (commune) system for *organization* of economic activity would surpass even technological advances in boosting production. His "theory of association" was to "triple the annual product of Industry or the wealth of nations" (in Poster, 1971, 23).

6. Stalin pushed Baconian projects in the extreme, as in Zhores Medvedev's comment on his "All-Union Program for the Transformation of Nature, including changing the climate, eliminating deserts, and constructing gigantic hydroelectric dams and canal systems. . . . " This megalomaniacal program was adopted in 1948. But in the central direction of all this, when figures such as Lenin, Stalin, Khruschev, or Mao held absolute power, it was likely to feed the illusion of their outstanding scientific judgment, and the resultant meddling with scientific research has had disastrous results for communist science (Medvedev, 1978, 61–62, 89, 92).

7. Marx only rarely commented on ecological abuse of nature, but too lightly assumed that only Capitalist profit motives could be a problem. Thus, Capitalist agriculture displaced the peasantry—among whom both food and

even clothing had eventually been recycled to the Earth—with chemical fertilizer substitutes that brought quicker enrichment of the soil but at the cost of long-term harm to its fertility (*Capital*, I, iv, 15, 10). The new Soviet and Eastern European liberalizations have brought us recurrent horror stories of ecological disasters within communist systems—stories long suppressed by the communist press. From the Baltics through Eastern Europe, vast areas of farmland have been contaminated by unfiltered industrial smokestack pollutants.

8. Against the Saint, and with both the Capitalist and the Socialist, few of us would deny the values of automation and robotization if the costs were not unfairly borne by those unemployed. Studs Terkel, in his *Working*, put it well: "In a world of cybernetics, of an almost runaway technology, things are increasingly making things. It is for our species, it would seem, to go on to other matters" (cited in Lea, 1982, 142–43).

9. To reject every view of Marx entails disagreement with many classical liberals. Figures such as Locke, Smith, and Ricardo preceded Marx in developing the labor theory of value, although the Capitalist abandons it once Socialists use it to support claims of labor as against owners (cf. Shaw, 1975, 75–83). Eugen von Böhm-Bawerk's critique of Marx's labor theory of value faults him for failure to attain what was not his aim. Marx was not trying to predict immediate market prices but to explain why freely reproducible commodities—such as found in, say, a K-Mart—keep within rough ranges in their ratios of exchange, these values being a "center of gravity" around which prices may fluctuate for myriad causes. For themselves, Capitalist theorists may be correct in saying that psychological propensities may better predict current prices, especially of rare collectibles; but they offer no alternative to incorporated labor time as an explanation of, say, why one VCR exchanges for about ten pairs of blue jeans or 200 ball-point pens (cf. Sweezy, 1984).

In the Capitalist's "fetishized" perspective, arbitrary and immediate mental states dominate prices (through the money that makes things commensurable), which dominate in turn exchange ratios of things and hence how much labor time is put into them. Marx turns this around: Average socially necessary labor time dominates normal relative price ranges and thereby the willingness of suppliers to sell or consumers to buy.

10. Rousseau saw us as divided in motives: By our merely "physical" nature, we would put our particular interest above the general interest; but by our "moral" nature we would put the general interest above our particular interest. In this last, we would put the more inclusive interest over the less inclusive one, and we would not exempt ourselves from rules applied to others. Not mere removal of inequalities, but also a lifting passion of either patriotism or love would make this spirit of the general will prevail (cf. Cook, 1975).

Perhaps pure egoism and pure altruism are both overrated as motives, since most motivation arises in a zone of overlap of self-regarding and other-regarding considerations. We at least like to think that in doing some good for ourselves we also are serving others.

11. Just as Socialist intellectuals have claimed that capitalism gets its longevity only by adopting some of their ideas (such as more welfare programs),

many Capitalists have claimed that only some penetration of market mechanisms has saved communist systems from total breakdown (e.g., Berger, 1986, 21). But the more extensive turn to market mechanisms brings new problems, including unemployment, inflation, advancing inequalities, and the like.

12.  Urging national self-reliance, Mao also favored severe social disruptions as often as every six to seven years to ward off any "capitalist roading," arguing that promotion of revolutionary consciousness could precede and beget great gains in production. His variant of the Socialist formula gave China neither.

# 9

# The Socialist and Democracy

> The first step in the revolution by the working
> class . . . is to raise the proletariat to the position
> of ruling class, to win the battle of democracy.
> The proletariat will use its political supremacy
> to wrest, by degrees, all capital from the bour-
> geoisie, to centralize all production in the hands
> of the State, i.e., of the proletariat organized as
> the ruling class; and to increase the total of
> productive forces as rapidly as possible.
>
> Karl Marx and Friedrich Engels,
> *Communist Manifesto*

Marx and Engels could not have been clearer in manifesting extreme
instrumentalism toward the democratic state. A workers' democracy
would be used as a tool for expropriating capital and replacing
Capitalist relations of production with Socialist ones. Then it guides
expansion of productive forces until the eclipse of property, classes,
and class conflict makes any state redundant, at least in the sense that
"the public power will lose its political character."

Having seen that each of the other primary paradigms of social
philosophy tended sometimes to reduce democratic freedoms to mere
means, we may expect that the same would apply to socialism. But in
Marx and Engels a more open and consistent instrumentalism regarding democratic government dominates at every phase: (1) in the use
of bourgeois democracy; (2) in the shift to the transitional state, the
"dictatorship of the proletariat"; and (3) in the prophesied "withering
away" of that state.

## The Attack on Formalism:
## Criticizing Yet Using Bourgeois Democracy

Although there are many nuances in contemporary Marxist theories of the state, Marx clearly understood the state in all of its

historical variants as being a direct or indirect tool of the dominant class (or classes) to repress other classes (cf. Jessop, 1982). It did not historically arise until emergence of private possessions of herds or lands and the availability of a social surplus to maintain state officials. Whatever its claim to wider legitimacy, the state essentially operates to protect or enlarge the relations of production favored by the hegemonic class or classes. While normally a single class or even fraction thereof may be dominant, Marx sometimes acknowledged the possibility of rule by a coalition of several classes.

I need not belabor the special case of the Bonapartist state—a state that gains some autonomy (usually with a strong autocrat relying on the bureaucracy and armed forces) because two major classes have neutralized each other, with neither able to rise to primacy at the level of civil society and thereby dominate the state apparatus. Although affirming that even such a state safeguarded property rights against the proletariat, Marx and Engels saw two phases of such standoffs in modern European history. One was the era of royal absolutism, when the rising bourgeois had not quite eclipsed the landowners, giving rise to such figures as Louis XIV of France in the seventeenth century. Once the bourgeoisie attain hegemony, a second period of stalemate occurs when they are in sharp conflict with the working class, as in the rise of Napoleon Bonaparte or Louis Bonaparte in the nineteenth century. In the latter case, in Marx's view, the propertied let lapse the parliamentary body that expressed the divisions among them, preferring a dictator who rather gave unity to property owners over the producers: "It was the only form of government possible at a time when the bourgeoisie had already lost, and the working class had not yet acquired, the faculty of ruling the nation." (*Civil War in France*, iii, in Tucker, 1978, 618–52). Many twentieth-century Marxists extend the model to explain fascist autocracies.

The usually short-lived Bonapartist transitions aside, beyond the core conception of the state as a repressive instrumentality in class-divided societies, there is little more that can be said about states *in general*. That is, the state otherwise assumes distinctive characteristic forms in the great historical modes of production. Although no uniform sequencing is to be expected, such social formations include variants of pastoralism, Asiatic society, ancient society, feudalism, capitalism, and then socialism in at least its lower phase.

### Denial That Bourgeois Democracy Protected Freedom

Marx recognized that the characteristic capitalist state differed from the feudal state in its relative separation of political and economic spheres. It had no equivalent of the feudal lord, who was both an economic figure and a localized political leader. In addition, the capitalist state characteristically sought to subordinate any provincial or more localized autonomy, working to create the larger market sphere of the nation-state. Finally, Marx was quite aware that capitalism shifted to competitive-consensual political procedures. Part of his critique of the liberal democratic state concerned the mystifications of its ideology: "Your very ideas are but outgrowth of the conditions of your bourgeois production and bourgeois property, just as your jurisprudence is but the will of your class made into a law for all" (*Communist Manifesto*, ii).

In Chapter 7, I have addressed several Marxist critiques of "bourgeois democracy," most of which stress that the merely formal equalities of rights conceal the substantive hegemony of capital in the influence, recruitment, and structures games. In my view, many of these critiques have considerable validity, although with the Saint I think the critique should emphasize the impact of economic inequalities rather than disparage the forms of freedom as such.

Some Marxist critiques seem overstated. Beyond the core consensus (protect private property, protect the inequalities of wealth and income associated with it, secure a political power distribution adequate thereto), the business world is often sharply divided over regulatory, revenue, and expenditure concerns. My prior analysis of self-interested efforts of all agents to shield themselves from market risks yet impose such on others leaves room for influence by nonbusiness actors—including labor, consumers, and public officials—often even being formalized in corporatist-oriented democracies such as Sweden. In other, noneconomic realms of policy, the business campaign contributions and other such influences are not always mobilized, and voting alone seems dominant, as in public transfer programs to the elderly or to the poor. Hence, the typical liberal democratic state cannot be adequately described as a mere capitalist tool, even if its overall operation must perform the function of protecting capital accumulation (cf. Offe and Offe, 1984; Offe, 1985).

If pressed, Marx could have admitted that the bourgeois state was not a monolith simply dominated by unified capital. Yet he recurrently disparaged its forms, as in arguing that there is no such thing as a "free state." Bourgeois parties had already demanded "the old democratic litany familiar to all: universal suffrage, direct legislation, popular rights, a people's militia, etc.," all being "pretty little gewgaws" of democratic republics (*Critique of the Gotha Programme*, iv, in Tucker, 1978, 525–41).

## Use of the Freedoms of Bourgeois Democracy

Yet Marx and Engels rejected the (perhaps overstated) tendency of many anarchists such as Proudhon or Bakunin to hold that states were states, that all were equally backward and vile. Marx and Engels regarded the bourgeois state as progressive. For one thing, it enabled the bourgeois to displace feudal relations of production. Hence, Marx and Engels favored liberal revolutions, and Engels himself bore arms in the 1848 insurgency in Germany, even if Marxists there and elsewhere joked about the importance of having the proletariat help the bourgeoisie to power so they could then overthrow them. The second major advantage of the bourgeois state—perhaps belying critical claims of its total political closure—is that it creates political space for the proletariat to carry on class struggle in its economic, political, and ideological forms (touching each liberal sphere, or Marxist levels of a social formation).

At the level of economic struggle, bourgeois republics can create the conditions for the establishment of trade unions. Marx believed that their economic potential is largely but defensive, unable to shape major changes in the working day, working conditions, or wages. Yet the activities of organizing and going on strike are important scenes for consciousness-raising, as described later.

As for political struggle, Marx and Engels believed that considerable violence would be necessary to overthrow a centralized, bureaucratic despotism. But they also favored, where liberal democratic conditions permit, the formation of an independent working-class political party that would run candidates for office. Although Marx talked of the possibilities of a peaceful transition—an electoral route to proletarian power for Great Britain, the Netherlands, or the United States (respectively, where he happened to live, where he was speaking in 1872, and where he was about to move the headquarters of the International)—it is doubtful that he really believed a wholly peaceful transition was possible. He probably shared the view much later expressed by Engels in the 1895 *Tactics of Social Democracy* (in Tucker, 1978, 556–73), which clearly endorsed pursuit of electoral opportunities but forecasted that, should the workers win, the bourgeoisie would "break the contract" or turn to a coup d'état. The bourgeoisie themselves would initiate the illicit violence, and the electorally victorious workers would merely defend the constitutional order (as attempted by the loyalist side of the 1936–39 Spanish Civil War).

For the most, Marx and Engels warned against expecting too much of democratic means, but they consistently said that electoral participation would be useful to promote organization, to count their numbers, and to boost consciousness-raising.[1] Much of Lenin's distinctiveness from Marx and Engels closely relates to his shift of the scene of revolution from advanced capitalist democracies to a backward autocracy, explaining in part his greater emphasis on violent initiatives. Yet even Lenin's essay "Left-wing Communism" (in Connor, 1968, 283–319) also endorses electoral activity for the purposes stated by Marx and Engels where such activity was feasible. For classical Marxism or Marxism-Leninism, bourgeois freedoms offered the opportunities for the proletariat to transcend bourgeois democracy.

## Strategies to Facilitate Entering the Dicatorship of the Proletariat

I earlier noted that by the mid-twentieth century many liberals in reaction to the fascists and communists had so fetishized the procedures of competition of ideas, of candidates, and of institutional units that they tended to forget that these were originally means to an end. Marx and Engels had long before contributed to that reaction by their disparagement of the forms of freedom and their fetishization, rather, of the substantive theory of democracy. In terms of the Lincoln phrase, "government of the people, by the people, and for the people," the substantive theory emphasizes the last (cf. Macpherson, 1966). Yet the "of" and "by" were also in view. At least when expressed in its transitional political character, this would involve the "dictatorship of the proletariat."

This Socialist phrase unfortunately borrowed from Blanqui was by no means a recommendation of a Stalin but was meant as a counterpart of the description of bourgeois democracy as in substance the dictatorship of the bourgeoisie. In any case, Marx and Engels made clear that the dictatorship of the proletariat was to be modeled along the lines of how Marx perceived the Paris Commune of 1871—that is, a radicalized democracy. But before touching on those forms, we should say something about how Marxism regards the strategic field of influence, since it is quite distinctive from the liberal "combat of ideas." Truth is discovered and actualized in the world in a very different way.

### *The Influence Strategy: Displacing Capitalist Combat of Ideas with Consciousness-raising*

Marx and Engels propose a distinctive view of the kind of discourse that may advance truth in the world—a praxeological model that may be called "consciousness-raising." Marxist thought differs from liberalism in each of the tactical subfields of the influence strategy, emphasizing more worker activity in creating messages, delivering them, and reinforcing them.

### The Creation of Messages

The term "consciousness-raising" implies the possibility of some higher consciousness as the target. Perhaps it also connotes the idea of agents engaged in the raising against others who are striving to keep consciousness low. For Marx and Engels, higher consciousness would ultimately involve effective universality—a lived rather than merely preached morality arising from the working class, a morality having no particularistic project of living off the labor of others. For the same reason, it would also be "scientific" or a view of the world emancipated from ideological distortion—a supposedly illusion-free perspective like that of Marx and Engels.

A scientific consciousness would include a scientifically valid account of ideas, of consciousness itself. Hegel had shown that idea systems are revolutionized through time, but he did so with an idealistic, or mystified, view—as if God were unfolding parts of his mind. This was a consequence of the fact that the penners of ideas had emerged as a distinct profession, in appearance separate from the power and the economic interests of a ruling class. Just as they were separate persons, it was easy to fall into the illusion of ideas floating free from any class moorings.

Marx stated his key premise in the famous preface to his *Contribution to the Critique of Political Economy*, "It is not the consciousness of men that determines their being, but, on the contrary, their social being that determines their consciousness." More specifically, it is one's economic conditions of existence as summarized by relationship to the means of production (or class membership) that determines how one will think. Although Marx and Engels never really explain their own emancipation from their bourgeois conditions of existence, class interests will cause distorted or unscientific perceptions of the world. The predictability from class to the relevant orientations seems arrayed on a continuum from stronger to weaker correlation as one moves from the class identity itself to economic policy preferences, preferences among political arrangements, and then what I call "justificatory languages" (cf. Feuer, 1975).

Any adequate theory of ideas would be historical, by which alone one may invalidate an idealistic causal misconstrual of any correlation of a set of ideas with a certain group—namely, that the idea comes first and shapes how people live. On the contrary, research would show that the class takes form and only later works up its characteristic ideology—the perception of the world that best suits its interest—helping to justify its economic and other preferences to itself as well as to other classes. Yet—in the other half of the dialectical ontology of Marx—once conditions of existence give rise to ideas, those ideas mediated by practical activity do shape the world that shapes us.

Marx and Engels make clear that an ideology for the most involves not cynical deception so much as self-deception, especially in the least intellectual members of a class. Thus, ordinary Capitalists are captives of their own illusions.

Even among intellectual advocates for a class, there would be considerable scientific content in its early period when it is criticizing the previously dominant ideology, as when Smith or Ricardo criticize feudalism. But the later intellectual apologists tend toward cynicism, since the world view has grown old and the practice to which it corresponds fully reveals its "contradictions." Marx held that the ratio of scientific content declines in later theorists such as Burke or Bastiat defending property against the working class: "It was . . . no longer a question, whether this theorem or that was true, but whether it was useful to capital or harmful, expedient or inexpedient, politically dangerous or not. In place of disinterested inquirers, there were hired prize fighters" (afterword to the second German edition of *Capital*).

Part of the creation of useful messages for the proletariat would be developing the science of ideas, since ideological distortions otherwise get in the way of scientific theory of economics, politics, and so on. Thus if Jeremy Bentham or Destutt de Tracy had, on behalf of the bourgeoisie, "unmasked" the ideas of the landlord class and its lawyers, bankers, and so on, Marx and Engels saw their task as "unmasking" the bourgeoisie in their turn, showing that—while progressive in their initial rising against feudalism—they did not in the last analysis really speak for "the people" but only for a class.

Every ideology involves false consciousness, but it also involves false *class* consciousness if one succumbs to the set of unscientific views that suits the interest of some class other than one's own. It is, so to speak, to have one's body (one's being, or conditions of existence) in one class, but one's mind (consciousness) in another. Thus Molière's *bourgeois gentilhomme* had the false class consciousness of a bourgeois who had incorporated the views (and behaviors) of the nobility. And so Marx believed that a proletarian who accepts Capitalist economic and political outlooks would also have false class consciousness.

The concept has been much critiqued by anti-Marxists, even by those who otherwise may acknowledge that mind-bending or indoctrination (often the right calls it "brainwashing") occurs in other settings, as when the Maoists supposedly cretinized the Chinese people (in fact, we now know that the Chinese never stopped thinking). But what disturbs the liberal even more is the idea that someone is trying to tell the workers what they really ought to prefer or, even worse, what they really want. There is something repugnant in telling others what their ultimate value judgments must be. They should be "free to choose" for themselves.

I fully share that repugnance, doubting the pretension of anyone to tell mentally competent adults what they must want. (Those who are value noncognitivists would be especially critical of such pretended knowledge.) Yet I would argue that the concept of false class consciousness is otherwise defensible when limited to saying, first, that some people hold scientifically invalid views and, second, that those views may promote the interests of some class other than their own.

Think of a continuum of kinds of statements, arrayed in rough order of increasingly manifest, more or less typical valuational content: discrete descriptive statements or isolated "facts," more general descriptive statements, statements of trends or correlations, causal judgments, statements about the future, prudential (or means–ends) judgments of value, and categorical (ultimate ought) judgments of value. Whatever my stated hesitation with regard to this last category, I would maintain that many workers do hold many *demonstrably* invalid beliefs of a descriptive, trend or correlational, causal, predictive, or prudential form. Further, many of such wrong beliefs quite plausibly suit the interests of the owners of means of production.[2]

If conditions of existence determine consciousness, Marx and Engels believed that unplanned changes in conditions of existence would more or less spontaneously lead workers to the more scientific outlook on the world. After all, workers were exploited at work, subjected to unemployment during business slumps, and otherwise exposed to consciousness-raising conditions, and were better able to communicate discontents because of their concentration in urban areas, unionization, and so forth. Marx and Engels expected workers to thus grow into a revolutionary consciousness. The left speaks of "maturation" as fighting inequalities, just as the right talks of "growing up" as accepting inequalities.

### *Delivery of Messages: From Promoting Consciousness to Stalinist Agitprop*

That proletarian class conditions of existence did not instantly or mechanically generate scientific consciousness was clear in the admitted existence of false class consciousness among the workers, or what our contemporaries may call "blue-collar bourgeoisie." For Marx and Engels this was at least temporarily possible because of a degree of autonomous impact of the ideological apparatuses dominated by the ruling class:

> The ideas of the ruling class are in every epoch the ruling ideas: i.e., the class, which is the ruling *material* force of society, is at the same time its ruling *intellectual* force. The class which has the means of material production at its disposal, has control at the same time over the means

of mental production, so that thereby, generally speaking, the ideas of those who lack the means of mental production are subject to it. (*German Ideology*, I, A, 2)

There was an "unequal combat" in the bourgeois combat of ideas, primarily because the owners rather than workers have hegemony over the mass media, the educational system, and so on.

Yet there has been much porosity in capitalist control over the production and dissemination of ideas. Not only were Marx and Engels able to publish their critical books about capitalism, but in their time market forces had not yet destroyed the once thriving working-class popular press, as noted in Chapter 7.

Imbalance of interclass message flows was clear enough in Marx's time just as in our own. If one were to count literally all politically relevant messages flowing between classes or other strata, the predominant pattern would be down more than up the stratification system (not only by class, but also by age, gender, race, etc.). At least on a per-capita basis, members of an upper class put their viewpoints before the lower class much more than the lower do to the upper. One may add that per-capita flows of primarily political messages among the upper class are also much higher than those moving among the lower.

If down-strata flows may aim at keeping lower-class consciousness low, then that is where consciousness-raising is important. In a reprise of the Saint's model of ideal communications, the dominated must be brought together for more horizontal message flows among themselves, especially in face-to-face meetings where they can neutralize propaganda from the dominant by exchanging *their own* experiences and interpretations of the world. But Saints want not just proletarians but a cross-section of the people at their meetings, even if these would often be relatively small in size. The Socialists target a specific class only, and may want mass meetings, save for a Leninist party in a conspiratorial mode. Also, the Saints would insist on the fullest truthfulness in political communications—something often set aside by Lenin and his similarly opportunistic followers. Finally, Saints would not want cultivation of class hatred, which a Socialist could favor.

For the Socialist, the practical activity of organization was needed for such communication as well as for coordination in action. Marx's own activities in journalism, in the First International, and in support of Socialist unions and parties are relevant here.

If part of the democratization of communication flows would occur before the revolution, part would occur after, in the period of the dictatorship of the proletariat similar to the Paris Commune. Marx had written one of his earliest essays against Prussian censorship; and in *The Civil War in France*, he claims much for the Paris Commune: "The Commune did not pretend to infallibility, the invariable attribute of all governments of the old stamp. It published its doings and sayings, it initiated the public into all its shortcomings" (in Tucker, 1978, 618–52).

### Leninism

Marx and Engels had expected workers to come eventually into a revolutionary consciousness not by tutelage by the few, but more by their mutual communication regarding their changed conditions of existence. However, as it turns out, not only would the advanced conditions of Capitalist development fail to create Socialist consciousness in the proletariat, even supposedly Socialist conditions of existence failed to do so (Heilbroner, 1980, 134–35, 166–70).

V. I. Lenin (d. 1924) had another view. Already in 1902, Lenin writing in *What Is to Be Done?* (1929) followed Karl Kautsky's suggestion that workers left to themselves could only rise to trade union consciousness—focused on improved wages, hours, and so forth, rather than on changed relations of production through revolution. Correct consciousness must be brought to the workers from without, from primarily nonproletarian intellectuals who understand the workers' conditions of existence better than do the workers themselves.

New attention is focused on the consciousness-raisers. Lenin distinguished agitation and propaganda. *Propaganda* accents the printed word, developing a system of ideas unlikely to be immediately understood by most workers. *Agitation*, by contrast, uses the living word or direct speech to present a single idea to mass audiences, concretizing some grievance in order to incite them to action (and perhaps here truthfulness is not always most effective). This distinction of levels of discourse is somewhat reminiscent of the Aristocrat's contrast of philosophic knowledge (accessible to the few) and true belief (appropriate for the many), except that Lenin makes clear that agitation is largely but a bridge toward propaganda. He even urged propagandists not to dwell too much in popularized pamphlets, seeing that "the workers do not confine themselves to the artificially restricted limits of *literature for workers* but that they study *general literature* to an increasing degree" (Lenin, 1929, 41n.).[3] Like the Capitalist in the Enlightenment, the Socialist believes that most can become philosophic.

But if Lenin wanted ultimately to transcend elite leadership, he believed that only a few had scientific consciousness and that only the correct theory should be disseminated within the Russian Social Democratic party. His rivals' espousal of the slogan "freedom of criticism" promoted bourgeois reformist illusions, for it implied "not the substitution of one theory by another, but freedom from every complete and thought-out theory; it implies eclecticism and absence of principle" (Lenin, 1929, 27). Trusting spontaneity would lead to dominance of bourgeois ideology, for it was advantaged by being older and more fully developed and by having more opportunities for diffusion. The Socialist movement was "in its infancy, and in order that it may grow up the quicker, it must become infected with intolerance against all those who retard its growth by subservience to spontaneity" (Lenin, 1929, 43).

### The Correct Line

Marx recurrently used the metaphor of bourgeois society as pregnant with the new society, with revolutionary action the midwife to the new birth. This suggests facilitating more than forcing the pace of events, which have their natural course of development.

In contrast, Lenin's master metaphor is a disciplined, military march up a mountainside to assault a fortress of class rule. Decisively forcing events, it is accompanied by a spirit of intolerance that becomes extreme under Stalin.

Lenin's marching column will have its elite of professional revolutionaries—its "vanguard of the proletariat"—who will define the "correct line" of march, the proper direction and velocity. The metaphor dominates the language that categorizes "deviations" from the correct line, although even Lenin acknowledges that it must admit of "zig-zags" to best ascend, or even use strategic retreats as necessary. Yet there are those who fall unnecessarily far behind (defeatists, atavists, rearguard) or rashly march too far forward (adventurists, avant-gardists, voluntarists). There are those who slip off the path to the left (infantilists, leftists, left-wing communists) or rather to the right (opportunists, economists, reformists, rightists). Only the party or, more precisely, the party leadership can define the correct line of march. While the metaphor fits with the Baconian emphasis on the correct method or pathway, its use also suggests the technocrat's illusion of the "one best way." Allan Bloom is correct in seeing Lenin's concept of the vanguard as an ingenious attempt to assert *leadership* without denying *democracy*: "The members of the vanguard have just a small evanescent advantage. They now know what everyone will soon know" (Bloom, 1987, 331).[4]

Military imagery fits poorly with any competition of ideas as part of such learning. Lenin's theory of "democratic centralism" within the Social Democratic party held that the party line would be discussed at all levels of the organization prior to a vote, but thereafter party policy decisions would no longer be criticized as such, limiting any further discussion to means of effective implementation. This makes it impossible to reconsider the party program, except when reconsideration is implemented from the top. But such an anomalous event usually supposed colossal error quite obvious to all, even its author (Lenin sometimes criticized himself, and Castro has done that often). In communist practice before recent reforms most public criticism has aimed downward, and occasionally laterally, but only rarely upward and even then usually sparing the top.

Lenin after the Bolshevik Revolution of November 1917 soon closed down opposition party presses, yet he did permit some discussion of alternatives within the top party organs such as the Central Committee as well as Politburo. But just after the end of the Civil War in 1921 he banned the organization of factions within the now renamed Communist party, and this blocked any really effective intraparty democracy. Free discussion vanished in the Central Committee and withered even within the committee-sized Politburo under Stalin.

Under Stalin's version of the Agitprop (agitation and propaganda department), the correct line was maintained by terror. If Lenin had spoken of tactical zig-zags, under Stalin one could be shot merely for continuing to zig when Stalin shifted to zag. The correct line by then made any inequality in the bourgeois combat of ideas seem mild, since Stalinist orthodoxy was maintained not only by economic constraints but by coercive and symbolic pressures as well.

It would require more than a half-century before the costs of such constrained communication became clear, especially in economic life. By 1990 Gorbachev permitted vigorous intraparty oppositions, as well as seeds of extraparty ones. Certainly, the relaxed censorship of glasnost brought into the open many latent conflicts within Soviet society (anti-Semitism and nationalistic ferment), but he had to court some risks to modernize the economy. The new freedoms are also compensatory for measures of economic austerity, such as raising subsidized prices of food, housing, and so forth, and lowering job security. In parts of Eastern Europe under Soviet influence, pressures for liberalization came not only from within but from the Soviet Union and from Western nations being asked for loans and other economic assistance.

### Reinforcement of Messages: From Discourse to Action

Having discussed creation and dissemination of persuasive messages, I will in brief address Marxist views on their reinforcement. Recall that Marx held that conditions of existence dominate formation of consciousness. This meant that one class would be easily persuaded to accept a scientific view of the world, while other classes would be largely beyond persuasion.

Workers would need little added reinforcement to accept and act on true consciousness, since they had no need to distort thinking to justify or conceal living off the labor of some other class. To get workers to act for their collective aims, Marx may have seen little need to apply symbolic, economic, or coercive pressure against fellow workers, but he may have underestimated the importance of individualized incentives in any effective organization.

As for nonproletarians, apparently by the emancipatory force of study a few such as Marx and Engels could come into true consciousness, but only through *attachment to the proletarian* class that had no need of ideological illusions—not by *detachment from all* classes.

Words alone—especially those of a few intellectuals, could not bring a new world into being. Only revolutionary action could do so, even if only as midwife to the new birth.[5] For Marx, action was necessarily a part of testing theory, as in showing that the supposed constants of the market "laws" of Capitalist economics are really variables subject to human transformation, or in showing that capitalists are no more socially indispensable than the feudal lords before them. Reification is mistaking alterable human artifacts with inalterable natural facts, and action to alter things could be viewed as dereification. Theory mediated by action changes the conditions of existence, and after observations of results (also understood as activity) one may make any needed correction of theory. Hence one of the *Theses on Feuerbach* rejected any passive way to knowledge: "The philosophers have only *interpreted* the world . . . ; the point, however is to *change* it." If disinterested philosophic dialogue (or indeed, the passive empiricism of the bourgeois positivist) blocked discovery of important truth, it is also unhelpful in promoting its realization in the world.

If class conditions of existence determine consciousness, it follows for Marx that just as persuasion of the proletariat is almost redundant (unnecessary except for acceleration of the inevitable when it fortunately happens to be good), so persuasion of many bourgeoisie is quite impossible. The conditions of their lives will not permit them to abandon cheerfully their ideology, control of the state, or the relations of production that ideology and state help maintain. Hence in books such as *The Holy Family* and *The German Ideology*, Marx and Engels make clear that their critique of bourgeois ideology is meant primarily for proletarian ears. Not argument but action will push the bourgeoisie out of the way. Marx and Engels are contemptuous of idealistic pseudoradicals ("critical critics") who think words alone can bring down capitalism.[6]

The Socialist's consciousness-raising is unlike that of the Saint in that it occasionally turns to secrecy in place of the Saint's openness. Further, as suggested, the Socialist directs persuasive efforts toward the dominated, not also to the dominant. In endorsing "class struggle," the Socialist abandons the Saint's dream of reconciliation with the adversary—a choice that as either cause or consequent rules out a turn to force. Lenin urged recognition of the class enemy behind the seeming propertied "friend," unlike Gandhi who wanted the oppressed to seek the potential friend within the "class enemy." As did Frantz Fanon in *The Wretched of the Earth*, a revolutionary Leninist would complain that the Saint's moderation permits the option of betrayal—a return to favor with the ruling class—while violently militant action normally permits no turning back.

One may object that the Marxist theory destroys the possibility of communication and community, since it precludes consideration that opponents could be correct. One need only explain bourgeois ideas, not refute them (Tinder, 1974, 554). But to be fair, Marx carefully read and sought to refute Capitalist economic treatises. While the objection properly warns us against the genetic fallacy of confusing origins of theories with validity, it succumbs to what I call the "projective fallacy" in holding Marx's theory invalid simply because it predicts some disturbing observations, such as the inability to persuade the propertied to let themselves be expropriated.

Landlords of Japan relinquished with compensation certain feudal rights under the Meiji, while capitalists sometimes accept social democratic "nationalizations," where compensation is often more than generous (at or even above "book value"). But most owners normally resist all "expropriations," or uncompensated assumptions of social ownership. That is, they *are* beyond persuasion when the goal is more than mild reform. Apart from some of their sons or daughters, very few of the propertied welcome socialism. Indeed, Latin American death squads decimate any who would agitate for even lesser infringements of property rights. There is very little "tolerance" of communication flows from radical Socialists.

Pushing against those beyond persuasion has often involved much violence, for as discussed before, often property abandons democracy for a police state. Rather than question the normal necessity of coercion in expropriations, critics are on better ground in asking whether the result is worth it, involving not only much dying but high destruction of means of production (recall what the Socialist formula was attempting to do).[7] Habermas notes that, if liberal theory fell into "decisionism" (what I called "proceduralism"), the equivalent folly of leftists may be "actionism," getting on with the means for change without asking whether the ends are justifiable (Habermas, 1973a, 142).

However, the same pushing rather than persuading may be turned by Socialists against other Socialists—as when Trotsky's Red Army repressed Ukrainian anarchists, or in the party purges under Stalin or Mao. Mao's campaigns involved more killing than anyone realized at the time, even if he did say that people are "re-educable" and are not like chives which can grow new heads.

### The Recruitment Strategy: The Turn to Noncompetitive Elections

Rather than persuading those with power, the recruitment strategy attempts to control policy by getting friends into power and rivals out. I noted that Marx and Engels saw electoral activity in bourgeois democracies as useful for independent organization, consciousness-raising, and assessing relative strengths of capitalist and socialist forces in case of armed struggle.

But Marx had warned against the "parliamentary cretinism" of taking electoral success as an end in itself. Even now, Marxist-Leninists sometimes debate whether to participate in bourgeois elections for the reasons Marx and Engels stressed, or rather to boycott elections to highlight denials of the legitimacy of a regime or its electoral procedures. Thus in 1969 the French Communist party used the slogan, "Let the bourgeoisie elect their own President," and I personally observed Parisian party cadres warning their members against voting. And again, in 1975 the leader of Portugal's Communist party, Alvaro Cunhal, displayed a Stalinist scorn: "We Communists don't accept the rules of the election game! You err in taking this concept for your starting point. No, no, no: I care nothing for elections. Nothing! Ha, ha!"[8] Other Communist parties of Western Europe were to follow the more serious electoral commitments of the liberalized Eurocommunists (especially the Italian and Spanish Communist parties) but with disappointing results in the 1980s. Voter bases of most Western European Communist parties have sharply contracted, obviously not helped by the unpopularity of communism in Eastern Europe.

For Marx's views of political recruitment under the transitional state, there is little to go by apart from how he perceived the Paris Commune (which matters here more than what it really was). Speaking of that short-lived rising of 1871 in *The Civil War in France* (in Tucker, 1978, 618–52), Marx saw a radically democratic model that was linked to a larger vision of nationwide ascending, delegated power (elaborated later). Since the emphasis was on plural bodies such as the Commune (or assembly), there was little place for leading individuals, and Marx complained of inept "bawlers" who got in the way.

Although figures associated with either the fallen autocracy of Louis Bonaparte or the new, rival republican regime of Thiers at Versailles were effectively ineligible, all male adults were eligible to vote or hold office. Public officials, however, were paid only the wage of ordinary workers. Further, representatives were clearly viewed in a Rousseauean delegate rather than Burkean trustee role. They were elected for short terms and with provision for removal by recall, said to be important for citizen protection against officials. Marx says little about competition of candidates, but we know that the few Marxists involved were almost irrelevant, while other ideological tendencies such as the Blanquists as well as a smaller group of Proudhonists were prominent.

### Lenin and Leadership

If the Bolshevik Revolution of 1917 aimed at that model, it missed by miles. Lenin's *State and Revolution* (1932) stressed that, to make way for the dictatorship of the proletariat, any existing state had to be smashed, even if liberal democratic. Even where it permitted universal suffrage, the bourgeois state was a sham democracy since the mass had no control over who would be in office:

> To decide once every few years which member of the ruling class is to repress and oppress the people through parliament—this is the real essence of bourgeois parliamentarism, not only in parliamentary-constitutional monarchies, but also in the most democratic republics. (Lenin, 1932, 40)

Lenin saw a structural shell-game, for—beyond the bourgeois parliamentary "talking shops"—the real work of the capitalist state was carried on behind the scenes through the executive departments and bureaucracy.

As if inverting the Capitalist "stake in society" theory, many communist regimes would for a time deny votes to the formerly propertied classes, or at least outlaw their political parties. *Inter*party competition was short-lived under Lenin, and *intra*party democracy did not replace it. Although he banned two rightist parties, he did allow prescheduled elections to the Constituent Assembly shortly after the Bolshevik seizure of power. But the Bolsheviks won less that a fourth of the vote and got only 170 of 707 seats. When Lenin proved reluctant to convene a body in which his forces were a minority, the non-Bolshevik delegates convened anyway at the preestablished date in January 1918. Lenin did not prevent this, yet he surrounded the assembly with armed forces. He himself visited the assembly, mocking it by stretching himself on a settee and pretending to sleep. Lenin eventually left. The meeting went on to 4 A.M., with recurrent Bolshevik disruptions, including the guards aiming and clicking their rifles at non-Bolshevik deputies. Eventually the guards dispersed the assembly, which never reconvened, and the action was one precipitant of the civil war of 1918–21.

Leninist rationalizations of the closure are unimpressive. They claimed that the election occurred prematurely, while Bolshevik support was just aborning, but Lenin did not call new competitive elections later. Or they said that at least the majority of *workers* backed the Bolsheviks, which was a thin claim when industrial workers were then only a small segment (perhaps 5 percent) of the largely peasant population.

As following years eliminated the allied left Social Revolutionaries and left Mensheviks from any independent existence, what remained was the Bolshevik party. The elimination of multiple political parties as the vehicle of competitions of ideas and candidates was then rationalized in a way later imitated by nationalistic socialist single-party systems of the Afro-Asian world.

The first argument is that the system, by the abolition of property, has eliminated classes and hence class conflict—the social base of Western multipartyism. This seems in apparent tension with the Stalinist stress on dangers of "capitalist survivals" within the Soviet Union (joining "capitalist encirclement" without). Another rejoinder is that given a division of labor and continued stratification, there remain more or less natural social cleavages that would be expressed in policy differences if not censored.

The second argument, perhaps only apparently in conflict, is that to allow two or more parties would cause any conflict to assume dangerous, artificial lines, such as fanning the embers of ethnic or regional animosities. Perhaps so, one may reply, but only full expression of such discords could make resolutions possible. As Frantz Fanon once noted regarding African single-party regimes, if a single party tribalized the central authority it would only encourage secession (Fanon, 1968, 183).

A third argument for single-party rule is that to have two or more parties means squandering scarce educated talent, since large numbers with university degrees would be left out of any government. But setting aside the possibility of coalition governments, there may be an even greater waste when talented critics of the single-party regime are exiled, jailed, or shot.

A fourth argument implausibly holds that a single party may by intraparty competition have more real democracy than in certain Western democracies, where the parties have only modest differences—especially in center-tending two-party systems such as the United States, where Democrats and Republicans are both thoroughly Capitalist.

In principle, the Leninist party was to feature intraparty democracy, but Lenin's mentioned ban on all organized factions in 1921 made effective competition impracticable, especially given the added blockage of other horizontal communications within the party structure. During the earlier Menshevik–Bolshevik rivalry within the Russian Social Democratic party, Leon Trotsky had in 1904 accurately predicted the future of the Leninist party model: "The party organization at first substitutes itself for the party as a whole; then the

Central Committee substitutes itself for the organization; and finally a single 'dictator' substitutes himself for the Central Committee" (in Howe, 1978, 16). That dictator eventually had Trotsky assassinated in Mexico.

Under Stalinist dictatorship, the view of democracy as a redundant tool becomes convenient for bureaucratic sycophants such as Lazar Kaganovich, as when he defended the Central Committee's 1930 purge of the All-Union Council of Trade Unions to put in Stalin's flunkies: "One might say that this is a violation of proletarian democracy, but comrades, it has long been known that for us Bolsheviks democracy is not a fetish; for us, proletarian democracy is a means for arming the working class for the better execution of its socialist tasks" (in Moore, 1987, 47–48).

The recruitment of top communist leaders became effectively co-optative: Those who are high determine who else ascends. Further—quite unlike the Paris Commune ideal—far from being rotated or readily removable by recall, the highest leaders would effectively serve for life, unless purged. This in the 1970s resulted in very old party leadership in both the Soviet Union and China, somewhat ameliorated since. In 1991 Castro had no Western equals in longevity in national leadership. In North Korea, the aging Kim Il Sung ("Great Leader") was attempting to pass the mantle of leadership to his publicly glorified son, Kim Chong Il ("Dear Leader"), as if a communist hereditary monarchy. While post-Stalinist Soviet communism starting with Khrushchev would call for collective leadership and avoidance of the dangers of the cult of personality, it was not until Gorbachev's recommendation that the Soviets began to consider limited tenure for the top party leader. Gorbachev got the Central Committee to accede to "the need to broaden inner-party democracy," although it balked at his proposal for multiple-candidate, secret-ballot elections in regional party committees. While encouraging competitive elections for Communist party posts, Gorbachev has long resisted the legalization of effectively emergent opposition parties. Within the Communist party, where he himself was resisted by "conservatives," he limited top party posts to two five-year terms, requiring a three-fourths majority for one additional five-year extension. Also, he encouraged a growing communist world tendency to permit competitive elections for local government and parliamentary posts.[9]

### Does Unchecked Power Corrupt?

Lenin's rule was harsh, even at the close of the Russian civil war. Perhaps his governance would have been nearly as harsh as Stalin's had he not then called for the partial economic liberalization of the New Economic Policy (in effect 1921–28) rather than Stalin's later collectivization of agriculture.[10] In a shallow apologia for his own powers, Lenin in his essay "Left-wing Communism: An Infantile Disease" castigated critics, saying that masses are divided into parties, parties are "directed by more or less stable groups composed of the most authoritative, influential, and experienced members, who are elected to the most responsible positions and are called leaders. All this is elementary. All this is simple and clear. Why replace this by some rigmarole?" (in Connor, 1968, 289). But it was also simple and clear that meaningful elections would have to involve some contest— not to be mere votes for or against one person proposed for each office, with the party secretariat guiding nominations and any vote against being open to view. Unchecked by legal opposition, leaders become tyrants. As Alexander Solzhenitsyn, Roy Medvedev, and many others have documented, Stalin's rule was murderously tyrannical, rivaled in our century only by that of Hitler. In the Khmer Rouge rule of Kampuchea (the government of Pol Pot and Ieng Sary), unknown numbers—perhaps hundreds of thousands—died during the massive famine in part caused by the sudden evacuation of Phnom Penh, motivated less by an urgent need to feed that population than to prevent political opposition there. While journalists may exaggerate the numbers, the most careful study suggests about 75,000–150,000 political executions. Yet the longer warring in that tragic country— which extended before and after Vietnam's 1976 invasion—decimated much of Kampuchea's male adult population (Kiljunen, 1984, 11, 30–31).

Beyond the mass murders, as under the autocracies of old, the absence of competitive elections for top leadership can also cause a downward spiral of corruption when accompanied by a high degree of the sycophancy found in virtually all hierarchical systems. Leaders extend privileges to toadies in exchange for inordinate public praise and other supports. As the Saint would say, such pandering to the powerful is morally devastating and socially disastrous; and Marx and Engels also detested sycophancy.

Any regime needs leaders, but we must beware when these are electorally unaccountable, overpowerful, and inflated to heroic proportions. If we must have heroes, we should choose them only from among the dead, when the whole pattern of their lives is complete and increasingly known.

### The Structures Strategy: The Costs of Centralization of Power

The structures strategy aims at control of policy by control over what institutional units make decisions. I have said that liberal democracy assumes pluralistic competition among units—just as among ideas and persons—but with popular sovereignty determining provisional precedence or allocations of powers among such alternative sites for making decisions.

Communist systems historically have tended toward consolidation of powers, in a pattern that even Leon Trotsky would call "totalitarian." After reviewing the record from the defeat of Nestor Makhno's Ukraine to the repression of Hungary, Trent Schroyer concludes, "A centralist model of revolution can be a justification for the most brutal kind of genocide" (Schroyer, 1973, 96).

### The Structures Strategy in the Struggle for Power

Major leaders of communist revolutions tend to be unusually ruthless players of the structures game, dropping all stable commitments to political procedures simply to put power where pals prevail. Thus before assuming power, Lenin found the Provisional Government's assembly, the Duma, hopelessly dominated by rival political forces such as the Kadets and rightist Mensheviks; and he turned more hopefully to the ex-officio *soviets* (Russian for "councils"), or assemblies of peasant, worker, and soldier representatives. Despite his slogan "All power to the Soviets," Bolshevik precedence in key urban councils was to grow slowly, leading him at one despairing moment to consider shifting power instead to the Bolshevik-dominated factory committees. But eventually the Bolsheviks and temporary coalition partners such as left Social Revolutionaries were able to dominate such key soviets as Petrograd and Moscow. Lenin then maneuvered to dominate the Congress of Soviets as well as its executive committee as he prepared to seize power. Once in power, as I have noted, he dissolved the Constituent Assembly of 1918; and he eventually weakened the authority of the soviets as well, pulling power to where he could surely prevail: the top organs of the Communist party.

Mao was at least as opportunistic in putting powers only where he won. It did not matter whether these were governmental or party organs:

> When he deemed a certain decision necessary to keep up the momentum of socialist construction, he submitted it to the decision-making body most likely to provide the needed support. If he felt he would be outvoted by the whole Politburo, he would convene a small group such as its Standing Committee. If he lacked support there, he might convene an expanded meeting of the Politburo with invited nonmembers; alternatively, he would turn to the entire Central Committee or even to ad hoc state conferences. Ultimately despairing of these groups, he undertook the Cultural Revolution as a means to achieve his goals. (Roth and Wilson, 1976, 294)

Such extreme instrumentalism regarding procedures can be even more ominous for democracy than the opposite extreme of procedural fetishism.

## State Control of the Economy

Recall that the Capitalist worked toward relative separation from the state of both the church and economy.

As for religion, Marx favored full separation of church and state, extending to secularization of education. He believed that, without repression, religion would cease to be attractive with correction of the conditions of existence (suffering, powerlessness) that caused this illusory consciousness.[11] Yet Marxist-Leninists in power were capable of harsh repression toward any autonomous religious institutions, even aiming at full-scale extirpation in the extreme case of the Albania of Enver Hoxha (d. 1985). As the Soviet Union and China have haltingly moved toward liberalization, their leaders have allowed more autonomy for religious organizations. The religious aspiration—perhaps linked more to our mortality than caused by economic suffering—has not waned under communism.

As for the economy, Marx and Engels clearly called in the *Communist Manifesto* for extensive state intervention in the economy during the transitional state. Although later acknowledging that the Paris Commune was not so Socialist as he had thought in 1871 (patriotism and antimonarchism were in fact more central motives than the vague Blanquist socialism), Marx approved of state seizures of abandoned factories for operation by workers cooperatives in one big union. Engels much later complained that one error of the Communards was failure to seize the Bank of France. (Having abolished conscription, the Communards worried about undermining confidence in the banknotes paid to their soldiers.)

Since statist dominance of economics in communist systems is well known, we touch here only on its political consequence. Even Friedrich Engels saw the danger in his 1891 critique of the Erfurt Program, where he said that Marxism "has nothing in common with the so-called State Socialism, that system of nationalization which puts the state in place of the private owner and by so doing concentrates the power of economic exploitation and the political oppression of the workers in one hand." While Engels's solution would be eventual abolition of the state, Max Weber sounded a similar warning with an implication of acceptance of some private sector:

> State bureaucracy would rule alone if private capitalism were eliminated. The private and public bureaucracies, which now work next to, and potentially against each other, and hence check one another to a degree, would be merged into a single hierarchy. This would be similar to the situation in ancient Egypt, but it would occur in a much more rational— and hence unbreakable—form. (Abrahamsson, 1977, 60)

I earlier said that the Capitalist formula had problems in that leaving giant corporations autonomous from the state permitted them—largely by the leverage of choosing when and where to invest or disinvest—to bend public policy to their purposes while giving them electorally unaccountable control over people's lives. But there are counterpart problems arising from the opposite approach of having the state dominate the economy. It becomes even less manageable when the state lacks liberal democratic competitions of ideas, candidacies, and institutional units and is dominated by the elite of a Communist party constitutionally designated as "leading," "guiding," or "hegemonic."

Thus statist socialism means undue control of apparatchiks over peoples' lives, as in the past routine Soviet practice of blocking dissidents from practice of their livelihoods.[12] To have both economic and coercive means of control in the same hands is bad news for elementary freedoms. Whatever one may think of global corporations lacking internal workers' control, some private sector may be needed for the alternative possible livelihoods that can embolden dissent.

### The Uses of Private Property in the Means of Coercion

The other consequence of statist socialism, especially when the regime is not liberal democratic, is that it permits those who control the state to secure to themselves a privileged share of the social product.

Whatever Plato's dream, historical evidence suggests that political power and economic privilege are not easily kept apart. If some come into economic wealth but lack power to protect and enlarge it, they have tended to use economic and other resources to seek power, as Marxists recognize of the rise of the bourgeois, who first used bribes and then bought cannons. But it is also true that if some come into power but lack economic privilege, they eventually tend to abuse their power to get a larger share of the social product. If this was the brief of classical liberalism against feudalism, it applies no less to communist systems.

Parlaying power in organizations into economic privilege can apply to primarily market economies as well, as witnessed by charges of "crony capitalism" against the Somoza regime of Nicaragua or the Marcos regime in the Philippines; but there is a "crony socialism" equivalent. This more personalized corruption of favoritism for kith and kin was much denounced by China's 1989 prodemocracy demonstrators. It is especially marked in the nationalistic Socialist systems of the underdeveloped nations, where nominally public ownership of mineral resources, manufacturing plants, and other means of production facilitates private plunder by the powerful. Someone has coined the term "kleptocracies" with reference to African regimes; but the same applies elsewhere, as witnessed by the massive corruption of both management and labor leaders in Mexico's state oil and gas monopoly, Pemex. Under circumstances of high corruption, socialism is not the solution to underdevelopment but just another part of the problem.

If property in the means of production is a kind of power, unchecked power can be the equivalent of property. Private property in the means of public coercion can be as effective as private property in the means of production in assuring a privileged share of the social product. These privileges—more than the power as such—can be partially passed on to children. Positions in party or government apparatuses thus displace the Capitalist possession of the means of production, yielding at least for the elite as a whole similar control over the social division of labor, assignments of persons within it, control over their wages and salaries, and thus control over differential standards of living. Under communist systems, the corruption may be more impersonal than under the typical nationalistic socialist regime, yet luxury indulgences of top leaders have been widely noted, especially in the wake of Eastern European upheavals. Soviet efforts toward "restructuring" (perestroika) find resistance among portions of the elite as well as the mass population.

With Albania and Cuba lagging, most contemporary communist systems have allowed some economic liberalization, as in Gorbachev's promotion of cooperative small-business ventures and leased farms, going beyond the earlier minimal autonomy for marketing the produce of collective farm private plots, and so on. Acceptance in both the Soviet Union and China of private initiative in such sectors as restaurants or food growing seems to be a major admission of productivity problems.

### Concentrated Governmental Powers

In Marx's view, the Paris Commune admirably avoided anything like the classic mixed regime as well as the U.S. variant of separation of powers with checks and balances. Marx endorsed, rather, unification of authority in a popular assembly:

> The Commune was to be a working, not a parliamentary, body, executive and legislative at the same time. . . . The judicial functionaries were to be divested of that sham independence which had but served to mask their abject subserviency to all succeeding governments to which, in turn, they had taken, and broken, the oaths of allegiance. Like the rest of public servants, magistrates and judges were to be elective, responsible and revocable. (*Civil War in France*, iii, in Tucker, 1978, 618–52)

Yet, Marx had admitted in the same essay that, before the Bonapartist dictatorship, conflicts among the propertied had limited state power. He implicitly recognized the liberal view that frictions had fostered (negative) freedoms. But he assumes that such freedoms become less necessary when the producing majority directly controls all state organs, with the unicameral assembly as the centerpiece of the popular will. There is no longer a question of professional politicians, standing army, and police, so the "repressive" aspect of the state is obliterated while "legitimate" functions are popularly controlled.

Leninist and later Stalinist state forms recall the ghost of this vision of the Commune. The Supreme Soviet obviously was understood as the rough parallel of the Commune, although its brief sessions, excessive decorum, and high representation of women (unlike the Politburo) all indicated absence of real power. Things changed with the new Gorbachev parliament, where sharp debate has occurred (as in the 1990 Communist Party Congress as well). Soviet constitutions had long maintained that over the unified state organs there would be "hegemony" of the Communist party. This meant that the secretary and Politburo presumed to act on behalf of the people, without any general elective accountability. While Lenin had said that a class could be led by as few as a dozen men (roughly the average number of voting members on the Soviet Politburo), there was no means of assessing the Soviet population's consent to it. Gorbachev chose to shift much power from the Communist party to the government organs, including the strong Soviet presidency that he occupied.

*Territorial Concentration: The Commune's Democracy as Lever*

The absence of any functional separation of powers went with rejection of any real territorial division of authority—that which would give meaningful autonomy to states or provinces, as in Western federal systems. Marx had approved the Commune's intent to extend its model beyond Paris to all of France, involving a pyramidal system of election from below, whereby delegates subject to instructions and recall would be locally elected and sent upward to the provincial and national levels—not unlike the similar ideas of Rousseau's *Poland*. Yet Marx approvingly notes that "the unity of the nation was not to be broken."

This was not to be the old Montesquieuan or Girondist dream of provincial autonomy, Marx says, since the "unity of great nations . . . , if originally brought about by political force, has now become a powerful coefficient of social production." The repressive, parasitic side of former concentration of power in Paris would be replaced by the legitimate, productive aspect—that is, Socialist relations of production and nationwide central planning.

Such instrumentality was clear in Marx's very language describing these "really democratic institutions," for the Commune was "the political form at last discovered under which to work out the economic emancipation of labour." It was "to serve as lever for uprooting the economical foundations upon which rests the existence of classes, and therefore of class-rule." The workers' democracy is thus but their "lever."

### Self-determination of Peoples?
Marx was by self-avowal an internationalist, and he probably envisaged an ultimate international parallel of the territorial model planned by the French Communards. But even international democratic arrangements would in the spirit of this theory be but instrumental to advance and sustain the socialist economic system. This becomes clear enough in Lenin: "The interests of socialism are above the interests of the right of nations to self-determination." Or again, Stalin: "There are cases when the right of self-determination conflicts with another, a higher right—the right of the working class that has come to power to consolidate that power" (cited in Conquest, 1986, 25, 33). Of course, the Capitalist has also recurrently subordinated the self-determination of small nations or of regions of large nations when the needs of capitalism required. But the Capitalist has been characteristically nationalist, lacking the Socialist's larger appeal to internationalism as justification. For Lenin and Stalin, it would seem that rational and reasonable people would only want self-determination as a "lever" to secure socialism.[13]

## Leaving the Dictatorship of the Proletariat: The Withering Away of the State

If the workers' democratic state is but a lever to complete the overthrow of capitalism and install socialism, the tool is regarded as ultimately disposable. Many in the nineteenth century mistakenly believed that not only religiosity and nationalism but even the state would become obsolete in the twentieth century. The state had been viewed as a parasitic excrescence on society, to be reabsorbed by a society returned to better health. The ultimate unimportance of the state usually assumed the solution of the problem that gave rise to it—namely, conflict born of economic scarcity. In Herbert Spencer or the individualist anarchists, this would be attained through capitalism, while for Marx and Engels it is only attainable through socialism. Engels even suggested that the state would become a museum piece, quite like other functionally obsolete instruments such as the spinning wheel or bronze axe.

The Socialist anarchists (e.g., Proudhon, Bakunin, and Kropotkin) accurately prophesied that the Marxist transitional democratic state would really become permanent and authoritarian. Believing that no

state immediately entailed no property, they hence would change the
first premise to begin with instant abolition of the state through
wholly nonpolitical means of direct action.[14] Otherwise they share the
basic chain of Marxist reasoning:

1. If one implements proletarian majority rule through a dictatorship
   of the proletariat, then Socialist relations of production will be put
   into effect.
2. If there is thus no longer any private property in means of
   production, and since class takes its meaning by differential relations to such means, there would then cease to be any distinctive
   classes.
3. If there are no classes, there could be no class conflict.
4. If there is no such conflict, none would have any use for a state—
   understood as a standing, separate apparatus by which one class
   represses another.
5. Hence, public authority loses all political character, or as Engels
   puts it in his *Anti-Duhring*:

As soon as there is no longer any social class to be held in subjection; as
soon as class rule, and the individual struggle for existence based upon
our present anarchy in production, with the collisions and excesses
arising from these, are removed, nothing more remains to be repressed,
and a special repressive force, a state, is no longer necessary. . . . State
interference in social relations becomes, in one domain after another,
superfluous and then dies out of itself; the government of persons is
replaced by the administration of things. (in Tucker, 1978, 713)

Louis Fischer notes that, with Lenin's victory, "withering away did
commence immediately, but what commenced to wither away was the
idea of withering away" (Fischer, 1965, 121). I will not belabor either
that fact nor its many explanations. Was it due to the conditions of
scarcity caused by having a Socialist revolution remain confined to the
inhospitable site of backward lands (Trotsky's explanation)? The error
of using political means or a transitional state (the anarchists')? The
administrative apparatus required by centrally planned socialism
(Hayek's)? Some mistake in the transitional state's political forms (as
per political science treatises celebrating American things such as
plurality voting and two-partyism, separation of powers, and federal-
ism)? Or some tragic error in philosophical first principles?

The important conclusion is that the Socialist paradigm—even
more than the other formulas—has proven to be a spectacular failure.
While efforts to implement it destroy vast means of production
created under private property, it does not itself assure great abundance or even equality, economic or political.

## Summary:
## Democracy and Economic Equality

The Marxists may underestimate the importance of liberal democratic forms in protecting or even promoting economic equality, even under capitalism.

Aggregate measures such as gross national product (GNP) mask what is happening to the distribution of that product. But income distribution has a more direct relation to satisfaction of basic bodily needs. It is logically possible and often empirically true that a higher GNP may mean *lower* real incomes for the poor, as illustrated by Brazil in the later 1960s. Even the 1980s growth in the United States corresponded with reported declines of real incomes for up to two-fifths of families, especially those that are black or Hispanic. It is also logically possible that, when dislocations of a revolution or other redistributional project cause slumped growth, more equal distribution could make the poorest sector better off.

If growth does not always entail more equality, perhaps democracy can help. Using only one-point-in-time (cross-sectional) data, earlier studies failed to show that any distinctively political variables—including presence or degree of democracy—made a difference on economic distributions. These were better predicted by levels of socioeconomic development, whether the units compared were the American states or rather nations. Broadly, the more affluent the society, the more egalitarian its income distribution and the more generous its welfare policies. However, such studies failed to take into consideration *duration* of democracy. It would be implausible to expect instantaneous income redistributions of democracies, especially if they are newborn or recurrently punctuated by military coups. A 55–nation study that looked at duration of democracy found that the *existence* of democracy (but not measures of level) did have a significant impact in equalizing income distribution, even after controlling for levels of economic development (as measured by energy consumption per capita). It apparently takes a few decades of democracy before vigorous unions, popular political mobilizations, and the like are able to flatten somewhat the income inequalities of a nation. Once that occurs democracy is better sustained, even where economic development is low. While equality of income distribution does not predict where democracy emerges, high inequality does predict where democracy is unstable (Muller, 1988).[15]

But especially the Marxist-Leninists among Socialists have not understood such possibilities of democracy. A theory that envisioned emancipation of human development through scientific administration of economic things culminates with very few people administering millions of people as if mere things.

While an overly instrumental view of democracy is part of the problem, I do not assume that democracy alone could salvage socialism. I just doubt that any formula—even if implemented at its best—could make democracy unneeded. If I suggested that the other three paradigms were also oversold, so with the Socialist formula.

Both the economy and the polity need major rethinking, avoiding the characteristic illusions of either the Capitalist or the Socialist. Rousseau taught that those who study morals and politics separately will never understand either. I say the same for economics and politics. If it seems that either economic or political inequality can readily extend to the other, the quest for more equality is difficult. Those who primarily pursue *either* political equality *or* economic equality on the misguided assumption that the one will automatically assure the other seem destined never to attain either.

## Notes

1. In 1850 Marx wrote, "Even where there is no prospect whatsoever of their being elected, the workers must put up their own candidates in order to preserve their own independence, to count their forces, and to bring before the public their revolutionary attitude and standpoint" (Marx and Engels, 1962, vol. 1, 114). In his essay *Tactics of Social Democracy* (in Tucker, 1978, 556–73), Engels in the last year of his life repeated the aims of electioneering to "count their numbers" and serve as the "best means of propaganda" in contact with the masses.

2. David Apter's critique has bite: "The concept of false consciousness seems merely a presumptuous convenience, adopted by messianic intellectuals as a warrant of superiority in a world which otherwise largely ignores them" (Apter, 1968, 314n.).

That sounds right when we think of some leftist intellectual telling the workers what their ultimate values or goals have to be, including those who use Marx's language describing the "historical mission" of the proletariat. But it loses its force if we shift to other kinds of statements about the world where we can empirically measure informational deficiencies of workers. Apter himself falls into "a presumptuous convenience" if he would ignore the massive class inequality in mass-media message flows. One should distinguish what is defensible and indefensible in the concept of false class consciousness.

3. Stalin's version of "socialist realism" in literature was to be often compared with Plato's noble lies, focused less on accurate depiction of the world than at shaping behavior to specific purposes.

4. In Mao's account, leaders theoretically clarify what the masses already vaguely knew. Mao's theory of the "mass line" holds that communists must go to the masses as listeners before they can articulate what the people are saying and return as teachers.

5. Plato wrote that dialectical discourse alone is on its negative side like a doctor's prescription, purging bowels constipated with falsehood. But on the

positive side, it is a midwife to the birth of truth (*Sophist*, 230d; *Theaetetus*, 148e and ff.).

6. "They are in no way combating the real existing world when they are merely combating the phrases of this world." Or again, "all forms and products of consciousness cannot be dissolved by mental criticism . . . , but only by the practical overthrow of the actual social relations which gave rise to this idealistic humbug; . . . not criticism but revolution is the driving force of history" (Marx and Engels, 1966, 6, 28–29).

7. Revolutionaries may retort that this makes redistribution impossible, since the only remaining options are either allowing continued private property in means of production or the alternative of compensating owners in nationalizations.

But a third way may be the long-term reality. Since property is essentially but a complex of governmentally enforced rights, gradual erosions of those rights (along with increments of duties on property) could culminate in a de facto expropriation. The right seems more aware of this possibility than is much of the left.

8. Interview with Oriana Fallaci, *New York Times*, July 13, 1975, sec. 6, p. 10.

9. There seems to be no consistent pattern in the introductions of competitive elections in communist systems. Castro chose to begin permitting multiple-candidate elections to local government after earlier frankly acknowledging that he would not want nationwide free elections until confident he would win. In China in 1988 the National Peoples' Congress allowed competitive elections for at least some of the 155 seats of its standing committee.

In Poland, in 1989 Solidarity won all but one of the legislative seats that the Communist party allowed to be contested, and then Solidarity won the Polish presidency. Communists were by 1990 electorally trounced in Hungary and Czechoslovakia, but allegedly reformed communists hung on in Bulgaria and Romania. Albania was the last regime to permit electoral competition.

10. Thus writes Barrington Moore: "The legend about his [Lenin's] being less authoritarian than Stalin stems from the fact that he was lucky enough to die before Russia had to face the crises of socialist construction" (Moore, 1972, 70).

11. As Engels wrote in his 1891 preface to Marx's *Civil War in France* (in Tucker, 1978, 618–52), religion was made a merely private matter in relation to the state, for "the Commune decreed the separation of the church from the state, and the abolition of all state payments for religious purposes as well as the transformation of all church property into national property." In the original essay, Marx had spoken of how these measures helped "break the spiritual force of repression," supplementing abolition of the previous regime's standing army and police; and he noted approvingly, "The priests were sent back to the recesses of private life, there to feed upon the alms of the faithful in imitation of their predecessors, the Apostles."

12. Many advocates of socialism want it both ways, citing socialism as the cause of any good things about past communist systems—such as more security of basic physiological needs of life (food, clothing, shelter, medical care)—yet denying that socialism was the cause of anything ugly. Anarchists,

Trotskyists, and some social democrats even denied that the Soviet Union was really socialist, as in claiming that the system was really just "state capitalism." In this sleight of hand, they can blame capitalism for whatever is deplorable in communist systems.

13. Currently there are major separatist strivings within the Soviet Union, Yugoslavia, and Tibetan China. In the past only pseudofederal, the Soviets may turn toward a loose federation in hopes of preventing secessionist moves, especially strong in the Baltics, which had been forcibly absorbed in 1940.

14. The extreme of political equality would constitute this instant abolition of the state. Leaving aside the question of whether success in it would soon elicit bullies nucleating new states, the anarchists are wrong to claim that statelessness has ever been attained outside of certain primitive peoples living in scattered bands. They may cite Makhno's Ukraine, Kronstadt, or parts of Spain during the Spanish Civil War, but the intact military apparatus essentially was the state in each case.

15. Others have presented theoretical reasons and some evidence to cast doubt on the claim that socialism is any more likely than capitalism to encourage economic equality. Rather, it is level of economic development that most strongly predicts higher equality, with personal freedoms, political participation, and social welfare expenditures also good predictors (Dye and Zeigler, 1988). But in view of remarks above, one wonders whether it is the lack of growth or the absence of liberal democratic freedoms that most limits more equality in communist systems.

# 10

# Epilogue

Does the end justify the means?
That is possible. But what will
justify the end? To that question,
which historical thought leaves pending,
rebellion replies: the means.

Albert Camus,
*The Rebel*

Most great social theorists have shared an interest in the problem of coping with scarcity to minimize human violence and attain other goals. But in large part because of identifications with different strata of society, they elaborated distinctive problematics, or special ways of restating the nature of that problem. These leaned strongly toward rather specific "solutions." Once fleshed out with answers, these solutions became the four great alternative paradigms of social theory.

Each paradigm attempted to shield its core assumptions by assuming for itself only ideal conditions for its application. Yet in the real world, each paradigm has had major failings. Also, each paradigm has had advocates who become critical of democracy as a threat to the paradigm. Further, while each social theory originally aimed to reduce human violence, often its avatars increased violence in the name of the paradigm corrupted into an end in itself.

If no paradigm has lived up to the promises of its advocates, then what is the solution? Perhaps one should question that question, for it may implicitly assume that there is some pre-established puzzle built into the nature of being.

Does this presuppose a divine being as the puzzle-maker? If so, could that divinity really be benevolent in not making the solution perfectly clear to all? Why do the gods hide their answers? And why

do they even hide themselves? Or could those believing in a nonprov-
idential god, as illustrated by Aristotle, yet believe in the puzzle that
must have a solution? Could even those who believe in no gods at all
assume that there are pre-established puzzles built into the very order
of nature? Even an atheist like Marx succumbed to such talk in
claiming, "Communism is the riddle of history solved, and it knows
itself to be this solution." Or might nonbelievers conclude, rather,
that there is no such "riddle of history," and that just as humans
created their own problem, only they can work toward a solution?
Thus the liberal Albert Camus claimed that, if we keep limits in our
own means, we constitute value by simply rebelling against what we
take to be evil. By saying no we really say yes to the limits that
constitute civilization, even helping to shape their specific contents.

Leaving aside such ultimate questions, perhaps the puzzle-solving
conception of the project of social thought leads many to think the
solution to the puzzle could be some kind of synthesis of two or more
of the four paradigms, such that the "pieces" could be made to "fit."

In passing, is it possible that any synthesis would bring together the
worst rather than best of each great alternative? While each paradigm
tends to ascribe fascism to the rival paradigms, one could argue that
Hitler's *Mein Kampf* really synthesized something of the worst of each
paradigm. While space precludes elaboration, readers may want to
make a list of characteristics of fascism and ask how these relate to
the four paradigms.

More hopefully, one can imagine a synthesis of the best, merging
two, three, or even all four of the paradigms. While I think each
paradigm does have a valid angle on how to deal with the problem of
scarcity and related violence, to think paradigms may be crisply
snapped together may assume the pre-established puzzle concept
already put in question.

Each of the six possible pairs of the four paradigms has major
tensions growing out of distinctive core assumptions. If only because
each paradigm makes exaggerated promises of its core assumptions,
it conflicts with any other paradigm. That the paradigms have incompatible needs becomes apparent in any close look at them paired:

1. The *Aristocrat* may regard the *Saint's* way not only as a personal
reproach, but also as a threat to the good order of hierarchical
deference and obedience to law. The Saint in turn was the classic
critic of the Aristocrats' pretension to a superior nature, and to their
hypocrisy in largely exempting themselves from the strict limitation
of economic aspirations imposed on others.

2. The *Socialist* is obviously the negation of the *Capitalist* in key
commitments other than a Baconian mastery of nature. The Capital-

ist correctly sees the Socialist as a threat to property as well as free markets.

3. The *Saint* would usually abhor the *Socialist's* turn to class hatred and violence, but the Socialist thinks the Saints' approach is futile in their hope of moderating elite wants—in part through religious appeals and persuasion of nonviolence.

4. The *Aristocrat* would denigrate the *Socialist* for threatening order by consciousness-raising, which in part consists in inflaming mass wants. The Socialist would view the Aristocrat as really looking for a caste system, as Marx said of Plato. Nor does the Socialist like the Aristocrat's elitism, religiosity, and traditionalism. Marx called Burke an "execrable cant-monger."

5. The *Aristocrat* and *Capitalist* agree on protecting property through unequal political power, but the former wanted the lower classes to want to live no better than their parents, while the Capitalist system *needs* rising economic aspirations.

6. The *Saint's* call for voluntary poverty among the rich and simple living among the poor sits poorly with the *Capitalist* need to well-reward those whom Locke called "the industrious and rational," while the giant, increasingly global corporations of the Capitalist make short work of the small peasant and artisan properties often praised by the Saints.

In view of such conflicts at the heart of the matter, one could at most hope for some adjustments of the paradigms to each other. But compromises would only be possible if each recalled its origin as primarily a means to social peace, and if each conceded its own limitations in attaining that end. This could also curb the tendency of each paradigm to exalt some special carrier of civilization: the Aristocrat's landed nobility and other old-wealth gentlemen; the Capitalist's mercantile and industrial entrepreneurs; the Saint's peasants and artisans; or the Socialist's proletariat. Most of us may not identify with any one of these categories, but will be some kind of salaried service worker or professional. But no class is the peculiar repository of virtue, and none has the corner on vice.

In historical experience, only minorities have zealously pursued each paradigm, while majorities have tended toward skepticism. Democracy may often frustrate the minority fixed on any paradigm. It may inflame popular wants (Plato); it may let the rich few practice too much exploitation or warring on its behalf (Thoreau); while strangely also said to be less responsive than the market, it may be too responsive to current majorities and encroach on the needs of capitalism

(Hayek); or it may threaten the survival of centrally planned socialism (Yegor Ligachev or any hard-line communist in the Soviet Union).

But if each paradigm has promised more than it can deliver, and if only a minority retains zealous commitment to a paradigm, a good argument for majority-rule democracy may be that it keeps each paradigm in its proper place. Only democratic freedoms permit each great alternative to be publicly advocated as well as exposed to public criticism by others, including advocates of all rival paradigms as well as those (such as this author) somewhat skeptical toward them all. Each paradigm needs to be humbled by such criticism, given the historical record of its failings. Democracy even assures exposure of itself to criticism, which is also healthy when it improves democracy.

I do not expect democracy itself to solve the problem of human conflict, but it can at best bring some civility to it. Even if there is no puzzle mysteriously embedded in the nature of things, our problems are real enough. Often our very efforts to solve some problem may create new problems by changing our distributions of resources, by changing our preferences, or even by changing the vulnerable biosphere about us. Perhaps certain problems will never be solved but at best just managed. It may be an error to "think of policy not as a temporary resting place but as a permanent cure" (Wildavsky, 1979, 82).

Shifting to a more positive mood, I trust democratic freedoms more than any formula that would sacrifice them to itself. Permitting all of us to get involved in the muddling through, democracy is not in itself a solution to our troubles, but it is the best corrective to the dogmatists who think they have got one.

# Bibliography

Abrahamsson, Bengt. 1977. *Bureaucracy or Participation: The Logic of Organization*. Beverly Hills, Calif.: Sage Publications.

Ackerman, Bruce. 1980. *Social Justice in the Liberal State*. New Haven, Conn.: Yale University Press.

Adler, Mortimer J. 1981. *Six Great Ideas*. New York: Macmillan.

Alt, James E. and K. Alec Chrystal. 1983. *Political Economics*. London: Harvester Press.

Althusius, Johannes. 1964. *The Politics*. London: Eyre and Spottiswoode.

Amalrik, Andrei. 1970. *Will the Soviet Union Survive until 1984?* New York: Harper & Row.

Apter, David. 1968. "Notes for a Theory of Nondemocratic Representation," in J. Roland Pennock and John W. Chapman, eds., *Representation*. New York: Atherton Press.

———. 1987. *Rethinking Development: Modernization, Dependency, and Postmodern Politics*. Beverly Hills, Calif.: Sage Publications.

Arendt, Hannah. 1958. *The Human Condition*. Chicago: University of Chicago Press.

———. 1961. *Between Past and Future: Six Exercises in Political Thought*. New York: Viking Press.

———. 1963. *On Revolution*. New York: Viking Press.

Aristotle. 1932. *The Rhetoric of Aristotle*. Lane Cooper, tr. New York: Appleton-Century-Crofts.

———. 1984. *The Politics*. Carnes Lord, tr. Chicago: University of Chicago Press.

Arnold, Thurman. 1935. *The Symbols of Government*. New Haven, Conn.: Yale University Press.

Ashcraft, Richard. 1986. *Revolutionary Politics and Locke's Two Treatises of Government*. Princeton, N.J.: Princeton University Press.

Aubrey, John. 1949. *Brief Lives*. London: Secker and Warburg.

Aurelius, Marcus. 1960. *The Meditations*. George Long, tr. Garden City, N.Y.: Doubleday, Dolphin.

Axelrod, Robert. 1984. *The Evolution of Cooperation*. New York: Basic Books.

Bachelor, Lynn. 1982. "Reindustrialization in Detroit: Capital Mobility and Corporate Influence," *Journal of Urban Affairs*, 4, No. 3.

Bachrach, Peter. 1967. *The Theory of Democratic Elitism: A Critique*. Boston: Little, Brown.

Bacon, Francis. 1955. *Selected Writings of Francis Bacon*. New York: Modern Library.

Bailes, Kendall E. 1978. *Technology and Society under Lenin and Stalin*. Princeton, N.J.: Princeton University Press.

Bailey, F. G. 1969. *Strategems and Spoils: A Social Anthropology of Politics*. New York: Schocken Books.

Bailyn, Bernard. 1967. *The Ideological Origins of the American Revolution*. Cambridge, Mass.: Harvard University Belknap Press.

Beard, Charles. 1914. *An Economic Interpretation of the Constitution of the United States*. New York: Macmillan.

Becker, Gary. 1976. *The Economic Approach to Human Behavior*. Chicago: University of Chicago Press.

Bell, Daniel. 1976. *The Cultural Contradictions of Capitalism*. New York: Basic Books.

Bentham, Jeremy. 1971. *The Handbook of Political Fallacies*. New York: Thomas Y. Crowell.

Berger, Peter L. 1976. *Pyramids of Sacrifice*. Garden City, N.Y.: Anchor Books.

———. 1986. *The Capitalist Revolution: Fifty Propositions about Property, Equality, and Liberty*. New York: Basic Books.

Berlin, Isaiah. 1969. *Four Essays on Liberty*. London: Oxford University Press.

Berns, Walter. 1957. *Freedom, Virtue, and the First Amendment*. Baton Rouge: Louisiana State University Press.

Berry, Wendell. 1986. *The Unsettling of America: Culture and Agriculture*. San Francisco: Sierra Club Books.

Béteille, André. 1983. *The Idea of Natural Inequality and Other Essays*. Delhi, India: Oxford University Press.

Birley, Anthony. 1987. *Marcus Aurelius: A Biography*. London: B. T. Batsford.

Bishop, Morris. 1974. *Saint Francis of Assisi*. Boston: Little, Brown.

Bloom, Allan. 1960. *Politics and the Arts*. Glencoe, Ill.: Free Press. Esp. pp. xv–xxxviii.

———. 1987. *The Closing of the American Mind*. New York: Simon and Schuster.

Boétie, Etienne de la. 1975. *The Politics of Obedience: The Discourse of Voluntary Servitude*. New York: Free Life Editions.

Bookchin, Murray. 1971. *Post-scarcity Anarchism*. Berkeley, Calif.: Ramparts Press.

Bowker, John. 1973. *Jesus and the Pharisees*. Cambridge, England: Cambridge University Press.

Bowles, Samuel and Herbert Gintis. 1986. *Democracy and Capitalism.* New York: Basic Books.

Brandon, S. G. F. 1967. *Jesus and the Zealots: A Study of the Political Factor in Christianity.* Manchester, England: Manchester Press.

Brittan, Samuel. 1975. "The Economic Contradictions of Democracy," *British Journal of Political Science*, 5, pp. 129–59.

Brown, Donald E. 1988. *Hierarchy, History, and Human Nature: The Social Origins of Historical Consciousness.* Tucson: University of Arizona Press.

Brown, Peter. 1981. *The Cult of the Saints: Its Rise and Function in Latin Christianity.* Chicago: University of Chicago Press.

Burke, Edmund. 1975. "Speech to the Electors of Bristol," pp. 156–58 in B. W. Hill, ed., *Edmund Burke on Government, Politics, and Society.* London: Harvester Press.

———. 1976. "Letter to a Member of the National Assembly," p. 342 in George Nash, *The Conservative Intellectual Movement in America.* New York: Basic Books.

Burke, Kenneth. 1945. *A Grammar of Motives.* New York: Prentice-Hall.

Burnheim, John. 1985. *Is Democracy Possible?: The Alternative to Electoral Politics.* Cambridge, Mass.: Polity Press.

Burtt, E. A. 1965. *In Search of Philosophic Understanding.* New York: New American Library.

Bury, J. B. 1924. *The Idea of Progress.* London: Macmillan.

Buultjens, Ralph. 1978. *The Decline of Democracy: Essays on an Endangered Political Species.* Maryknoll, N.Y.: Orbis Books.

Cabet, Etienne. 1848. *Voyage en Icarie.* Paris: Bureau du Populaire.

Calhoun, John C. 1953. *A Disquisition on Government.* Indianapolis, Ind.: Bobbs-Merrill.

Camus, Albert. 1956. *The Rebel: An Essay on Man in Revolt.* Anthony Bower, tr. New York: Vintage Books.

———. 1986. *Neither Victims nor Executioners.* Dwight McBride, tr. Philadelphia: New Society Publishers.

Canovan, Margaret. 1983. "Arendt, Rousseau, and Human Plurality in Politics," *Journal of Politics*, 45, No. 1, pp. 286–302.

Carcopino, Jerome. 1951. *Cicero: The Secrets of His Correspondence.* Volumes 1 and 2. New Haven, Conn.: Yale University Press.

Catton, William R., Jr. 1980. *Overshoot: The Ecological Basis of Revolutionary Change.* Urbana: University of Illinois Press.

Chappell, David W., ed. 1987. *Buddhist and Taoist Practice in Medieval Chinese Society.* Honolulu: University of Hawaii Press.

Cicero, Marcus Tullius. 1947. *De Officiis.* Cambridge, Mass.: Harvard University Press, Loeb Classical Library.

———. 1956. *De Re Publica, and De Legibus.* Cambridge, Mass.: Harvard University Press, Loeb Classical Library.

————. 1970. *De Oratore*, in J. S. Watson, tr., *Cicero on Oratory and Orators*. Carbondale, Ill.: Southern Illinois Press.

Cingranelli, David L. and Richard I. Hofferbert. 1988. "Human Rights and Democracy: Life, Liberty, and the Pursuit of Happiness," delivered at the Annual Meeting of the Western Political Science Association, San Francisco.

Clark, Kenneth. 1964. *Ruskin Today*. New York: Holt, Rinehart, and Winston.

Colburn, Forrest D. 1986. *Post-revolutionary Nicaragua*. Berkeley: University of California Press.

Connor, James. 1968. *Lenin on Politics and Revolution*. New York: Pegasus.

Conquest, Robert. 1986. *The Harvest of Sorrow: Soviet Collectivization and the Terror-famine*. New York: Oxford University Press.

Cook, Terrence E. 1975. "Rousseau: Education and Politics," *Journal of Politics*, 37, pp. 108–28.

————. 1980. "Political Justifications: The Use of Standards in Political Argument," *Journal of Politics*, 42, pp. 511–37.

————. 1983a. "The Courtship of Capital: Political Implications of Increasingly Portable Capital and Fixed Territorial Jurisdictions of Government," *Policy Perspectives*, 3, No. 1, pp. 69–105.

————. 1983b. "'Misbegotten Males?' Innate Differences and Stratified Choice in the Subjection of Women," *Western Political Quarterly*, 36, pp. 194–220.

Cook, Terrence E. and Patrick M. Morgan, eds. 1971. *Participatory Democracy*. San Francisco: Canfield Press.

Corancez, "Citizen." 1798. *Anecdotes of the Last Twelve Years of the Life of J. J. Rousseau*. London: James Wallis.

Coser, Lewis. 1984. *Refugee Scholars in America*. New Haven, Conn.: Yale University Press.

Cowell, F. R. 1967. *Cicero and the Roman Republic*. Baltimore, Md.: Penguin Books.

Croly, Herbert. 1963. *The Promise of American Life*. New York: E. P. Dutton.

Crossman, R. H. S. 1959. *Plato Today*. New York: Oxford University Press.

Curran, James. 1979. "Capitalism and Control of the Press, 1800–1975," pp. 195–230 in James Curran, Michael Gurevitch, and Janet Woollacott, eds., *Mass Communications and Society*. Beverly Hills, Calif.: Sage Publications.

Curry, Jane Leftwich, ed. and tr. 1984. *The Black Book of Polish Censorship*. New York: Random House.

de Tocqueville, Alexis. 1945. *Democracy in America*. 2 Volumes. New York: Random House, Vintage Books.

Deutsch, Karl W. 1969. "On Methodological Problems of Quantitative Research," pp. 19–39 in Mattei Dogan and Stein Rokkan, eds., *Quantitative Ecological Analysis in the Social Sciences*. Cambridge, Mass.: MIT Press.

Deutsch, Kenneth L. and Walter Soffer, eds. 1987. *The Crisis of Liberal*

*Democracy: A Straussian Approach.* Albany: State University of New York Press.

Dolan, Jay P. 1985. *The American Catholic Experience.* Garden City, N.Y.: Doubleday.

Dolbeare, Kenneth M. 1984. *Democracy at Risk: The Politics of Economic Renewal.* Chatham, N.J.: Chatham House Publishers.

Dorfman, Joseph. 1967. "The Regal Republic of John Adams," pp. 114–38 in John P. Roche, ed., *Origins of American Political Thought.* New York: Harper & Row.

Douglas, Jack D. 1976. *Investigative Social Research.* Beverly Hills, Calif.: Sage Publications.

Dow, F. D. 1985. *Radicalism in the English Revolution 1640–1660.* Oxford, England: Basil Blackwell.

Doyle, Michael W. 1983. "Kant, Liberal Legacies, and Foreign Affairs, Part I," *Philosophy and Public Affairs,* 12, No. 1, pp. 205–25.

Drucker, H. M. 1974. *The Political Uses of Ideology.* London: Macmillan.

Drury, Shadia B. 1988. *The Political Ideas of Leo Strauss.* New York: Macmillan.

Dumm, Thomas L. 1985. "Friendly Persuasion: Quaker, Liberal Toleration and the Birth of the Prison," *Political Theory,* 13, No. 3, pp. 387–407.

Dunn, John. 1979. *Western Political Theory in the Face of the Future.* Cambridge, England: Cambridge University Press.

Durkheim, Emile. 1964. *The Division of Labor in Society.* George Simpson, tr. New York: Free Press.

Dye, Thomas R. and Harmon Zeigler. 1988. "Socialism and Equality in Cross-national Perspective," *PS,* 21, No. 1, pp. 45–56.

Earland, Ada. 1971. *Ruskin and His Circle.* New York: AMS Press.

Elgin, Duane. 1981. *Voluntary Simplicity.* New York: William Morrow.

Elster, Jon. 1983. *Sour Grapes: Studies in the Subversion of Rationality.* Cambridge, England: Cambridge University Press.

———. 1989. *Nuts and Bolts for the Social Sciences.* Cambridge, England: Cambridge University Press.

Emerson, Ralph Waldo. 1960. "On Politics," pp. 241–52 in Stephen E. Whicher, ed., *Selections from Ralph Waldo Emerson.* Boston: Houghton Mifflin.

Engels, Friedrich. 1973. *The Condition of the Working Class in England.* Moscow: Progress Publishers.

Erikson, Erik. 1969. *Gandhi's Truth.* New York: W. W. Norton.

Etzioni, Amitai. 1984. *Capital Corruption: The New Attack on American Democracy.* New York: Harcourt Brace Jovanovich.

Fan, K. T. 1972. *Mao Tse-tung and Lin Piao: Post-revolutionary Writings.* Garden City, N.Y.: Doubleday Anchor.

Fanon, Frantz. 1968. *The Wretched of the Earth.* New York: Grove Press.

Feuer, Lewis S. 1958. *Spinoza and the Rise of Liberalism.* Boston: Beacon Press.

——. 1975. *Ideology and the Ideologists.* New York: Harper and Row.

Feuerbach, Ludwig. 1957. *The Essence of Christianity.* New York: Harper & Row.

Figgis, John Neville. 1916. *Gerson to Grotius.* 2nd Edition. London: Cambridge University Press.

Finkelstein, Louis. 1962. *The Pharisees: The Sociological Background of Their Faith.* 2 Volumes. Philadelphia: Jewish Publication Society of America.

Fischer, Louis. 1950. *The Life of Mahatma Gandhi.* New York: Harper & Brothers.

——. 1965. *The Life of Lenin.* New York: Harper & Row.

Fishkin, James S. 1979. *Tyranny and Legitimacy: A Critique of Political Theories.* Baltimore: Johns Hopkins University Press.

Foucault, Michel. 1979. *Discipline and Punish.* New York: Vintage Books.

——. 1980. *Power/Knowledge.* New York: Pantheon Books.

Freedman, Daniel G. 1979. *Human Sociobiology: A Holistic Approach.* New York: Free Press.

Freire, Paulo. 1970. *Pedagogy of the Oppressed.* New York: Herder and Herder.

Friedman, Milton and Rose Friedman. 1980. *Free to Choose.* New York: Harcourt Brace Jovanovich.

Fromm, Eric. 1961. *Marx's Concept of Man.* New York: Ungar Publishing.

Fukuyama, Francis. 1989. "Have We Reached the End of History?" Rand Corporation. Reprinted in the *National Interest,* Summer Issue.

Galbraith, John Kenneth. 1958. *The Affluent Society.* Boston: Houghton Mifflin.

Galston, William A. 1988. "Liberal Virtues," *American Political Science Review,* 82, No. 4, pp. 1277–90.

Gandhi, Mohandas. 1973. Quoted on p. 33 in E. F. Schumacher, *Small Is Beautiful.* New York: Harper & Row.

Geertz, Clifford. 1983. *Local Knowledge.* New York: Basic Books.

Gerth, Hans and C. Wright Mills. 1946. *From Max Weber: Essays in Sociology.* New York: Oxford University Press.

Ginsburg, Christian D. 1956. *The Essenes: Their History and Doctrines.* London: Routledge and Kegan Paul.

Gitlin, Todd. 1980. *The Whole World Is Watching.* Berkeley: University of California Press.

Gödel, Kurt. 1970. "Some Metamathematical Results or Completion and Consistency," pp. 83–108 in Jean van Heijenoort, ed., *Frege and Gödel: Two Fundamental Texts in Mathematical Logic.* Cambridge, Mass.: Harvard University Press.

Goldstone, Jack A. 1986. "State Breakdown in the English Revolution: A New

Synthesis," *American Journal of Sociology*, 92, No. 2.

Goodman, Paul and Percival Goodman. 1947. *Communitas: Means of Livelihood and Ways of Life*. Chicago: University of Chicago Press.

Goodman, Robert. 1979. *The Last Entrepreneurs: America's Regional Wars for Jobs and Dollars*. New York: Simon and Schuster.

Gorz, André. 1980. *Ecology as Politics*. Boston: South End Press.

Green, Martin. 1983. *Tolstoy and Gandhi: Men of Peace*. New York: Basic Books.

Grimke, Archibald A. 1891. *William Lloyd Garrison: The Abolitionist*. New York: Funk and Wagnalls.

Gunn, J. A. W. 1969. *Politics and the Public Interest in the Seventeenth Century*. London: Routledge and Kegan Paul.

Gunnell, John. 1979. *Political Theory: Tradition and Interpretation*. Cambridge, Mass.: Winthrop Publishers.

Gupta, Shanti S. 1971. "Gandhi on Labor–Capital Relations," *American Journal of Economics and Society*, 30, No. 4.

Habermas, Jurgen. 1973a. *Legitimation Crisis*. Boston: Beacon Press.

———. 1973b. *Theory and Practice*. Boston: Beacon Press.

Hansen, Susan B. 1983. *The Politics of Taxation*. New York: Praeger Publishers.

Harrington, James. 1901. *Oceana*, pp. 183 ff. in Henry Morley, ed., *Ideal Commonwealths*. Revised edition. New York: Colonial Press.

Harris, Marvin. 1977. *Cannibals and Kings, The Origins of Cultures*. New York: Random House.

Hayek, Friedrich. 1972. *The Constitution of Liberty*. Chicago: Henry Regnery.

———. 1978. *New Studies in Philosophy, Politics, Economics, and the History of Ideas*. London: Routledge & Kegan Paul.

Heilbroner, Robert. 1966. *The Limits of American Capitalism*. New York: Harper & Row.

———. 1980. *Marxism: For and Against*. New York: W. W. Norton.

Held, David. 1987. *Models of Democracy*. Stanford, Calif.: Stanford University Press.

Held, David and Christopher Pollitt, eds. 1986. *New Forms of Democracy*. Beverly Hills, Calif.: Sage Publications.

Herman, Edward S. 1982. *The Real Terror Network: Terrorism in Fact and Propaganda*. Boston: Beacon Press.

Hirsch, Fred. 1976. *Social Limits to Growth*. Cambridge, Mass.: Harvard University Press.

Hirschman, Albert O. 1977. *The Passions and the Interests: Political Arguments for Capitalism before Its Triumph*. Princeton, N.J.: Princeton University Press.

———. 1989. "Reactionary Rhetoric," *Atlantic Monthly*, 263, No. 5, pp. 63–70.

Hobbes, Thomas. 1968. *Leviathan*. New York: Penguin Books.

Hofstadter, Richard. 1959. *Social Darwinism in American Thought*. Revised edition. New York: George Braziller.

Holmes, Oliver W., Jr. 1955. "Natural Law," pp. 118–23 in Julius J. Marke, ed., *The Holmes Reader.* New York: Oceana Press.

Hooker, Richard. 1963. *Of the Laws of Ecclesiastical Polity.* Volumes 1 and 2. New York: Everyman's Library.

Howe, Irving. 1978. *Leon Trotsky.* New York: Penguin Books.

Hsiao, Kung-chuan. 1979. *A History of Chinese Political Thought.* Princeton, N.J.: Princeton University Press.

Hume, David. 1965. *A Treatise of Human Nature.* Oxford, England: Clarendon Press.

Inglehart, Ronald. 1977. *The Silent Revolution.* Princeton, N.J.: Princeton University Press.

International Confederation of Free Trade Unions. 1986–87; 1988; 1989. "Annual Survey of Violations of Trade Union Rights."

Jackson, Samuel Macauley, ed. 1901. *Selected Works of Huldreich Zwingli.* Philadelphia: University of Pennsylvania Press.

Jacobi, Jolande, ed. 1951. *Paracelsus: Selected Writings.* New York: Pantheon Books.

Jacobs, Jerry A. 1989. "The English Landed Aristocracy and the Rise of Capitalism: Status Maximization and Economic Change," pp. 180–99 in Harold J. Bershady, ed., *Social Class and Democratic Leadership.* Philadelphia: University of Pennsylvania Press.

Jencks, Christopher et al. 1972. *Inequality: A Reassessment of the Effect of Family and Schooling in America.* New York: Basic Books.

Jessop, Bob. 1982. *The Capitalist State: Marxist Theories and Methods.* New York: New York University Press.

Johnson, Curtis. 1986. "Aristotle on Popular Rule," delivered at the Pacific Northwest Political Science Association, Vancouver, Wash.

Josephus, Flavius. 1830. *The Antiquities of the Jews,* in *Works of Flavius Josephus,* Volume 2. Glasgow, Scotland: Blackie and Sons.

————. 1981. *The Jewish War.* Revised edition. G. A. Williamson, tr. London: Penguin Books.

Kant, Immanuel. 1949. *Fundamental Principles of the Metaphysic of Morals.* New York: Bobbs-Merrill.

Kiljunen, Kimmo, ed. 1984. *Kampuchea: Decade of the Genocide.* Helsinki: Report of Finnish Inquiry Commission.

Koestler, Arthur. 1963. Untitled essay, in Richard Crossman, ed., *The God That Failed.* New York: Harper & Row.

Korner, Peter, Gero Maas, Thomas Siebold, and Rainer Tetzlaff. 1986. *The IMF and the Debt Crisis: A Guide to the Third World's Dilemma.* London: Zed Books.

Kuttner, Robert. 1984. *The Economic Illusion: False Choices between Prosperity and Social Justice.* Boston: Houghton Mifflin.

Laing, R. D. 1969. *The Politics of Experience.* New York: Ballantine Books.

Lakey, George. 1973. *Strategy for a Living Revolution*. San Francisco: W. H. Freeman.

Lao Tzu. 1955. *The Way of Life*. R. B. Blackney, tr. New York: New American Library.

Lappé, Frances Moore and Joseph Collins. 1979. *Food First: Beyond the Myth of Scarcity*. New York: Ballantine Books.

Laski, Harold. 1936. *The Rise of Liberalism: The Philosophy of a Business Civilization*. New York: Harper & Brothers.

Lea, James. 1982. *Political Consciousness and American Democracy*. Jackson: University Press of Mississippi.

Leiss, William. 1972. *The Domination of Nature*. New York: George Braziller.

Lenin, V. I. 1929. *What Is to Be Done?* New York: International Publishers.

———. 1932. *State and Revolution*. New York: International Publishers.

———. 1939. *Imperialism: The Highest Stage of Capitalism*. New York: International Publishers.

Lentin, A., ed. 1985. *Enlightened Absolutism (1760–1790): A Documentary Sourcebook*. Newcastle-upon-Tyne, England: Avero Publishers.

Lieberman, Jethro K. 1979. *The Tyranny of Experts*. New York: Walker.

Lijphart, Arend. 1984. *Democracies*. New Haven, Conn.: Yale University Press.

Lindblom, Charles E. 1977. *Politics and Markets*. New York: W. W. Norton.

Lipset, Seymour Martin. 1963. *Political Man: The Social Bases of Politics*. Garden City, N.Y.: Anchor Books.

Lively, Jack. 1975. *Democracy*. New York: St. Martin's Press.

Locke, John. 1965a. *Essays on the Law of Nature*. Oxford, England: Clarendon Press.

———. 1965b. *Two Treatises of Government*. New York: New American Library, Mentor.

———. 1967. *Two Tracts on Government*. Cambridge, England: Cambridge University Press.

Lovejoy, Arthur O. 1936. *The Great Chain of Being*. Cambridge, Mass.: Harvard University Press.

Lucas, Robert. 1983. *Studies in Business-cycle Theory*. Cambridge, Mass.: MIT Press.

McCombs, Maxwell E. and Donald Shaw. 1972. "The Agenda-setting Function of Mass Media," *Public Opinion Quarterly*, 36, No. 2, pp. 176–87.

McDonald, Forrest. 1958. *We the People*. New York: Stratford Press.

Machiavelli, Niccolo. 1975. *The Prince*. New York: Penguin Books.

MacIntyre, Alasdair. 1981. *After Virtue: A Study in Moral Theory*. Notre Dame, Ind.: University of Notre Dame Press.

McLaughlin, Elizabeth T. 1974. *Ruskin and Gandhi*. Lewisburg, Pa.: Bucknell University Press.

McNeill, William H. 1980. *The Human Condition: An Ecological and Historical View*. Princeton, N.J.: Princeton University Press.

Macpherson, C. B. 1966. *The Real World of Democracy*. Oxford, England: Oxford University Press.

———. 1967. "The Maximization of Democracy," pp. 83–103 in Peter Laslett and W. G. Runciman, eds., *Philosophy, Politics, and Society*, 3rd Series. New York: Barnes & Noble.

———. 1977. *The Life and Times of Liberal Democracy*. Oxford, England: Oxford University Press.

Maine, Henry S. 1888. *Ancient Law*. New York: Henry Holt.

Malthus, Thomas R. 1976. *An Essay on the Principle of Population: Text, Sources and Background, Criticism*. Philip Appleman, ed. New York: Norton.

Mansbridge, Jane J. 1980. *Beyond Adversary Democracy*. New York: Basic Books.

Mara, Gerald. 1988. "Socrates and Liberal Toleration," *Political Theory*, 16, No. 3, pp. 468–95.

Marx, Karl. 1967. *Capital*. 3 Volumes. New York: International Publishers.

Marx, Karl and Friedrich Engels. 1962. *Selected Works*. Volume 1. Moscow: Foreign Languages Publishing House.

———. 1966. *The German Ideology*. New York: International Publishers, New World Paperbacks.

Maslow, Abraham. 1954. *Motivation and Personality*. New York: Harper & Row.

———. 1971. *The Farther Reaches of Human Nature*. New York: Viking Press.

Mazlish, Bruce. 1976. *The Revolutionary Ascetic: Evolution of a Political Type*. New York: Basic Books.

Medvedev, Zhores. 1978. *Soviet Science*. New York: W. W. Norton.

Mehring, Franz. 1962. *Karl Marx: The Story of His Life*. Ann Arbor: University of Michigan Press.

Merchant, Carolyn. 1980. *The Death of Nature: Women, Ecology, and the Scientific Revolution*. San Francisco: Harper & Row.

Mewes, Horst. 1988. "The Green Party Comes of Age," pp. 110–18 in Christian Soe, ed., *Comparative Politics 87/88*. Guilford, Conn.: Dushkin Publishing Group. First printed in *Environment*, June 1985, pp. 12–17.

Mill, James. 1966. "An Essay on the Impolicy of a Bounty on the Exportation of Grain," pp. 41–84 in Donald Winch, ed., *James Mill: Selected Economic Writings*. Chicago: University of Chicago Press.

———. 1971. *The Principles of Toleration*. New York: B. Franklin.

Mill, John Stuart. 1961. "Nature," from his *Three Essays on Religion*, pp. 445–88 in Marshall Cohen, ed., *The Philosophy of John Stuart Mill*. New York: Modern Library.

———. 1974. *On Liberty, Representative Government, The Subjection of Women: Three Essays by John Stuart Mill*. London: Oxford University Press.

Miller, Perry and Thomas H. Johnson. 1938. *The Puritans*. New York: American Book.

Milton, John. 1957. *Complete Poems and Major Prose*. New York: Odyssey Press.

Montesquieu, Baron de. 1965. *The Spirit of the Laws*. Thomas Nugent, tr. New York: Hafner Publishing.

Moore, Barrington. 1969. *Social Origins of Dictatorship and Democracy*. Boston: Beacon Press.

———. 1972. *Reflections on the Causes of Human Misery and upon Certain Proposals to Eliminate Them*. Boston: Beacon Press.

———. 1987. *Authority and Inequality under Capitalism and Socialism*. London: Oxford University Press.

Morrow, Glenn R. 1960. *Plato's Cretan City: A Historical Interpretation of the Laws*. Princeton, N.J.: Princeton University Press.

Muhaiyaddeen, Muhammed Roheem Bawa. 1987. *Islam and World Peace: Explanations of a Sufi*. Philadelphia: Fellowship Press.

Muller, Edward. 1988. "Democracy, Economic Development, and Income Inequality," *American Sociological Review*, 53, pp. 50–68.

Nash, George. 1976. *The Conservative Intellectual Movement in America*. New York: Basic Books.

Neusner, Jacob. 1973. *From Politics to Piety: The Emergence of Pharasaic Judaism*. Englewood Cliffs, N.J.: Prentice-Hall.

Newman, Graeme. 1979. *Understanding Violence*. New York: J. B. Lippincott.

Niebuhr, Reinhold. 1941. *The Nature and Destiny of Man: A Christian Interpretation*. New York: Charles Scribner's Sons.

Nietzsche, Friedrich. 1968. "On the Prejudices of Philosophers," in Walter Kauffman, ed., *Basic Writings of Nietzsche*. New York: Modern Library.

North, Douglass C. 1981. *Structure and Change in Economic History*. New York: W. W. Norton.

North, Douglass C. and Robert Paul Thomas. 1973. *The Rise of the Western World: A New Economic History*. Cambridge, England: Cambridge University Press.

Nozick, Robert. 1974. *Anarchy, State, and Utopia*. New York: Basic Books.

O'Connor, James. 1973. *The Fiscal Crisis of the State*. New York: St. Martin's Press.

Offe, Claus. 1985. *Disorganized Capitalism*. Cambridge, England: Polity Press.

Offe, John and Claus Offe. 1984. *Contradictions of the Welfare State*. London: Hutchinson.

Okun, Arthur M. 1975. *Equality and Efficiency: The Big Tradeoff*. Washington, D.C.: Brookings Institution.

Ollman, Bertell and Edward Vernoff, eds. 1984. *The Left Academy: Marxist Scholarship on American Campuses*. Volume 2. New York: Praeger Publishers.

Olson, Mancur. 1982. *The Rise and Decline of Nations*. New Haven, Conn.: Yale University Press.

Ooms, Herman. 1985. *Tokugawa Ideology: Early Constructs 1570–1680*. Princeton, N.J.: Princeton University Press.

Ophuls, William. 1977. *Ecology and the Politics of Scarcity: Prologue to a Theory of the Steady State*. San Francisco: W. H. Freeman.

Orwin, Clifford. 1978. "Machiavelli's Unchristian Charity," *American Political Science Review*, 72, No. 4, pp. 1217–28.

Paine, Thomas. 1942. *Age of Reason: Being an Investigation of True and Fabulous Theology*. New York: Willey Book.

Pantham, Thomas. 1986. "Beyond Liberal Democracy: Thinking with Mahatma Gandhi," pp. 325–46 in Thomas Pantham and Kenneth L. Deutsch, eds., *Political Thought in Modern India*. Beverly Hills, Calif.: Sage Publications.

Parekh, Bhikhu. 1986. "Some Reflections on the Hindu Tradition of Political Thought," pp. 17–31 in Thomas Pantham and Kenneth L. Deutsch, eds. *Political Thought in Modern India*. Beverly Hills, Calif.: Sage Publications.

Parenti, Michael. 1988. *Democracy for the Few*. New York: St. Martin's Press.

Parkin, Frank. 1971. *Class Inequality and Political Order*. London: MacGibbon & Kee.

Parrott, Bruce. 1983. *Politics and Technology in the Soviet Union*. Cambridge, Mass.: MIT Press.

Pascal, Blaise. 1941. *Pensées and the Provincial Letters*. New York: Modern Library.

Pateman, Carole. 1979. *The Problem of Political Obligation: A Critical Analysis of Liberal Theory*. New York: John Wiley & Sons.

Pennock, J. Roland. 1979. *Democratic Political Theory*. Princeton, N.J.: Princeton University Press.

Petty, William. 1899. *The Economic Writings of Sir William Petty*. Cambridge, England: Cambridge University Press.

Philips, C. H. 1961. *The East India Company, 1784–1834*. London: Manchester University Press.

Pitkin, Hanna Fenichel. 1967. *The Concept of Representation*. Berkeley and Los Angeles: University of California Press.

Piven, Frances Fox and A. Cloward. 1982. *The New Class War*. New York: Pantheon Books.

Plato. 1968. *Republic*. Allan Bloom, tr. New York: Basic Books.

———. 1984. *The Collected Dialogues of Plato*. Edith Hamilton and Huntington Cairns, eds. First published, New York: Pantheon Books, 1964. Reprinted, Princeton, N.J.: Princeton University Press.

Polanyi, Karl. 1957. *The Great Transformation*. Boston: Beacon Press.

Popkin, Samuel L. 1979. *The Rational Peasant: The Political Economy of Rural Society in Vietnam.* Berkeley: University of California Press.

Popper, Karl. 1957. *The Poverty of Historicism.* London: Routledge and Kegan Paul.

————. 1968. *The Logic of Scientific Discovery.* New York: Harper & Row.

————. 1979. *Objective Knowledge: An Evolutionary Approach.* Oxford, England: Clarendon Press.

Poster, Mark, ed. 1971. *Harmonian Man: Selected Writings of Charles Fourier.* Garden City, N.Y.: Anchor Books.

Poulantzas, Nicos. 1978. *State, Power, Socialism.* London: NLB.

Rapoport, Anatol. 1960. *Fights, Games, and Debates.* Ann Arbor: University of Michigan Press.

————. 1989. *The Origins of Violence: Approaches to the Study of Conflict.* New York: Paragon House.

Rawls, John. 1971. *A Theory of Justice.* Cambridge, Mass.: Harvard University Press.

Redner, Harry. 1982. *In the Beginning Was the Deed: Reflections on the Passage of Faust.* Berkeley: University of California Press.

Rescher, Nicholas. 1976. *Plausible Reasoning.* Assen/Amsterdam: Van Gorcum.

Riddel, David. 1968. "Social Self-government: The Background of Theory and Practice in Yugoslav Socialism," *British Journal of Sociology*, 19, No. 1, pp. 47–75.

Riker, William H. 1982. *Liberalism against Populism.* San Francisco: W. H. Freeman.

Riley, Patrick. 1981. *The Political Writings of Leibniz.* Cambridge, England: Cambridge University Press.

Rogowski, Ronald. 1974. *Rational Legitimacy: A Theory of Political Support.* Princeton, N.J.: Princeton University Press.

Ross, Nancy Wilson. 1966. *Three Ways of Asian Wisdom.* New York: Simon and Schuster.

Roth, David F. and Frank L. Wilson. 1976. *The Comparative Study of Politics.* Boston: Houghton Mifflin.

Rotunda, Ronald. 1968. "The 'Liberal' Label: Roosevelt's Capture of a Symbolic," *Public Policy*, 17, pp. 377–408.

Rousseau, Jean-Jacques. 1964. *Oeuvres Complètes.* Volume 3. Paris: Bibliothèque de la Pléiade.

Ruskin, John. 1851–53. *The Stones of Venice.* 3 Volumes. London: Smith and Eder.

————. 1978. *Praeterita.* New York: Oxford University Press.

Rydenfelt, Sven. 1984. *Pattern for Failure: Socialist Economics in Crisis.* San Diego: Harcourt Brace Jovanovich.

Sabato, Larry J. 1989. *Paying for Elections.* New York: Priority Press Publications.

Sahlins, Marshall D. 1976. *The Use and Abuse of Biology: An Anthropological Critique of Sociobiology.* Ann Arbor: University of Michigan Press.

Santayana, George. 1905–6. *The Life of Reason.* 5 Volumes. New York: Charles Scribner's Sons.

Schacht, Richard. 1971. *Alienation.* Garden City, N.Y.: Doubleday.

Schell, Jonathan. 1982. *The Fate of the Earth.* New York: Avon Books.

Schmitter, Philippe. 1981. "Interest Intermediation and Regime Governability in Western Europe and North America," in Suzanne Berger, ed., *Organizing Interests in Western Europe.* Cambridge, England: Cambridge University Press.

Schomer, Karine and W. H. McLeod, eds. 1987. *The Saints: Studies in a Devotional Tradition in India.* Berkeley, Calif.: Religious Studies Group.

Schopflin, George. 1983. *Censorship and Political Communication in Eastern Europe.* New York: St. Martin's Press.

Schouls, Peter A. 1989. *Descartes and the Enlightenment.* Kingston and Montreal: McGill-Queen's University Press.

Schroyer, Trent. 1973. *The Critique of Domination: The Origins and Development of Critical Theory.* New York: George Braziller.

Schumacher, E. F. 1973. *Small Is Beautiful: Economics as if People Mattered.* New York: Harper & Row.

Schwarzchild, Leopold. 1947. *The Red Prussian: The Life and Legend of Karl Marx.* New York: Charles Scribner's Sons.

Secretería General de Gobierno. 1972. *Los Documentos Secretos de la ITT y La República de Chile.* Santiago: Empresa Nacional Quimantu.

Serba, Gregor. 1982. "Prelude and Variations on the Theme of Eric Voegelin's Thought: A Critical Appraisal," pp. 3–65 in Ellis Sandoz, ed., *Eric Voegelin's Thought: A Critical Appraisal.* Durham, N.C.: Duke University Press.

Sharp, Gene. 1970. *Exploring Nonviolent Alternatives.* Boston: Porter Sargent.

———. 1979. *Gandhi as a Political Strategist.* Boston: Porter Sargent.

———. 1980. *Social Power and Political Freedom.* Boston: Porter Sargent.

———. 1985. *Making Europe Unconquerable: The Potential of Civilian-based Deterrence and Defence.* London: Taylor and Francis.

Shaw, George Bernard. 1921. *Ruskin's Politics.* Folcroft, Pa.: Folcroft Press.

Shaw, Martin. 1975. *Marxism and Social Science: The Roots of Social Knowledge.* London: Pluto Press.

Simpson, John and Jana Bennett. 1985. *The Disappeared: Voices from a Secret War.* London: Robson Books.

Smith, Adam. 1937. *An Inquiry into the Nature and Causes of the Wealth of Nations.* New York: Random House, Modern Library.

Spencer, Herbert. 1910a. *Social Statics, together with Man versus the State.* New York: D. Appleton.

———. 1910b. *Essays.* Volume 3. New York: D. Appleton.

Spinoza, Benedict. 1951. *The Political Treatise, and Theologico-Political Treatise,* in *Chief Works of Benedict de Spinoza.* Volume 1. New York: Dover Publications.

Spitz, Elaine. 1984. *Majority Rule.* Chatham, N.J.: Chatham House Publishers.

Spragens, Thomas A., Jr. 1981. *The Irony of Liberal Reason.* Chicago: University of Chicago Press.

Stone, I. F. 1988. *The Trial of Socrates.* Boston: Little, Brown.

Strauss, Leo. 1952. *Persecution and the Art of Writing.* Glencoe, Ill.: Free Press.

———. 1953. *Natural Right and History.* Chicago: University of Chicago Press.

———. 1959. *What Is Political Philosophy?* New York: Free Press.

———. 1962. "Epilogue," in Herbert J. Storing, ed., *Essays on the Scientific Study of Politics.* New York: Holt, Rinehart, and Winston.

———. 1964. *The City and Man.* Addison, Ill.: Rand McNally.

———. 1965. *Spinoza's Critique of Religion.* New York: Schocken Books.

———. 1975. *The Argument and Action of Plato's Laws.* Chicago: University of Chicago Press.

Sweezy, Paul. 1980. *Post-revolutionary Society.* New York: Monthly Review Press.

———, ed. 1984. *Karl Marx and the Close of His System and Böhm-Bawerk's Criticism of Marx.* Philadelphia: Orion Editions.

Sydney, Algernon. 1805. *Discourses on Government.* Volume 1. New York: Deare and Andrews.

Thapar, Romila. 1966. *A History of India.* Volume 1. Baltimore, Md.: Penguin Books.

———. 1978. *Ancient Indian Social History: Some Interpretations.* Bashir Bagh, Hyderabad, India: Orient Longman.

Thoreau, Henry David. 1950. *Walden and Other Writings of Henry David Thoreau.* New York: Modern Library.

Thurow, Lester. 1981. *The Zero-sum Society.* New York: Penguin Books.

Tinder, Glenn. 1974. "Transcending Tragedy: The Idea of Civility," *American Political Science Review*," 68, No. 2, pp. 547–60.

Tolstoy, Leo. 1962. *War and Peace.* New York: Modern Library.

———. 1966. *Resurrection.* Rosemary Edmonds, tr. Baltimore: Penguin Books.

———. 1983. *Confession.* New York: W. W. Norton.

Trenchard, John and Thomas Gordon. 1965. *Cato's Letters,* in David Jacobson, ed., *The English Libertarian Heritage: From the Writings of John Trenchard and Thomas Gordon in the Independent Whig and Cato's Letters.* Indianapolis, Ind.: Bobbs-Merrill.

Trotsky, Leon. 1965. *The Revolution Betrayed: What Is the Soviet Union and Where Is It Going?* New York: Merit Publishers.

Troyat, Henri. 1967. *Tolstoy*. Garden City, N.Y.: Doubleday.

Tucker, Robert C. 1978. *The Marx-Engels Reader*. 2nd. Edition. New York: W. W. Norton.

Turnbull, Colin M. 1972. *The Mountain People*. New York: Simon and Schuster.

Vaughan, Charles E., ed. 1915. *The Political Writings of Jean-Jacques Rousseau*. 2 Volumes. Cambridge, England: Cambridge University Press.

Vaughan, Frederick. 1982. *The Tradition of Political Hedonism: From Hobbes to J. S. Mill*. New York: Fordham University Press.

Veblen, Thorstein. 1915. *Imperial Germany and the Industrial Revolution*. New York: Macmillan.

Venable, Vernon. 1966. *Human Nature: The Marxian View*. Cleveland, Ohio: World Publishing.

Vlastos, Gustav. 1973. "Does Slavery Exist in Plato's *Republic*?" pp. 140–46 in Vlastos, *Platonic Studies*. Princeton, N.J.: Princeton University Press.

Voegelin, Eric. 1952. *The New Science of Politics*. Chicago: University of Chicago Press.

———. 1956–87. *Order and History*. 5 Volumes. Baton Rouge: Louisiana State University Press.

Walzer, Michael. 1983. *Spheres of Justice*. New York: Basic Books.

Weinstein, Donald and Rudolph M. Bell. 1982. *Saints and Society: The Two Worlds of Western Christendom, 1000–1700*. Chicago: University of Chicago Press.

Wesson, Robert. 1987. *Democracy: A Worldwide Survey*. New York: Praeger.

Wildavsky, Aaron. 1979. *Speaking Truth to Power: The Art and Craft of Policy Analysis*. Boston: Little, Brown.

———. 1980. "The 1980's: Monopoly or Competition," *Intergovernmental Perspectives*, 6, No. 3, pp. 15–18.

Wildes, Harry Emerson. 1965. *Voice of the Lord: A Biography of George Fox*. Philadelphia: University of Pennsylvania Press.

Wilensky, Harold and Lowell Turner. 1987. *Democratic Corporatism and Policy Linkages*. Berkeley, Calif.: Institute of International Studies.

Williams, George Huntson. 1962. *The Radical Reformation*. Philadelphia: Westminster Press.

Williams, Robin M., Jr. 1979. "Change and Stability in Values and Value Systems: A Sociological Perspective," pp. 15–46 in Milton Rokeach, ed., *Understanding Human Values*. New York: Free Press.

Williams, Roger. 1963. *The Bloudy Tenent, of Persecution, for Cause of Conscience*, in *The Complete Writings of Roger Williams*. New York: Russell and Russell.

Wilson, Edward O. 1975. *Sociobiology*. Cambridge, Mass.: Harvard University Press.

Winch, Donald. 1978. *Adam Smith's Politics: An Essay in Historiographic Revision*. Cambridge, England: Cambridge University Press.

Winspear, Alban. 1940. *The Genesis of Plato's Thought*. New York: Dryden Press.

Wolfe, Don M., ed. 1967. *Leveller Manifestoes of the Puritan Revolution*. New York: Humanities Press.

Wood, Neal. 1984. *John Locke and Agrarian Capitalism*. Berkeley: University of California Press.

————. 1988. *Cicero's Social and Political Thought*. Berkeley: University of California Press.

Wood, Neal and Ellen Meiskins Wood. 1978. *Class Ideology and Ancient Political Theory*. New York: Oxford University Press.

Yoder, John H. 1971. *Nevertheless*. Scottsdale, Pa.: Herald Press.

# Index

# About the Author

TERRENCE COOK, a Phi Beta Kappa undergraduate in International Relations from the University of Wisconsin–Madison, eventually completed a Master's and Ph.D. (1971) with the Department of Politics, Princeton University, where he was a participant in their interdepartmental political philosophy program. He has since taught most of Western political thought at Washington State University, where he is currently preparing to add a course in human civilization.

Cook has published in such journals as *The Journal of Politics* and *The Western Political Quarterly*, and he co-edited a book on democratic theory (*Participatory Democracy*, Canfield, 1971). That interest continues in a current book project comparing appropriate roles of experts, elective officials, and citizens in modern democracy. Other books in progress include a work on American political thought and another that is an empirical theory of nested political choice.